THE NEUROSCIENCE
OF PSYCHOTHERAPY

Building and Rebuilding the Human Brain

THE NEUROSCIENCE
OF PSYCHOTHERAPY

Building and Rebuilding the Human Brain

Louis Cozolino, Ph.D.

W. W. Norton & Company
New York • London

For information about permission to reproduce
selections from this book, write to
Permissions, W. W. Norton & Company, Inc.
500 Fifth Avenue, New York, NY 10110

Composition and book design by Ecomlinks, Inc.
Manufacturing by Haddon Craftsman
Production Manager: Leeann Graham

Library of Congress Cataloging-in-Publication Data
Cozolino, Louis J.
  The neuroscience of psychotherapy : building and rebuilding the human brain / Louis J
Cozolino.
      p.   cm.
  Includes bibliographical references and index.
  ISBN 0-393-70367-3
  1. Psychotherapy. 2. Neurosciences. 3. Brain research. I. Title.
RC480.5 .C645   2002
616.89'14—dc21   2002071818

W. W. Norton & Company, Inc., 500 Fifth Avenue, New York, NY 10110
www.wwnorton.com
W. W. Norton & Company, Ltd., Castle House, 75/76 Wells Street, London W1T 3QT
7 8 9 0

This book is dedicated to my family: my mother's courage,
my father's determination, and the memory of
my grandparents. Together they somehow instilled within
me the belief that all things are possible.

Contents

Foreword

by Daniel J. Siegel, M.D.

A s clinicians, we immerse ourselves in the stories of individuals who come to us for help in feeling better and developing beyond old, maladaptive patterns of thought, behavior, emotion, and relating. Over the years, the field of psychotherapy has developed numerous approaches that help people change. Whatever the approach, lasting change in therapy occurs as a result of changes in the human mind. Such development can be said to involve changes in the structure and thus function of the brain that gives rise to the mind. Exactly how the mind changes during the psychotherapeutic process is the fundamental puzzle that the exciting new synthesis of neuroscience and psychotherapy seeks to solve.

Human growth across the life span within psychotherapy involves the strategic catalyzing of this development of the mind. But what is the mind? Conceptualizing the mind as emanating from the processes of the brain, some scientists take a "single-skull" view of the psyche by examining the neural activity that gives rise to mental processes such as memory, emotion, and thought. However, clinicians know full well that these fundamental aspects of mind are profoundly influenced by interpersonal relationships and the patterns of communication that connect people to each other which occur within families and in psychotherapy. The differences between the single-skull view of mind and the social perspective can be reconciled by defining the mind as the flow of energy and information. Energy and information flow within the brain as well as between and among brains. The view from an interpersonal neurobiology perspective enables clinicians to embrace the powerful findings of neuroscience and incorporate them into their understanding of the nature of the subjective and social lives of human minds. This perspective can provide powerful new insights into how the mind develops within psychotherapy.

We are at an exciting moment in the history of psychotherapy as we now have the ability to integrate the clinical field of mental health with the independent field of neuroscience. In this volume, Lou Cozolino boldly explores the findings of neuroscience that bring to light some exciting new insights into the possible mechanisms underlying how psychotherapy works. In psychotherapy, we strive to find ways to help patients heal and overcome barriers to attaining flexible and balanced self-regulation. In neuroscience, we develop testable hypotheses and explanatory theories to help understand the brain and how neurons create the processes of mind. Recent technological advances have allowed us to peer beneath the skull and observe the functioning of a previously hidden normal human brain. These intriguing advances have enabled us to conceptualize in new and emerging ways how systems of neurons create mental processes.

How can the two independent fields of therapy and brain science be brought together in a meaningful way to effect a body of knowledge that is valid and useful? Each field explores reality in such different ways. Psychotherapy emphasizes the importance of *subjective* human experience and the power of relationships to transform the growing mind. Neuroscience focuses on quantifiable, *objective* data and the scientific method to create models of mind and brain. Embracing the view that subjective experience is as real as the quantifiable data of science is a first step in finding a convergence of knowledge across the two disciplines. We must learn the language that each field uses in order to understand their different conceptualizations of the world. The aspect of the world we focus on may be the external reality of physical events, or the internal reality of mental life. Though we cannot see the mind, it is as real as the processes of the kidney or the lungs or the heart. Understanding the mind as a process, and how the mind grows in response to experience, requires that we acknowledge the importance of both the objective and the subjective sides of reality.

The Neuroscience of Psychotherapy offers a unique perspective for clinicians, focusing on the growth of the mind by integrating neuroscience and psychotherapy research findings with the wisdom of an experienced and compassionate clinician. The book opens with an extremely useful review of the independent research findings from the fields of therapy and brain science. This is an invaluable resource for an up-to-date synthesis of our current knowledge in these fields. Next, Lou Cozolino creates a model of the possible neurobiological mechanisms underlying how people change. This model is an important and courageous step in advancing our understanding of the process of psychotherapy. Building on the foundation in neuroscience and psychotherapy, he also draws on the basic principles of a number of sciences, including those of evolution, developmental psychology, psychopathology, and linguistics, to establish his compelling model of how psychotherapy works.

In Cozolino's framework, neural integration plays a central role in the growth process. Integration is important because it enables the differentiated components of a system to achieve coherent levels in their functioning. In the therapeutic relationship, interpersonal communication promotes an integrative process within the client/patient's emerging mind. The text reviews some of the major approaches that have influenced the practice of psychotherapy, such as cognitive, behavioral, psychodynamic, and attachment based views. Focusing on such conditions as anxiety, depression, trauma, and personality disorders, the book also applies this model to an understanding of the nature and origins of mental dysfunction. Each chapter then offers a practical approach to how therapists can incorporate a neuroscience perspective into their daily clinical work. Finally, the book provides a glimpse into the future that might allow researchers and clinicians ways to consider new avenues for exploring the nature of human growth within psychotherapy.

These are exciting times and we must take bold integrative steps to move the field of mental health forward. Lou Cozolino guides us along this important path. Enjoy!

Preface

It takes ages to destroy a popular opinion.
(Voltaire, 1976)

I initially suspected that an exploration of neuroscience might lead me to reject psychotherapy and join those predicting its demise. Hard-core science types almost always seem hostile to psychotherapy, and I feared I'd fall prey to their way of thinking. After spending all of my life studying humanities and the softer side of science, I couldn't resist finding out what the other side was up to. Imagine my surprise to find that many recent discoveries in the neurosciences seem to support the value of psychotherapy. I've come to believe that the current convergence of neuroscience and psychotherapy is driven by the fact that both strive to explain the impact of the evolution, development, and functioning of the brain on human experience.

Why is it important to know anything about neurons or neural networks to understand the problems, passions, and aspirations of human beings? Wouldn't it be better to study poetry, world history, or even the stock market to get a handle on humanity? Although I agree that all of these are important, I also feel that understanding our brain is a vital addition to a comprehensive appreciation of who and what we are. I feel that it may help us to better understand where, as a species, we have come from, and where we may be headed. When we consider that every experience, memory, and behavior we have is encoded within neural networks, it is difficult to discount the importance of the nervous system, especially the brain.

Despite their shared focus, psychotherapy would not have survived as a branch of neurology during the 20th century. Although many factors contribute to their lack of compatibility, cultural and professional biases against brain-based explanations for personality have played a major role. Perhaps more importantly, the brain has been viewed as a relatively static entity, determined by the interaction of genetic preprogramming and early childhood experience. This attitude of neural pessimism is essentially incompatible with psychotherapy.

Psychotherapy is an optimistic endeavor that demands the possibility of change. Freud had to abandon his colleagues' view of the brain (and the field of neurology) in order to pursue the idea that the "talking cure" could alter neural connections and change the nature of psychological experience. It took many decades before the study of the brain could catch up with Freud's radical ideas. More recent research reflects an openness to the brain's role in all domains of human experience, including love, empathy, and spirituality. There is also a new optimism concerning the brain's ability to remain flexible and to benefit from enriched environments throughout life.

Psychotherapy is just such an enriched environment, tailored to encourage the growth and integration of neural networks regulating memory, cognition, emotion, and attachment. In the following pages, I will make a case for the theory that all forms of psychotherapy— from psychoanalysis to behavioral interventions—are successful to the extent to which they enhance change in relevant neural circuits. I will also make a case for the notion that the "unscientific" use of language and emotional attunement (for which psychotherapists are often criticized by those in the hard sciences) actually provides the best medium for neural growth and integration. This way of thinking about psychotherapy is as fascinating as it is speculative.

The Brain

The brain is neither predetermined nor unchanging, but rather is an *organ of adaptation*. The brain and nervous systems are built and sculpted, neuron by neuron, through the interaction of our genetic programming and environmental influences (Changeux & Danchin, 1976) in what is now called *use-dependent development*. The architectural sculpting of our brain determines the shape of all of our experiences. Neuroscience helps us to understand the process of how the brain is built and shaped by early interpersonal experiences, and how psychotherapy creates an interpersonal matrix capable of rebuilding it (Schore, 1994; Siegel, 1999).

Although the idea that the brain is built by experience during development and rebuilt during psychotherapy feels new, it was in fact suggested by Freud at the end of the 19th century. We know that learning and memory are encoded within the nervous system, and it is this learning that organizes the neural architecture and functioning of the brain. During childhood, the growth and organization of the brain are paralleled by the rapid development of skills and abilities (Fischer, 1987). In psychotherapy, subtle changes in thinking, feeling, and behavior are slower to occur but still vitally important. Therapy is a learning environment that targets specific skills and abilities, organized by specific neural systems that neuroscience is in the process of discovering.

The movement to integrate psychotherapy and neuroscience has gradually gained momentum throughout the last decade. The expansion of psychopharmacology during the 1980s and the development of brain-scanning techniques in the 1990s have both contributed to the convergence of psychotherapy and the biological sciences. Courses in pharmacology and neurobiology are now common at psychoanalytic institutes; training in psychotherapy increasingly includes attention to the underlying neurobiology of brain development, parent–child bonding, and mental illness. Over the next few years, courses in biological psychology will shift from the traditional focus on sensation, perception, and neurochemistry to areas of applied cognitive and affective neuroscience. In the not-too-distant future, an understanding and application of the neuroscience of psychotherapy will become an accepted standard of practice (Kandel, 1998).

Unfortunately, many psychotherapists have a bias against neuroscience. They describe it as confusing and irrelevant to their work. Although I agree that it can be confusing, it is extremely relevant to the process of psychotherapy. My primary goal in writing this book is to encourage you to include knowledge of the brain in your overall understanding of human growth and development. I will present information about the neuroscience behind human experience and provide examples of why and how it may apply to psychotherapy. Remember that we need to approach our struggle to understand the role of the brain in human experience with a balance of enthusiasm and skepticism. Although there are thousands of research studies and many theories, few definitive answers exist about the causes and treatment of mental illness.

Psychiatric disorders, like mental health, are the result of multiple interacting processes. Our present knowledge is a patchwork of symptom clusters, etiological theories, medication reactions, and brain-scanning data. Some diagnoses, such as posttraumatic stress disorder, are relatively straightforward, and the connections between symptoms and their neurobiological mechanisms are fairly well understood. Others, like schizophrenia and autism, are far more complex, and elude satisfactory and comprehensive descriptions. Neuroscience offers an additional perspective to the diagnosis and treatment of psychiatric disorders. Although much about mental illness remains a mystery, advances in theory and technology promise to bring us closer to a more complete understanding. In the chapters to come, we will explore the neural networks that have evolved to perform functions especially relevant to psychotherapy.

The Book

In Part I, we begin with the birth of psychotherapy and the discovery of the unconscious, while taking a first look at the brain from an evolutionary point of view. The next two chapters discuss psychotherapy from the perspective of neuroscience. Some basic overlapping principles of psychotherapy and neuroscience are presented to propose a theory of how and why therapy works. These principles are then applied to specific forms of therapy, translating the language of psychology to neuroscience. This presentation of the theoretical outline before the more detailed discussion of neuroscience will allow us to then discuss the hard science with an idea of its applicability to psychotherapy.

In Part II we will get down to some of the details of how the brain works, from the basic neuronal building blocks to complex systems of memory, language, and the organization of experience. Although this section contains a great deal of research information, the science is applied, wherever possible, to day-to-day experience and clinical practice. Part III will focus on the development and organization of the healthy brain. Specific networks related to social functioning will be explored in relation to attachment and how the brain constructs stories for private and public consumption. Knowing how these networks function will help us understand defense mechanisms, perceptual distortions, and the experience of the private and social selves.

Part IV focuses primarily on common problems such as anxiety, trauma, and codependency, from a scientific perspective. Anxiety, stress, and trauma are areas in which neuroscience can be especially helpful in educating and treating clients, and in which the bridges between psychotherapy and science are the most developed. The last section, Part V, will focus on the emerging paradigm of psychotherapist as neuroscientist, and some practical applications of neuroscience to psychotherapy. Finally, I argue for the use of a neuroscience perspective to serve as the foundation for a rational and scientific synthesis among the various modes of psychotherapy presently in use. Competing schools of psychotherapy may ultimately need to give way to multimodal interventions based on principles of neurobiological growth, regulation, and integration.

What follows is one psychotherapist's view of the vast field of neuroscience. No attempt was made to be comprehensive or even-handed in the selection of the materials presented. I included what I thought would be most interesting and relevant to both practicing clinicians and others interested in the relationship between the mind and brain. Although I discuss a variety of psychiatric disorders—and neural systems that are relevant to them—a comprehensive examination of this rapidly growing area of research is beyond the scope of the present work.

I hope that this book will stimulate your interest in neuroscience and encourage you to seek out some of the many excellent books referenced in the chapters ahead. I further hope that you will go out on a limb and speculate about new applications of neuroscience to psychotherapy. Keep in mind that the tools and theories at our disposal are primitive relative to the complexity of what we are attempting to understand. There is much to be discovered about the human brain. Future advances will require the interaction of scientific studies from the laboratory, case studies from clinical practice, and the imagination of theoreticians who will make sense of it all. This is, after all, the process that characterizes the history of scientific progress.

Acknowledgments

I would like to thank my editor at Norton Professional Books, Deborah Malmud, and her associates Regina Dahlgren Ardini and Anne Hellman for their consistent encouragement and assistance in the preparation of this book. Many thanks also go to Jennifer Goldman, Lisa McDonald, Lauri Mattenson, Joanna Wertheimer, and Bruce Singer for their editorial and creative contributions.

In my journey to link mind and brain, I have been fortunate to find fellow travelers who have become both intellectual comrades and supportive friends. I have been inspired by Dan Siegel's enthusiasm for the integration of psychotherapy and neuroscience. Many of the concepts described here have emerged from our discussions and Dan's writings and seminars over the past decade. In the same spirit, I am thankful to Allan Schore for his friendship, intellectual fervor, and ability to motivate me when I falter. Both Dan and Allan provided invaluable suggestions during the preparation of this manuscript.

John Schumann has been a good friend and teacher for many years, and I thank him for his encouragement and extremely helpful input. Hans Miller has taught me much over the years and I thank him for his many excellent suggestions. I am also deeply appreciative of the considerable moral support and intellectual horsepower contributed to this book by my friend John Wynn.

My appreciation also goes to Aleen Agranowitz, Alex Caldwell, Antonio deNicolas, Drew Erhardt, Michael Goldstein, David Foy, Marvin & Shelia Lieberman, Brendan Maher, Michael McGuire, Keith Neuchterlien, Regina Pally, Arnold Scheibel, Edward Shafranske, and Fredrick Silvers for their combined support, inspiration, and intellectual input over these many years.

I owe much to my friends, students, and colleagues at Pepperdine, UCLA, and Morning Sky School, who provide me with a stimulating mixture of challenge, struggle, and laughter. Special thanks go to all of my clients who, through the years, have shared this journey with me. Finally, I want to thank Susan for her caring and support during this all-too-consuming process.

THE NEUROSCIENCE
OF PSYCHOTHERAPY
Building and Rebuilding the Human Brain

PART I

NEUROSCIENCE AND PSYCHOTHERAPY: AN OVERVIEW

The Entangled Histories of Neurology and Psychology

> The seemingly irreconcilable dichotomies and paradoxes
> that formerly prevailed with respect to mind vs. matter . . .
> become reconciled today in a single comprehensive and
> unifying view of mind, brain, and man in nature.
> (Sperry, 1981)

How does the brain give rise to the mind? Where do the brain and mind meet, and by what means do they interact? These are difficult questions—so difficult, in fact, that most academics ignore them and move on to safer topics. The popular choice is to focus on either the mind *or* the brain and act as if the other doesn't exist. The problem with this dichotomous approach is that it creates a barrier to understanding what is essentially a unified process (Cobb, 1944). Fields of study related to neurology and psychology are simultaneously pushed apart by academic and intellectual politics, and drawn together by the common elements of human experience and behavior. The entangled histories of neurology and psychology are a reflection of these opposing forces (Ellenberger, 1970; Sulloway, 1979).

Freud started out as a rebel, a neurologist who wanted to understand the mind. I suspect he was extremely frustrated with the mind–brain partisanship of medical school, and longed to study and work with others who shared his interests. At the age of 29, Freud won a traveling fellowship and decided to spend the fall and winter of 1885 at the Salpetriere Hospital on the left bank of Paris (Sulloway, 1979). The choice of the Salpetriere was based on the reputation of one professor, Jean-Martin Charcot. Through the preceding decades, Charcot had become an expert in both neurology and psychology, but one of his specialties was using hypnotism to demonstrate the power of the mind over the body. In Charcot, Freud sought a teacher who was well established, confident, and unafraid of the "no man's land" between mind and brain. Imagine Freud's excitement as he rode through the streets of Paris to meet with the great man, hoping he had found a kindred spirit.

Charcot specialized in patients suffering from what was then called *hysteria*. These patients had symptoms, such as seizures or paralysis, that mimicked neurological illnesses but were without apparent physical cause. A classic example is the condition called "glove anesthesia," in which feeling is lost in one or both hands, beginning at the wrist. This condition cannot be explained by the neural structures within the arms and hands, and thus necessitates a psychological explanation. In these patients, the hands take on some symbolic meaning; perhaps they have been used to commit some taboo act filled with guilt and fear. The 1880s were also a time when hypnosis and the mind's ability to control behavior and awareness first burst into popular culture. Charcot used hypnosis in lectures and demonstrations to illustrate his beliefs about mind–body interactions.

The months spent at Salpetriere with Charcot had a profound effect on Freud. He came to believe that hidden mental processes exerted powerful effects on consciousness, and that hysterical symptoms resulted not from malingering or feigning illness, but instead from the subtle and powerful neurological structures of the brain.

Hysteria was a reflection of the capacity of the brain to reorganize as a result of stress and trauma. Dissociative splits between consciousness and behavior demonstrated to Freud that the brain is capable of multiple levels of conscious and unconscious awareness; in the years to come, he would use language and emotion (in the context of psychoanalysis) to reconnect them. Freud returned to Vienna in February 1886, opening his own clinical practice two months later. Despite his entry into the medical establishment, he continued his rebellion later that year, with the presentation of a paper on the existence of hysteria in males (Sulloway, 1979). Freud, so fascinated by the unconscious, remained its most ardent explorer until his death in 1939 (Ellenberger, 1970).

In the years that followed his time at Salpetriere, Freud expanded on Charcot's thinking in many significant ways. He placed the unconscious in a developmental context by tracing the genesis of hysterical symptoms to childhood experiences. He came to believe that hysterical patients suffered from the unconscious emotional aftereffects of repressed childhood memories. Furthermore, Freud connected the development of the individual to the evolution of the species. Influenced by the ancient idea that we contain within us the biological history of our primitive ancestors, Freud included the importance of instinctual drives such as sexuality, rage, and envy into his theories about the construction of the brain and the development of the mind. Freud believed that beneath our civilized exteriors, there exists within us a primitive savage, which accounts for some of the contradictions in human nature.

Freud's message was that in order to understand who and what we are, we need to understand the part of us that is still animalistic. He called this the id—the primitive and uncivilized life energy that we share with our reptilian and mammalian ancestors. This concept was met with understandable hostility by Freud's civilized and repressed contemporaries. At that time, physicians were pillars of European culture, highly invested in their superiority over wild animals and steadfast in their right and obligation to subjugate the "primitive" people of the world. Needless to say, linking civilized humans to animals (to say nothing of his idea that children have sexual desires) made Freud and his theories scandalous in "respectable" circles.

Freud's Abandoned Project

In the late 1800s, the doors to the microscopic world of the nervous system opened for the first time. Technical improvements in the microscope and newly developed staining techniques led to the discovery of both neurons and the synapses through which they communicate. The existence of synapses revealed that the nervous system is not a single structure, but instead is made up of countless microscopic processing units. Furthermore, that humans shared these neurons with all other living creatures supported the radical idea of a common evolutionary ancestry with other animals. Around this same time, the work of Wernicke and Broca showed that specific areas of the brain were responsible for different aspects of language. The dual neuroanatomical notions of synaptic transmission and localization provided rich theoretical soil for new models of the brain.

Inspired by Darwin, Charcot, and the opening of the microscopic neural world to investigation, Freud wrote *The Project for a Scientific Psychology* (Freud, 1895). In the "Project," Freud postulated that what we witness of conscious and unconscious processing is reflected in the neural architecture of the brain and nervous system. As part of this work, he drew simple sketches of interconnecting neurons to represent human emotions, behaviors, and psychological defenses. These sketches depicted the interactions among drives, the organs of the senses, impulses, and mechanisms of inhibition. According to his colleagues, Freud became obsessed with the idea of constructing a model of the mind in terms of its neurobiological mechanisms (Schore, 1997b).

Despite his enthusiasm, Freud realized that his dream for a psychology based in an understanding of the nervous system was too far ahead of its time, and he suppressed the publication of the "Project" until his death. He decided to instead utilize the more palatable and accessible models of literature and anthropology to provide the primary metaphors for psychoanalysis. Freud, the neurologist, became all but forgotten as his complex psychological theories moved increasingly further from their neurobiological roots. Freud's shift away from neurological explanations was based primarily on the lack of scientific knowledge and the constraints he must have felt in battling a conservative medical establishment. Because it was so scientifically and politically difficult to study the brain, Freud chose to study the mind.

Perhaps Freud felt that his "Project" would be relegated to the same sort of obscurity as the case of Phineas Gage. Gage, a 19th-century railroad foreman, had a metal bar pass completely through his head, causing the destruction of the middle portions of his frontal cortex. This particular area of the brain has been shown to be involved with judgment, planning, and emotional control. Although Gage had no specific sensory, motor, or language deficits, the reports of those who knew him said that "Gage was no longer Gage" (Benson, 1994). His emotionality, relationship abilities, and the quality of his experience were all dramatically altered. Because Gage's symptoms involved his personality and emotions, the publication reporting his case received little attention for most of the 20th century. Not only did it not fit well into the realm of behaviors that neurology felt comfortable addressing, but there was also a bias against relating human personality to neurobiological mechanisms (Damasio, 1994).

Unfortunately, Freud's shift from the brain to metaphors of mind opened psychoanalysis to all sorts of criticism throughout the 20th century. Metaphors such as the Oedipal and Electra complexes were seen as contrived fictions, which shielded them from scientific evaluation (Sulloway, 1979). Freud felt that psychoanalysis would eventually be reunited with its neurobiological origins when the time was right for a synthesis, rather than being taken over by the biological sciences (Pribram & Gill, 1976). Many, including myself, feel that the time is now. A respect for psychological processes has taken a strong enough hold within the scientific community and general culture to avoid a reduction of the mind to biological processes.

It is in this spirit that we turn our attention to ways of thinking about the brain that enhance our understanding of human experience. We begin with a model of the brain that provides a bridge between the fields of neurology and evolution, and the origins of the unconscious and internal conflicts.

The Triune Brain

In the 1970s, the neuroscientist Paul MacLean presented a model of the brain that emphasized the conservation of more primitive evolutionary structures within the modern human brain. *Conservation*, in this context, refers to the modification of earlier evolving brain structures for new applications in networks dedicated to more complex functions (Taylor, 1999). MacLean called his model the *triune brain*, and it is very much in line with the theories of both Darwin and Freud. The triune brain presents an evolutionary explanation that may account for some of the contradictions and discontinuities of human consciousness and behavior (MacLean, 1990).

MacLean described the human brain as a three-part phylogenetic system reflecting our evolutionary connection to both reptiles and lower mammals. Think of it as a brain within a brain within a brain. Each successive layer is devoted to increasingly complex functions and abilities. At the core is the *reptilian brain*, which has changed little through evolutionary history and is responsible for activation, arousal, homeostasis of the organism, and reproductive drives. The *paleomammalian brain* (or *limbic system*)—involved with learning, memory, and emotion—wraps around the reptilian brain. The highest layer, the *neomammalian brain*—primarily the cerebral cortex and a large portion of the corpus callosum (the bands of nerve fibers connecting the left and right hemispheres)—is required for conscious thought and self-awareness (MacLean, 1985).

MacLean suggested that our three brains don't necessarily work well together. He thought that the linkup among the three brains is problematic because of their differing "mentalities" and the fact that only the neomammalian brain is capable of consciousness and verbal communication (MacLean, 1990). What Charcot and Freud called dissociation and hysteria could be the result of inadequate or problematic linkups between these different, cohabitating brains. MacLean's description of the non-verbal reptilian and paleomammalian brains as unconsciously influencing processing in the neomammalian brain parallels Freud's distinction of the conscious and the unconscious minds.

The model of the triune brain serves the valuable function of providing a connective metaphor among the artifacts of evolution, the contemporary nervous system, and some of the inherent difficulties related to the organization and disorganization of human consciousness. This inner menagerie confronts the therapist with the challenge of simultaneously treating a human, a horse, and a crocodile (Hampden-Turner, 1981).

Ah, If It Were Only so Simple!

If three different brains controlling the same body weren't complex enough, it turns out that, in reality, the reptilian and paleomammalian brains continued to evolve along with the neomammalian brain. Later systems, emerging to address new survival requirements, conserved and modified components of already existing systems. Thus, all three layers gradually linked together in complex vertical and horizontal neural networks. This conservation and modification of neural networks has led to an amazingly complex set of convoluted neural networks, connecting multiple regions of the brain and performing an array of functions from monitoring respiration to performing mathematical computations. This makes the study of functional neuroanatomy a complex puzzle.

An example from space exploration may prove useful for an understanding of the evolution of the brain. As *Apollo 13* approached the moon, difficulties with the air supply system left the crew with just a few hours of oxygen (Lovell & Kluger, 1994). In the face of this crisis, scientists on earth removed all non-essential pieces from a mock spacecraft and constructed a new air supply system. Pieces of upholstery, plastic bags, duct tape, and electrical wiring were used in ways quite different from their original intent. The instructions on how to build this makeshift system were then conveyed to the *Apollo 13* crew. This scenario is much closer to the crafting of the modern brain than imagining a computer engineer sitting down to construct a new motherboard for a specific function.

An engineer presented with this bootstrapped air purification system would most certainly wonder how and why things were done the way they were. Although there are obvious differences between the *Apollo 13* scenario and natural selection, what *is* the same is an adaptation to an environmental crisis given existing material. It is in this context that a clearly divided triune brain is misleading. A superficial reading of MacLean's model might lead us to the idea that each layer of the triune brain evolved independently and sequentially, and that they all cooperate in a hierarchical fashion like a military chain of command. Ah, if it were only so simple!

The multiple roles played by the cerebellum offer a prime example of both neural conservation and adaptation. The cerebellum is a very old part of the brain that expanded during the evolution of the cerebral cortex. The vermis, involved with balance, is the oldest portion of the cerebellum. The newer portions—the cerebellar lobes— evolved along with the cerebral cortex, and are involved in neural networks of language, memory, and reasoning (Schmahmann, 1997). The cerebellum's ability to process vast amounts of information has been utilized by the evolving brain in increasingly higher cortical processes.

Just as balance requires constant monitoring of posture and the inhibition of unnecessary and distracting movements, so, in their own ways, do memory, attention, concentration, and language. The same timing mechanisms involved in locomotion seem to have been conserved for sequential processing in thought and language (Schmahmann, 1997). Although the cerebellum is considered by some as a primitive brain structure, its evolution and development reflect its networking with highly evolved areas of the neocortex. In order to study the brain we can't simply divide it into horizontal layers; we must also explore the vertical networks that interconnect the layers of the triune brain (Alexander, DeLong, & Strick, 1986; Cummings, 1993).

In fact, there are many ways to partition and understand the brain. Besides horizontal and vertical analysis, evolution has also selected for increasing differentiation between the left and right hemispheres. Certain areas of the brain have become specialized for specific skills such as language and spatial abilities. Still other areas serve to organize and control the activity of multiple regions.

Neural networks relevant to psychotherapy exist throughout the brain and nervous system. Some are evolutionarily primitive, whereas others have developed more recently. Some are fully functional from birth, whereas others take decades to mature. This is why an understanding of evolution and development is so vital in capturing the full picture of human experience. In the chapters to follow, we will pay special attention to networks that organize memory, attachment, emotion, and conscious awareness. Although these particular networks have been chosen because of their relevance to the psychotherapeutic process, keep in mind that there are many more. Also remember that although they are separated for the purpose of discussion, all neural systems are interconnected and are constantly interacting and influencing one other.

The Interpersonal Sculpting of the Brain

The theory that ontogeny recapitulates phylogeny refers to the concept that the evolution of the species is recreated in the gestation and development of each individual. To use MacLean's terms, we pass through the reptilian and paleomammalian stages before we develop into a full human. Although the theory of recapitulation is in many ways incorrect (Gould, 1977), some interesting parallels exist between our evolutionary history and the process of human development. At birth, the reptilian brain is fully functional and the paleomammalian brain is ready to be organized by early experiences.

The cortex, although active at birth, is much slower to develop than are most other areas of the brain, and is still forming in the third decade of life. Much of our most important emotional and interpersonal learning during our first few years occurs when our primitive brains are in control. The result is that a great deal of learning takes place before we have the necessary cortical systems for conscious awareness and memory. Thus, many of the most important aspects of our lives are controlled by reflexes, behaviors, and emotions learned and organized outside of our awareness. To a great extent, psychotherapy may owe its existence to these artifacts of evolution: the sequential development of the brain, its multiple processing systems, and their tendency to become dissociated.

The slow development of the brain maximizes the influence of environmental factors, increasing its chances to survive in the face of radical changes from generation to generation. That so much of the brain is shaped after birth is both *good and bad news*. The good news is that the individual brain is built to survive in a particular environment. Culture, language, climate, nutrition, and each set of parents shape each of our brains in a unique way. In good times and with good parents, this early brain building may serve the child well throughout life. The bad news comes when factors are not so favorable, such as in times of war or in the case of parental psychopathology. The brain is then sculpted in ways that can become maladaptive. It is in these instances that a therapist attempts to restructure neural architecture. Building the human brain is vastly complex; rebuilding it is a difficult and fascinating challenge.

In the course of evolution, primates have experienced increasingly long periods of maternal dependence. In fact, a portion of the brain called the *anterior cingulate*—centrally involved with maternal behavior, nursing, and play—begins to appear in the evolution of early mammals (MacLean, 1985). Before this, animals had to be prepared to survive at birth. A good example are sea turtles that hatch from their eggs high on a beach and make a mad instinctual dash toward the ocean. With the evolution of maternal care, children are allowed to develop more slowly within a supportive, scaffolding environment. This luxury leads to the increasing impact of parenting and early experiences on the building of the brain.

Konrad Lorenz (1991) found that geese imprint on an attachment object during a limited period of time soon after birth. If baby geese saw Lorenz instead of their mothers during this period, they would follow him as if he were their mother. Lorenz also found that when these geese reached sexual maturity 2 years later, they would "fall in love" with the kinds of geese they had been exposed to during their imprinting period. He even noted that a baby goose, who originally imprinted on him, fell in love with a human girl from the next town upon reaching sexual maturity! These early experiences seemed to be permanently etched into the brains of Lorenz's geese.

This principle of *imprinting* may exist in a more flexible and complex manner in humans, in the form of attraction to physical characteristics and attachment patterns. The early interpersonal environment may be imprinted in the human brain by shaping the child's neural networks and establishing the biochemical setpoints for circuitry dedicated to memory, emotion, and attachment. These structures and processes then serve as the infrastructure for later-developing intellectual skills, affect regulation, attachment, and the sense of self (Schore, 1994; Siegel, 1999).

Prolonged dependence in childhood allows for the development of a neocortex so complex that we have become capable of spoken language, multiple systems of memory and consciousness, and the construction of both private and social selves. These abilities create the possibility of generating inventions, imaginary internal environments, and many potential selves. Although these skills and abilities create tremendous possibilities, brainpower does have its downside. We are now also capable of becoming anxious about things that will never happen, and depressed by imagined slights and potential losses. Our imaginations can create exciting new lives, but they also generate fears that prevent us from living these lives. It is obvious that despite the massive development of the cortex, our primitive emotional brains continue to exert great influence over us.

Summary

Evolution's legacy is a complex brain, vulnerable to a variety of factors that can disrupt the growth and integration of important neural networks. The field of psychotherapy has emerged because of the brain's vulnerability to developmental and environmental risks. Although Freud began his career attempting to create a brain-based psychology, the theories and technology available to him did not allow him to carry out this project. Various ways of thinking about the brain (like MacLean's), although limited, provide models that bridge the gap between psychology and neurology, between mind and brain. How can the psychotherapist as neuroscientist synthesize these two ways of thinking? The following chapter will present a model of neural networks, how they develop, and how psychotherapists attempt to alter them during treatment. It is from this perspective that we will then examine the relevance of the nervous system to the process of psychotherapy.

Rebuilding the Brain: Neuroscience and Psychotherapy

I know of no more encouraging fact than the unquestionable
ability of man to elevate his life by a conscious endeavor.
(Henry David Thoreau)

Although psychotherapy was born of neurology in the 19th century, differences in language and world view resulted in little collaboration between scientists in these two fields for most of the 20th century. During this time, psychotherapists developed a rich metaphoric language of mind while neurologists built a detailed knowledge of brain–behavior relationships. As we begin the 21st century, neuroscience provides us with theoretical models and research data that allow us to begin to understand what happens in the brain during psychotherapy. A return to Freud's "Project" of a biological psychology is finally at hand.

At the heart of the interface of neuroscience and psychotherapy is the fact that human experience is mediated via two interacting processes. The first is the expression of our evolutionary past via the organization and functioning of the nervous system—a process resulting in billions of neurons organizing into neural networks, each with its own developmental timetable and requirements for growth. The second is the shaping of this neural architecture within the context of significant interpersonal relationships. The human brain is an "organ of adaptation" to the physical and social worlds; it is stimulated to grow and learn through positive and negative interactions. The quality and nature of our relationships are translated into codes within neural networks that serve as the infrastructure for both brain and mind. Through this translation of experience into neurobiological structures, nature and nurture become one.

When one or more neural networks necessary for optimal functioning remain underdeveloped, underregulated, or underintegrated with other networks, we experience the complaints and symptoms for which people seek psychotherapy. At the heart of psychotherapy is an understanding of the interwoven forces of nature and nurture, what goes right and wrong in their developmental unfolding, and how to reinstate healthy neural functioning. When psychotherapy results in symptom reduction or experiential change, the brain has, in some way, been altered (Kandel, 1998).

In this chapter we will explore ideas and data from neuroscience to form an explanation for how psychotherapy changes the brain. We will discuss the building and rebuilding of neural networks, the role of enriched environments, and the part played by stress in changing the brain. We will also explore the central role of the therapeutic relationship in this change process, as well as the importance of the expression of emotion and the use of language in therapeutic success.

Neural Networks

So far we have used the term *neural networks* in a general way; I would like now to get a bit more specific. *Neurons* are the microscopic processing units that make up all parts of the nervous system. When we talk of the frontal cortex, amygdala, or hippocampus, we are literally talking about large numbers of individual neurons organized to perform a set of functions. The neurons within these systems need to be able to organize and reorganize in such a way as to allow us to learn, remember, and act as we adjust to different situations. Although each individual neuron is limited to either firing or not firing, the diverse capabilities of the nervous system come from the complex interaction of individual neuronal signals. A simplistic analogy is an old-fashioned billboard consisting of rows and columns of thousands of light bulbs. Although each individual bulb is limited to being either on or off, the pattern created by these lights can spell out words, form images, and create the illusion of movement. In a similar fashion, patterns of neural firing come to have meaning within the flow of information throughout the nervous system.

To accomplish the complexity required of the nervous system, neurons organize into *neural networks*. A neural network can range from just a few neurons in a simple animal to trillions of neural interconnections in brains such as our own. Neural networks encode and organize all of our behaviors from basic reflexes, such as pulling our hand away from a hot plate, to our ability to simultaneously comprehend the visual, emotional, and political significance of Picasso's *Guernica*. Single neurons or neural networks can interconnect with multiple other neural networks, allowing for interaction and integration. Because we will be referring to neural networks throughout the chapters to come, it is important to keep a good visual image in our minds as we proceed.

Figures 2.1 and 2.2 depict simple neural networks with each circle representing an individual neuron. Starting with Figure 2.1, you will notice that the flow of information moves from left to right across the four columns of neurons. On the left, some of the *input neurons* are firing in response to some stimulus (1 = firing/0 = nonfiring). In turn, their firing stimulates the activation of some set of neurons within the *hidden layers* of processing. Finally, a combination of *output neurons* fire, resulting in some experience or reaction. Figure 2.2 represents a step toward a more accurate model, with information flowing in both directions and an increased level of interaction among neurons. Each of the connections will have either

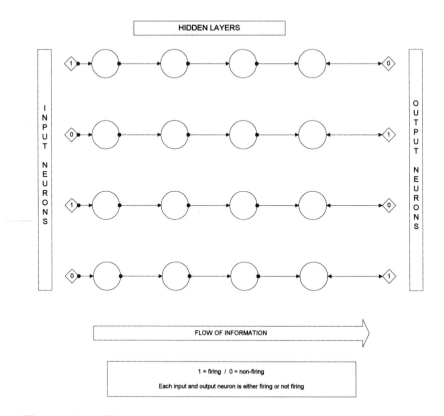

Figure 2.1   The feedforward neural network

A depiction of sixteen neurons in a simple feedforward circuit.

an excitatory or inhibitory effect on other neurons. This mosaic of firing patterns, the network's *entanstiation*, will determine which set of output neurons fire. Making things slightly more complicated, instead of 16 neurons there are millions, and each neuron can be connected to thousands of other neurons.

Entanstiations are sculpted by experience and encode all of our capabilities, emotions, memories, and dreams. It is the consistency of these firing patterns that results in the patterns of our behaviors and experience. Once these neural patterns are established, new learning modifies the relationship of neurons within these networks. When we

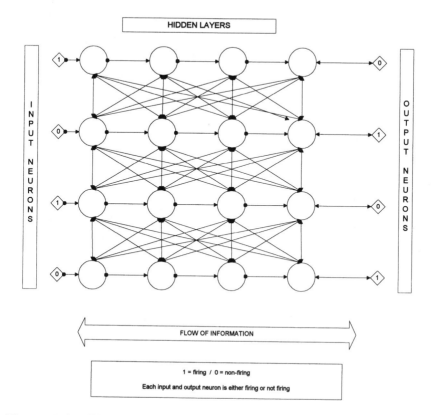

Figure 2.2   The feedforward and feedback neural network
A slightly more complex model in which information is fed backwards and each neuron can communicate with all of its neighbors.

talk of building and rebuilding the brain, neurons are our basic building blocks and neural networks are the structures that we sculpt and resculpt.

Learning within neural networks occurs as a result of trial and error. Feedforward and feedback information loops form complex patterns of excitation and inhibition among neurons within the hidden layers. This process eventually leads to consistent and adaptive output. This is demonstrated in a soon-to-be toddler, who repeatedly tests and refines her balance, leg strength, and coordination with each new attempt to walk. Her brain drives her to keep trying while recording her successes and failures within neural networks responsible for balance, motor coordination, and visual tracking. In this same way, neural networks organize behaviors, emotions, thought, and sensations that are built and rebuilt throughout life.

I remember being surprised to find a table of random numbers in an appendix of my college statistics textbook. At first, I thought this to be a waste of paper, assuming that anyone could generate random numbers on their own. When I shared my thoughts with the professor, he assured me that much research had gone into demonstrating that we are incapable of generating random numbers. He said that as hard as we might try, we can't avoid falling into patterns of certain numbers. This finally makes sense to me based on neural network organization: We are unable to engage in random actions because our behaviors are guided by patterns established through previous learning to which we automatically return.

Neural Network Growth and Integration

The growth and connectivity of neurons is the basic mechanism of all learning and adaptation. Learning can be reflected in neural changes in a number of ways, including the growth of new neurons, the expansion of existing neurons, and changes in the connectivity between existing neurons. All of these changes are expressions of *plasticity*, or the ability of the nervous system to change. The birth of new neurons, or *neurogenesis*, is a controversial field of study. Some recent research suggests that new neurons are generated in different areas of primate and human brains, especially in regions involved with ongoing learning, such as the hippocampus, the amygdala, and the frontal and temporal lobes (Eriksson et al., 1998; Gould, Reeves, Graziano, & Gross, 1999; Gould, Tanapat, Hastigs, & Shors, 1999; Gross, 2000).

Existing neurons grow though the expansion and branching of the dendrites they project to other neurons. There is sufficient evidence that neurons demonstrate growth and changes in reaction to new experiences and learning (Purves & Voyvodic, 1987). This process is reflected in the connectivity among neurons in our simple schematic diagrams. Neurons interconnect to form neural networks, and neural networks, in turn, integrate with one another to perform increasingly complex tasks. For example, networks that participate in language, emotion, and memory need to become integrated in order for us to recall and tell an emotionally meaningful story with the proper affect, correct details, and appropriate words.

Association areas within the brain serve the roles of bridging, coordinating, and directing the multiple neural circuits to which they are connected. Although the actual mechanisms of this integration are not yet known, they are likely to include some combination of communication within and between neurons, the relationships among local neuronal circuits, and the interactions between functional brain systems (Trojan & Pokorny, 1999). Changes in the synchrony of activation of multiple neural networks may also play a role in the coordination of their activity (Crick, 1994; Konig & Engel, 1995).

Gene Expression

The growth and organization of the brain is a function of the interaction of genetic and environmental influences. It is helpful to think of genes in terms of serving both a *template* and a *transcription* function (Kandel, 1998). As templates, genes provide the organization of the uniform structures of brain anatomy that are relatively unimpacted by environmental influences. These structures and functions, such as the organization of the triune brain and our basic reflexes, are shared by all members of our species. Transcription genes, on the other hand, depend on environmental triggers in order to be expressed (Black, 1998). Transcription genes control the more subtle aspects of the brain's organization, such as the specific sculpting of later developing neural networks and the levels of specific neurotransmitters available to different brain systems. In fact, 70% of our genetic structure is added after birth (Schore, 1994).

At our present level of understanding, experience appears to play a vital role in gene expression via the activation of neural firing and a cascade of biochemical processes. For example, although identical twins raised in the same household may have identical genes for schizophrenia, only one may develop the illness. This is believed to be the result of the triggering of different gene expression based on the unique interactions between each child and his or her environment. It is through gene transcription that new neurons grow, existing neurons expand, and environmental stimulation continues to build the brain. The transcription function of genes allows for ongoing neural plasticity throughout life, and provides the basis for enriched experiences like psychotherapy to benefit both the adolescent and adult brain (Black, 1998).

The Role of Enriched Environments

The brain continually changes to reflect aspects of its environment. In other words, its neural architecture comes to reflect the environment that shapes it. An enriched environment is one that is characterized by a level of stimulation and complexity that enhances learning and growth; an impoverished environment presents little stimulation, novelty, or challenge.

In studies that examine the effects of the environment on animals, enriched environments take the form of more diverse, complex, colorful, and stimulating habitats. The brains of these animals are compared with those raised in relatively empty monochromatic enclosures. Animals raised in enriched environments have more neurons, more synaptic connections among neurons, a greater number of blood capillaries, and more mitochondria activity (Diamond, Krech, & Rosenweig, 1964; Kempermann, Kuhn, & Gage, 1997, 1998; Kolb

& Whishaw, 1998; Sirevaag & Greenough, 1988). These findings reflect a brain that is more complex, active, and enriched.

For humans, enriched environments can include the kinds of challenging educational and experiential opportunities that encourage us to learn new skills and expand our knowledge. Higher levels of education, practicing skills, and continued engagement in mental activities also correlate with more neurons and neural connections (Jacobs & Scheibel, 1993; Jacobs, Schall, & Scheibel, 1993). Higher levels of education and reading ability have been shown to correlate with a diminished impact of dementia later in life (Schmand, Smit, Geerling, & Lindeboom, 1997). Areas of the brain dedicated to certain skills can actually adopt cells in adjacent neural areas to serve their expanded needs (Elbert, Pantev, Wienbruch, Rockstroh, & Taub, 1995). The human brain does, indeed, grow in response to challenge and new learning.

Psychotherapy can be thought of as an enriched environment that promotes the development of cognitive, emotional, and behavioral abilities. The way the brain changes during therapy depends on the neural networks involved in the kinds of problems addressed in treatment. The available data, although limited, support the theory that neuronal growth and enhanced interconnection among neurons and neural networks parallel the experiential and symptomatic changes we witness in psychotherapy. These neuronal changes coincide with changes in glucose metabolism (Baxter et al., 1992), concentrations of neurotransmitters, and blood flow. Perhaps, in the future, these biochemical changes will become part of an accepted method for determining the success of psychotherapy.

Learning and Stress

During periods of stress, changes in the biochemical environment of the brain shifts its focus to new learning (Gould, McEwen, Tanapat, Galea, & Fuchs, 1997). Although extreme stress inhibits new learning and brain growth, mild to moderate stress stimulates neural growth hormones and leads to increased production of cells in brain areas involved in learning (Pham, Soderstrom, Henriksson, & Mohammed, 1997). These and other studies suggest that stress may be utilized to enlist naturally occurring neurobiological processes involved in the growth and connectivity of neurons and neural circuits. Furthermore, moderate stress triggers the release of neurohormones that enhance cortical reorganization and new learning (Cowan & Kandel, 2001; Jablonska, Gierdalski, Kossut, & Skangiel-Kramska, 1999; Myers, Churchill, Muja, & Garraghty, 2000; Zhu & Waite, 1998). Stressful and dangerous situations alert and prepare the brain to pay attention and learn.

Dissociation is a common symptom in reaction to traumatic experiences. It is characterized by disorientation and a disconnection among thoughts, behaviors, sensations, and emotions. Dissociation demonstrates to us that the neural networks organizing these functions are, in fact, separate. Because they are seamlessly interwoven during normal states of awareness, we fail to understand that their integration is an active, if unconscious, process. Dissociation reflects a pathological expression of the plasticity that organizes and integrates neural networks.

The power of stress to trigger neural plasticity is a key element in the success of psychotherapy. As opposed to traumatic experiences, the controlled exposure to stress during therapy is a way in which therapists have attempted to harness the interaction of stress and learning in order to change the brain in a manner promoting mental health. As therapists, we work against dissociation to integrate neural networks. Integration is essentially the opposite of the dissociation observed in reaction to trauma.

Psychopathology and Neural Network Integration

If everything we experience is represented within neural networks, then psychopathology of all kinds—from the mildest neurotic symptoms to the most severe psychosis—must be represented within and among neural networks. Healthy functioning requires proper development and functioning of neural networks organizing conscious awareness, behavior, emotion, and sensation. In line with this theory, psychopathology is a reflection of suboptimal integration and coordination of neural networks. Patterns of dysregulation of brain activation in specific disorders support the theory of a brain-based explanation for the symptoms of psychopathology.

In the chapters ahead, we will explore how the formation and integration of neural networks is facilitated through nurturing relationships during sensitive periods of development (Schore, 1994; Siegel, 1999). Difficulties in early caretaking, genetic and biological vulnerabilities, or trauma at any time during life can result in the lack of integration among networks. Unresolved trauma results in information processing deficits that disrupt integrated neural processing. Evidence for this comes from a variety of sources. Dissociative symptoms following trauma—reflecting the disconnection among networks of behavior, emotion, sensation, and cognition—predict the later development of posttraumatic stress disorder (Koopman, Classen, & Spiegel, 1994; McFarlane & Yehuda, 1996). Children victimized by psychological, physical, and sexual abuse have a greater probability of demonstrating electrophysiological abnormalities in executive regions of the brain vital to neural network integration (Ito et al., 1993; Teicher et al., 1997). *These studies reflect the central relationship between neural network integration and mental health.*

In general, psychological integration suggests that the cognitive functions of the executive brain have increasing access to information across networks of sensation, behavior, and emotion. A primary focus of neural integration in psychotherapy is between networks of affect and cognition. Dissociation between the two occurs when biochemical changes caused by high levels of stress inhibit or disrupt the brain's integrative abilities. The circuits of the reptilian and paleomammalian brains can be "unlinked" from the conscious neomammalian cortex under stress.

This unlinking may not be accidental. As valuable as language can be, evolution appears to have selected for the shutdown of language (and a decrease in cognitive processing) when confronted with threat. When in danger, it is better to shut up and act! The resulting disruption of the integration of information processing may be the most common cause of neural network dissociation. Cortical networks responsible for memory, language, and integration become inhibited and underperform during times of overwhelming stress. The very way that the brain has evolved to successfully cope with immediate threat creates a vulnerability to longer-term psychological problems: Enter psychotherapy.

Applying this model, psychotherapy is a means of creating or restoring neural network integration and coordination among various neural networks. Research has demonstrated that successful psychotherapy correlates with changes in activation in areas of the brain hypothesized to be involved in disorders such as obsessive compulsive disorder and depression (Baxter et al., 1992; Brody et al., 2001; Schwartz, Stoessel, Baxter, Martin, & Phelps, 1996). The return to normal levels of activation results in reestablishing positive reciprocal control among relevant neural structures and networks.

Psychotherapy and Neural Network Integration

A basic assumption of both neuroscience and psychotherapy is that optimal health and functioning are related to increasingly advanced levels of growth and integration. On a neurological level, this equates to the integration and communication of neural networks dedicated to emotion, cognition, sensation, and behavior. On a psychological level, integration is the ability to experience the important aspects of life while employing a minimum of defensiveness. Growth and integration are optimized by a positive early environment, including stage-appropriate challenges, support, and parents who are capable and willing to put feelings into words. These factors lead to positive affect regulation, biological homeostasis, and a quiet "internal milieu" allowing for the consolidation of the experience of subjectivity and a positive sense of self.

From the perspective of neuroscience, psychotherapy can be understood as a specific kind of enriched environment designed to *enhance the growth of neurons and the integration of neural networks*. The therapeutic environment is individually tailored to fit the symptoms and needs of the client. Although interventions can be based on any theory of change, I propose here that all forms of therapy, regardless of theoretical orientation, will be successful to the degree to which they foster neural growth and integration. *Neural growth and integration in psychotherapy are enhanced by*:

1. The establishment of a safe and trusting relationship.
2. Gaining new information and experiences across the domains of cognition, emotion, sensation, and behavior.
3. The simultaneous or alternating activation of neural networks that are inadequately integrated or dissociated.
4. Moderate levels of stress or emotional arousal alternating with periods of calm and safety.
5. The integration of conceptual knowledge with emotional and bodily experience through narratives that are co-constructed with the therapist.
6. Developing a method of processing and organizing new experiences so as to continue ongoing growth and integration outside of therapy.

Although psychotherapists do not generally think in "neuroscientific" terms, I believe this is essentially what we do, regardless of theoretical orientation. We provide information to clients about our understanding of their difficulties in the form of psychoeducation, interpretations, and/or reality testing. We encourage clients to engage in behaviors, express feelings, and become conscious of aspects of themselves of which they may be unaware. We dare them to take risks. We guide them back and forth between thoughts and feelings, trying to help them establish new connections between the two. We help clients alter their description of themselves and the world, incorporating new awareness and encouraging better decision making. With successful treatment, the methods being used are internalized so that clients can gain independence from therapy. This process occurs across psychodynamic, systems, and cognitive–behavioral approaches to treatment.

The broad context in which these processes can successfully occur is one of increasing levels of *affect tolerance and regulation* and the development of *integrative narratives* that emerge from the client–therapist relationship. In the context of empathic attunement within a safe and structured environment, clients are encouraged to tolerate the anxiety of feared experiences, memories, and thoughts. In this process, neural networks that are normally inhibited become activated and available for inclusion into conscious processing (Siegel, 1995). Interpretations in psychodynamic therapy, exposure in behavioral therapies, or experiments in differentiation from a family systems perspective all focus on this goal. Through the activation of multiple cognitive and emotional networks, previously dissociated functions are integrated and gradually brought under the control of cortical executive functions. Narratives co-constructed with therapists provide a new template for thoughts, behaviors, and ongoing integration.

Pathways of Integration

Remember how information flows simultaneously in multiple directions through many neural networks? Optimal integration likely involves maximum flow and efficient interconnection (Pribram, 1991). Using the model of neural network integration, psychopathology doesn't exist in a specific brain area, but rather is the result of unhealthful mutual interactions among participating systems (Mayberg, 1997; Mayberg et al., 1999). Numerous processing networks combine affect, sensation, behavior, and conscious awareness into an integrated, functional, and balanced whole. The integration and organization of these multiple and complex networks is the neural substrate for what Freud called the *ego*. The ego is essentially a shorthand for how the organization of the self comes to be expressed in dimensions such as personality, affect regulation, coping styles, and self-image.

For the purpose of psychotherapy, information flow and integration may best be described as a set of neural information loops. The primary directions of flow are top-down (cortical to subcortical and back again) and left–right (across the two halves of the brain). Keep in mind that these information loops need to communicate with each other as well as with many other processing systems.

Top-down integration would include MacLean's linkup among the three levels of the triune brain and the unification of the body, emotion, and conscious awareness. This is called top-down because these circuits form loops that go from the top of our head down and back up again. Top-down integration includes the ability of the cortex to process, inhibit, and organize the reflexes, impulses, and emotions generated by the brain stem and limbic system (Alexander et al., 1986; Cummings, 1993). Frontal lobe disorders often result in a disinhibition of impulses and movements normally under its control. Obsessive-compulsive and attention deficit disorders fall within the category of dysregulation of top-down neural circuitry. Within this category I include what has been referred to as *dorsal-ventral integration* connecting cortical with limbic processing (Panksepp, 1998; Tucker, Luu, & Pribram, 1995).

Left–right integration involves abilities that require the input of both the left and right cerebral cortex and limbic regions for optimal functioning. For example, adequate language production requires an integration of the grammatical functions of the left and the emotional functions of the right. Left-right integration allows us to put feelings into words, consider feelings in conscious awareness, and balance the positive and negative affective biases of the left and right hemispheres (Silberman & Weingartner, 1986). Alexithymia (the inability to put words to feelings) and somatization disorder (the conversion of emotional conflicts into bodily illness) may reflect left–right dissociation (Hoppe & Bogen, 1977). There is also evidence that depression and mania correlate with dysregulation of activation between the left and right areas of the frontal cortex (Baxter et al., 1985; Field, Healy, Goldstein, Perry, & Bendell, 1988).

The right hemisphere is more highly connected with the body and the more primitive and emotional aspects of functioning. The left hemisphere is more closely identified with cortical functioning, whereas the right is more densely connected with limbic and brain stem functions (Shapiro, Jamner, & Spence, 1997). For example, states of stress, anxiety, and fear result in more activation in both the right cerebral hemisphere and right subcortical structures (Rauch et al., 1996; Wittling, 1997). This bias is also relevant to the organization of social emotional attachment patterns, transference, and affect regulation. Much of the integration of top-down and left–right systems is mediated through interactions among regions of the frontal cortex, our primary executive system.

Due to the interconnectivity between left–right and top-down neural networks, examining integration from either the vertical or horizontal dimension alone is overly simplistic. Studies of metabolism in specific areas of the brain in pathological states, such as depression and obsessive compulsive disorder, reveal differences in both cortical and subcortical structures on both sides of the brain. This research suggests that restoring neural integration requires the simultaneous re-regulation of networks on both vertical and horizontal planes. It is also important to remember that neural networks vary in their use of neurotransmitters that allow psychiatric medications to rebalance neural functioning. Although we have been discussing brain functioning from the perspective of neural networks, an equally meaningful discussion could examine the impact of pharmacological interventions on the mutual modulation and restoration of homeostatic balance among networks (Coplan & Lydiard, 1998). This helps us to understand why both psychotherapy and medication are capable of restoring network balance and symptom reduction (Andreasen, 2001).

Integration is accomplished through the simultaneous or alternating activation of conscious language production (top and left) with more primitive, emotional, and unconscious processes (down and right) that have been dissociated due to undue stress during childhood or trauma later in life (Siegel, 1995, 1999). Depending on their theoretical orientation, therapists facilitate this process through supplying challenges of all kinds. An analyst may use interpretations and reality testing to enhance awareness of inhibited, repressed, or dissociated thoughts and emotions. A cognitive–behavioral therapist will expose a client to a feared stimulus after providing him or her with education and relaxation skills, thereby activating normally inhibited cortical circuitry to allow for descending cortical control of fear. Research across most forms of therapy supports the hypothesis that positive outcomes in psychotherapy are related to the combined engagement of thought and affect, utilizing both support and challenge (Orlinsky & Howard, 1986).

Emotion: Tolerance, Regulation, and Integration

Although emotions are the stock and trade of psychotherapy, mainstream neuroscience has yet to become comfortable with them. This is primarily because affect is a complex subjective phenomenon, lacking a good animal model (Plutchik, 2001). Emotions reflect our ability to subjectively experience states of our nervous system (Panksepp, 1998). These states, which we describe with words such as *elation, fear, shame, rage*, and *love*, are experienced as either good or bad, leading us to approach or avoid other people or specific situations (Rolls, 1999).

Assistance with experiencing increasing levels of positive and negative affect is a vital component of both parenting and psychotherapy. The gradual increasing tolerance for stress builds our brains, expands neural organization of emotional and cognitive integration, and creates networks of descending control to help inhibit and regulate affect (Schore, 1994). Emerging from childhood with an ability to experience a range of emotions and tolerate stress serves both as a means of brain growth and continued development throughout life.

In the absence of adequate assistance in making sense of emotions, the brain organizes a variety of coping strategies and defense mechanisms. These strategies and defenses vary in the degree to which they distort reality in order to achieve their goal of reducing anxiety. This distortion is accomplished in circuits of unconscious memory that control anxiety and fear (Critchley et al., 2000). The neural connections that result in defenses shape our lives by selecting what we approach and avoid, where our attention is drawn, and the assumptions we use to organize our experiences. Our cortex then provides us with rationalizations and beliefs about our behaviors that help keep our coping strategies and defenses in place, possibly for a lifetime. These neural and psychic structures can lead to psychological and physical health, or symptoms and disability.

Fritz Perls used the term *safe emergency* for the experience that psychotherapists strive to create in treatment (Perls, Hefferline, & Goodman, 1951). A safe emergency is a challenge for growth and integration in the context of guidance and support. It is also a wonderful way to describe an important aspect of good parenting. Therapists create this emergency by exposing clients to unintegrated and dysregulating thoughts and feelings while offering to clients the tools and nurturance with which to integrate the experiences. Psychodynamic therapies alternate confrontations and interpretations with a supportive and soothing interpersonal environment (Weiner, 1998). The systematic desensitization of cognitive behavioral therapy pairs exposure to feared stimuli with psychoeducation and relaxation training in the presence of a coach and ally (Wolpe, 1958). Bowen's family systems approach focuses on pairing anxiety reduction with experiments in increasing levels of independent and differentiated behavior (Bowen, 1978). All forms of successful therapy strive to create these safe emergencies in one form or another.

As in development, the repeated exposure to stress in the supportive interpersonal context of psychotherapy results in the ability to tolerate increasing levels of arousal. This process reflects the building and integration of cortical circuits and their increasing ability to inhibit and regulate subcortical activation. Flexible and balanced affect regulation enhances continued cortical processing in situations that evoke strong emotions, allowing for the flexibility to permit ongoing learning and neural integration.

In this process the therapist plays essentially the same role as a parent, provides and models the regulatory functions of the social brain. As affect is repeatedly brought into the therapeutic relationship and managed through a variety of stabilizing mechanisms, the client gradually internalizes these skills while simultaneously sculpting the neural structures necessary for the autoregulation of emotions. Increased affect regulatory function and a distribution of regulators in the client's life through networking and skill building are core components of successful psychotherapy (Bradley, 1990; Pipp & Harmon, 1987). As in childhood, the repeated cycle of attunement, rupture of the attunement, and its reestablishment gradually creates an expectation of reconnection (Lachmann & Beebe, 1996). The learned expectation of relief in the future enhances the ability to tolerate more intense affect in the midst of the stressful moment.

As a therapist, one of my primary goals has been to shift my clients' experience of anxiety from an unconscious trigger resulting in avoidance into a conscious cue for curiosity and exploration. One of my patients described it metaphorically as using anxiety as a compass to help guide him to his unconscious fears. Becoming aware of anxiety is then followed with an understanding of what we are afraid of and why. The next step is to move toward the anxiety with an understanding of its meaning and significance. In this way, anxiety becomes woven into a conscious narrative as opposed to being an unconscious trigger for avoidance. This process reflects the integration of cortical linguistic processing with conditioned subcortical arousal in the service of inhibiting, regulating, and modifying maladaptive reactions.

As we will see later, when discussing the building of the social brain, biological and environmental factors during childhood can result in long periods of dysregulation. Deprivation and/or chronic stress during childhood increase the chances of simultaneous damage to the brain and the utilization of primitive defenses. Brain structures vital to memory and reality testing can be damaged by sustained high levels of stress hormones (Sapolsky, 1985). With increased nurturance and support, stress hormone levels decrease; physical comfort and soothing talk with caretakers helps the brain to integrate experience.

The Role of Language
and the Co-Construction of New Narratives

Although growth and development occur at all levels of neural processing, language appears to be a key mechanism of integration. As the language areas of the left hemisphere enter their sensitive period during the middle of the second year of life, grammatical language in the left integrates with the interpersonal and prosodic elements of communication already well developed in the right. As the cortical language centers mature, words are joined together to make sentences, and can be used to express increasingly complex ideas.

As the frontal cortex continues to expand and interconnect, memory improves. A sense of time slowly emerges with autobiographical memory beginning to connect places, events, and the self in time. The narratives that emerge from this process combine events with emotional value and begin to organize the nascent sense of self. Storytelling weaves together sensations, feelings, thoughts, and actions in ways that organize both one's internal and external worlds. These autobiographical memories are at the core of our sense of history, our conscious connections with others, and our sense of self in interpersonal and physical space.

Language draws on (and is able to integrate) multiple processing networks throughout the brain. Children are told by others, and gradually begin to tell others, who they are, what is important to them, and what they are capable of. These self-stories are shaped by the children's interactions with parents, peers, and available cultural models. In this process, stories serve to perpetuate both healthy and unhealthy forms of self-identity. The recognition of the power of negative self-statements resulted in the development of cognitive therapies (Ellis, 1962). The role of language and narratives in neural integration, memory formation, and self-identity make them a powerful tool in the creation and maintenance of the self (Bruner, 1990). And although it does sometimes seem that children are little scientists discovering the world, what we often miss is that they are primarily engaged in discovering what the rest of us already know, especially about them (Newman, 1982).

Narratives allow us to place ourselves within a story. Through these stories, we have the opportunity to ponder ourselves in an objective way within an infinite number of contexts. We can escape our bodies and the present moment in imagination to create other possible selves, ways of being, and worlds that have yet to be created.

Have you have ever watched the faces of small children as they listen to a gifted and dramatic storyteller? You can see the drama being lived within their eyes, on their faces, and throughout their bodies as the story unfolds. Listeners will experience a range of drastically shifting emotions, listen intensely to absorb every detail, even shout out warnings to one of the characters in the story.

Hearing and telling stories calls upon the brain to perform multiple simultaneous tasks. Storytelling requires sustained attention; memory for the plot; keeping track of time and sequences; evoking the emotions, facial expressions, postures, and movements of the characters; and paying attention to the listeners' reactions. The process of listening to and telling stories brings together behavior, affect, sensation, and conscious awareness in a way that maximizes the integration of a wide variety of neural networks. Through stories, we connect with others, share the words, thoughts, and feelings of the characters, and provide the opportunity for moral lessons, catharsis, and self-reflection.

Although stories may appear imprecise and unscientific (Oatley, 1992), they serve as powerful tools for the work of neural network integration at a high level (Rossi, 1993). The combination of a goal-oriented linear storyline with verbal and nonverbal expressions of emotion activates and utilizes processing of both left and right hemispheres and cortical and subcortical processing (Siegel, 1999). This cooperative and interactive activation may be precisely what is required for sculpting integrated neural networks. An inclusive narrative structure provides the executive brain with the best template and strategy for the oversight and coordination of the functions of mind. There is evidence that these narratives aid in emotional security while minimizing the need for elaborate psychological defenses (Fonagy, Steele, Steele, Moran, & Higgitt, 1991).

Through psychotherapy and self-reflection, most of us become aware that we seem to shift back and forth among different perspectives, emotional states, and the way we use language. Looking closely at this provides a window to shifts in states of mind that reflect the use of different neural networks and levels of integration. There appear to be at least three levels of language functioning accessed during psychotherapy. There is a reflexive social language, an internal dialogue, and a language of self-reflection. *Reflexive social language* is a stream of words that function primarily in the maintenance of ongoing social communication and relatedness.

As primate groups grew larger, reflexive social language most likely evolved from social grooming and hand-gestures (Dunbar, 1996; Rizzolatti & Arbib, 1998). This form of language mirrors the external interpersonal world and provides a matrix for ongoing communication with others. Unconscious reflexes and learned reactions in response to social situations and constraints "lubricate" our interpersonal relationships. Most of us experience this whenever we find ourselves automatically saying something positive to avoid or reduce tension.

We are all aware of the voices we hear and the conversations we carry on within us as we struggle with the weighty issues of our lives or even decide where to go for dinner. This *internal dialogue*, guiding (or being guided by) our thoughts and behaviors, often departs from what we say socially. This level of language is also primarily reflexive and may have evolved on a separate track from social language, allowing for survival-enhancing deception. These two levels of language are like over-learned motor skills that usually serve as mechanisms to maintain preexisting attitudes, behaviors, and feelings. Most of our ongoing verbal production is habitual and continues to keep us in the mode in which we have been shaped. We hear in our heads the supportive or critical voices of our parents, and we speak the language of our group. Like reflexive social language, internal dialogue is based on semantic routines and habits that reflect our thoughts, behaviors, and social presentation.

Much of therapy consists of examining and attempting to understand reflexive social language and internal dialogue. This process expands perspective on many aspects of the unconscious aspects of the self. In therapy, a *language of self-reflection* is either enhanced or created for the first time. This third level of language is less a mechanism of control than a vehicle of consideration and potential change. As this language is expanded and reinforced, clients learn that they can first evaluate and then choose whether to follow their thoughts or what others expect of them. The language of self-reflection, when contrasted with social language and internal dialogue, most likely reflects a higher level of integration of top-down and left–right processing. In this language, cognition is blended with affect so that there can be feelings about thoughts and thoughts about feelings.

Abbey

Abbey, an extremely bright and charismatic woman, came in to the consulting room with a smile on her face, even though she was obviously close to tears. Before she had even sat down, Abbey launched into a description of all the positive events that had occurred to her and her family over the last week. Seeing the pain in her eyes and the rigidity throughout her body, I suspected that my face reflected the sadness I was feeling. My expression seemed to make Abbey avoid my eyes and speak more quickly. From time to time, I would attempt to break in and ask her what *she* was feeling.

Abbey ignored my questions and, with a voice increasingly filled with pressure, described her family in even greater detail. As I listened to her, I remembered how, as a child, I would cover my ears and sing when my mother began to hint that it was time for bed. Abbey's talk went on through the first half of the session as I realized that all I could do was sit, listen, and wait and see. As I sat quietly, she gradually slowed, became quiet, and hung her head looking at the floor. It seemed that her feelings had finally caught up with her conscious awareness. Abbey had shifted from reflexive social language.

I was considering what to say when she told me, "I caught myself blabbing on." I asked her what she had been thinking about while she sat there in silence. Abbey replied, "I was thinking of what an idiot I am and how I must bore you with my endless prattle about my stupid life." She seemed deflated now, depressed and lost. "What a stupid job you have," she suddenly said, "sitting in this office every day, listening to people's problems. Why don't you get out of here and live?" At this point, Abbey lowered her face into her hands and began to sob. I could see that not only was she sharing with me the voices in her head and her fears and doubts, but she was also projecting onto me her anger, confusion, and frustration. Her internal dialogue was hurting her and she wanted to hurt me so that I would know how she felt.

When she finally spoke again, she told me of the emptiness she felt from the loss of her father a few months earlier (until this point she had denied its having much impact on her). It had become clear to her over the last few minutes that she had been coping with her sadness by burying herself in a flurry of words, social activities, and caretaking. After a few minutes of silence and deep sighs, Abbey began to talk about how much she missed her father, his strong hugs, good advice, and the profound feeling of safety he was able to create with his loving gaze. She began the mourning process in the context of self-reflection.

When clients shift to this level of language in the consulting room, the change is palpable. This is when I feel most confident about a client's willingness to join me as a collaborator in the therapeutic process. I imagine at this moment that clients have the clearest perspective on their thoughts, behaviors, and feelings. They speak more slowly because the organization of sentences is difficult when not relying on semantic habits and cliches. Emotions bubble up and clients feel safe enough to express them in a process that enhances self-reflective capacity. These states are usually fleeting and not supported by friends, family, popular culture, or the day-to-day demands of life. The greatest challenge to increased self-awareness is to remember the difference between unconscious reflexes and conscious consideration (Ouspensky, 1954).

Psychotherapy and Parenting

We've talked a little about the parallels between positive parenting and successful psychotherapy; these similarities reflect the commonality of the conditions required for building and rebuilding the brain. Mutual eye gaze and escalating positive emotional interactions between parent and child stimulate the growth and organization of the brain. In the future, we may discover scientific evidence that the interpersonal experience of psychotherapy impacts the neurobiological environment of the brain in ways that stimulate neural plasticity and neurogenesis. Although the various schools of therapy tend to accentuate their differences, the therapeutic relationship itself may be the most powerful curative agent.

The warmth, acceptance, and unconditional positive regard demonstrated by Carl Rogers' work embodies the broad interpersonal environment for the initial growth of the brain and continued development later in life (Rogers, 1942). Having spent a brief period of time with Dr. Rogers when I was a student, I can attest to the power of his interpersonal style and therapeutic technique. I'm sure he left many, including myself, with the fantasy of being available for adoption.

In a review of hundreds of studies examining the outcome of psychotherapy, Orlinsky and Howard (1986) looked for those factors that seemed to relate to success. They found that the factors related to the quality of the emotional connection between the patient and the therapist were far more important than the theoretical orientation of the therapist. Patients who work more collaboratively with their therapists also do better. Therapists' professional experience was positively related to success, as were the use of interpretation, a focus on transference, and the expression of affect. The continual involvement of both cognitive and emotional processing during treatment seems essential for positive change.

Primary goals of parenting include providing a child with the capacity for self-soothing and the ability to form positive relationships. This allows the child to face the challenges of life and benefit from healing life experiences. The successful mastery of challenges throughout life leads to taking on even more complex challenges that will promote increasingly higher levels of neural network development and integration. When internal or external factors prevent an individual from approaching challenging and stressful situations, neural systems will tend to remain underdeveloped or unintegrated.

Psychotherapy, like parenting, is neither mechanical nor generic. Each therapist–client pair creates a unique relationship resulting in a particular outcome. The importance of the unconscious processes of both parent and therapist is highlighted by their active participation in the co-construction of new narratives of their children and patients. As we will see in research on attachment, each parent's unconscious plays a role in the creation of the child's brain, just as the therapist's unconscious contributes to the context and outcome of therapy. This underscores the importance of the proper training and adequate personal therapy for therapists who will be putting their imprint on the hearts, minds, and brains of their clients.

Sam and Jessica

One of my most powerful learning experiences as a therapist didn't take place in a consulting room or seminar, instead, it was at the home of a friend one weekday afternoon. I had volunteered to watch his two young children for a few hours while he ran some errands. I had known Jessica and Sam, four and six years old, all their lives. I was someone on an outer ring of their universe, an attractive combination of familiar and new, and completely unprepared for what was about to happen. The minute their father left, they began shifting from low to medium to high gear, their excitement escalating and their level of physical activity increasing to near frenzy.

Toys began flying out of closets and storage containers; games were begun and tossed aside; videos were started, stopped, and replaced; Indian princes were followed by mermaids, lion kings, ladies, and tramps. After what felt like an hour I glanced at my watch to find that only 15 minutes had gone by! I feared I couldn't survive four more hours at this pace. I repeatedly tried to refocus their activity, to no avail. At one point, as we dashed from bedroom to den to living room, I sank to the floor in the hall, and propped myself up against the wall. When Jessica and Sam realized that I wasn't right behind them, they ran back to find me.

On either side of me now, they stood panting, wondering what new game I had concocted. I suggested that we sit and talk for awhile. From the look on their faces, it seemed that I had spoken some unfamiliar language. After a few seconds, Sam looked at his sister and said, "Show Lou how you burp your dolly!" Both let out a scream and Jessica returned in a flash with an adorable squishy doll. As I reached for the doll to hold and admire it, Jessica threw the doll on the floor face first and drove her fists into its back. As Jessica and Sam took turns, screeching with delight, they flattened the doll into the carpet. I watched, horrified, holding back my urge to save this poor doll from its attackers.

I reminded myself that I was feeling sorry for a ball of cotton and that I should turn my attention back to the children. I also realized that to rescue the doll was to scold Sam and Jessica for their behavior, which I did not want to do. I struggled to make sense of what was happening and tried to understand it from a different perspective. I asked myself if there might be some symbolic value in the way they were treating this doll and how might knowing this be helpful to these two beautiful children. Jessica and Sam had experienced a great deal of stress in their brief lives in the forms of severe physical illness, surgery, drug addiction in the family, and an understandably over-whelmed support system. The frantic activity I was witnessing was the accumulated anxiety from all they had gone through, mixed with normal childhood exuberance.

As I reflected on these things I was hit by the notion that perhaps the doll represented Sam and Jessica. This doll needed to be burped. It needed the help of an adult to alleviate its discomfort and regain a sense of safety and equilibrium. Perhaps they were showing me that when they needed to be comforted, they were met with more pain, or, at the very least, insufficient help. Their behavior might have been a message: "Please, we need nurturance and healing!" Their world seemed chaotic and unsafe, a whirlwind; these were the same feelings they had created within me during the last half-hour.

I noticed they had each taken a number of turns "burping" the doll and that their attention would soon be turning to me. What to do or say? I didn't want to burp the baby their way and I couldn't share the thoughts I was having with them; my interpretation of what was hap-pening would be meaningless. Finally, they both turned to me and cried in unison those dreaded words, "Your turn!" I hesitated. The chant of "Burp the baby, burp the baby" began to rise. I hesitated for another moment and said, "I know another way to burp a baby. Here's how my mom burped me." A cheer went up. I think they assumed that I was going to set the doll on fire or put it in the microwave.

I gently picked up the doll and brought it to my left shoulder. Rubbing its back in a circular motion using my right hand, I said to the doll, "This will make you feel better." As I said these words, a silence fell over the hallway. I looked up to find Jessica and Sam transfixed, as if hypnotized. Their gaze followed the movement of my hand, their eyes traveled in slow circles, heads tilted like puppies. Their bodies looked relaxed, their hands limp at their sides, calm!

After following the movement of my hand for about 30 seconds, Jessica looked up at me and softly asked, "Can I have a turn?" "Of course you can," I told her. Then carefully, almost respectfully, she took the doll from me and placed it on the floor with its back against the wall. She stepped over to me, climbed over my crossed legs and put her head on my shoulder where the doll's head had been. She turned to me and almost inaudibly said "I'm ready now." As I rubbed Jessica's back, I felt her growing heavier, more and more limp as if melting into me. I half expected Sam to tear her off and climb on himself. When I looked over to him, I could see that he was in the same emotional state he had been in watching me burp the doll. He seemed to come to for a moment and asked, "Can I have a turn?" Before I could answer, Jessica lifted her head slightly and told him "In a minute."

After a while, she gave up her spot on my shoulder and Sam had his turn being "burped." It felt wonderful to hold them in this way and give them something they seemed to need so badly. After a few turns for each of them, we went into the den, curled up on the sofa, and watched a movie. Correction—I watched the movie—they both dozed off after a few minutes. While my eyes followed the frenetic animation on the screen, I paced my breathing with theirs and shared the peace they seemed to be feeling.

I marveled at how they managed to communicate their pain and confusion by creating these same feelings in me. By playing along with them for a while, I told them I respected their way of dealing with things. Through the use of the doll, they said that when they need soothing their pain was often met with more pain. When I burped their doll, I showed them that I was capable of soothing them if they were feeling bad. By asking me to burp them, they told me I was trusted. In falling asleep, they said, "We feel safe, we need some rest, and we know you will watch over us while we rest."

The interpretation I made though our interactions with the doll changed Sam and Jessica. Their words clearly reflected a shift from reflexive to reflective language. I believe that it not only impacted their attitudes and behaviors that afternoon, but may have also changed their brains in some more permanent way. I could see this reflected in their faces and hear it in the tone of their voices; something fundamental had changed that affected their entire beings. I provided them with a metaphor through which they could reorganize their experience, get their needs met, and regulate their emotions. Together, the three of us co-constructed a new narrative for them to use as an avenue to sooth themselves and each other.

Were this process to be repeated enough times, their brains could reorganize around this metaphor of nurturance and holding; it would enhance communication between networks of cognitive and emotional processing. This type of process is at the heart of all forms of psychotherapy, regardless of philosophy or technique. All forms of therapy have their own versions of integrative metaphors, serving to reorganize neural networks and human experience.

Summary

In this chapter we have explored an integration of psychotherapy and neuroscience based on common principles within both fields. Using the concept of neural networks, we have equated psychological health with optimal neural network growth and integration. The psychological difficulties for which patients seek psychotherapy are a function of inadequate growth and integration within and between these same networks. The aspects of development that foster positive brain development and those in therapy that promote positive change are emotional attunement, affect-regulation, and the co-construction of narratives.

In the following chapter, we turn our attention to major models of psychotherapy in use today. By examining their theories and techniques, we will see how they have been shaped by underlying principles related to the growth and integration of neural networks. It is my belief that the development of psychotherapy has always been implicitly guided by the principles of neuroscience. All forms of therapy are successful to the degree to which they have found a way to tap into processes that build and modify neural structures within the brain.

Neural Integration
in Different Models
of Psychotherapy

3

The techniques of behavior therapy and psychotherapy
have relied on the principles of brain plasticity, generally
without realizing it, for nearly one hundred years.
(Andreasen, 2001)

The major forms of psychotherapy in use today have survived
because they have proven helpful to patients in the relief of
symptoms or in an improved quality of life. Like other scientific discoveries, psychotherapy developed from a combination of trial-and-
error learning, intuition, and plain good luck. Each school of
psychotherapy offers an explanation as to why its strategies and techniques are effective. Fortunately, the effectiveness of an intervention
does not necessarily depend on the accuracy of the theory used to
support it. For example, there was a time when psychoanalysts attributed the success of electro-shock therapy to the need of a depressed
person to be punished. The treatment worked despite the lack of a
viable causal explanation.

Although each approach to psychotherapy is experienced as a
fundamental truth by its disciples, all modes of therapy are actually
"heuristics." Heuristics are interpretations of experience or ways of

understanding various phenomena. The value of a heuristic lies in its ability to explain and predict what we observe. Neuroscience is another heuristic, one that we are using in the present discussion to explain psychotherapy. It is my belief is that it will lead us to a fuller understanding of how psychotherapy attains its results, and may also serve as a means of organizing and combining treatment modalities. From the perspective of neuroscience, all psychotherapists are in the brain rebuilding business.

In this chapter we will examine, in broad strokes, some of the primary approaches to psychotherapy. These overviews are presented in order to provide a context in which to understand and organize the neuroscience in the chapters to come. In taking a sample of general theoretical approaches to psychotherapy, we will look for common elements among them and how these elements may relate to neural network development and change.

Psychoanalytic Therapy

Freud's psychoanalysis, the original form of psychodynamic therapy, has spun off countless variants in its century-long existence. Ego-psychology, self-psychology, and schools of thought connected to names such as Klein, Kernberg, and Kohut have all attracted considerable followings over the years. Despite their differences, psychodynamic forms of therapy generally share similar theoretical beliefs, including the existence of a conscious and unconscious mind, the importance of early childhood experiences, an understanding of mental illness based in developmental processes, and the existence of defenses that distort reality to reduce anxiety and enhance coping.

The exploration of the unconscious and its connection to our evolutionary past is perhaps Freud's greatest professional and cultural legacy. He remained true to his teacher Charcot by exploring the functioning of multiple systems of memory and levels of awareness. Many psychoanalytic techniques were specifically designed to expose the unconscious and bring it to awareness. The power of childhood experiences and their ability to shape the subsequent organization of the mind were also examined in great detail. Psychodynamic therapies assume that early attachment and relational difficulties, neglect, or trauma result in developmental arrests or "fixations" that delay or derail the ability of the adult to love and work. From the standpoint of neurobiology, most of Freud's work addressed the discontinuities and dissociations between networks of conscious and unconscious processing, and between conscious awareness and the emotional aftereffects of past experience. Freud focused on the role of overwhelming emotion as the cause of unintegrated neural processing.

Freud's psychic self contains the primitive drives (id), the demands of civilization to conform for the benefit of the group (superego), and those parts of the self (ego) that attempt to negotiate the naturally occurring conflicts between the two. In its attempt to be diplomatic in the fight between id and superego, the ego utilizes many elaborate defenses to help cope with reality. Ego strength, or the ego's ability to navigate reality with a minimum of defensiveness, reflects the integration of neural networks of emotion and thought, and the development of mature defenses. The more primitive or immature the defense mechanism, the more reality is distorted and the more functional impairment occurs. Mature defenses, such as humor and intellectualization, allow us to lessen strong feelings, keep in contact with others, and remain attuned to a shared reality. Sublimation allows us to convert the energy connected with unacceptable impulses into a constructive focus.

Less mature defenses, such as denial and dissociation, result in greater distortion of reality and difficulties in both work and relationships. People often seek treatment when their defense mechanisms cannot adequately cope with repressed emotions, or when symptoms become intolerable. Defenses are often invisible to their owners because they are organized by layers of neural processing that are inaccessible to conscious awareness. Essentially, what Freud called defenses are ways in which the neural networks have organized in the face of difficulties during development. Defenses are ways in which thoughts, feelings, sensations, and behaviors have been thwarted from becoming integrated within conscious awareness.

Despite a conscious awareness that something may be wrong, the hidden layers of neural processing continue to organize the world based on the prior experiences that shaped them. Part of therapy is an exploration and uncovering of this unconscious organization of experience. Freud's theory of the *projective hypothesis* described the process by which our brains create and organize the world around us. As the clarity of situations decreases, the brain naturally generates structure and projects it onto the world. The way we organize and understand ambiguous stimuli gives us clues about the architecture of the hidden layers of neural processing (how our unconscious organizes the world). From the projective hypothesis comes projective tests such as Rorschach's ink blots, free association, and an emphasis on the importance of dreams as the "royal road to the unconscious."

As part of the projective hypothesis, psychodynamic therapists often provide minimal information about themselves, allowing the client to project onto them implicit (unconscious) memories from past relationships. This form of projection, *transference*, results in the client's placing expectations and emotions from earlier relationships onto the therapist, which allows them to be experienced and worked on firsthand. It is through this transference that early relationships are brought fully into the therapy, and unconscious attachment schema within the neural networks of the social brain are made available for analysis. Freud felt that the evocation and resolution of the transference was a core component of a successful analysis. Because learning from early relationships is usually established before explicit conscious memory is fully formed, transference allows access to otherwise hidden learning. In Freud's words, only transference renders "the invaluable service of making the patient's buried and forgotten love emotions actual and manifest . . ." (Freud, 1912, p. 115).

Emotions play a central role in the success of dynamic therapies. The neural networks that organize emotions are shaped by early experiences to guide us away from thoughts and feelings for which we are punished, made uncomfortable, or led to neglect by others. Anxiety signals continue to shape our behavior at an unconscious level throughout life, leading us to remain on tried-and-true paths and avoid situations that trigger our unremembered past. An emphasis on the evocation of emotion and cognition is a primary contribution of psychoanalysis and reflects fundamental underlying neurobiological processes of growth and change.

Resistance represents aspects of implicit memory that the client presents for the therapist to decipher. An interesting example of this is captured in the Groucho Marx line, "I don't want to belong to any club that would accept me as a member." Early experience of the parents as rejecting, critical, or neglectful can result in the development of a negative self-image. This resultant self-doubt and self-criticism manifest themselves in a disrespect for anyone who loves or respects us. The unconscious logic may be to not trust anyone who loves us because either they "don't truly know us" or "their judgment is terrible." In therapy, this may manifest as a strong distrust of the therapist's intentions or his or her ability to be of help. Resistance and transference can both be understood as forms of implicit memory providing a window to the client's experience of his or her early development.

Interpretation is one of the most important techniques of the psychodynamic therapist. Sometimes called the "therapist's scalpel," interpretations attempt to make the unconscious conscious. Based on observations of all levels of the client's behavior, the therapist attempts to bring the processing of the hidden layers to the client's attention. Repeated attention to unconscious material via confrontations, clarifications, and interpretation results in a gradually expanding awareness of unconscious processes and the integration of top-down and right–left processing networks.

Accurate successful interpretations are sometimes accompanied by feelings of disorganization, anger, or depression on the part of the patient. Making defenses conscious serves to make them lose their effectiveness as coping strategies. Conscious awareness of the defenses often leads to experiencing the feelings against which the patient has been defending. The networks containing the negative emotions become disinhibited and activated. For example, if intellectualization is being used to avoid the shame and depression related to early criticism, a recognition of the defense will bring these feeling memories to awareness.

Across psychodynamic forms of therapy, emotional expression is encouraged, thoughts are explored, and awareness expanded. Feelings, thoughts, and behaviors are repeatedly juxtaposed, combined, and recombined in the process of *working through*. The conscious story of the past is reedited based on new information, and assumptions about the present and future self are reconsidered. From the perspective of neuroscience, the techniques of psychodynamic therapy focus on releasing emotion via uncovering unconscious material in the context of a supportive relationship. The overall goal is combining emotion with conscious understanding, and rewriting the story of the self. These factors enhance the growth and integration of neural networks.

Rogerian or Client-Centered Therapy

Against the background of the dominant analytic psychotherapies, Carl Rogers (1942) emerged with a new form of therapy he referred to as "client-centered." In stark contrast to focusing on a theory-based analysis of the patient, Rogers emphasized creating an interpersonal context that maximized the individual's opportunity to discover his or her inner world. Rogers' approach gained increasing acceptance in the non-medical community and by the 1960s came to be the dominant conceptualization for counseling of all kinds (Gilliland & James, 1998).

When different approaches to therapy are compared for effectiveness, the general agreement is that the perceived quality of the client–therapist relationship has the highest correlation with reported treatment success. Some have gone as far as to say that the relationship itself is the curative element, and not the specific techniques. This would certainly have been Rogers' opinion. He believed that it was through warmth, acceptance, genuineness, spontaneous prizing, non-possessive love, and unconditional positive regard that clients improve. His emphasis on congruence between client and therapist foreshadowed the focus on empathic attunement in object-relations and intersubjective forms of psychotherapy (Kohut, 1984; Stolorow & Atwood, 1979).

The therapist attributes suggested by Rogers and what we would think of as the best possible attitudes for optimal parenting are essentially identical. From Rogers' perspective, parenting coincides with the behaviors and attitudes attributed to secure attachment between children and their parents. Rogerian principles would lead to a minimization of defensiveness and shame while maximizing expressiveness, exploration, and risk taking. Rogers may have described the best interpersonal environment for brain growth during both development and change in psychotherapy. For Rogers, psychotherapy

> aims directly toward the greater independence and integration of the individual rather than hoping that such results will accrue if the counselor assists in solving the problem. The individual and not the problem is the focus. The aim is not to solve one particular problem, but to assist the individual to grow, so that he can cope with the present problem and later problems in a better-integrated fashion. (Rogers, 1942, p. 28).

While in my psychotherapeutic training, I was struck by the power of Rogers' approach. I found it immensely difficult to maintain his supportive stance, and often struggled to keep myself from pushing my clients to change. To my astonishment, I found that providing clients with a supportive relationship where defenses were unnecessary led to insights on their part that mirrored the interpretations I struggled to keep to myself. Clients often expressed a great deal of sadness when they realized how much they longed to be listened to without the worry of being judged or shamed. Many memories emerged concerning experiences of pain and isolation in the absence of support, and the struggle to make sense of life without adequate help.

What might be going on in the brain of a client in Rogerian therapy? In the Rogerian interpersonal context, a client would most likely experience the widest range of emotions within the ego-scaffolding of an empathic other. The activation of neural networks of emotion make feelings and emotional memories available for reorganization. Rogers' supportive rephrasing and clarification of what the client says may also optimize cortical executive functioning in the face of these emotions. This simultaneous activation of cognition and emotion, enhanced perspective, and the emotional regulation offered by the relationship may provide an optimal environment for neural change. By being non-directive, Rogers' method creates the necessity of executive networks and the self-reflective functions of the client to become activated. The client, guided by the therapist's support and encouragement, can then work to reorganize and rewrite his or her story.

We know that social interactions early in life result in the stimulation of both neurotransmitters and neural growth hormones that participate in the active building of the brain (Schore, 1994). Is it possible that the empathic connectedness promoted by Rogers actually stimulates biochemical changes in the brain capable of enhancing new learning in adolescents and adults? Can emotional nurturance by an attuned therapist trigger biochemical processes that increase brain plasticity? Surprisingly, the answer to these questions may be yes!

Studies with birds have demonstrated that the ability to learn their "songs" can be enhanced when exposed to live singing birds versus tape recordings of the same songs (Baptista & Petrinovich, 1986). Other birds are actually unable to learn from tape recordings and require positive social interactions and nurturance in order to learn (Eales, 1985). We will see later how maternal contact and nurturance serves to protect the brain from the damaging effects of stress (Meaney, Aitken, Vian, Sherman, & Sarrieau, 1989; Plotsky & Meaney, 1993). Studies such as these suggest that the proper social relationship may stimulate the neural plasticity required for new learning. The therapeutic relationship, referred to as a *non-specific factor*, may be a necessary element for both psychological and neurological adaptation. Unfortunately, the social isolation created by certain psychological defenses reinforce the fixity of neural organization as the client avoids the interpersonal contexts required to stimulate growth and healing.

Cognitive Therapies

Cognitive therapies highlight the centrality of a person's thoughts, appraisals, and beliefs in determining his or her feelings and actions. Faulty appraisals are believed to lead to dysfunctional thoughts that, in turn, create and exacerbate psychiatric symptoms. Active interventions in cognitive therapy focus on the identification of these dysfunctional thoughts, and educating clients to test and modify them as they arise (Beck, Rush, Shaw, & Emery, 1979; Ellis, 1962). The primary targets of cognitive behavioral therapy have been disorders such as depression, anxiety, obsessive compulsive disorder, phobias, and panic disorders.

Depressed patients tend to evaluate their world in absolute terms, taking details out of context, and experiencing neutral comments and events as negative. Common depressive thoughts include the expectation of failure despite many past successes, and thoughts that one is alone despite being surrounded by friends and family. In cognitive therapy, the patient is educated about these common distortions and encouraged to engage in reality testing and self-talk designed to counteract negative reflexive statements.

In patients with anxiety-related disorders, fear comes to organize and control the patients' lives to the extent of severe functional impairment. High levels of anxiety inhibit and distort rational cognitive processing. Cognitive interventions with these patients often include educating them about the physiological symptoms of anxiety such as a racing heart, shortness of breath, and sweaty palms. These patients are taught that feelings of dread are secondary to autonomic symptoms and should not be taken as seriously as they feel. A focus on understanding normal biological processes usually redirects the client away from catastrophic attributions of serious illness.

The boost of cortical processing from *psychoeducation* is combined with *exposure and response prevention*. Exposure and response prevention means that the client faces the feared stimulus (e.g., germs or venturing outside) without being allowed to retreat back to the safety of the bathroom or home. Exposure is usually systematic, gradual, and paired with *relaxation training* used to aid in the down-regulation of affective arousal. This process combines increased cortical processing (thought) with the result of exposure (affect), allowing fear circuitry to integrate with cortical circuitry in order to permit inhibition, habituation, and increased conscious control.

How does this translate into what is going on in the brain during cognitive therapy? Research has demonstrated that disorders of anxiety and depression correlate with changes in metabolic balance within the brain. For example, symptoms of depression correlate with changes in activation in the frontal cortex—lower levels of activation in the left and higher levels in the right (Baxter et al., 1985; Field, Healy, Goldstein, Perry, & Bendell, 1988) have been found. Alternately, the imbalance in functioning may be due to dysregulation among different regions within the frontal cortex (Brody et al., 2001).

Symptoms of obsessive compulsive disorder correlate with heightened activation in the medial (middle) portions of the frontal cortex and a subcortical structure called the *caudate nucleus* (Rauch et al., 1994). Posttraumatic flashbacks and states of high arousal correlate with higher levels of activation in right-sided limbic and medial frontal structures. Importantly, high arousal also correlates with decreased metabolism in the expressive language centers of the left hemisphere (Rauch et al., 1996).

Of all the different types of therapy, a specific link has been found between successful cognitive behavioral therapy and changes in brain functioning (Schwartz, 1996). As described in the last chapter, changes in brain functioning and symptomatology in both obsessive compulsive disorder and depression have been found after successful psychotherapy (Baxter et al., 1992; Brody et al., 2001; Schwartz et al,. 1996). These findings strongly suggest that therapists can utilize cognition to alter the relationship among neural networks in such a manner as to impact relative levels of activation and inhibition. In striving to activate cortical processing through conscious control of thoughts and feelings, these therapies enhance left cortical processing, inhibiting and regulating right hemispheric and subcortical activation. The reestablishment of hemispheric and top-down regulation allows for increases in positive attitudes that counteract the depressing effects of right hemisphere dominance.

Cognitive behavioral therapy, although stressing an interpersonal context of support and collaboration, places far less emphasis on the interpersonal elements of the therapeutic process than do Rogerian or psychodynamic approaches. The inherent wisdom of this approach with depressed and anxious patients lies in the fact that disorders of affect need activation of cortical executive structures. A deeper emotional connection might result in the therapist attuning to dysregulated states and sharing in the patient's depressed, anxious, and panicky feelings. While emotional attunement with these feelings is helpful, it has been my experience that after the working relationship is established, challenging thoughts and encouraging new behaviors can often be far more beneficial to the therapeutic process than empathy alone.

Systemic Family Therapy

There is an increasing awareness that neural networks throughout the brain are stimulated to grow and organize by interaction with the social environment. Early relationships become neurally encoded in networks of sensory, motor, and emotional learning to form what dynamic therapists call *inner objects*. These inner objects have the power to soothe or dysregulate, depending on the quality of our attachment experiences with significant others. These unconscious memories organize our inner worlds both when we are alone and when we are in proximity to others. Given the essential social organization of the brain, at some level we always experience ourselves in the context of others.

In line with this, systems therapists question the validity of diagnosing and treating people in isolation. They believe that we exist simultaneously in the multiple contexts of our present families and our multigenerational histories. This perspective is especially relevant when working with children who have yet to form clear ego boundaries between themselves and their family. Other adult patients who have not successfully individuated also demonstrate unclear boundaries between their own thoughts and feelings and those of family members.

Murry Bowen, a prime contributor to systems therapy, presented a model that is compatible with an exploration of the underlying neuroscience of psychotherapy. His perspective on systemic therapy is based on the recognition that a family provides both emotional regulation and a platform for differentiation. He defines *differentiation* as the development of *autonomy*—a balance between the recognition of the needs of self and others, and the ability to emotionally self-regulate and be available for others. Differentiation involves the balance and integration of affect and cognition. Bowen would say that anxiety is the enemy of differentiation. That is, the more frightened people are, the more dependent and primitive they become in their interaction with others (Bowen, 1978). These ideas parallel those described in cognitive therapy but are applied within an interpersonal context across a wide variety of psychological symptoms.

When individuals become anxious and this processing regression occurs, family members try—consciously and unconsciously—to shape the family in a manner so as to reduce their own anxiety.

Dysfunctional family patterns are those that sacrifice the growth and well-being of one or more members (often the children) to reduce the overall level of anxiety in the family. A classic example is a family in which one or both parents are alcoholics. The cognitive, emotional, and social world of the family is shaped by the avoidance of feelings, thoughts, and activities that expose their shameful secret to conscious awareness. The development of the children, on all levels, is shaped and distorted by all of the adaptations necessary for their emotional survival within the family. The family is maintained by roles, behaviors, and defenses designed to decrease anxiety but in fact result in a dysfunctional homeostatic balance.

Over time, the dysfunction becomes embedded in the personality and neural architecture of all of the individuals; they collude to maintain the homeostasis because now they all require it in order to feel safe. These processes shape individuals to survive in the context of particular dysfunctions, and may also keep them from adapting to healthier relationships. As a result, many of us recreate the dysfunction from our family of origin in our choice of partners and in our shaping of relationships. The problems of each family are determined through a series of successive childhoods; it is a multigenerational unconscious shaping of neural structure passed on from generation to generation. If brains are sculpted in the context of dysfunctional families, then the functioning of these brains reflect how they have been organized. The dysfunctional brain, like the dysfunctional family, is determined by the avoidance of thoughts and feelings, resulting in the dissociation of neural systems of affect, cognition, sensation, and behavior.

As in other forms of psychotherapy, the goal of systems therapy is to integrate and balance the various cortical and subcortical, left and right hemisphere, processing networks. This process requires a decrease in anxiety from high to moderate levels. High levels of affect block thinking, whereas moderate levels can result in cognition combined with emotion. In essence, Bowen is highlighting the fact that the simultaneous activation of cognition and emotion will lead to neural integration. Increased differentiation of individuals within a family will decrease the overall rigidity of the system. This process also allows family members to become more responsive to the needs of others and less reactive to their own inner conflicts.

The first step in systems therapy is to educate the family about these ideas and to explore the history of both sides of the family through a few generations. In the context of theory and history, the problems of a family are often more understandable, and it becomes more difficult to scapegoat individual family members. Uncovering family secrets and reality testing around the myths and projections of each family member allow for cortical processing of primitive and unconscious defenses. The process of family therapy is a series of experiments with increasingly higher levels of differentiation. Communication skills, assertiveness training, and exercises in new forms of cooperation can all increase cortical involvement with previously reflexive and regressive emotions and behaviors. Often the person with the symptoms needs to take more responsibility, while caretakers learn to accept nurturance. Ultimately, each member of the family needs to achieve a balance between autonomy and interdependence. Psychological, interpersonal, and neural integration are different manifestations of the same process.

Reichian and Gestalt Therapy

Wilhelm Reich, one of Freud's early disciples, felt that memory and personality are shaped and stored not just in the brain but throughout the entire body. Because of this, Reich not only paid careful attention to his clients' musculature, posture, and breathing, but also encouraged them to express themselves physically during analysis. By beating their fists, stomping their feet, and using exaggerated breathing techniques, they were encouraged to release emotions that were normally inhibited. Reich's theories led to the development of Rolfing (which uses deep body massage to evoke and process memories) and Gestalt therapy (which often focuses on drawing attention to nonverbal aspects of communication). From a neurobiological perspective, Reich highlighted the importance of the therapist's interpretation of the nonverbal messages of the body, making them available for conscious consideration.

Reich (1945) felt that the major focus of psychotherapy should be the analysis of the character, something he saw as similar to Freud's notion of ego. His major contribution was to focus on the nonverbal and emotional aspects of the therapeutic interaction versus the conscious verbal content. The problems people bring to therapy are embedded in their *character armor*, shaped during development as an adaptation against real or imagined danger. Character armor forms as a result of misattunement, neglect, or trauma at the hands of important others. This armor is preverbal and organizes during the first years of life. According to Reich, early defenses take shape at all levels of the nervous system, become encoded in our entire being, and are, like the air we breathe, utterly invisible. The defenses identified by Reich reflect emotional memories from early preverbal experiences that are stored in sensory, motor, and emotional networks of early memory. Because character armor is invisible to its owner, the therapist's job is to make the client aware of it.

A particular spinoff of the Reichian perspective is Gestalt therapy. Although Gestalt therapy is not widely practiced, it is a unique expression of psychodynamic therapy that is particularly relevant to the notion of neural integration. *Gestalt*, a German word meaning "whole," reflects the orientation of bringing together an awareness of conscious and unconscious processes. Gestalt therapy's charismatic founder, Fritz Perls, described the therapist's job as creating a *safe emergency* for the patient. Safety is provided in the form of a supportive and collaborative therapeutic relationship, often in the context of a group. The emergency is created by an unmasking of defenses, making unacceptable needs and emotions conscious, and by bringing into awareness dissociated elements of consciousness.

The stories a patient tells about his or her problems are often seen, in the Gestalt context, as self-deceptions. They serve to keep from awareness those feelings that are more relevant but less acceptable. Unconscious gestures, facial expressions, and movements are first brought to awareness, then exaggerated, and finally given a voice with the purpose of understanding and integrating experience. The therapist points out such contradictions as making positive statements while shaking the head "no," or smiling while talking of a painful experience. These contradictions are explored as indications of internal conflicts to be brought into awareness. Again, the focus is on bringing to conscious awareness the automatic, nonverbal, and unconscious processes organized in right hemisphere and subcortical neural networks.

Gestalt therapy emphasizes the identification and exploration of projection, identifying it as an avenue for discovering aspects of the self that have been difficult or impossible to accept. The popular "empty chair" technique explores the projective process. In the empty chair, patients alternately play the role of different parts of themselves to fully articulate the different sides of inner conflicts. The Gestalt therapist believes that maximizing awareness of all aspects of the self—including cognition, emotion, behavior, and sensation—will result in increased maturation and psychological health. This process depends on the integration of the neural networks responsible for each of these functions.

Summary

In reviewing these various modes of psychotherapy, a number of principles emerge to help us understand more deeply the factors that unify the various therapeutic schools. Each form of psychotherapy creates an individualized experience designed to examine conscious and unconscious beliefs and assumptions, expand awareness and reality testing, and encourage the confrontation of anxiety-provoking experiences. Each perspective explores behavior, emotion, sensation, and cognition in an attempt to expand awareness of previously unconscious or distorted material. The primary focus of psychotherapy appears to be the integration of affect and cognition.

Intellectual understanding of a psychological problem in the absence of increased integration with emotion, sensation, and behavior does not result in change. All forms of treatment recognize the need for stress, from the subtle disruption of defenses created by the compassion of Carl Rogers, to the exposure to feared stimuli in cognitive therapies. There is a recognition that the evocation of emotion coupled with conscious awareness is most likely to result in symptom reduction and personal growth.

When theories of neuroscience and psychotherapy are considered side by side, a number of working hypotheses emerge:

1. We appear to experience optimal development and integration in a context of *a balance of nurturance and optimal stress.* The disruption of this balance during development can result in symptoms, maladaptive defenses, and psychopathology. The creation of this balance in the therapeutic relationship optimizes the neurobiological environment for neural growth and integration. Although stress appears important as part of the activation of circuits involved with emotion, *states of moderate arousal* seem optimal for consolidation and integration. In states of high arousal, sympathetic activation inhibits optimal cortical processing and disrupts integration functions. States of moderate arousal maximize the ability of networks to process and integrate information. The ebb and flow of emotion over the course of therapy reflects the underlying neural rhythms of growth and change.

2. *Empathic attunement* with the therapist provides the context of nurturance in which growth and development occur. By activating processes involved in attachment and bonding, as well as moderating stress in therapy, empathic attunement may create an optimal biochemical environment for enhancing neural plasticity.

3. The involvement of *affect and cognition* appears necessary in the therapeutic process in order to create the context for inte-

gration of dissociated neural circuits. It has been said that, in psychotherapy, "understanding is the booby prize": It is a hollow victory to end up with a psychological explanation for problems that remain unchanged. On the other hand, catharsis without cognition does not result in integration, either. The mutual participation of affect and cognition are required for optimal neural functioning.

4. Repeated *simultaneous activation* of networks requiring integration with one another most likely aid in their integration. The repetitive play in children and the phrase "working through" in therapy best reflect this process. This concept parallels the principle from neuroscience that "neurons that fire together, wire together" (Hebb, 1949; Shatz, 1990). The simultaneous activation of neural circuits allows them to stimulate the development of connections within association areas to coordinate and integrate their functioning.

5. The ability to tolerate and regulate affect creates the necessary condition for the brain's continued growth throughout life. Increased integration parallels an increased ability to experience and tolerate thoughts and emotions previously inhibited, dissociated, or defended against. *Affect regulation* may be the most important result of the psychotherapeutic process across orientations, because it allows for a reconnection with the naturally occurring growthful experiences in life.

6. Language is an important tool in both neurological and psychological development. The *co-construction of narratives* between parent and child or therapist and client provides a broad matrix supporting the integration of multiple neural networks. Autobiographical memory creates stories of the self capable of supporting affect regulation in the present and the maintenance of homeostatic functions into the future. Memory, in this form, may maximize neural network integration as it organizes vast amounts of information across multiple

processing tracks. *Stories serve to bridge and integrate neural networks* both in the present moment and through time (Siegel, 1999).

In this chapter we have discussed some of the basic principles connecting the historical and conceptual connections between psychotherapy and neuroscience. In the chapters to come, we will explore the components and organizing principles of the nervous system. These basic concepts will help us understand the neural mechanisms of the building and rebuilding of the brain.

PART II

HOW THE BRAIN WORKS: EVOLUTION'S LEGACY

The Human Nervous System: From Neurons to Neural Networks

All functions of mind reflect functions of brain.
(Eric Kandel, 1998)

Studying the human brain is a daunting task, and many turn away assuming that it is just too difficult to understand. In fact, the human nervous system is so vastly complex that it would take thousands of pages to do justice to what is known about its structure and function. But how much do we really need to know about the brain to help us in our work as therapists? My feeling is that a basic understanding of the nervous system, without getting lost in the details, can be very helpful. Neuroscience can aid us in understanding what is happening in the brain while we attempt to influence the mind. With this as our goal, we will move through a thumbnail sketch of the basic theories of the structure, function, and development of the nervous system. Focus on getting a feel for neurons, neural networks, and how they operate. If you find certain topics to be especially interesting, I encourage you to follow up by reading some of the source materials referenced throughout this book. If you find what follows here to be too basic a review, you may want to skip ahead to the next chapter. Let's begin with some basic facts about the structures of the brain.

Neurons

The basic unit of the nervous system is the *neuron*, which receives and transmits signals via chemical transmission and electrical impulses. There are approximately *12,000,000,000* neurons in the brain, with between 10 and 100,000 synaptic connections each, creating an almost unlimited number of associations among them (Post & Weiss, 1997). Neurons have fibers called *axons* covered with *myelin*, which serves as an insulator and enhances the efficiency of communication. Because neurons myelinate as they develop, one way of measuring the maturity of a neural network is to measure its degree of myelinization. Multiple sclerosis—a disease that breaks down myelin—results in a decrease in the efficiency of neural communication, negatively impacting cognition, affect, and movement (Hurley, Taber, Zhang, & Hayman, 1999). The *white matter* of the brain is white because myelin is white (or at least light in color). *Gray matter* consists primarily of neural cell bodies.

When a neuron fires, information is carried via an electrical charge that travels down the length of its axon. Neurons communicate with one another across *synapses* (the spaces between neurons) via chemical messengers called *neurotransmitters*. The combination of these two complimentary processes creates the brain's *electrochemical* system. Many neurons develop elaborate branches, called *dendrites*, that can interconnect with thousands of dendrites from other neurons. The relationships formed among these dendrites organize the complex networking of the nervous system.

One-half of the volume of the central nervous system consists of neurons; the other half is made up of a variety of cells known as *glia*. More is known about neurons because they are about 10 times larger than glia and easier to study. Glia cells appear to have a role in the construction, organization, and maintenance of neural systems. Our knowledge of the role glia play in behavior and awareness remains limited, although it is suspected that they participate in neural network communication and plasticity (Pfrieger & Barres, 1996; Sontheimer, 1995; Vernadakis, 1996).

Neurogenesis

Neurogenesis—the growth of new neurons by cell division—is an area of ongoing controversy. The traditional wisdom concerning neurogenesis in vertebrates, and especially primates, has been that new neurons are no longer created after early development (Michel & Moore, 1995; Rakic, 1985). However, recent research has demonstrated that new neurons grow in the brains of adult birds (Nottebohm, 1981), tree shrews (Gould et al., 1997), primates (Gould et al., 1999a), and humans (Gould et al., 1999b). The importance of these discoveries and the abandonment of the old dogma cannot be underestimated. Nobel-prize-winning neuroscientist Eric Kandel referred to Nottebohm's discovery of seasonal neurogenesis in birds as having resulted in one of the great paradigm shifts in modern biology (Specter, 2001).

Some fish and amphibians, demonstrating ongoing neurogenesis, possess nervous systems that continue to grow in size throughout life (Fine, 1989). During evolution, primates may have given up some of their capacity for neurogenesis in order to retain more of their past learning. Dendrites, which change in reaction to new experience, may be capable of more refined learning if retained and continually modified instead of being replaced (Purves & Voyvodic, 1987). Humans have, however, maintained the ability to create neurons in areas involved with new learning, such as the hippocampus, the amygdala, and the cerebral cortex (Eriksson et al., 1998; Gross, 2000). The debate about neurogenesis is especially relevant to those of us attempting to change the brain through psychotherapy and education.

Neural Systems

Neurons organize in more and more complex neural networks that are genetically tailored to carry out the numerous functions of the nervous system. The two most basic divisions of the nervous system are the *central nervous system* (CNS) and the *peripheral nervous system* (PNS). The CNS includes the brain and spinal cord, whereas the

PNS is comprised of the *autonomic nervous system* and the *somatic nervous system*. The autonomic and somatic nervous systems are involved in the communication between the CNS and the sense organs, glands, and the body (including the heart, intestines, and lungs).

The autonomic nervous system has two branches, called the *sympathetic* and *parasympathetic* nervous systems. The sympathetic system controls the activation of the nervous system in response to a threat or other forms of motivation. The parasympathetic system balances the sympathetic system by fostering conservation of bodily energy, immunological functions, and repair of damaged systems. These two systems will be of particular interest in later chapters, when we discuss attachment and the effects of stress and trauma on the brain.

Although MacLean's formulation of the triune brain is no longer supported by most neuroscientists, they still recognize a tripartite division of the brain into the cerebral cortex, the limbic system, and the brainstem. Each layer is thought of as having different responsibilities. The *brainstem*—the inner core of the brain—oversees the body's internal milieu by regulating temperature, heart rate, and basic reflexes such as breathing and coughing. The functions of the brainstem are based in our genetic history and function well at birth. The reflexes we see in the newborn who grasps her mother, sucks at her mother's nipple, and even holds her breath when put under water are useful genetic memories retained from our tree-dwelling ancestors.

The outer layer of the brain, the *cerebral cortex*, organizes our experiences and how we interact with the world. As we grow, the cortex allows us to form ideas and mental representations of ourselves, other people, and the environment. As opposed to the brainstem, the cortex is primarily shaped through countless positive and negative interactions with our social and physical worlds.

The two halves of the cerebral cortex have gradually differentiated during primate evolution to the point where some functions have become lateralized to one side or the other. *Laterality* has allowed for a division of labor and specialization within the brain. Language is the best-understood example of lateral specialization. The two cerebral hemispheres communicate with each other primarily via the corpus callosum. The *corpus callosum* consists of long neural fibers connecting the corresponding areas of the left and right cerebral hemispheres. Although the corpus callosum is the largest and most efficient mode of communication between the hemispheres in adults, there are a number of smaller cortical and subcortical interconnections between the two halves of the brain (Myers & Sperry, 1985; Sergent, 1986, 1990). We will discuss the issue of laterality in greater detail in chapter 6.

The cortex has been subdivided by neuroanatomists into four lobes: frontal, temporal, parietal, and occipital (Figure 4.1). Each is represented on both sides of the brain and specializes in certain functions: the *occipital* lobe comprises the areas for visual processing; the *temporal* lobe for auditory processing, receptive language, and memory functions; the *parietal* lobe for linking the senses with motor abilities and the creation of the experience of a sense of our body in space; and the *frontal* lobe for motor behavior, expressive language, executive functioning, abstract reasoning, and directed attention. The term *prefrontal* cortex is often used to refer to the foremost portion of the frontal lobe.

Between the brainstem and the cortex lies a region referred to as the *limbic system*. The limbic system, which includes the amygdala and hippocampus, is involved with learning, motivation, memory, and emotion. The limbic system can be thought of as an intersection of the internal and external worlds where the primitive needs of the organism negotiate with the requirements of the outside world. Because this book focuses on development and psychotherapy, you will notice repeated references to limbic structures involved with attachment, emotion, and memory. The *amygdala* is a key component in neural networks involved with fear, attachment, earlymemory, and emotional experience throughout life. The *hippocampus* organizes explicit memory in collaboration with the cerebral cortex.

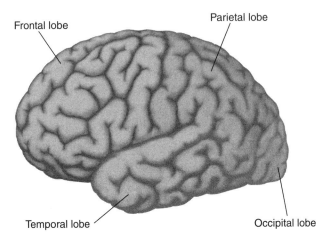

Figure 4.1   The four lobes of the cerebral cortex
The four lobes of the cerebral cortex as seen from the left side of the brain.

These neurobiological details are particularly important for psychotherapists.

Neurotransmitters and Neuromodulators

Recall that, within the nervous system, neurons communicate with one another via chemical messengers called neurotransmitters. Different neural networks tend to utilize different sets of neurotransmitters, which is why certain *psychotropic* medications impact different symptoms. Chemicals that serve as neurotransmitters include monoamines, neuropeptides, and amino acids. Neuromodulators (e.g., the hormones testosterone, estrogen, cortisol, and other steroids) regulate the effects of the neurotransmitters on receptor neurons. *Amino acids* are the simplest and most prevalent neuromodulators. *Glutamate* is the major excitatory amino acid in the brain, and structurally related to N-methyl-D-aspartate (*NMDA*), which is of particular importance in learning and neural change. Evidence suggests that NMDA receptors are involved with enhancing of connection between neurons and the plasticity of neural networks (Cowen & Kandel, 2001; Malenka & Siegelbaum, 2001).

The *monoamines*—including dopamine, norepinephrine, and serotonin—are very relevant to psychotherapy because of their role in the regulation of cognitive and emotional processing. All three are generated in different areas of the brainstem and are carried upward via ascending neural networks through the limbic system to the cortex. *Dopamine* (DA), produced in the substantia nigra and other areas of the brainstem, is a key neurotransmitter in motor action and the reward system. Too much dopamine can result in changes in mood, increased motor behavior, and disturbed frontal lobe functioning; these can result in symptoms such as depression, memory impairment, and apathy. Parkinson's disease results from damage to the substantia nigra and a consequent loss of dopamine. Many believe that schizophrenia is caused by too much dopamine, which overloads sensory processing capabilities.

Norepinephrine (NE), produced in the locus coeruleus and other brain regions, is a key component of the emergency fight–flight system of the brain and is especially relevant for understanding stress and trauma. High levels of NE result in anxiety, vigilance, and attacking or defense behavior. NE also serves to enhance memory for stressful and traumatic events. *Serotonin* (5HT), generated in the raphe nucleus, is distributed widely throughout the brain and plays a role in arousal and the sleep–wake cycle. Serotonin is involved in the mediation of mood and emotion. Popular antidepressant medications such as Prozac and Paxil cause higher levels of available serotonin in the synapses and greater activation of serotonergic neural networks.

The group of neurotransmitters known as *neuropeptides* includes endorphins, enkephalins, oxytocin, vasopressin, and neuropeptide-Y. These compounds work together with neuromodulators to regulate pain, pleasure, and reward systems. The endorphins tend to modulate the activity of monoamines, making them highly relevant for understanding psychiatric illnesses. *Endogenous endorphins* (endorphins produced by the body) serve as an analgesic in states of physical pain.

They are also involved with dissociation and self-abusive behavior, as we will discuss in later chapters on stress and trauma. The relationship between the monoamines and neuropeptides is vitally important to the growth and organization of the brain.

The production and availability of these neurochemicals shape all of our experience, from bonding and affect regulation to cognitive processing and our sense of well-being. Regulation of these neurochemicals to control psychiatric symptomatology is the focus of the field of psychopharmacology (Gitlin, 1996).

Brain Development and Neural Plasticity

Experience sculpts the brain through selective excitation of neurons and the subsequent shaping of neural networks. Paradoxically, the number of neurons decreases with age while the size of the brain increases. The surviving neurons continue to grow from what look like small sprouts into what seem like large oak trees. This process of growth and connectivity is sometimes referred to as *arborization*. Just as we survive and thrive through our relationships with others, neurons survive and grow as a function of how "well connected" they are.

In order for a neuron to survive and grow, it must wire with other neurons in increasingly complex interconnections. Through what appears to be a competitive process referred to as *neural Darwinism*, cells struggle for connectivity with other cells in the creation of neural networks (Edelman, 1987). Cells connect and learning occurs through changes of synaptic strength between neurons in response to some inner or outer stimulus. Repeated firing of two cells results in metabolic changes in both cells, producing an increased efficiency in their joint activation. In a process called *long-term potentiation* (LTP), excitation between cells is prolonged, allowing them to become interconnected and synchronized in their firing patterns. Repeated simultaneous firing of two neurons results in an increase of their joint effectiveness (Hebb, 1949).

Through LTP, cell assemblies organize into neural networks. This is only one small piece of a vastly complex set of processes and interactions involving the connection, timing, and organization of the firing within and between the billions of interconnected neurons in the CNS (Malkena & Siegelbaum, 2001). LTP is believed to be the fundamental principle of learning in all neural systems. Neural *plasticity* refers to the ability of neurons to change the way they behave and relate to one another as the brain adapts to the environment through time.

Early in development, there is an initial overproduction of neurons that gradually decreases through the process of *pruning*, or *apoptosis*. Neural Darwinism applies to both the survival of neurons and of synaptic connections among them. Synapses that are formed may be subsequently eliminated if they become inactivated or inefficient (Purves & Lichtman, 1980). In fact, elimination of synaptic connections in the cortex continues to shape neural circuitry well into adolescence (Huttenlocher, 1994).

In contrast to the brainstem, which is fully functional at birth (and the limbic system, which is in the process of rapidly wiring), the cortex is immature at birth and continues to develop through the first two decades of life (Thatcher, 1980). Because of this developmental timing, the behavior of a newborn is dominated by subcortical activity. Brainstem reflexes, having been shaped by evolution, organize much of the infant's early behaviors. The neonate will orient to the mother's smell, seek the nipple, gaze into her eyes, and grasp her hair. All of these are brainstem reflexes. A good example of this is the Moro reflex, by which the infant reaches out with open hands and legs extended, putting the infant into a position for grasping and holding (Eliot, 1999). These reflexes enhance physical survival and "jump start" the attachment process. The child's eyes orient to his or her mother's eyes and face. A baby's first smiles are also a reflex controlled by the brainstem to attract caretakers. In fact, children born with a genetic malformation resulting in them having only a brainstem, still show smiling patterns (Herschkowitz, Kegan, & Zilles, 1997).

Well before birth, the fetus begins to engage in spontaneous activity. In-utero images show consistent movements of the arms and hands. Newborns continue to move all parts of their bodies, allowing them to discover their hands as they pass in front of their faces or feet to put in their mouths. Although these movements are seemingly random, they serve a developmental purpose: It has been suggested that they are actually the brain's *best guess* at which movements will eventually be needed for the gross and fine motor skills necessary for survival (Katz & Shatz, 1996).

These best guesses become shaped into purposeful and intentional behaviors, just as spontaneous neural activity results in the structuring of network connections (Shatz, 1990). As sensory systems develop, they provide more precise input to guide neural network formation and increasingly complex patterns of behavior. Motor circuits gradually become less dependent on spontaneous activity. As positive and negative values are connected with certain perceptions and movements—such as the appearance of the mother and reaching out to her—emotional networks will integrate with sensory and motor systems. In the development of these and other systems, we find the sequential activation of reflexive and spontaneous processes priming neural development (which is later shaped by interpersonal and environmental experiences).

Cortical Inhibition and Control

The gradual attenuation of neonatal reflexes and spontaneous behavior corresponds with increasing levels of cortical activity. As the cortex develops, vast numbers of top-down neural networks connect it with subcortical areas. These top-down networks provide the information pathway for inhibiting reflexes and bringing subcortical functions under cortical control. Thus, a vital aspect of the development of the cortex is *inhibitory*. This theory is supported by the effects of cortical damage in adults. Individuals with Alzheimer's disease, for example, experience significant cell death in their cortex. As this occurs, the descending circuits dedicated to inhibiting early reflexes break down, resulting in the reemergence of reflexes more typical of a newborn. Early reflexes that reemerge after brain damage in an adult are referred to as *cortical release signs* (Chugani, Phelps, & Mazziotta, 1987). These release signs demonstrate that the inhibitory capacity of the cortex is decreasing.

As the cortex develops, both inhibitory abilities and memory skills increase, allowing the gradual emergence of behaviors that require a delayed response and the inhibition of incorrect responses (Goldman-Rakic, 1987). An example of this is the development of the fine motor movements between the thumb and forefinger that are required to hold a spoon. Primitive grasping reflexes allow only for the spoon to be held in a tight fist, rendering it useless as a tool. As the cortex develops, the grasping reflex is inhibited while cortical networks dedicated to finger sensitivity and hand–eye coordination mature.

Only through repeated trial and error are early clumsy movements slowly shape into functional skills. For example, when we attempt to help, a child's impatient protest of "Let me do it!" reflects his or her instinctual wisdom of the importance of trial and error in the growth of neural networks. Another good example of this growth is the ability to swim. The newborn's brainstem reflex to hold its breath and paddle when dropped into water is lost (inhibited by higher brain circuitry) just weeks after birth. The skills involved with swimming need to be relearned as cortically organized skills in years to come.

Why does the cortex make the inhibition of primitive reflexes one of its first orders of business? After all, it seems that most reflexes continue to be useful for quite a long time. Although the answer to this question can only be speculative, an educated guess is that, in the long run, human survival is better served by cortical control of these processes. In order for the cortex to take control, it has to first inhibit basic reflexes that organize gross motor programs. Thus, although the grasping of the hands and feet may best serve the young ape in navigating its environment, the ability to develop complex manual dexterity and smooth upright walking requires freedom from these more primitive brainstem programs.

The disappearance of reflexes is only one indication of brain development. We see the changes in motor control and posture as a child moves from being able to sit upright without help at about six months, to crawling at about nine months, and then to walking without help by about one year. At two years, a child will walk up and down stairs; by three she can peddle a tricycle. As these skills are shaped, so too are brain systems dedicated to balance, motor control, visual–spatial coordination, learning, and motivation. The growth, development, and integration of neural networks continue to be sculpted by environmental demands. In turn, neuronal sculpting is reflected in increasingly complex behavioral patterns.

Cortical inhibition and descending control are central to affect regulation. The rapidly changing and overwhelming emotions displayed by very young children reflect this lack of control. As the middle portions of the frontal cortex expand and extend their fibers down into the limbic system and brainstem, children gradually gain increasing capacity to regulate their emotions and find ways to gain soothing, first through others, and eventually by themselves. When these systems are damaged or developmentally delayed, we witness symptoms related to deficits in attention, emotional regulation, and impulse control.

Sensitive Periods

Brain development occurs during periods of exuberant neural growth and connectivity called *sensitive periods* (traditionally called *critical periods*) that greatly facilitate learning. These sensitive or critical periods occur early in pre- and postnatal development, accounting for the higher level of metabolism in the brains of infants as compared to adults. In rats' brains, for example, it is estimated that 250,000 synaptic connection are formed every second during the first month after birth (Schuz, 1978). The timing of sensitive periods varies across neural systems. This is the reason why different abilities appear at different points during development. The most widely recognized sensitive period is the development of language in children at about age two. At 24 months, a child can understand and use about 50 words; this increases to 1,000 words by 36 months (Dunbar, 1996). Because of the timing of extremely active periods of neural growth, learning during sensitive periods has a greater impact on neural structure and behavioral functioning than experiences during non-sensitive periods.

New research has resulted in differences in our attitudes about the importance of sensitive periods. Although initially thought to reflect only genetically timed growth, it is now clear that sensitive periods are also influenced by experience as well as the nature of what is being learned (Greenough, 1987; ten Cate, 1989). As we learn of the brain's ability to create new neurons and retain plasticity throughout life, the importance of sensitive periods takes on new meaning. The question for therapists is: How amenable are these established structures to modification?

During the first years of life, the growth of neurons and the development of increasingly complex neural networks require large amounts of energy. Patterns of increasing glucose metabolism during the first year of life proceed in "phylogenic order," meaning that the development of more primitive brain structures precedes later-evolving ones (Chugani, 1998; Chugani & Phelps, 1991). Networks dedicated to individual senses develop before the association areas that connect them (Chugani et al., 1987). The growth and coordination of the different senses parallel what we also witness in such behavioral changes as hand–eye coordination (Fischer, 1987) and the ability to inhibit incorrect movement (Bell & Fox, 1992). As the frontal and occipital cortices mature, a child at eight months is able to distinguish faces and compare them to his or her memory of other faces. It is around this period that *stranger* and *separation anxiety* develop. As the brain matures, we witness increasing activation of the cortex and the establishment of more efficient neural circuitry working in increasingly synchronous patterns.

Although both the left and right cerebral hemispheres are developing at very high rates during the early years of life, the right hemisphere appears to have a relatively higher rate of growth during the first three years (based on measures of blood flow; Chiron et al., 1997). At around age three, this asymmetry shifts to the left hemisphere. The difference in the rate of growth of the hemispheres turns out to be a recent development in evolution. Instead of having two equivalent and redundant hemispheres, humans have evolved in such a way as to slow the growth of the left hemisphere so that neural space can be preserved for the development of language and other functions (Gould, 1977).

The maturation and sculpting of the cortex and limbic system after birth allow for highly specific environmental adaptations. The caretaker relationship is the primary means by which physical and cultural environments are translated to infants. It is within the context of these close relationships that networks dedicated to feelings of safety and danger, attachment, and the core sense of self are shaped. The first few years of life appear to be a particularly sensitive period for the formation of these networks. It may be precisely because there is so much neural growth and organization during sensitive periods that early interpersonal experiences are far more influential than are those occurring in later life. The fact that they are visceral and preverbal make them even more resistant to change. Because our networks are unconsciously sculpted during early interactions, we all emerge into self-awareness preprogrammed by unconsciously organized neural networks. The organization of these neural networks—the infrastructure of our human brain—contains the core structures of our experience of self.

Views of the Brain

Over the years, the structures and functions of the brain have been studied using an increasingly sophisticated variety of techniques. For most of the history of neurology, however, the structure of the human brain was only examined after death. Findings concerning the location of brain damage during autopsy were linked to the nature and severity of the patient's clinical symptoms during her or his lifetime. The development of the brain was studied by examining and comparing the brains of humans and animals at different ages. These brains were compared for size; the number of neurons, synapses, and dendrites; the degree of myelinization; and other details that reflect maturation.

Fortunately, newer techniques allow us to examine the structure of the brain without waiting for the patient to die. Through the use of *computerized tomography* (CT) and *magnetic resonance imaging* (MRI), we are able to see two- and three-dimensional pictures of the living brain. Both of these techniques provide a series of cross-sectional images of the brain through its different layers. CT scans do this via multiple x-rays, whereas MRI scans utilize radio waves and a magnetic field to study the magnetic resonance of hydrogen molecules in the water present in the different structures throughout the brain. In determining brain–behavior relationships, these measures need to be evaluated on the basis of whether they are causes or correlates of the disorder being studied (Davidson, 1999). In their present practical applications, radiologists learn to read these images for the presence and locations of tumors or lesions in order to assist surgeons in their work. These scans have become an indispensable tool in neurology by providing a picture of the brain of a patient who can still be treated.

The *functioning* of the brain can also be measured in many ways. The clinical exam, tests of strength and reflexes, mental status exams, and neuropsychological testing all require a patient to perform physical or mental operations that are tied to known neurobiological systems. These clinical tests are supplemented and informed by a number of laboratory tests that measure different aspects of brain functioning. The *electroencephalograph* (EEG) measures patterns of electrical activity throughout the cortex. There are characteristic brainwave patterns in different states of arousal and stages of sleep. Epilepsy or the presence of tumors will demonstrate characteristic alterations of normal electrical functioning allowing EEGs to be used as diagnostic tools. EEGs can also be used to measure brain development, because neural network organization is characterized by the replacement of local erratic discharges with more widespread and constant wave patterns.

The most exciting new tools in neuroscience are the various brain-scanning techniques providing us with a window to the brain in action. *Positron emission tomography* (PET), *single photon emission tomography* (SPECT), and *functional magnetic resonance imaging* (FMRI) measure changes in blood flow, oxygen metabolism, and glucose utilization; they can be used to assess the relative activity of different regions of the brain. Using these techniques, neuroscientists can now explore complex activation–deactivation patterns of brain activity in subjects performing a wide range of cognitive, emotional, and behavioral tasks (Drevets, 1998). Most of these newer scanning techniques are still somewhat experimental, and methodological standards regarding their use and interpretation are still evolving. These methods, and those yet to be developed, will vastly enhance our understanding of the brain. As they grow increasingly more accurate and specific, so too will our knowledge of the functioning of neural networks.

Summary

All our experiences are encoded by the interconnection of neurons within neural networks. Neural networks grow and organize in the interactive matrix of genetically programmed sensitive periods interacting with our social and physical worlds. The most powerful environment is the one created within intimate relationships with caretakers. These relationships stimulate the brain to grow and determine the shape it takes. Although the brain remains plastic throughout life, these early experiences have a lasting and powerful impact on our experience. Memory, in its many forms, determines all of our experiences and behaviors. We now turn our attention to an exploration of memory.

5

Multiple Memory Systems in Psychotherapy

"... to 'do memory' is essentially to engage in a cultural practice."
(Gergen, 1994)

Just about everything we do in therapy depends on the patient's memory. Yet, despite its central role, the majority of clinical psychologists, psychiatrists, family therapists, and social workers have little or no training about how memory works. This lack of training has been recognized as a critical deficit, and in recent years efforts have been made to remedy the problem (Yapko, 1994). In this chapter we will explore some aspects of memory and their application to development, psychological illnesses, and psychotherapy. Some of these concepts may be difficult to grasp at first, but I encourage you to put in the time to learn them; they can be quite helpful in understanding ourselves and our clients.

Since Freud, psychotherapists have traditionally been taught to divide memory into the broad categories of conscious, preconscious, and unconscious. In psychotherapy, conscious memory is expressed in the form of recollections of things past, the content of previous therapy sessions, and reports of day-to-day life. The preconscious contains memories that can be brought easily into conscious awareness. Unconscious memory manifests in behaviors, postures, attitudes, and feelings as well as in more complex forms such as defenses, self-esteem, and transference.

Freud believed that a fundamental goal of therapy is to make the unconscious conscious. From the perspective of rebuilding the brain, this goal can be described as increasing the interconnection and integration of neural networks dedicated to unconscious and conscious memory. This makes understanding the evolution, development, and functioning of the various systems of memory crucial to conceptualizing and treating psychological illnesses. It also aids in explaining to clients some of the paradoxes and confusion they experience based on the way their brains process information.

Resistance to Therapy or Memory Deficit?

For almost a year, I treated a woman named Sophia who had experienced repeated traumas and chronic stress dating back to early childhood. Sexual abuse, family difficulties, and relationship problems as an adult were all aspects of the conscious memories she brought to treatment. One of Sophia's long-standing complaints had been severe memory difficulties, especially when it came to names, dates, and appointments. Sophia told me that her teachers in elementary and high school had told her she was "stupid" because she wasn't able to remember class material from one day to the next. She still carried the shame of these memories and the fear that what her teachers had said was true. Her emotional memory, on the other hand, especially for experiences in which she had felt shame, seemed to function at a superior level.

Sophia had gone to many therapists throughout her adult life and was repeatedly told she missed appointments because she was resistant to treatment. Sophia found this understandably frustrating, and each time she terminated treatment after just a few sessions. Based on her history, these therapists assumed that her problems with memory were caused by a defensive style of denial and repression, and encouraged her to face her fears. This way of understanding and treating her memory problems had obviously not worked. Certain that it was her fault, Sophia's treatment failures led her to feel increasingly hopeless about ever finding the help she needed. Although she feared our work together would meet the same fate, she was willing to give therapy another try.

After learning about her history, I shared with her the destructive role of early and prolonged stress on the development of the neural networks that organize the types of explicit memory with which she was having trouble (Bremner, Scott, Delaney, Southwick, Mason, Johnson, et al., 1993). I suggested that we begin therapy by studying memory together and exploring memory aids from the field of cognitive rehabilitation. Daytimers, watches with alarms, personal digital assistants (PDAs), and computer programs with timed reminders were all tried and proved helpful for different applications. For the first two months of treatment, Sophia and I would schedule telephone contact every other day for a few minutes. During these contacts, we exercised her memory, checked on the various strategies we had set up during our previous session, and reinforced her successes. Sophia needed to learn to remember to use her strategies to help her remember. Utilizing her memory aids had to become automatic even if, in the moment, she'd forget *why* she was checking her book or calling me.

By using these strategies for about six weeks, Sophia was consistently able to remember appointments. This allowed her to gain confidence in therapy and learn that these specific memory problems in no way meant she was stupid. On the contrary, her self-respect increased as she realized how much she had accomplished during her life despite her traumatic history and memory deficits. Once memory-related issues were no longer an impediment to maintaining consistent contact, we shifted the focus of treatment to the impact of her life experiences on her relationships and career. The initial focus of therapy, using a formulation from neuroscience, turned out to be the necessary first step in a sustained and successful therapeutic relationship. From this point the therapeutic relationship was characterized by a more traditional psychodynamic approach.

There are many psychological disorders that present with a variety of memory deficits. Depression, for example, results in a negative bias in the recollection and interpretation of past, present, and future events (Beck, 1976). Depression convincingly demonstrates the influence of emotional states in the organization of conscious memory, sometimes called *state-dependent memory*. Clients report that if they wake up depressed, everything looks worse than it did the day before, even though they know, intellectually, that nothing has changed. The rapid (and unconscious) networks of emotion shape our understanding of the world microseconds before we become aware of our perception. Through identical mechanisms, our past experiences create our expectations for the future. This *memory for the future* (Ingvar, 1985) created in dysfunctional situations can repeatedly recreate unsuccessful but familiar patterns.

Multiple Memory Systems

Research and clinical experience support the existence of multiple memory systems, each with its own domains of learning, neural architecture, and developmental timetable (Tulving, 1985). Learning within all systems of memory is dependent on the process of LTP and the Hebbian synapses we have already discussed (Hebb, 1949). The two broadest categories of memory are explicit and implicit. The concepts of explicit and implicit memory, although similar to Freud's concept of conscious and unconscious memory, do not directly overlap. *Explicit memory* describes conscious learning and memory, including semantic, sensory, and motor forms. These memory systems allow us to recite the alphabet, recognize the smell of coconut, or play tennis. Some of these memory abilities remain just beneath the level of consciousness until we turn our attention to them (the preconscious). *Implicit memory* is reflected in unconscious patterns of learning stored in hidden layers of neural processing, largely inaccessible to conscious awareness.

Many of our daily experiences make it clear that we have multiple systems of explicit and implicit memory. For example, it sometimes helps to recall a phone number by moving your fingers over the keypad of an imaginary phone. This process demonstrates that systems of unconscious motor and visual memory can aid in the conscious recall of numbers. Another example is a phenomenon common among the elderly—having difficulty learning new information but easily recalling stories from their youth in great detail. Networks involved in the storage of long-term memory are distributed throughout the cortex and are more resistant to the effects of aging than are those responsible for short- and medium-term memory (Schacter, 1996).

Thinking back to the triune brain, each tier is involved with different aspects of memory functioning. The reptilian brain contains instinctual memories, the lessons of past generations (genetic memory) that control reflexes, and inner bodily functions. The paleomammalian brain (limbic system) contributes to emotional memory and conditioned learning—a mixture of primitive impulses and survival programs sculpted by experiences. These two systems are nonverbal and together comprise the majority of what Freud would have called the unconscious. The neomammalian brain, although largely unconscious in its processing, controls networks responsible for explicit memory.

Because of the order in which they develop, implicit and explicit memory (detailed in Table 5.1) are referred to as early and late memory. Systems of implicit memory are active even before birth, as demonstrated in the newborn's instincts to orient to the sound of her mother's voice (deCasper & Fifer, 1980). During the first months of life, basic sensory memories combine with one another and with bodily and emotional associations (Stern, 1985). These networks allow for the sight of one's father to be paired with raised arms, a smile, and a good feeling. Somatic, sensory, motor, and emotional experience help sculpt neural networks during the first few years into a sense of a physical self.

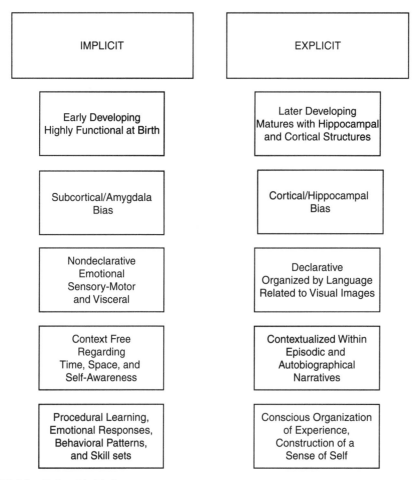

IMPLICIT	EXPLICIT
Early Developing Highly Functional at Birth	Later Developing Matures with Hippocampal and Cortical Structures
Subcortical/Amygdala Bias	Cortical/Hippocampal Bias
Nondeclarative Emotional Sensory-Motor and Visceral	Declarative Organized by Language Related to Visual Images
Context Free Regarding Time, Space, and Self-Awareness	Contextualized Within Episodic and Autobiographical Narratives
Procedural Learning, Emotional Responses, Behavioral Patterns, and Skill sets	Conscious Organization of Experience, Construction of a Sense of Self

Table 5.1 Multiple memory systems

A number of the basic distinctions between implicit and explicit systems of memory.

Because explicit memory requires networks involving the hippocampus and higher cortical structures, the development of conscious memory parallels the maturation of these systems over the first years of life (Fuster, 1996; Jacobs, van Praag, & Gage, 2000; LeDoux, 1996; McCarthy, 1995). *Childhood amnesia,* or the absence of explicit memory from early life, results from this maturational delay. In the absence of explicit memory, however, we learn how to walk and talk, whether the world is safe or dangerous, and how to attach to others. These vital early lessons, stored in networks throughout our brain and body, lack *source attribution*; that is, we don't remember how we learned them. Although many of us think we have explicit memories from the first years of life, these are most likely constructed later on and attributed to an earlier time in our life.

Explicit memory can be either sensory or linguistic. We associate sights, sounds, and smells with words to organize them in conscious memory. For most of us, words and visual images are, in fact, the keys to conscious memory. Different types of semantic memory include episodic, narrative, and autobiographical; these forms of explicit memory have the additional quality of being organized sequentially through time to become the basic structure of story-telling. We usually have source attributions for these memories. This form of memory is especially important for the formation and main-tenance of emotional regulation and self-identity. Autobiographical memory is characterized by the narrator being at the center of the story and combines episodic, semantic, and emotional memory with the self-awareness needed for maximal neural network integration.

Overall, the development of the different systems of memory reflects the early primacy of implicit memory for learning in sensory, motor, and emotional networks. These early-forming neural net-works depend on the more primitive brain structures such as the amygdala, thalamus, and middle portions of the frontal cortex (Figure 5.2). As the cortex and the hippocampus expand and mature over the first few years of life, there is a gradual maturation of the net-works of explicit memory. These systems provide for conscious, con-textualized learning and memory that become more consistent and stable over time.

Memory Is Distributed Throughout the Brain

Even though we are focusing on the memory systems most relevant to psychotherapy, it is important to remember that the systems of

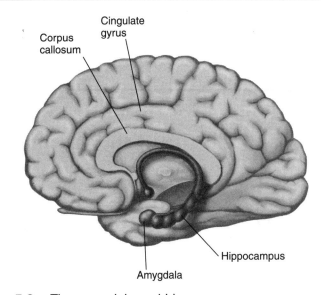

Figure 5.2   The amygdala and hippocampus

The right half of the brain viewed from the left side. The hippocampus and the amygdala are located on the inferior and medial aspects of the temporal lobes.

memory are distributed throughout the entire brain and nervous system. Systems of memory bridge top-down and left–right pathways. Where memory is stored depends on the type of memory and how the brain and body encode its component parts (McCarthy, 1995).

A good example comes from an experiment conducted by Martin and his colleagues. While measuring cerebral blood flow, they showed subjects pictures of animals and hand tools and asked them to name what they saw (Martin, Wiggs, Ungerleider, & Haxby, 1996). Naming both animals and tools resulted in increased activity in the temporal lobes and Broca's area. This makes sense, because the temporal lobes are known to be important for the organization of memory whereas Broca's area controls verbal expression. In addition, naming tools (but not animals) activated areas in the left motor cortex involved in hand movements (Martin et al., 1996).

Although there is overlap of activation during picture naming, the nature of the visual image triggers brain areas relevant to what is depicted. The portion of the occipital lobe (visual cortex) activated with animals is an area involved with very early stages of visual processing. This may be a reflection of how evolution has shaped the primitive areas of our visual brains to recognize and react quickly to threats from possible predators (animals chosen for this study happened to be a bear and an ape, both evolutionarily relevant predators). Activity occurring in the motor cortex while the subject is naming tools suggests that part of our "tool" memory is stored in neural networks that use them. Research has consistently demonstrated that the occipital lobe becomes activated when something is seen and, later, imagined. In the case of the imagined memory, the prefrontal area also becomes activated, reflecting its role in processing the instructions, staying on task, and accessing imagination. How neural networks in the prefrontal cortex know how to do this is as yet unknown (Ungerleider, 1995).

Although these studies focus primarily on activity in the cortex, psychotherapy often relates to the storage and retrieval of subcortical emotional memories. Emotional memories involve networks that include limbic structures such as the amygdala and hippocampus, both central to our later discussions of psychopathology and the impact of childhood experiences, stress, and trauma on adult functioning.

Amygdaloid Memory Networks

The amygdala is located within the limbic system and beneath the temporal lobes on each side of the brain. It is well developed at birth and has a significant role in the networks involved with emotional learning (Brodal, 1992). Portions of the amygdala (the basolateral areas) have evolved in tandem with the expansion of the cerebral cortex in humans (Stephan & Andy, 1977). The amygdala's neural connectivity supports its participation in the integration of the different senses with a special emphasis on vision (van Hoesen, 1981). The amygdala functions as an organ of appraisal for danger, safety, and familiarity in approach-avoidance situations (Sarter & Markowitsch, 1985). The amygdala, in association with medial areas of the frontal cortex, connects emotional value to the object of the senses based on both instincts and learning history (Davis, 1992; LeDoux, 1986), and translates these appraisals into bodily states. It is a central neural player in translating the sight of danger into preparing to fight or flee.

Two circuits of sensory input reach the amygdala in the adult brain. The first comes directly from the thalamus and the second loops first through the cortex and hippocampus (LeDoux, 1994). The first system serves to make rapid survival decisions with a minimum of information, whereas the second system adds cortical processing (context and inhibition) to appraise ongoing behavior. The amygdala's direct neural connectivity with the hypothalamus (Amaral, Veazey & Cowan, 1982) and limbic-motor circuits allows it to trigger rapid action. The power of phobias and flashbacks is greatly enhanced by the involvement of immediate and intense somatic activation provided by this direct connectivity.

Thus, the amygdala is one of the key components of affective memory, not just in infancy but throughout life (Ross, Homan, & Buck, 1994). In the fully developed brain, the amygdala enhances hippocampal processing of emotional memory by stimulating the release of *norepinephrine* and *glucocorticoids* via other brain structures (McGaugh, 1996; McGaugh et al., 1993). Through these chemical messages, the hippocampus is put on notice that what is being experienced is important to remember. As we discussed in chapter 2, this process represents a key component of new learning. The activation of the sympathetic nervous system alters the chemical environment within and between neurons, enhancing LTP, neural plasticity, and, possibly, neurogenesis. We will return to this topic in greater detail in later chapters, when we discuss the impact of stress and trauma on the brain.

The Amygdala and Unusual Experiences

The amygdala is a central neural hub of emotional experience, suggesting that it may be involved with some of the more unusual human experiences. Electrical stimulation of the amygdala results in a wide variety of bodily sensations (Halgren, Walter, Cherlow, & Crandall, 1978). Feelings of anxiety, déjà vu, and memory-like hallucinations have also been reported with stimulation of the amygdala (Chapman, Walter, Markham, Rand, & Crandall, 1967; Penfield & Perot, 1963; Weingarten, Cherlow, & Holmgren, 1977). Because of its low seizure threshold, subtle seizure activity may trigger the amygdala to activate normally inhibited sensory and emotional memories that then break through into conscious awareness (Sarter & Markowitsch, 1985). These primitive memories may also become activated in states of stress and posttraumatic arousal (van der Kolk & Greenberg, 1987). Individuals under stress may be particularly vulnerable to the intrusion of powerful memories from early childhood (Cozolino, 1997).

Primary process thinking and dreamlike experiences are more likely to merge with conscious awareness in situations of decreasing contextual cues, as in near-sleep states or conditions of sensory deprivation (Schacter, 1976). Decreasing contextual cues lessen the ability of the cortico-hippocampal systems to utilize past learning to make sense of present experience. This may account for the success of projective testing in tapping into unconscious processing. In attempting to make sense of ambiguous situations, subcortical circuits are more likely to guide conscious awareness.

Individuals with temporal lobe epilepsy (TLE) often experience extreme religiosity (Cummings, 1985), suggesting that stimulation of the amygdala can impart everyday experience with deep significance. In other words, its appraisal function can be applied in an inappropriate manner not based on external realities. The central nucleus of the amygdala also has a high density of *opioid receptors* (Goodman, Snyder, Kuhar, & Young, 1980), which are biochemical mechanisms of bonding and attachment behavior (Herman, & Panksepp, 1978;

Kalin, Shelton, & Lynn, 1995; Kalin, Shelton, & Snowdon, 1993) but also result in alterations of consciousness. This suggests that unregulated activation of the amygdala may be a neurobiological trigger for the religious preoccupations occurring in some individuals with TLE. The fact that hypergraphia (writing a lot) can also be a symptom of TLE may lead us to speculate that some religious texts have been motivated by the authors' unusual amygdala activation.

Hippocampal Memory Networks

The hippocampi, shaped like seahorses on either side of the human brain, are essential structures for the encoding and storage of explicit memory and learning (Zola-Morgan & Squire, 1990) and play a central role in the organization of spatial and temporal information (Edelman, 1989; O'Keefe & Nadel, 1978; Olton, 1986; Selden, Everitt, Jarral, & Robbins, 1991; Sherry, Jacobs, & Gaulin, 1992). The hippocampus also participates in our ability to compare different memories and make inferences from previous learning in new situations (Eichenbaum, 1992). Damage to the hippocampus can prevent any new learning from occurring, condemning the victim to forgetting everything seconds after it is experienced (Squire, 1987).

The hippocampus is noted for its late maturation, with the myelination of cortical–hippocampal circuits continuing into late adolescence (Benes, 1989). The late development of the hippocampus and its connectivity with the cortex reflects both its delayed functional availability and prolonged sensitivity to developmental disruption and traumatic insult. It remains particularly vulnerable to hypoxia (lack of oxygen caused by decreased blood supply) throughout life. Gradual atrophy of the hippocampus appears to be a natural component of aging, corresponding with gradually decreasing explicit memory abilities (Golomb et al., 1993).

Research suggests that sustained stress results in excessive exposure of the hippocampus to glucocorticoids, released in the response to acute stress (Sapolsky, 1987). Prolonged high levels of glucocorticoids can result in dendritic degeneration, increased vulnerability to future neurological insult, inhibited hippocampal functioning, and cell death (Wantanabe, Gould, & McEwen, 1992). Patients suffering from post-traumatic stress disorder (PTSD) secondary to childhood trauma or combat exposure, prolonged depression, temporal lobe epilepsy (de Lanerolle, Kim, Robbins, & Spencer, 1989), and schizophrenia (Falkai & Bogerts, 1986; Nelson, Saykin, Flashman, & Riordan, 1998) have also been shown to have hippocampal cell loss. Decreases in hip-pocampal volume have been shown to correlate with deficits of encoding short-term into long-term memory (Bremner, Scott, Delaney, Southwick, Mason, Johnson, Innis, McCarthy, & Charney, 1993). Given that chronic stress correlates with decreased hippocampal volume, and that so many patients in psychotherapy have experienced chronic stress, it is logical to assume that many patients (like Sophia) have difficulty in those functions in which the hippocampus plays a role.

Amygdaloid–Hippocampal Interaction

The relationship between the amygdala and hippocampus contributes to the top-down and left–right integration discussed in chapter 2. The participation of the amygdala is biased toward right and down systems, whereas the hippocampus plays a larger role in left and top processing. Put another way, the amygdala has a central role in the emotional and somatic organization of experience, whereas the hippocampus is vital for conscious, logical, and cooperative social functioning. Their proper functioning and mutual regulation are central to normal functioning.

Douglas and Pribram (1966) suggested that the amygdala and hippocampus play opposite roles in an attention-directing process. By accentuating small differences among inputs, the amygdala heightens awareness of specific aspects of the environment (attention) whereas the hippocampus inhibits responses, attention, and stimulus input (habituation; Douglas, 1967; Kimble, 1968; Marr, 1971). The amygdala is involved with generalization, the hippocampus with discrimination (Sherry & Schacter, 1987). The amygdala will make us jump at the sight of a spider, whereas the hippocampus will allow us to remember that this particular spider is not poisonous, so we shouldn't worry.

We can immediately see the relevance of these two systems to psychotherapy. The amygdaloid memory system, organizing early memories of abandonment, makes the patient with borderline disorder react to the *perception* of abandonment where little or none exists in reality. Therapy with this patient would utilize the hippocampal–cortical systems to test the reality of their amygdaloid cue for the experience of abandonment in order to organize and inhibit inappropriate reactions. This serves to distinguish real abandonment from innocent triggers such as someone showing up a few minutes late for an appointment. It can also inhibit affective dyscontrol triggered by early memories of abandonment stored in amygdaloid networks. Remember, for a young primate, *abandonment means death*. The catastrophic reaction of borderline patients to abandonment is a result of the fact that, to them, it is experienced as life threatening.

Flashbacks from traumatic experiences likely reside in amygdaloid memory networks. PTSD victims describe flashbacks as powerful, and multisensory, often triggered by stress, and experienced as if they were occurring in the present (Gloor, 1978; LeDoux, Romanski, & Xagoraris, 1989; van der Kolk & Greenberg, 1987). These flashbacks also have the characteristic of being stereotyped and repetitive (van der Kolk, Blitz, Burr, Sherry, & Hartmann, 1984), suggesting that they are not subject to the assimilating and contextualizing properties of hippocampal memory networks. A model of dual memory processing, paralleling the amygdala hippocampal distinction made here, has been previously proposed as underlying mechanisms in both PTSD (Brewin, Dalgleish, & Joseph, 1996) and the reemergence of past fears and phobias (Jacobs & Nadel, 1985).

Given the reciprocal nature of amygdaloid and hippocampal circuits, impairment of the hippocampus should lead to the increased influence of the amygdala in directing memory, emotion, and behavior, and would certainly disrupt affect regulation. Depressed patients are overwhelmed by their negative feelings and unable to engage in adequate reality testing. Indeed, Sheline and her colleagues noted both decreased hippocampal (Sheline, Wang, Gado, Csernansky, & Vannier, 1996) and amygdaloid (Sheline, Gado, & Price, 1998) volume in depressed patients. Dysregulation of hippocampal-amygdaloid circuits are likely involved in depressive symptomatology.

Research with rats has found that increased levels of serotonin leads to enhanced neurogenesis in the hippocampus (Jacobs et al., 2000). This suggests that Prozac and Paxil may be effective in treating depression because they boost hippocampal volume and its ability to moderate amygdala activation.

The Intrusion of Early Implicit Memory Into Adult Consciousness

Early implicit learning and memory intrude into adult consciousness in many ways that are relevant to psychotherapy. Children who suffer early abuse may enter their school-age years agitated, aggressive, and destructive, frequently engaging in fights, property damage, and animal torture. Their behavior results in such consequences as constant trouble, criticism, and punishment. This feedback, in combination with the emotional memories of their abuse, naturally evolves into a self-image of a bad person. In the absence of memory of their trauma, these childrens' behavior is not experienced as a reaction to a negative event, but instead as an indication of their essential badness. Because these experiences date back to the formation of preverbal sensory, motor, and affective memory systems, victims often report feeling "evil to the core." This is common in children who grow up in cults or with highly authoritarian or abusive parents.

The formation of attachment schema (a form of implicit memory) guides and shapes relationships throughout life. Given that so many clients come to therapy with relationship difficulties, this implicit memory system may be one of the most common themes in psy-chotherapy. These networks of social memory give rise to the phe-nomenon of transference. We have all experienced having our "buttons pushed" by someone; many of these "buttons" are the emo-tional traces of personal experiences, stored in implicit systems of memory.

"Overreacting" to something implies that the difference between an appropriate reaction and how we *actually* react is attributable to a sensitivity based on our learning history. The most common distor-tions based on the input of early memory are in the direction of shame, a primary socializing affect starting at about 12 months (Schore, 1994). Individuals who are "shame based" (Bradshaw, 1990) can find criticism, rejection, and abandonment in nearly every inter-action, resulting in a life of chronic anxiety, a struggle for perfection, exhaustion, and depression. Chapter 10 provides a detailed descrip-tion of this process.

Silence may be golden, but in therapy it evokes a variety of implicit memories. During periods of silence, many clients assume that the therapist is thinking critical thoughts. They report being afraid that the therapist is thinking they are boring, stupid, a waste of time, or a bad client. These feelings usually mirror those they have had in a problematic relationship with one or both parents. Furthermore, these feelings are deep seated and tenacious, often tak-ing many years to reorganize. On the other hand, some clients find silence to be a form of acceptance and, as such, a relief from the pres-sures of being articulate and communicative.

These stark differences in reactions to the same situation are con-vincing evidence of the workings of implicit memory and their effects on conscious experience. Silence is an ambiguous stimulus that acti-vates systems of implicit memory. The projection of the client into the silence teaches us something of their emotional history. A similar phenomenon occurs in individuals who become uncomfortable when they try to relax without any distractions. The emotions, images, and thoughts that emerge in conditions of low stimulation (or the absence of distraction) may hold clues to the workings of our brains and the aftereffects of early learning.

The Malleability of Memory

The false memory debate of recent years has clearly highlighted deficits in the knowledge and sophistication of therapists concerning memory. Highly publicized legal cases of repressed memory and clinician contribution to the co-construction of false memories has resulted in increased understanding and training focused on the processes of memory. Most therapists are now aware of the vulnerability of conscious memory to suggestion, distortion, and fabrication from both the client and therapist (Loftus, 1988). Research has demonstrated that memory can be implanted in experimental situations where the subject soon becomes certain that the false memories have actually occurred (Ceci & Bruch, 1993; Loftus, Milo, & Paddock, 1995). A therapist's belief that her client has been abused may influence that patient to unconsciously fabricate a memory that they both then come to believe as true. This process is a clear demonstration of both the malleability of memory and the power of co-constructed narrative in shaping experience.

Given that the organization of memory is encoded among neurons and within neural networks, the malleability of memory is a behavioral manifestation of the plasticity of neural systems. Because our ethics and legal system are based on objective truth, the fact that memory is so malleable and imperfect is a stumbling block in the pursuit of objective truth. From the perspective of psychotherapy, however, the plasticity of memory provides an avenue to the alteration of neural systems. Revisiting and evaluating childhood experiences from an adult perspective often leads to rewriting history in a creative and positive way. The introduction of new information or scenarios about past experiences can modify affective reactions and alter the nature of memories.

The Magic Tricycle

Sheldon was a man in his late 60s who came to therapy for help with his many anxieties and fears. As a child, his parents had hidden him from the Nazis in a storage room behind the home of family friends. One day, after finding out that she and Sheldon's father would soon be taken to the concentration camps, Sheldon's mother told him to be a good boy, said goodbye, and left. While the family friends were kind to him, he spent his days alone with few toys, his small tricycle, and some scraps of food. Describing these days, Sheldon recalled alternating states of terror, boredom, and half-sleep during which he would either sit and rock or ride his tricycle around in slow tight circles. The slightest noise would startle him and he feared that each passing siren might be the police coming for him. Each day, exhausted by fear, he would eventually fall asleep.

The intervening decades had not diminished the impact of his experiences during the war; 60 years later, he still found himself reflexively rocking or walking in small slow circles when he became frightened. His life felt like one long day of fear.

In repeatedly recalling these experiences, he sometimes mentioned how he wished he could have left the house where he was hidden and traveled down the narrow streets to his grandmother's house. Sheldon remembered long afternoons before the war when he sat there and listened to stories of her childhood on her father's farm. His grandmother and his parents perished in the war, and he never saw them again.

One day, I asked him for permission to change his memories just a bit. After a few quizzical looks he agreed to close his eyes and tell me the entire story again, during which time I would interrupt him and make some suggestions. As he came to the part of the story where he rode around in circles, I asked him, "What would you do if this were a magic tricycle and it could take you through walls without getting hurt?" I felt Sheldon had sufficient ego strength to allow him to simultaneously engage in the role play while staying fully in touch with present reality.

After some hesitation, Sheldon said, "Ride right through the house and out onto the sidewalk."

"Fine," I said, "Let's go!" Sheldon had been primed for our imaginary therapy play because he had spent many enjoyable hours of storytelling, cuddling, and laughing with his grandchildren. He had described these pleasures to me and I felt that an imaginative task like this was not only accessible to him but would also serve the purpose of bridging the positive affect from his grandchildren to his lonely and frightened experiences as a child. Imagining he was making up the story for his grandchildren might also help him cope with the embarrassment of doing this with another adult.

After some mild hesitation, he pedaled through the house. As he got close to the door, however, he said, "They'll see me and kill me."

"What if the magic tricycle has the power to make you invisible?" I asked.

"I think that'll do," said Sheldon, and he pedaled through the front of the house and out onto the sidewalk. Once he got out of the house, he knew what to do. He described the street to me as he pedaled toward his grandmother's house. The storekeepers, the neighbors, the park, his rabbi, even some of his young friends were all alive in his memories of those streets. Sure enough, when he finally got to his grandmother's house she was home and, as always, happy to see him. He told his grandmother about his invisible tricycle and how scared he was in his hiding place. He went on to tell her of the end of the war, his travels, and raising his family. Finally, almost like a prayer, Sheldon told her how, many years from now, she would have the most beautiful great-great-grandchildren who would somehow make her suffering worthwhile.

Over the next few months, whenever Sheldon experienced his childhood fears and anxieties, we would revisit his story and modify different details. These changes seemed to grow deeper in his mind, more detailed, and more vivid. His imagination gave him the power to master many of his past fears. Because memory is modified each time it is remembered (Bruner, 1990), Sheldon's brain was able to gradually contaminate his painful childhood with his present safety and joy. He even began to tell his grandchildren stories about a little boy with a magic tricycle who accomplished great things with his courage and wit. Sheldon was a very special man who was able to take advantage of the malleability of memory to make his inner world a safer place. Nothing had changed about his childhood except that now, when he remembered his hiding place, he also remembered his magic tricycle.

Summary

The construction of autobiographical narratives requires that the semantic processing of the left hemisphere integrate with the emotional networks in the right. Storytelling also invokes participation of the body as we gesture and act out the events we are describing. As such, narratives are a valuable tool in the organization and integration of neural networks throughout the nervous system. Memories are distributed throughout the brain and body and are subject to modification. Because we can write and rewrite the stories of ourselves, new stories hold the potential for new ways of experiencing ourselves and our lives. In editing our narratives, we change the organization and nature of our memories and, hence, reorganize our brains as well as our minds. This is a central endeavor in many forms of psychotherapy.

As a boy in the early 1960s, I remember being fascinated by news stories of Japanese soldiers attacking tourists in the South Pacific. During World War II, their navy had apparently left soldiers on many small islands throughout the Pacific but had never retrieved them. Decades later, pleasure craft would innocently land on these islands only to be attacked by soldiers who thought the war was still being fought. They had dutifully kept guns oiled and remained vigilant for decades in anticipation of an American attack. I was awed by their loyalty and saddened by the thought of the years they spent fighting a war that no longer existed.

Like these soldiers, early memory systems retain struggles, stress, and trauma from a time before we can remember. Our conscious awareness may move on to new lives and challenges while our implicit memory systems retain fears and pain, remaining vigilant for signs of attack. Therapists land on these beaches, attempting to convince the loyal soldiers trapped within implicit systems of memory that *the war is over.*

Laterality:
One Brain or Two?

In the last chapter, we explored our multiple and diverse systems of memory. Another aspect of neural network complexity is the difference between the two cerebral hemispheres. Because most neural processing requires the contribution of both hemispheres, smooth neural functioning requires the coordination of both halves of the brain. There are situations, however, when the hemispheres not only "think" differently but also compete with one another. This unconscious neurobiological tension may be one cause of our internal struggles, and give new meaning to why we sometimes feel we are "beside ourselves." By the end of this chapter, you may be left wondering whether we have one brain or two.

John Hughlings Jackson, the eminent 19th-century neurologist, believed that the left side of the brain was, for most people, the "leading" side. This seemed logical given the findings that the left hemisphere was responsible for our ability to use language, as was reported by Broca in the 1860s (Springer & Deutsch, 1998). Jackson later suggested that the right hemisphere was the leading side of the brain in visual-spatial abilities. These concepts were the beginning of the notion of *cerebral dominance*. Since then, the picture of cerebral dominance has grown increasingly complex. In this chapter we will explore some of the clinical phenomena and scientific theories that have emerged from the study of our two brains.

Laterality

The human brain is divided into two hemispheres, referred to as right and left (when looking from back to front). Each cerebral hemisphere controls the opposite side of the body. *Laterality* is the assignment of tasks to one side of the brain or the other, and is reflected in the fact that the right and left hemispheres differ in their organization, processing strategies, and neural connectivity. Keep in mind that laterality demonstrates considerable variation among individuals.

Most neural systems integrate circuitry from both the left and right sides of the brain. Because of this, research attempting to localize functions in one hemisphere or the other often results in "untidy" findings (Christman, 1994). When we speak of functions of the right or left brain, we are more accurately referring to functions that are represented more fully in one hemisphere than the other. Over the past 40 years, much has been written about the artistic right brain and the logical left. Although this view may be appealing to the imagination, it is far too simplistic. Assigning specific functions to particular areas of the brain needs to be done with both caution and the recognition that our knowledge is still evolving.

Evolution and Development

During evolution, the right and left cerebral hemispheres have become increasingly dissimilar (Geschwind & Galaburda, 1985). Although having redundant hemispheres provides a backup system in case of injury, natural selection appears to have favored hemispheric specialization in humans to provide for more complex neural organization and higher-level functions. For example, areas of the left and right cortices have become specialized to serve the formation of the conscious linguistic self in the left and the physical emotional self in the right.

During the first 2 years of life, the right hemisphere has a growth spurt that parallels the rapid development of sensory, motor, and emotional capabilities (Chiron et al., 1997; Thatcher, Walker, & Guidice, 1987). The child learns hand–eye coordination, crawling, and walking while becoming acquainted with his or her world. An organized sense of the body in space forms in subcortical and cortical networks involving the thalamus, cerebellum, and parietal cortex. At the same time, portions of the cortex are maturing along with the other circuitry of the social and fearful brains to establish the basic structures of emotional regulation and attachment (Schore, 1994). During this period, the development of the left hemisphere is slowed and reserved for later-developing functions (Gould, 1977).

In the middle of the second year, a growth spurt occurs in the left hemisphere. An explosion in language comprehension and expression, and increased locomotion, propel the child into an extended exploration of the physical and social worlds. In the frontal lobes, there is a shift to development in the dorsolateral areas, linking back to other cortical regions, that sculpt the language network (Tucker, 1992) while connecting the movements of hands and eyes to visual stimuli and words. The corpus callosum begins to develop at the end of the first year, is significantly developed by age four, and continues to mature past the age of ten. Because of this slow maturation, the two hemispheres at first function more autonomously, gradually gaining coordination through childhood (Galin, Johnstone, Nakell, & Herron, 1979).

The neurology literature contains countless examples of conscious experience being disturbed by trauma to both sides of the brain (Benson, 1994). A great deal of what is known about the functions of the different hemispheres has been the result of the "split brain" research of Sperry and his colleagues (Sperry, Gazzaniga, & Bogen, 1969). *Split brain* patients suffer from epilepsy that cannot be treated successfully with medication. These patents have their corpus callosum surgically severed to limit seizures to one side of the brain. Presenting information separately to each hemisphere has revealed divisions of awareness (as well as specialization in a range of cognitive and emotional tasks) that have expanded our knowledge of hemispheric specialization (LeDoux, Wilson, & Gazzaniga, 1977; Ross et al., 1994; Sperry, 1968).

Lateral Asymmetry

The earliest forms of language in evolutionary history were most likely hand gestures. This may explain why handedness and language functions are linked in the brain. Most of us are right-handed (controlled by the left brain) and have language that is lateralized in the left hemisphere. During evolution, as the semantic functions of the cortex expanded, and language became more descriptive and useful, words gradually replaced gestures in importance. Our present use of hand gestures to augment spoken language reflects these evolutionary origins. The fact that we tend to use hand gestures even when talking on the telephone suggests that they also play a role in organizing our thinking. We may use gestures to help ourselves think, stay on task, and communicate with ourselves as well as others. Coordinated use of words and bodily gestures may reflect the simultaneous participation of both hemispheres in communication and thought.

Language functions are located in the left hemisphere for most adults, using both spoken and sign language (Corina, Vaid, & Bellugi, 1992). In left-handed or ambidextrous individuals, lateralization of language is somewhat less clear. Damage to the left hemisphere usually results in language disturbances as in the various forms of aphasia. The left hemisphere appears to be more involved in conscious coping and problem solving than is the right, most likely a function of its language skills. The left hemisphere functions best within the middle range of affect and is biased toward positive and prosocial emotions (Silberman & Weingartner, 1986). Strong affect, especially anxiety and terror, appear to inhibit left hemisphere functions of language and logic—hence, the experience of *stage fright* and *speechless terror*.

The right hemisphere is generally responsible for both appraising the safety and danger of others and organizing the sense of the corporeal and emotional self (Devinsky, 2000). *Appraisal* simply means whether we have positive or negative associations to a stimulus, resulting in an approach or avoidance response (Fox, 1991). Emotion is the conscious manifestation of this mostly unconscious appraisal process (Fischer, Shaver, & Carnochan, 1990). The vast majority of appraisal occurs at an unconscious level, guiding our thoughts and behavior outside of our awareness. This is why the right hemisphere is generally associated with the unconscious mind.

The bias against left-handedness across many cultures may reflect an intuitive understanding of the left hand's (right-brain's) relationship to the uncivilized and uncooperative parts of our nature. Some of these biases could date back into prehistory, when the left hemisphere may have exerted less control over the right. By offering the right hand in greeting, early humans may have been more likely to be civilized, while less likely to act out primitive and dangerous impulses. An examination of cave drawings suggests that the bias toward right-handedness has existed for at least the last 5,000 years (Coren & Porac, 1977).

Although the left hemisphere generally produces language, it is unclear whether it has any advantage in language comprehension. The right hemisphere may, in fact, be better at comprehending emotionally laden language (Searleman, 1977). Emotions in general, the ability to evaluate emotional facial expressions, and visual-spatial and musical abilities are primarily right-hemisphere processes (Ahern et al., 1991). Damage to the right hemisphere results not only in an impairment in our ability to assess facial gestures, but also to comprehend other nonverbal aspects of communication such as hand gestures and tone of voice (Blonder, Bowers, & Heilman, 1991).

For most individuals, the right hemisphere processes information in a holistic fashion (Nebes, 1971) and is densely connected to the limbic systems and the viscera. The left hemisphere, on the other hand, processes information in a linear, sequential, language-based manner and is less densely connected with the body. The right hemisphere is heavily wired to the limbic system and is more directly involved in the regulation of the endocrine and autonomic nervous systems than is the left hemisphere (Wittling & Pfluger, 1990). The right hemisphere also contains centers within the parietal lobes that integrate the experience of our body as a whole. The representation of the entire body, contained primarily in the right hemisphere, is an important aspect of laterality.

It has been suggested that Wernicke's area in the left temporal lobe, known to be centrally involved in language comprehension, acts as a probability calculator for other forms of behavior as well as language (Bischoff-Grethe, Proper, Mao, Daniels, & Berns, 2000). Given the rapidity with which we process speech, Wernicke's area may process what is heard based as much on what it *expects* to hear as what is actually said. This would certainly help to explain why human communication can be so problematic and misunderstandings so common.

The Integration of the Body in the Right Hemisphere

The parietal lobes, located above our ears toward the top of our heads, are at the crossroads of neural networks responsible for vision, hearing, and sensation. They serve as a high-level association area for the integration and coordination of these functions. Although the anterior (front) portion of the parietal lobes organize tactile perception, the posterior (back) portion interconnects the senses to organize sensory-motor with conceptual events (Joseph, 1996). Accordingly, cells in the parietal lobes respond to hand position, eye movement, words, motivational relevance, body position, and many other factors relevant to the integration of experience.

The purpose of the association of all of these high-order process-ing networks is to provide an integrated awareness of one's own body and its relation to the external environment (Adams, Victor, & Ropper, 1997). This makes sense in that the parietal lobes have evolved from the hippocampus, which, in lower mammals, serves as a cognitive map for foraging territory (O'Keefe & Nadel, 1978). Damage to the parietal lobes, especially on the right, results in a wide range of disruptions to the organization of conscious experience of the self and the world.

Hemi-neglect, or the denial of the existence of the left side of the body, is a dramatic neurological syndrome resulting from lesions to the right parietal lobe. When neglect is severe, the patient behaves as if the left half of his or her world has stopped existing, and may have difficulty with leftward shifts of attention (Mesulam, 1985). Patients with neglect will dress and put makeup only on the right side of their bodies, denying ownership of their left arm or leg. Asked to draw the face of a clock, they may put all 12 numbers on the right side. The result of damage to the right parietal lobes strongly suggests that it contains an internal representation of the entire body (both left and right sides) in space. Although the left hemisphere seems to contain a network to monitor attention on the right side of the body, the right hemisphere of right-handers has a specialized ability to direct atten-tion bilaterally to both the right and left sides of "extrapersonal space" (Mesulam, 1981).

Amazingly, the phenomenon of hemi-neglect not only exists in regard to bodily space, but also in imaginary space. Bisiach and Luzzatti (1978) examined two patients with left-sided neglect who were asked to describe the Piazza del Duomo in Milan. The Piazza was very familiar to both patients throughout their lives prior to experiencing the injuries that led to their hemi-neglect. When asked to imagine the Piazza from one end, they could recall and describe the details on their imagined right side but not their left. Later, they were asked to imagine the Piazza from the other end. Looking back to where they previously pictured themselves sitting, they were able to accurately describe what was on the right side but not on the left. In other words, once they imagined turning around 180 degrees, they now had access to memories that they were unable to remember just a short while earlier. Further, the information they just provided was no longer accessible. This remarkable demonstration suggests neural networks that organize and attend to the body in space are also utilized in imagination.

In later research, Bisiach and his colleagues (Bisiach, Rusconi, & Vallar, 1991; Cappa, Sterzi, Vallar, & Bisiach, 1987; Vallar, Sterzi, Bottini, Cappa, & Rusconi, 1990) found that vestibular stimulation via cold water irrigation of the left ear (the caloric test) in patients with right parietal lobe lesions resulted in temporary remission of their left hemi-neglect. Putting cold water into the left inner ear stimulated areas within the right temporal lobe and caused the patients to orient toward the left (Friberg, Olsen, Roland, Paulsen, & Lassen, 1985). Although the mechanism of action is not certain, one possible explanation could be that activation of the right temporal lobe resulted in a reintegration of right and left hemispheric attentional processes. This reintegration of attention may have temporarily counteracted the loss of the body integration resulting from right parietal damage (Rubens, 1985).

Although the right hemisphere specializes in the organization of the experience of the body and other visual-spatial abilities, the left hemisphere appears to be generally dominant for comprehending and expressing language.

The Language Network

Although the semantic aspects of language are usually lateralized to the left hemisphere, the right contributes the emotional and prosodic element of speech. The left-hemisphere language network relies on the convergence of auditory, visual, and sensory information from the temporal, occipital, and parietal lobes, respectively. Wernicke's area in the temporal lobe receives input from the primary auditory area, and organizes it into meaningful bits of information. The convergence zone connects sounds, sights, and touch so that cross-modal connections can be made, allowing us to name things we touch and hear without visual cues. It is also necessary for the development of sign language, where words take the form of gestures. This sophisticated and highly processed information projects forward to Broca's area, where expressive speech is organized.

Nerve fibers linking language areas to the rest of the frontal lobes allow both spoken and internal language to guide behavior and regulate affect. The integrative properties of language may be unequaled by any other function of the brain. Creating and recalling a story requires the convergence of multisensory emotional, temporal, and memory capabilities that bridge all vectors of neural networks. In this way, language organizes the brain and can be used to reorganize it in psychotherapy.

The Left-Hemisphere Interpreter

Working with split-brain patients, Gazzaniga and his colleagues found that the left hemisphere could create an explanation of experience when right-hemisphere information was unavailable (Gazzaniga, LeDoux, & Wilson, 1977). This strategy of filling in gaps in experience and memory, and making a guess at an explanation, parallels confabulatory processes seen in patients with dementia and psychosis. *Confabulation* appears to be a natural and reflexive function of the left-hemisphere interpreter. This function is likely related to Freudian defense mechanisms that distort reality in order to reduce anxiety; it is also the core mechanism of reflexive social language discussed earlier.

After extensive observation of split-brain patients, Gazzaniga (1989) developed the concept of the *left-hemisphere interpreter*. He postulated that one function of the left-hemisphere interpreter is to synthesize available information and generate a coherent narrative for the conscious social self. The consistency of findings across a variety of settings led to a general acceptance that the verbal neocortex organizes conscious experience (Nasrallah, 1985) and embodies the "social self" as arbiter of rules, expectations, and socio-emotional presentation (Ross et al., 1994). The left-hemisphere interpreter is the spokesperson for our conscious reflexive self.

The Woman in the Mirror

S.M. was a 77-year-old patient suffering from atrophy of the parietal and temporal lobes of her right hemisphere. One day, she was seen using sign language in front of the mirror in her bedroom (Feinberg & Shapiro, 1989). When asked what she was doing, the patient reported to her son that she was communicating with the "other S.M." The patient stated that there was another S.M. who was identical to her in appearance, age, background, and education. The other S.M. was always seen in a mirror. She and the other S.M. had gone to the same school, but did not know each other. The other S.M. had a son of the same name and identical in appearance to the patient's own son.

Feinberg and Shapiro (1989) reported that S.M. and her double were virtually identical in every respect, except that S.M. stated that the other S.M. had a tendency to talk too much and did not communicate as well in sign language. When presented with a mirror, S.M. would generally identify her image as the other S.M. If the patient's son or the examiner appeared behind the patient in the mirror, the patient would correctly label that person's mirror reflection. Thus, the phenomenon was only evident for her own image. When it was pointed out to S.M. that this was indeed her own mirror image, she would say to her son, "Oh sure, that's what you think" (Feinberg & Shapiro, 1989, p. 41). While S.M.'s comprehension of herself and the world had been disrupted by her right-hemisphere lesion, her left-hemisphere interpreter remained intact. It is sad, if somewhat comical, to think that she experienced her reflection in the mirror as talking too much and being less skilled in sign language.

This confabulation and positive bias of S.M. versus her reflection is a perfect example of the left-hemisphere interpreter at work. It also reflects the brain's basic instinct to engage in explanatory behavior for things it cannot understand. Some version of the interpreter concept has previously been used to explain the development of paranormal beliefs (Cozolino, 1997), schizophrenic delusions (Maher, 1974), and religious beliefs (Gazzaniga, 1995). The concept is especially relevant to psychotherapy, because the construction of reality is at work in the world views of patients with character disorders, the defense mechanisms of neurotics, and the day-to-day reality of healthy individuals. The left-hemisphere interpreter is an internal press secretary for the self, putting a positive spin on what is experienced and how it is presented to others. If the interpreter is not doing its job adequately, such as in the case of left-hemisphere damage or decreased activation of the left frontal cortex, we become pessimistic and depressed.

Communication and Coordination Between the Hemispheres

As our left and right hemispheres differentiated during evolution, each may have come to gain dominance for specific functions after failed experiments with transcortical democracy (Levy, Trevarthan, & Sperry, 1972). Lateral dominance now appears to depend on the functional domain in question (Cutting, 1992; Goldberg & Costa, 1981; Semmes, 1968). The blending of the strengths of each hemisphere allows for the maximum integration of our cognitive and emotional experience with our inner and outer worlds. When we are awake, the right hemisphere constantly provides information to the left, although that hemisphere may not necessarily register, understand, or allow the information into consciousness. Nasrallah (1985) suggested that this input relates to intuition, feelings, fantasy, and visual images. The momentary "bubbling up" of feelings or images, which are then quickly lost, may reflect this neural process.

The filtration of right-hemispheric processes may be necessary to allow us to remain focused on the tasks in which we are engaged.

What happens when the hemispheres find themselves disconnected from one another? Jason and Pajurkova (1992) reported a case of a 41-year-old right-handed man who suffered damage to both the front portion of his corpus callosum and the medial portion of his frontal cortex. The most salient aspect of his behavior after his injury was the fact that the two sides of his body seemed to be in conflict with one another. During neuropsychological testing, the patient's right hand would perform a task while the left would move in and disrupt what had been accomplished. When he would try to go down a set of stairs, his right foot would lead but then his left hand would grab the doorjamb and refuse to let him move forward. He found himself unable to do tasks where both hands had to cooperate.

The patient reported, "My left foot and my left hand want to do the opposite of what my right one does all the time" (Jason & Pajurkova, p. 252). In another situation he stated, "My left hand doesn't go where I want it to" (p. 249). It seemed that in each of these situations, the right hand and side (controlled by the left hemisphere) attempted to carry out the conscious will of the patient. But the left side (controlled by the right hemisphere) would have no part of it. The authors reported that it seemed as if the right hemisphere was acting like a spiteful sibling, fighting for control or attention (Jason & Pajurkova, 1992).

Because of the absence of any psychiatric disorder, this unusual behavior was considered to be solely a function of the brain damage the patient had sustained. The authors reported that although this "conflictual" behavior decreased over time, it was still evident six months after the injury. Although similar left–right conflicts have been reported in split-brain patients, it usually resolves in the first few weeks after surgery.

It is clear in this case, as it has been with many split-brain patients, that the left hemisphere was experienced by the client as his conscious self (ego) while the behavior of the right hemisphere was experienced as a force from outside the self (ego-alien). The experience and behavior of such patients suggests not only alternate ways of processing information, but also another "will" residing in the right hemisphere (Jason & Pajurkova, 1992). The unconscious and oppositional quality of the behavior of this client's right hemisphere suggests that the left hand may have been acting out unconscious emotional judgments or appraisals. The right hemisphere may have sensed danger in walking down stairs, or was unhappy about the patient's test performance. The prosocial left hemisphere may have been struggling to be a good testing client while the right may have been frustrated and ashamed by his poor performance on neuropsychological testing.

Right-Left Integration and Psychopathology

I postulated in chapter 2 that neural network integration corresponds to ego strength, the use of mature defenses, and mental health. If this is the case, dissociation or imbalance among networks should correlate with mental illness. Based on what we know about hemispheric specialization, we have to assume that integration between the right and left hemispheres is a vital element of healthy brain functioning. Anxiety and affective disorders, psychosis, alexithymia, and psychosomatic conditions have all been hypothesized to be causally related to deficits in the regulation and integration of neural networks connecting the hemispheres. Although each of these conditions may have far more complex causes, understanding the lateralized aspects of these disorders may provide important information concerning etiology and treatment.

Anxiety and Depression

The proper integration and balance between right and left hemisphere functioning allows us to experience a healthy mixture of positive and negative emotional experiences, as well as to regulate and manage anxiety. The left hemisphere's bias toward positive affective and prosocial behavior helps us to connect with others and decrease anxiety. The right hemisphere's bias toward anxiety, suspiciousness, and negativity keeps the body alert to danger. Dysregulation between the two hemispheres results in a loss of balance between positive and negative affect states (Silberman & Weingartner, 1986).

Frontal lobe activation, when biased toward the right hemisphere, correlates with the signs and symptoms of depression. Research has shown that anesthesia of the left hemisphere results in greater expressions of negative emotions and less prosocial explanations of experience (Dimond & Farrington, 1977; Ross et al., 1994). Orienting eye gaze to the left (stimulating the right hemisphere) results in decreased optimism, while the opposite is true with rightward eye gaze (Drake, 1984; Thayer & Cohen, 1985). Right-hemisphere-biased neural processing, measured in a variety of ways, has been shown to correlate with low self-esteem (Persinger & Makarec, 1991), less prosocial explanation of events (Ross et al., 1994), and depression (Nikolaenko, Egorov, & Freiman, 1997).

The same phenomena holds true for anxiety. Primates with extreme right frontal activity are more fearful and defensive, and have higher levels of stress hormones, than do those with activity biased toward the left hemisphere (Kalin, Larson, Shelton, & Davidson, 1998). Adults with a history of childhood trauma demonstrate a significantly greater shift to right hemispheric processing when asked to change their thinking from neutral to unpleasant memories (Schiffer, Teicher, & Papanicolaou, 1995). Activation of many structures of the right hemisphere is also evident during posttraumatic flashbacks (Rauch et al., 1996).

If anxiety and depression are, in part, the result of a bias toward right-hemisphere processing, then any form of successful treatment will enhance a rebalancing of these systems. Cognitive therapies for both anxiety and depression utilize rational thought that may work by activating left-hemisphere processes and regain lateral balance.

Symptomatic relief can also be achieved by a downregulation of the right-hemisphere processes through relaxation training.

Because neurons communicate via electrochemical processes, magnetic stimulation can enhance activity in targeted areas of the brain. *Transcranial magnetic stimulation* (TMS), utilizing pulsed magnetic fields to stimulate brain activity, has been the focus of recent experimentation with psychiatric patients (Bohning, 2000). Research with patients suffering from depression and mania has shown some promising results (Klein et al., 1999). Successful magnetic stimulation of the left hemisphere of depressed patients (Pascual-Leone, Rubio, Pallardo, & Catala, 1996; Teneback et al., 1999) and the right hemisphere of patients with mania (Grisaru, Chudakov, Yaroslavsky, & Belmaker, 1998) supports the theory that affective symptoms are related to lateral imbalance. Lateral stimulation of the brain to balance functioning is a possible focus of future treatment and could potentially become interwoven with other psychological interventions.

An unfortunate artifact of the evolution of laterality may be that the right hemisphere is biased toward negative emotions and pessimism (unfortunate because the right prefrontal cortex also appears to have primary control over emotional self-awareness; Keenan et al., 1999). This aspect of laterality may create a bias toward shame, guilt, and depression and explain the neurobiological mechanism underlying Nietzsche's statement that "Man is the only animal who has to be encouraged to live."

Psychosis

Whereas normal consciousness is comprised of an integration of right- and left-hemisphere processing, one aspect of the complex neurobiology of psychosis may be a bias in the direction of increased right-hemisphere control. Hyperactivation of the right hemisphere (or a decrease in the inhibitory capacities of the left) may result in intrusion of right-hemisphere processing, which is usually inhibited or filtered out of consciousness by the left. This shift in right–left bias may occur for many reasons, including changes in levels of important neurochemicals such as dopamine, metabolic abnormalities, or changing activation in subcortical brain areas such as the thalamus. Schizophrenic patients and their close relatives have been shown to have reduced left-hemisphere volumes in a number of brain areas, including the hippocampus and the amygdala (Seidman et al., 1999). There is a significant correlation between increases in thought disorder and decreases in left-hemisphere neuronal volume (Shenton et al., 1992).

Auditory hallucinations, or hearing one or more voices talking, is a core symptom of schizophrenia. This aberrant perceptual experience may be seen as right-hemisphere language (related to primary process thinking and/or implicit memories) breaking into left-hemisphere awareness. These voices are experienced as ego-alien by the left hemisphere and, in the past, were thought to be signs of demonic possession. These voices are often heard as single words with strong emotional value. For example, patients report hearing critical words (*jerk, idiot*) as people walk by them on the street. Command hallucinations have this same quality, usually to hurt oneself or others, or to engage in dangerous behaviors. Schizophrenic patients often appear to struggle with negative and shameful aspects of their inner world, against which the rest of us are better defended.

In psychosis, primary process thinking breaks into normal states of awareness to create what we see, clinically, as deficits in reality testing and thought disorders. Patients report dreaming while they are awake and struggling to make sense of and integrate the superimposition of both primary and secondary process experiences. This attempt to make sense out of nonsense leads to the elaboration of bizarre delusions (Maher, 1974). Although a hemispheric model of psychosis is still speculative, tests of lateral dominance (measured by a listening task) have been given to both psychotic and depressed patients. Results showed that less lateral dominance in these patients correlated with more severe psychotic symptoms (Wexler & Heninger, 1979).

Inspired by both split-brain research and his readings of ancient texts, the neuropsychologist Julian Jaynes (1976) developed a theory of the evolution of human consciousness based on the increasing ability of the left hemisphere to inhibit input from the right. Jaynes argued that prior to 1000 B.C., the two halves of the human brain acted more separately; the right hemisphere unconsciously controlled the body, while the left witnessed and described the social environment and actions of the body. This division of labor has been supported by current research in the lateral dominance of different functions.

Jaynes suggested that in situations of extreme stress, such as hunting or combat, the right hemisphere provided auditory commands to the left, which were experienced as ego-alien or coming from outside the self. These commands are similar to the command hallucinations reported by schizophrenics. With the expansion of the corpus callosum and increasing dominance of the left hemisphere, a more unified sense of self has gradually evolved. Jaynes felt that psychotic symptoms seen in patients in modern times result from of a breakdown of the left hemisphere's capacity to inhibit communications from the right.

Alexithymia and Psychosomatic Illness

Alexithymia—the inability to consciously experience and describe feelings—is characterized by deficits in functions most usually identified with the right hemisphere. Patients with alexithymia are also described as having concrete or stimulus-bound cognitive style, restricted imagination, and a lack of memory for dreams (Bagby & Taylor, 1997). Patients with alexithymia have been described as having a "bidirectional interhemispheric transfer deficit" (Taylor, 2000). Clients who suffer from alexithymia often recognize that others have feelings, but report that they are unable to locate feelings within themselves. It is as if feelings have been excluded from conscious awareness.

From a psychodynamic perspective, these patients seem trapped in secondary process thinking, disconnected from their inner physical and emotional worlds. They have difficulty benefiting from traditional modes of talk therapy because of their inability to bring emotions into the session, or to use imagination or roleplaying to expand their thinking about themselves. Although the neurological origins of this disorder are still unknown, alexithymia may reflect a lack of transfer or integration of right-hemisphere emotional and somatic information with the linguistic cognitive systems of the left (Taylor, 2000). This leaves the conscious self of the left hemisphere with little input from the emotional, intuitive, and imaginative processing of the right.

Examining patients with psychosomatic illness reveals patterns similar to patients with alexithymia. Hoppe (1977) found psychosomatic patients to also have impoverished dreams, a paucity of symbolic thinking, and difficulty putting feelings into words. Similar difficulties were also found in Holocaust survivors and split-brain patients (Hoppe & Bogen, 1977). Hoppe and Bogen hypothesized that problems during development could result in the two hemispheres organizing and functioning autonomously. Their autonomy would then lead to a lack of integration in those processes requiring their mutual input, such as a coherent sense of self. The theory of such an "interhemispheric transfer deficit" was supported by findings with patients who suffered from PTSD with and without alexithymia. Those with alexithymia were found to have deficits in transferring sensory-motor information between hemispheres, whereas those without alexithymia did not (Zeitlin, Lane, O'Leary, & Schrift, 1989).

Laterality and Psychotherapy

Examples from psychiatry and neurology strongly suggest that psychological health is related to the proper balance of activation, inhibition, and integration of systems biased toward left- and right-hemisphere control. Genetic and neuroanatomic factors can combine with early neglect or trauma to interfere with the development of optimal neural network integration and regulation. Based on what is known about the functions of the right and left hemispheres, we have found that a number of psychiatric disorders appear to correlate with a disruption of integrated processing between left and right hemispheres. Psychotherapy can serve as a means to reintegrate the patient's disconnected hemispheres through reality testing, emotional expression, interpretations, and putting words to feelings.

The similarity between hemispheric specialization and Freud's notion of the conscious and unconscious mind has not been lost on psychotherapists. Right-hemisphere functions are similar to Freud's model of the unconscious in that they develop first and are emotional, nonverbal, and sensory-motor (Galin, 1974). This nonlinear mode of processing allows the right hemisphere to contain multiple overlapping realities, similar to Freud's primary process thinking most clearly demonstrated during dream states. The linear processing of conscious thought in the left hemisphere parallels Freud's concept of secondary process, which is bound by time, reality, and social constraints (Galin, 1974).

When patients come to therapy, the left-hemisphere interpreter tells its story. But something is usually wrong; the story doesn't fully account for what is happening in their lives. The narratives that organize their identities are inadequate to account for their experiences, feelings, and behaviors. The right hemisphere also "speaks" via facial expressions, body language, emotions, and attitudes. Thus, we listen to both stories for the congruence between the verbal narrative and nonverbal and emotional communication. In this process, we analyze the integration and coherence of left–right and top-down neural networks. A primary tool across all models of therapy is editing and expanding the self-narrative of the left hemisphere to include the silent wisdom of the right.

Another way of describing therapy from the perspective of laterality is that we teach clients a method by which they can learn to attend to and translate right-hemisphere processing into left-hemisphere language. We teach them about the limitations and distortions of their own conscious beliefs presented by their left-hemisphere interpreter. Many clients need to become suspect of the ideas that their left hemispheres offer them. This is why reality testing is so important to treatment success. It is the therapist's job to hear what is *not* said, resonate with what the client is unable to consciously experience, and communicate it back to him or her in a way that will allow it to become integrated. This process serves to increase hemispheric integration.

Clients come to therapy to learn how the therapist gathers and interprets the information presented to them (Gedo, 1991). This process closely parallels what is done during positive interactions with parents during childhood. If the method taught during childhood is maladaptive, it leaves the child (later the adult) in a state of limited self-awareness and neural network dissociation (Siegel, 1999). The learning of these skills in therapy occurs in the context of emotional and cognitive integration, requiring the participation of both hemispheres, reflective language, feelings, sensations, and behaviors. In the language of neuroscience, we are integrating systems of memory and dissociated neural processing networks by teaching methods of attention and information processing. These processes aid in the construction of a more inclusive and integrative self-narrative, which, in turn, supports ongoing neural integration.

Summary

In this chapter, we have explored some of the basic building blocks of the brain, including the fundamental divisions between systems of memory and the two halves of the brain. In the next section, we will examine some of the systems and processes responsible for the organization and integration of these diverse neural networks. It is the role of the executive networks of the brain to organize and govern the many legacies of evolutionary adaptation. Design compromises (and the primacy of unconscious processing within hidden layers) has created a brain in need of proper shaping during development, and reshaping over time, as it—and the world around it—matures and changes. The primary role of interpersonal experience in shaping the brain will also become clear in our discussion of the interpersonal sculpting of the brain.

PART III

THE ORGANIZATION
OF EXPERIENCE
AND THE HEALTHY BRAIN

The Executive Brain

7

Ongoing adaptation during evolution has resulted in an ever-expanding human brain. Networks have organized and reorganized, and new networks have formed and combined to form still newer and more complex neural structures. In this process, some executive functions were assumed by the expanding cortex, while others were left to older subcortical networks. As part of evolution's legacy, various areas of the brain play executive roles for different skills and abilities. The control of most functions is carried out unconsciously. We pay almost no attention to our breathing, walking, talking, or thousands of other tasks in which we regularly engage. We can drive a car safely for hours while having conversations, listening to music, even daydreaming, without having an accident. In fact, we focus our conscious attention on just a small fraction of what we are actually accomplishing in any given moment.

The executive brain contains the control mechanisms that allow us to attend to and focus on a particular activity, filter out distractions, make decisions, and act. If these functions are carried out successfully, we feel calm and safe enough to turn our attention inward for contemplation, imagination, and self-awareness. These capabilities, in turn, create the possibility for art, religion, philosophy, and other endeavors thought to be uniquely human. The executive cortical areas of the human brain were the last to evolve and are the slowest to develop as we grow into adults. In fact, they probably continue to develop throughout life, allowing the potential for increasing perspective, compassion, and wisdom.

Executive areas of the brain provide direction and coordination of the neural networks they oversee. Although they are traditionally linked to our rational abilities, they actually involve much more. Executive networks combine sensory, motor, memory, and appraisal (emotional) information to shape plans, actions, thoughts, and fantasies. This broader view of executive functioning has been propelled by an increasing appreciation of emotional intelligence (Goleman, 1995), the contribution of intuition in decision making (Damasio, 1994), and the role of early relationships in sculpting the frontal cortex (Schore, 1994). The processes in psychotherapy geared toward neural network integration call on the executive brain to reorganize the relationship among the networks they oversee.

Think for a moment of a large corporation with a CEO at the top of its executive hierarchy. Lower-level executives, who specialize in particular areas of the company's operations, are employed to control thousands of diverse functions. Utilizing multiple lower-level executives frees the CEO to monitor market forces, keep an eye on the competition, and plan for the future. Just as a CEO is freed from the everyday concerns of production, building maintenance, and bill paying, the executive areas of the cerebral cortex have been freed from attention to basic bodily functions, well-learned motor behavior, and visual-spatial organization. The executive brain participates in more basic functions only in novel situations or when problems arise.

Our comparison of the executive brain with a corporate CEO only works up to a point. Because so much of brain functioning is unconscious, nonverbal, and hidden from conscious observation, the conscious components of the executive brain are directed and controlled by hidden layers of processing. So, in truth, the executive brain may function more like the boss' son-in-law—he's allowed to think he is an executive while, in actuality, he has relatively little control. Given the state of our present knowledge, the real relationship between the different executive functions of the brain remains unclear.

For the purpose of the present discussion, we will focus on the role of the executive functions of the primate cerebral cortex, primarily the frontal and prefrontal cortices. What we know about these areas is based on a combination of primate and human research, naturalistic observations, and clinical evidence with human patients. Although the focus will be on the frontal and prefrontal cortices, I will return to the idea of multiple executives later in the chapter, in a discussion of the parietal lobes.

The Frontal and Prefrontal Cortices

The frontal and prefrontal cortices are the prime candidates for behavioral and emotional executive functioning. The connectivity and organization of the prefrontal cortex provide for the highest level of integration of cognitive and emotional processing (Fuster, 1997). Because there are no primary sensory areas in the frontal cortex, they are entirely dedicated to the association of highly processed information from other neural systems and the direction of motor activity (Nauta, 1971). For example, projections to the frontal areas from the parietal regions have already combined visual, motor, and vestibular information, whereas those from the temporal lobe have integrated sensory information with socio-emotional appraisal.

Human frontal areas initially evolved as a motor cortex in mammals (Fuster, 1997). As the frontal cortex expanded, they created the possibility for increasingly complex behaviors. Broca's area, for example, controlling expressive speech, is located adjacent to the area of the motor cortex that controls the lips and tongue. This proximity reflects the co-evolution of spoken language and fine motor control. Because of the evolutionary links between motor behavior and cognition, some theorists consider cognition to be a derivative of motor behavior (Wilson, 1998). Support for this idea may exist in the fact that much of our symbolic and abstract thinking is organized by visceral, sensory, and motor metaphors that permeate our oral and written communication (Johnson, 1987).

As we have seen, transcortical networks in both hemispheres feed highly processed sensory-motor information forward to the frontal cortex. Simultaneously, multiple hierarchical networks, which loop up and down through the cortex, limbic system and brainstem, provide the frontal cortex with visceral, behavioral, and emotional information (Alexander et al., 1986). It is through the convergence of all of these networks that the frontal areas synthesize numerous diverse sources of information and coordinate our attention, emotions, and cognition with action. Neurons and neural networks within the frontal cortex organize our behavior through time (Fuster, Bonder, & Kroger, 2000) by sustaining a memory for the future (Ingvar, 1985) that keeps in mind the eventual consequences of behaviors about to be performed (Dolan, 1999; Wantanabe, 1996). The ability to remember the past and predict the future is essential for survival.

The prefrontal cortex participates in constructing ideas about the beliefs, intentions, and perspective of others (Goel, Grafman, Sadato, & Halletta, 1995; Stuss, Gallup, & Alexander, 2001). Damage to the prefrontal cortex in early childhood results in deficits in the development of empathic abilities (Dolan, 1999). Damage in the same areas later in life can also result in decreased empathic capacity. Because empathy requires conceptual understanding, emotional attunement, and the ability to regulate one's own affect, damage to either the dorsolateral or orbitofrontal areas will impair different aspects of empathic behavior (Eslinger, 1998). Empathic thinking requires the cognitive flexibility and affect regulation to pull back from the environment, put our needs aside, and imagine the feelings of others.

The act of murder is the ultimate lack of empathy. Murderers, as a group, have demonstrated significantly lower glucose metabolism in both dorsal and orbital portions of the frontal areas. This finding exists in the absence of indications of brain damage or decreased metabolism in other areas of the brain (Raine et al., 1994). Damage to the orbitofrontal cortex has been correlated with acquired antisocial personality (Meyers, Berman, Scheibel, & Hayman, 1992). Although antisocial behavior is a complex phenomenon, correlations exist between deficits in affect regulation and impulse control, and the inability to relate to the experience of others (Nauta, 1971).

Injury to the Frontal Cortex

A young man named Luis was in a serious auto accident soon after his 20th birthday. He and his family came to see me 18 months after the accident. I opened the door to my office to find eight people tightly packed into my small waiting room. Luis had been brought to me by his parents and five younger siblings after his neurologist suggested they might benefit from family therapy. As they filed into my office, I noticed the scars and indentations across Luis' forehead and imagined the damage beneath them. I knew from talking with his neurologist that Luis had sustained severe injuries to his frontal cortex and that his family experienced him as impulsive, irritable, and, sometimes, violent. The damage to his executive brain left Luis with limited self-reflective abilities; reasoning with him about his behavior seemed to be of no help. A year after the accident he returned to his auto repair job but was soon fired because he was unable to complete his work or get along with customers. All of these symptoms are typical of frontal injury. Although he had always been somewhat impulsive, his parents claimed that he was now far worse than before the accident.

After we settled down in my office, I turned to the father and asked how I could help him help his family. He immediately became tearful, shook his head slowly from side to side, and rubbed his hands together. "He drives too fast," he said quietly. "I don't!" exclaimed Luis. "Except for that one time!" Everyone in the family looked embarrassed. It was immediately clear that talking back to their father was a violation of the family culture. I suspected that no matter how impulsive Luis might have been before the accident, this "disrespectful" behavior was new. The effects of Luis' accident became apparent just a few seconds into the session.

As the family slowly relaxed, I found out that Luis' parents had moved to the United States from Mexico shortly before his birth, and had been successful in acclimating to their adopted home. Despite their acculturation, they remained true to traditional Mexican values centering on loyalty to the family and respect for elders. In this context, Luis' reflexive and loud contradiction of his father was a source of shame for everyone in the family except Luis. His injury had damaged the networks that allowed him to monitor his own behavior and the expectations of others.

Luis didn't remember much about his accident except that he and a friend were racing against each other. He lost consciousness for a few days after the accident, and all his memories of the days immediately before and after the accident were gone. He had read in the police reports how he had lost control of his car and hit a pole. His injury was worsened because he wasn't wearing a seat belt and had installed a custom steering wheel without an airbag.

His mother said that Luis had tried to go back to work six months ago, but was fired because he couldn't concentrate. She reported that he spent most of his time at home, and that his behavior was sometimes frightening. At times he would cry for no reason, yell at her and the others, and jump in her car and race off. A few times, he went into a rage and threw things. He had also made sexual statements and cursed using Jesus' name, upsetting everyone in this conservative religious family. The family members were torn between loyalty to their oldest child and their disgust with many of his behaviors.

As society moves faster and becomes more dangerous, the opportunity for severe head injury also increases. Automobile, industrial, and recreational accidents, and community and domestic violence, all contribute to the number of people who experience traumatic brain injury. Because the frontal areas are located directly behind the fore-head, they are also most likely to be damaged.

Although patients with head injuries come from all walks of life, young males seem to be disproportionately represented. This is partly due to youthful impulsivity, risk taking, and a lack of judgment, all of which are related to frontal lobe functions. The massive reorganization of the frontal areas during adolescence likely contributes to these behavioral phenomena (Spear, 2000). Many of these young men may have already had frontal deficits or slowed frontal development prior to their accidents, amplifying more typical adolescent, risk-taking behavior. In this way, frontal injuries often compound preexisting deficits of impulse control and judgment, thus complicating treatment and recovery.

Treatment with Luis and his family was multifaceted. I began by educating the entire family about the brain and Luis' particular injuries. The specific information was less important than connecting his symptoms with the injury. I specifically targeted symptoms such as his cursing and sexual statements, which had, in their minds, been connected to his character. By sharing case studies with them, I was able to show that Luis' symptoms were part of an illness pattern related to frontal damage and not caused by immorality or bad parenting.

More specific interventions included enrolling Luis in an occupational therapy program to help him toward developing the skills needed to start a new career. As the oldest son, it was very important for him to feel productive and regain his sense of pride. One of my goals was to reduce his resistance to taking medication for his anxiety and depression caused by a combination of his head injury and the life changes that flowed from it. I also worked with Luis and his whole family to develop skills related to stress reduction and anger management. We turned these exercises into family role-playing games that alleviated some of the tension and allowed everyone to participate in helping Luis. The structure and permission provided by the education and the exercises allowed the entire family to serve some of the executive functions damaged in Luis' brain.

Over time, Luis was able to apply his love and knowledge of cars to a job in an auto parts store. His occupational therapist helped to establish routines that allowed Luis to use the computer and help customers. Antidepressants proved helpful, and the family games became woven into the family's everyday interactions. All of these improvements made the occasional outbursts more tolerable and seen as part of his illness. Luis was very fortunate to have the unquestioning love and support of a strong family.

The Orbitofrontal and Dorsolateral Regions of the Prefrontal Cortex

Luis had a serious accident that damaged many areas of his brain, including most of his frontal cortex. The frontal areas are not uniform structures but instead are diverse in their structure, function, and neurochemistry. The mixture of symptoms seen as a result of most frontal brain injury is the result of simultaneous damage to multiple areas. The dorsolateral and orbitofrontal regions form the main division between the prefrontal areas (Figure 7.1). In humans, the dorsolateral areas perform executive functions biased toward the left hemisphere.

The orbitofrontal areas, first to evolve in our species and to develop in the individual, perform the executive functions biased toward the right hemisphere (Schore, 1994). The orbitofrontal areas sit at the apex of the limbic system and are richly connected with subcortical networks of learning, memory, and emotion (Barbas, 1995). These connections, and their role as executive of the right hemisphere, account for the bias of emotional processing toward the right hemisphere. Orbitofrontal regions are also often referred to as the *medial* prefrontal areas in the research literature and in the chapters to come.

Although the dorsolateral and orbitofrontal frontal regions are physically contiguous, they differ in their connectivity, neural archi-

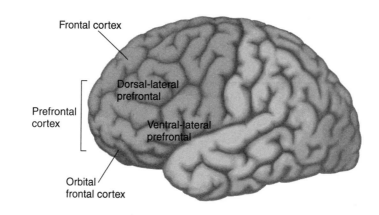

Figure 7.1 The frontal and prefrontal lobes

The general topography of the frontal and prefrontal lobes, looking at the brain from the left.

tecture, biochemistry, and function (Wilson, O'Scalaidhe, & Goldman-Rakic, 1993). Research with primates has demonstrated that although both dorsolateral and orbitofrontal frontal areas play a role in inhibition and control, the dorsolateral areas are involved when the decision is attentional; the orbitofrontal regions become involved when the decision is based on affective information (Dias, Robbins, & Roberts, 1996; Teasdale et al., 1999). Damage to these different regions in humans results in different clinical syndromes, reflecting their different executive roles (Malloy, Bihrle, Duffy, & Cimino, 1993).

The Orbital Prefrontal Cortex

Tucked under the frontal cortex and sitting directly above the eyes, the orbital areas of the prefrontal cortex (Ofc) are densely connected to both the anterior cingulate and the amygdala. These networks coordinate affect regulation via reward and punishment, conditioned fear, and bonding and attachment. The anterior cingulate—involved with attention, maternal behavior, reward-based learning (Shima & Tanji, 1998), and autonomic arousal (Devinsky, Morrell, & Vogt, 1995)—first appeared during evolution in animals demonstrating maternal behavior (MacLean, 1985).

Consequently, damage to either the Ofc or the anterior cingulate results in deficits of maternal behavior, emotional functioning, and empathy. Disorders of emotional control are also seen with damage to these regions, including inappropriate social behavior, impulsiveness, sexual disinhibition, and increased motor activity (Price, Daffner, Stowe, & Mesulam, 1990). The overlapping functions of these neural systems reflect the fundamental neural unity of attachment, the experience of fear, and affect regulation. These functions, in turn, serve as the precursors and foundation of the development of self-identity emerging from the success or failure of early social interactions.

The classic example of damage to the Ofc is the case of Phineas Gage (Harlow, 1868). As you may remember from the beginning of this book, Mr. Gage was a young and well-respected New Hampshire railroad foreman who was known for his maturity, organizational abilities, and "well-balanced" mind. An accident at the job sent an inch-and-a-quarter-wide iron bar up through his head, obliterating much of his orbitofrontal cortex. Although free of any "neurobehavioral" deficits from the accident (such as aphasia, paralysis, or sensory loss), his workmates reported that Gage was "no longer Gage." After the accident he was unable to control his emotions, sustain goal-oriented behavior, or adhere to the conventions of social behavior. He went from being a young man with a promising future to the life of an aimless and unsuccessful drifter (Benson, 1994).

The Ofc appears to be vital in interpreting complex social events and linking them with their emotional value (a skill referred to as *appraisal*). This network bridges advanced cortical analysis with primitive emotional reactions mediated by the amygdala and auto-nomic nervous system. The Ofc also has the ability to modulate the amygdala's reaction to fearful faces (Hariri, Bookheimer, & Mazziotta, 2000) based on the context in which the faces are pre-sented. For example, the amygdala will alert us to the sight of an angry face, whereas the Ofc will include information about *how* dan-gerous it is. If the Ofc adds to the amygdala's alarm that it is the face of a feared predator, the fight-or-flight response will be activated. If, on the other hand, the Ofc adds that it is the face of a baby, we may approach the baby to find out what is wrong. Damage to either the amygdala or Ofc results in the inability to organize this information in a useful manner, resulting in deficits in social relatedness.

Research has demonstrated that the Ofc both mediates the reward value of voluntary actions and calculates the magnitude of reward or punishment value, such as winning or losing money (O'Doherty, Kringelback, Rolls, Hornak, & Andrews, 2001; Rolls, 2000; Tremblay & Schultz, 1999; Wantanabe, 1996). Much of this analysis occurs out of conscious awareness and is commonly called *intuition.* Those of us who are good at gambling or "reading" people might just be aware of having a sense for these things. In actuality, our neural networks are capable of appraising huge amounts of information that provide us with a "feeling" about what to do even if it is sometimes contrary to our conscious and logical thought processes.

The Dorsolateral Prefrontal Cortex

The dorsolateral regions of the prefrontal cortex (DlPfc) integrate information from the senses, the body, and memory in order to guide behavior. The DlPfc performs a variety of functions, including direct-ing attention (Fuster, 1997), organizing working memory (Rezai et al., 1993), learning motor sequences (Pascual-Leone, Rubio, Pallardo, & Catala, 1996), and organizing temporal experience (Knight &

Grabowecky, 1995). The dorsolateral region is the slowest to be myelinated in the cerebral cortex and does not fully mature until the middle to late teens (Schore, 1994). This gradual maturation maximizes specific environmental adaptation. The role of the DlPfc in interacting and coping with the environment is highlighted by the effects of damage to these regions. Dorsolateral damage results in decreased interaction with the environment, symptoms of depression, reduced spontaneity, and flattened affect.

A primary component of the integration between cortical and limbic processing (top-down) occurs in the communication between orbital and dorsal regions within the frontal cortex. The fact that these regions are biased toward the right and left hemispheres results in the communication between them also providing integration across both the top-down and left–right axes of information processing. In addition, the dorsal and lateral areas of the frontal cortex evolved and networked with the hippocampus while the medial regions developed along with the amygdala. Thus, the communication between dorsal and medial frontal regions provides pathways of integration for the hippocampal and amygdaloid memory systems described in chapter 5.

Orbitofrontal–Dorsolateral Integration

The dorsolateral and orbitofrontal areas can demonstrate various degrees of integration and dissociation. The cognitive and emotional intelligences in which they specialize have different developmental timetables and learning contexts. Orbital prefrontal areas begin to organize emotional development—in the context of interpersonal relationships—from the first moments of life. During the first 18 months of life, these areas share a sensitive period of exuberant development with the right hemisphere. Dorsolateral areas exhibit an initial lag and then a growth spurt with the development of language and the exploration of the physical and conceptual worlds.

The relationship between the medial and dorsal regions of the prefrontal cortex is of particular interest for understanding human executive functioning. Medial prefrontal regions serve an executive function for the sensory and motor programs organized by the lateral regions (Starkstein & Robinson, 1997). In other words, emotional and motivational information stored in the limbic system may direct behavior via connections with the medial frontal areas; they, in turn, activate or inhibit behaviors organized in the lateral frontal regions. Research also suggests that the right prefrontal area plays a dominant role in mediating the effects of emotion on behavior. The fact that more patients with right hemisphere lesions suffer from symptoms of emotional dyscontrol and mania supports this theory.

I'm Up Here!!!

Jimmy, an elfin eight-year-old, was referred to me to assess whether or not he had attention deficit hyperactivity disorder (ADHD). Before meeting him, I read notes from his parents, teachers, and soccer coach that described his behavior. All agreed he was far more distracted, restless, and energetic than what is expected from a child his age. His coach noted Jimmy's inability to stay focused on the game; one teacher described him as a bundle of energy; his father wrote, in big letters, "Exhausting!" Jimmy's restlessness and impulsivity made it difficult for other kids to interact with him, and his mother felt he was becoming isolated.

I walked into the testing room to find Jimmy's mother slumped in a chair with her face in her hands. She didn't react when I entered the room and I thought she might be crying. I scanned the room, looked behind the chair and small sofa, but couldn't see Jimmy. Before I could speak, Jimmy shouted, "I'm up here!!!" Startled, I looked up and saw him perched on the top of a six-foot storage unit that he had somehow managed to scale. Looking over to his mother, I saw her momentarily pick up her head, roll her eyes, and lower it back down. It was clear that while making a diagnosis might not be too difficult, just getting through the assessment would take strength and patience.

Jimmy did have ADHD, with the same symptoms his father had when he was a boy. ADHD does sometimes run in families. Apparently, his father still suffered from many symptoms of distractibility and restlessness that created difficulties in his work and relationships. After many failed career attempts, he found considerable success in real estate. The constant movement and brief contact utilized his energy and personality, while his choice of a partner—who excelled at handling the details of sales—protected him from his deficits in attention. The treatment for Jimmy included behavioral therapy to help with his attention and social skills, martial arts classes, and stimulant medications. These and other interventions were designed to boost frontal functioning through biochemical and psychosocial interventions (social skills and teaching him to stop and think), and by giving him constructive avenues through which to channel his considerable energy.

Individuals like Jimmy who suffer with ADHD are characterized by an inability to sustain attention and inhibit extraneous thought and behavior. They can be easily lost in daydreams, or be in constant motion. There is the dangerous problem of leaping before they look. In fact, Jimmy had been injured a year earlier when he raced into a neighbor's backyard and jumped into the pool before noticing that it had been drained for repair. It is not surprising that individuals with ADHD often show deficits on tests measuring frontal abilities (Faraone & Biederman, 1999).

Brain scans of ADHD sufferers show altered functioning in prefrontal regions and reduced volume in right prefrontal areas (Casey, Castellanos, & Giedd, 1997). Stimulant medications (such as Ritalin) enhance frontal functioning through the stimulation of dopamine and norepinephrine, the neurochemicals that drive these brain regions (Arnsten, 2000). Stimulants intensify activity in under-performing regions, reestablishing neural network balance. In Jimmy's case, the enhancement of activation of the prefrontal cortical regions increased focused attention and cortical inhibition over cortical and subcortical motor networks.

The Prefrontal Cortex and Conscious Awareness

The prefrontal cortices oversee and organize countless functions, including attention, monitoring the environment for danger, affect regulation, and negotiating social relations. Most of the time, these functions are performed automatically and unconsciously. Although individuals with severe damage to the frontal areas retain consciousness, previously automatic processes become obstacles to successful functioning. Attention, concentration, affect-regulation, and motivation can all become problematic and sometimes impossible to perform. As we have seen, depression, anxiety, emotional dyscontrol, and socially appropriate behavior are all related to the functioning of the frontal cortex.

An interesting view of the role of the prefrontal cortex is that it allows us to escape from the present moment (Knight & Grabowecky, 1995). The prefrontal cortex's adequate and automatic negotiation of most of our moment-to-moment needs allows us to turn our attention from the survival demands of the outer world. Put another way, an adequately functioning prefrontal cortex regulates sensory input, behavioral inhibition, and affect regulation, allowing for sustained and focused attention to tasks unrelated to physical survival. In this way, a quiet internal world can be organized and revisited through time, and can serve as a context for private thought separate from external problem solving. These quiet moments serve as the grounds for imagination and creativity, and are especially important for imagining and consolidating the self (Winnicott, 1958).

A damaged or compromised prefrontal cortex does not lead to an absence of conscious experience. It does, however, "ensnare" the victim in "a noisy and temporally constrained state, locking the patient into the immediate space and time with little ability to escape" (Knight & Grabowecky, 1995, p.1368). This phenomenon is seen in victims of frontal brain injury who are constantly distracted by emotional and sensory experience, unable to maintain focus, and suffer deficits in imaginative abilities. A similar experience is shared by children like Jimmy who exhibit a loss of impulse control, or individuals with borderline personality disorder who are consumed and overwhelmed by abandonment fears. All of these individuals can become trapped in present time by an inability to unhook from the constant stream of sensations, emotions, and the demands of their inner and outer worlds. Without the ability to cancel "evolving motor plans" or predetermined emotional responses, there is little *response flexibility* or freedom from environmental constraints (Schall, 2001).

Problem solving—which requires cognitive flexibility and emotional regulation—is a central component of executive functioning. All of these functions become impaired with traumatic or developmental damage to the frontal cortex. Individuals with frontal damage will get stuck in a particular way of thinking or have difficulty thinking in ways that are separate from the demands of their environment (concrete thinking). They have a hard time monitoring social interactions, such as keeping the listener in mind when talking and not referring to situations of which the listener is unaware. They will also have difficulty in remembering the outcome of past behaviors and repeatedly apply the same unsuccessful solutions to problems (perseveration).

Because these problems come from damage to the frontal areas, it is generally assumed that the lost abilities arise from the frontal areas. This, however, is not necessarily the case. Although some specific functions—like temporal and sequential organization—may, in fact, be organized primarily by the frontal areas, abilities like problem solving, creativity, and imagination emerge from the overall organization and integration of neural networks throughout the brain.

Proper frontal functioning alone cannot account for the highest levels of human functioning. But if the frontal cortex only creates the conditions for processes such as imagination, empathy, and spirituality, how do these abilities and functions emerge? The answer is, we don't yet know.

The Parietal Lobes

Without question, the frontal lobes are predominant in the direction and organization of behavior, judgment, and affect regulation. Individuals with frontal damage experience disturbances in their ability to successfully function in the contexts of both work and relationships. Because behavior is easily observable and measured, neurologists have focused primarily on the behavioral aspects of brain injury. However, there is more to human experience than behavior; there are also the experiences of self in the world and inner subjective space. These more subtle and subjective aspects of human experience have received little attention in neurological examinations.

Although it is not common to think of the parietal lobes as providing executive functions, in fact they may organize body image and inner subjective experiences. Like the frontal lobes, the parietal lobes become activated during novel activities (e.g. visual search) but not during behaviors that have already been learned (Walsh, Ashbridge, & Cowey, 1998). The parietal lobes also appear to be involved in coding intentions (Snyder, Batista, & Andersen, 1997) and calculating the probability of success or correctness of a choice (Platt & Glimcher, 1999). Although neither of these abilities qualify the parietal lobes as an executive area akin to the frontal lobes, they suggest that it is far more than a simple association area. Curiously, studies of skulls reflecting different stages of primate evolution suggest that expansion of the parietal and not the frontal lobes is most characteristic of the human brain (von Bonin, 1963).

Parietal damage resulting in disturbances to body image, neglect of one side of the body, and confabulation of missing information has been witnessed with fascination and confusion by neurologists and patients' families. The patients themselves, however, seem generally oblivious to their deficits, or at least tend to deny the disruption to the organization of their world. These symptoms suggest that the parietal lobes may serve an executive function in the organization of the experience of inner and outer space (both physical and imaginal), but may not be involved with conscious or self-reflective awareness.

The neural connectivity of the parietal lobes appears to provide us with an awareness of the body and its relation to extrapersonal space (Adams et al., 1997). Cells in inferior parietal regions respond to hand position, eye movement, words, motivational relevance, body position, and many other factors relevant to the integration of experience. Damage to the parietal lobes disrupts the experience of location and identity, such as where and who we are. The fact that we don't think of the parietal lobes as a component of the executive brain may reflect a cultural bias of equating individuals with their external behavior over their inner experiences. Future research may demonstrate that the parietal lobes play a large role in the more subjective executive elements of human experience.

Winnicott (1962) suggested that the ego and one's sense of self consolidate during periods of quiescence. Periods of quiescence are made possible when a child feels calm and safe, and is not impinged on by the demands of the environment or responding to physical or emotional needs. In neurological terms, this may correspond with the frontal lobes having done their job in managing the social and physical environments to the point where the child is able to go "inside" and rest in imagination and the experience of self (Stern, 1985). Dawson and her colleagues demonstrated that infants who were expressing emotion demonstrated frontal activation, whereas parietal lobe activation went in the opposite direction or remained relatively unaffected (Dawson, Panagiotides, Klinger, & Hill, 1992). During periods of quiescence, there may be a shift in the focus of cortical processing toward the parietal lobes.

When the frontal lobes have done their job well, attention can be shifted from interacting with the environment to a focus on internal space. One study has shown that when experienced meditators engage in meditation, the parietal and frontal lobes show a significant negative correlation in their level of activity (Newberg et al., 2001). This means that as the frontal lobes become less active, the parietal lobes become more active. In psychological terms, decreased need for attention to the environment, as Winnicott suggested, may be a prerequisite to the parietal activation related to the consolidation of the self.

You may remember from our discussion on the left and right brain that the parietal lobes evolved from the hippocampus (Joseph, 1996), which, in lower mammals, organizes cognitive maps of the self in space (O'Keefe & Nadel, 1978). Johnson (1987) asserted that the experience of our bodies provides the internal basis for meaning and reasoning. The brain's ability to take our physical experience and use it metaphorically is the basis of imagination. Bungee jumping may serve as a metaphor for falling in love. The child's experience of emerging from under the covers into the light of day provides a sensory-motor metaphor for religious enlightenment later in life. The balance provided by the vestibular system may serve as a visceral model for the psychological balance provided by the ego (Frick, 1982). Perhaps the experience of constantly maintaining balance also provides us with the core physical sense of what it would mean to live a balanced life. Physical metaphors provide a contextual grounding in time and space that help us to understand our experience. These schema may reflect cognition's emergence from bodily experiences and motor movement. The organization of the body in conscious processing may be a primary contribution of the parietal lobes.

Albert Einstein—who, as we all know, did poorly in math classes during his early education—ended up solving complex problems of mathematics and physics using visual imagery. Many of his intuitive theories about the relationship among time, matter, and energy have been proven accurate with the development of more sophisticated technology and space exploration. Examination of his brain revealed differences in the inferior parietal area in the ratio of neurons to glia cells when compared to both other areas of his brain and to control subjects (Diamond, Scheibel, Murphy, & Harvey, 1985). Diamond and her colleagues (Diamond et al., 1966) suggested that these lower ratios represent the capacity for higher levels of neuronal activity. An examination by another research group concluded that Einstein's brain differed from 91 brains to which it was compared only in the size of the inferior parietal lobe (Witelson, Kigar, & Harvey, 1999).

These findings concerning Einstein's neuroanatomy are interesting in light of Einstein's reporting that he often arrived at the answers to complex mathematical questions based on vague mental images and bodily sensations. Based on his report, and the findings concerning his brain, it would appear that Einstein's unique parietal lobes may have been at the core of his genius. His difficulty in navigating day-to-day life (he was the archetypical absent-minded professor) supports the idea that his frontal areas may not have been anywhere near as successful in coping with moment-to-moment survival needs, but, instead, provided him with the type of internal environment he required to go deep within his imaginative capabilities. Mental images and bodily sensations are the building blocks of the internal representation of the self. The construction of inner imaginal space creates the possibility for perspective and empathy for others as well as for ourselves.

The Executive Brain in Psychotherapy

Given their role as high-level association areas, the regions of the frontal cortex are primarily sculpted by experience and most likely possess a high degree of plasticity relative to other areas in the brain. Their role in the analysis of highly abstract social information and affect regulation shapes the networks of our social brain and, because of their involvement in the stimulation of biochemical growth factors, they also play a role in the overall growth and expansion of the cortex (Schore, 1994). One goal of psychotherapy, then, is to help the frontal areas do their many jobs more effectively and gain access to the imaginal capabilities involving the parietal areas and other processing networks.

Although demands on the executive brain vary widely depending on the form of psychotherapy, all forms of talk therapy rely on executive functioning. Individuals with frontal brain damage have been traditionally considered poor clients for psychotherapy because they often have low levels of insight and self-perspective. Being tied to immediate experience by poor frontal lobe functioning separates us from self-perspective and a useful imaginal world. Psychotherapy often requires that we step away from reflexive behavior and the immediate demands of the environment to manipulate ideas, theories, and feelings in order to "try on" new truths. Consider my client Sandy, who needed help to gain perspective on a mysterious cycle of changes in her attitudes and mood.

I Just Lose the Will to Live

Sandy was a successful woman in her mid-40s who came to therapy with concerns about relationships, family, and career. We soon developed a good relationship, and she seemed to be benefiting from our work together. Although her mood was generally upbeat and positive, she occasionally came to sessions feeling irritable, deflated, and hopeless. My first assumption was that she was struggling with mood swings that were as yet too difficult to discuss. As I continued to point out these mood fluctuations, she gradually became more aware of them.

Once Sandy was able to talk about these moods, she realized that they seemed to come out of nowhere and disappear just as mysteriously. During her down moods she felt like a fraud and planned to quit her job and leave her husband. I remember her sighing as she said, "When I feel this way I just lose the will to live."

We were able to discuss her experiences through two or three mood cycles as she struggled to find the things in her life that would precipitate them. Their timing didn't coincide with anything related to her work, family, menstrual cycle, exercise patterns, or diet. Her only other complaint was that she had developed some new allergies and suffered increasingly frequent sinus infections. On the outside chance there was some relationship between her use of antihistamines and her mood changes, we created a mood chart that included her use of medication. One of the things she marked on this chart was an estimate of her will to live.

Although we didn't find any connection between mood and medication, it did turn out that she lost the will to live a day or two before a sinus infection. Her mood would then improve shortly after the onset of the nasal symptoms and headaches. Once we made this connection, we anxiously waited for the next dip in her mood to see if it would be again followed by a sinus infection. Sure enough, the same pattern emerged! Although we still didn't know what affected her mood, the timing did suggest that it was related to the cycle of her allergies and sinus infections. It was now time to develop Sandy's memory for the future.

The plan was to anticipate her next dip in mood with a new plan. We agreed that she would stop evaluating her life on days where she lost the will to live. She was not allowed to think about leaving her husband, her job, or assess her worth as a person. Instead, the mood dip would be a cue for her to go to the health food store, buy bottles of vitamin C and zinc tablets, and rearrange her schedule so as to reduce stress. Her assignment was to remember the future in the present. Sandy had to keep in mind that what she experienced as negative emotions was really a result of biological changes related to a physical illness process and not some collapse of her character.

For some unknown reason, Sandy's system reacted to infection with certain biochemical changes that caused her mood to change. Most likely these changes were within systems related to neurotransmitters that control her mood and motivation, such as serotonin, dopamine, and norepinephrine. The psychological depression experienced as a result of these changes led her to reinterpret, in a negative way, the value of all aspects of her existence. How she dealt with these feelings was neither pleasant nor adaptive. By using her cortical executive functions to associate experiences with new meanings, she was able to engage in a different plan of action and a different set of behaviors. We converted her existential dilemma into a trigger for medical management.

Sandy needed to learn how to be consciously aware of her feelings, to think about them and what they meant, and then to follow a plan of action that was contrary to her reflexive thoughts and feelings. These important frontal functions allowed Sandy to escape from automatic and detrimental behaviors. Through these frontal processes she was able to change reflexive stimulus-response connections by escaping the present moment and imagining a new scenario. We wrote a new narrative, with a new ending, for her experiences.

Summary

In this chapter, we've explored aspects of the executive regions of the brain and their role in integrating and organizing the multitude of the brain's neural systems. Their role in concentration, memory, emotional regulation, and abstract thinking make them primary participants in the psychotherapeutic process. As Sandy learned to understand the functioning and fluctuations of her brain, she was able to utilize executive functions for insight, perspective, and control. In this way, therapy utilized executive functions to increase the integration of cognition and emotion. In the next chapter, we will explore aspects of the construction of the self, with a special focus on the hidden layers of neural processing. The ability to discern what is stored in these layers, and make it available for conscious consideration and/or modification, is a primary task of most psychotherapy.

The Construction
of the Narrative Self

8

> Self is a perpetually rewritten story.
> (Bruner, 1994)

A s we have seen, what is known about the brain does not support the idea that consciousness and the self arise from any single region or neural network. Rather, both appear to emerge from the integration and synchrony of cycle upon cycle of neural processing up and down the axis of the nervous system (Scott, 1995). This is why consciousness is sometimes referred to as an *emergent function* or an ability that arises from the combined interaction of other functions. All neural systems appear to contribute in unique ways to the construction of the self and to our experience of the world (Feinberg, 2001). Just how the nervous system accomplishes the task of binding these processes to achieve a unified experience of conscious awareness is the focus of ongoing debate (Crick, 1994; Revonsuo, 1999; Treisman, 1996; von der Malsburg, 1995).

Neisser (1994) suggested that the self consists of the integration of five separate functions, including: (a) the temporally extended self or the experience of self in time, (b) the ecological self or the experience of self in the environment, (c) the interpersonal self, (d) the private self, and (e) the conceptual self or the idea of "me." Neisser's model contains an appreciation of the interaction of the somatic, temporal, interpersonal, and narrative aspects of the construction of the self. Our sense of time, for example, includes such influences as the reflexive beating of our heart controlled by our brainstem, motor programs for walking stored in our cerebellum and cortex, counting down from 10 to 0 from networks of semantic memory, and our expectations and dreams for the future from somewhere in our cortex.

For our present purposes, we will focus on aspects of the self suggested by Neisser's last three categories, considering the self primarily as a matrix of conscious and unconscious memories organized into episodes, stories, or narratives. These narratives are either shared with others, held internally, or codified into our public and private identity. Underlying and shaping these narratives is a vast amount of neural processing hidden from conscious observation. The nature of this hidden processing results in a number of illusions, distortions, and self-deceptions that influence our narratives and are a focus of many forms of psychotherapy. The centrality of narratives to memory, development, and psychotherapy derives from the influence of language and storytelling in the building and organization of our brains during evolution.

From Grooming to Gossip

One way in which cohesion is maintained in primate groups is through social grooming. Grooming involves the manual inspection of each other's fur for insects and other possible problems. Although grooming may have originally developed to protect primates from small pests, over time it appears to have become a mechanism of bonding and cooperation (Dunbar, 1992). Time spent in social grooming increases with the size of the group or tribe. As human groups grew increasingly large, grooming as a means of group cohesion became unmanageable. Grooming may have gradually evolved into gestures, sign language, and the use of words under the demands for a more time-efficient means of social bonding (Dunbar, 1993).

As the number of individuals in social groups expands, so does the ratio of the size of the neocortex to the entire brain (Dunbar, 1992). The larger and more complex the social group, the more brainpower is required of its members; the more sophisticated the brain, the larger the social group can become. Given that larger groups increase the probability of success in warfare and competition for resources, the brain, language, and group size had to evolve together. Hemispheric specialization and the expansion of the neocortex created neural space for the development of more complex forms of social communication. Gestures and sign language may have become fairly complex before the adoption of a primarily verbal mode of communication (Wilson, 1998). Hand gestures and other nonverbal aspects of communication continue to be an important aspect of communication today.

Because 60% of our language production involves gossip and sharing non-essential personal information, its role in social coherence cannot be doubted (Dunbar, 1996). The acquisition and production of language are instincts requiring little conscious attention. Most speech production is quite predictable and repetitive, containing stock phrases that fill silences and stall for time as we think of new things to say. The left-hemisphere interpreter, discussed in a previous chapter, may be the present-day descendant of the first evolving language system. The specialization of the left hemisphere in navigating the social world supports this idea. Its role in social cohesion and group function is entirely in line with confabulation, defense mechanisms, and its positive affective bias. This is the language of the public self.

Although it is impossible to know its order in evolution, an internal language or inner dialogue also emerged from the use of words. The first role of inner language may have been to direct and organize behavior in longer sequences than is possible through basic motor programs. Perhaps it even served as an inner control for coordinated group behavior (Jaynes, 1976). This inner track of language may have evolved into what we now call *introspection*, or the private self. The vast expansion of the neocortex allowed for its use in internal processing, private planning, and the ability to analyze social interations.

Internal language may have also evolved from the need to have thoughts that were not safe or advantageous to share with others. We see primates practicing deception in situations in which they trick one another to obtain food or favor. For example, when some monkeys see food on the ground, they give the warning call for snake, sending their troopmates scampering up trees. Evolutionary psychologists suggest that denial and repression may have evolved to make us better at deceiving others by fooling ourselves (Nesse & Lloyd, 1992).

The existence of a conscious self most likely depends on language. Neisser's (1994) division between the interpersonal and private selves, as well as the presentation of the "me," reflect different aspects and levels of language production. Although other species may have some form of consciousness based in their particular forms of communication and social structure, it is almost certainly quite different from our own. The debate about whether animals have consciousness is a tricky and often emotional subject. I am convinced that my own understanding of the internal world of animals has been so shaped by Walt Disney that I fear I can do nothing but project my own way of thinking onto mice, ducks, and dogs.

Despite the number of voices in our heads and our changing feelings, thoughts, and sensations, we generally experience ourselves as stable and consistent through time. The stories we tell about ourselves have a unified agent—a single self that is the protagonist of our stories. Deviations from our usual behavior are either discounted or accounted for by various narrative twists and turns. If we act in ways inconsistent with our habitual identity, we say things like "I am not myself today" or "I am beside myself." Although our actual memories are fragmented, disorganized, and contain huge holes, we assume a continuity of our bodies through time and graft the pieces of our remembered self onto them (Albright, 1994). Evolution may, in fact, have selected for a single self-identity as a means of behavioral continuity within each individual as well as for the necessity of identity, predictability, and accountability within larger groups.

The idea of "me," or the objective construction of self-identity, was Neisser's final aspect of self. This self seems to serve more of a conceptual function and is most likely the last to have evolved. This is the self most closely identified with the everyday notion of self-identity. Dennett (1991) proposed the useful concept of this self as *the center of narrative gravity*. That is, our identity consists of a matrix of memories that include thoughts, feelings, and sensations woven into the narratives we tell about ourselves. The difference from the traditional view that we are the conscious authors of our own story is that we don't spin these tales, but rather the tales spin us. "Our human consciousness, and our narrative selfhood, is their product, not their source" (Dennett, 1991, p. 418). These tales are spun by culture and family (Howard, 1991); we come into consciousness as a story that, in many ways, has already been written.

The spinning of these tales is influenced by multiple factors related to both the way narratives are cocreated with parents and how the brain organizes and processes information. The combined influence of these factors leads to the creation of narratives and self-identity that can be either supportive or deleterious to mental health. The analysis and editing of the narratives of self-identity is a central component of therapy. Illusions are automatically woven into our experience of reality and the construction of the self by layers of hidden neural processing.

The Brain as Illusionist

How the brain constructs the self results in many common illusions. One illusion is that our consciousness comes together at some location within our heads where the totality of experience is presented to us on a screen. This Cartesian theater (Dennett, 1991), in reference to

Descartes' mind–body dualism, results in the view of consciousness as being a spirit inhabiting the body as opposed to being one with it. This fundamental disconnection between mind and body reflects how we in the Western world experience ourselves: We experience consciousness in this way despite the fact that there is no single area of the brain capable of performing this function (Damasio, 1994). The Cartesian theater is a subjective illusion—an experience with no specific or dedicated neural substrate. Yet, despite the experienced separation of mind and body, we also view ourselves as single, continuous, and unified entities through time and space (Erdelyi, 1994).

A second illusion created by our brains is that conscious awareness leads us through time. That is, our moment-to-moment thinking occurs first and guides our feelings and actions, as opposed to the other way around. This results in a third illusion, which is that the processes of the brain and mind are under our control (Bargh & Chartrand, 1999; Langer, 1978). This *illusion of control* leads us to consistently overestimate our control over an outcome and to underestimate the role of chance or factors beyond our control (Taylor & Brown, 1988). All three of these illusions can be exposed and successfully defeated on both cognitive and neurological grounds. Thus, although we feel convinced we are driving, actually we may be dozing in the backseat merely dreaming that we are driving.

Despite the fact that the vast majority of the information we acquire and encode is both outside of conscious awareness and processed *prior* to conscious awareness (Bechara, Damasio, Tranel, & Damasio, 1997), we feel and act as if we have all the necessary information and have made a conscious choice. In truth, we have little or no conscious access to the information or the logic on which most of our decisions are based (Lewicki, Hill, & Czyzewska 1992). What we call intuition is the result of rapid and unconscious decisions that guide our thoughts, feelings, and actions without our conscious knowledge (Damasio, 1999). Nonconscious decision-making penetrates and shapes the construction of the self.

Although some illusions are stable, others break down or dissolve with new information or insight. In life and in psychotherapy, we find that what we thought was true actually turns out to be a fabrication of our self, our family, or our culture. Our brains, like the Wizard of Oz, present an image of existence designed to create certain effects. For the residents of Oz, the purpose of the illusions created by the great wizard was to make his subjects feel that they were guided by a powerful force, providing them with both confidence and direction. Evolutionary psychologists feel that the illusions created by our brains serve a similar function. People often enter therapy with an intuitive sense that their own inner wizard has lost his or her power.

Hidden layers of neural processing (including the Freudian unconscious) predigest and organize our experience before it emerges into awareness. Their organization results in perceptual biases and distortions, including those with seeming genetic origins, such as fears of spiders and snakes related to the evolutionary history of our species. They also include biases laid down by experience during early development, subsequent trauma, and day-to-day learning. Much of psychotherapy is involved with detecting, understanding, and correcting the content and organization of these hidden layers.

Why Hidden Layers?

When a male lizard feels the urge to mate, it finds a nice sunny rock and does a few pushups for the benefit of whatever females may be watching. For some reason, female lizards find this appealing, and a courtship ritual ensues. In this way, reptiles demonstrate instinctual and automatic behavioral programs connected to specific sensations and environmental cues. The sight of food, a dangerous predator, or, in this case, a suitable mate triggers stereotyped reactions showing little cross-situation variability. These stimulus–response connections result in rapid and predictable processing and reactions in the absence of conscious cognition.

The evolution of mammals and primates and the expansion of the cerebral cortex correlate with increased variation of behavioral responses to similar situations. In other words, we sometimes have the option to ignore the pushups of an attractive other. More brain dedicated to high-level neural integration means more behavioral options and flexibility. This response flexibility requires layers of intermediate neural processing dedicated to calculating probabilities of success based on accumulated experience. Hidden layers allow for an increased ability to remember and apply what we've learned.

Through trial-and-error learning, experiences are translated into the strength and connectivity of neurons with neural networks allowing for alternative behavioral patterns to be stored and activated. All neural networks that organize information below the level of conscious evaluation have hidden layers. *Hidden layers* (also called *hidden units* in cognitive science) are those neural structures that serve as connectors between sensation and conscious awareness that are "completely internal and always one step removed from either input or output" (Ashcraft, 1994, p. 119). Because both *response speed and flexibility* are vital to survival, primate evolution reflects a compromise between the two (Mesulam, 1998). Each neural network reflects elements of this compromise and, like most design compromises, results in some functional shortcomings. The impact of these shortcomings is almost certainly responsible for most of the difficulties people bring to psychotherapy.

Our memories, self-awareness, and what is presented on the screen of our Cartesian theater are generated from the landscape of this complex and invisible neural world. What appears to us as inner and outer reality is instead the result of considerable filtration and organization prior to conscious awareness. In the few hundredths of a second it takes for us to become consciously aware of a sensation, the hidden layers of neural processing shape and organize it, trigger related networks, and select an appropriate presentation for conscious awareness (Panksepp, 1998). Because of this, the senses themselves can be considered to be a type of perceptual system and a form of implicit procedural memory (Gibson, 1966).

In these and many other ways, the hidden layers—in connection with executive and memory systems—create both a conscious and unconscious memory for the future (Ingvar, 1985). Through the nearly instantaneous processes of the hidden layers, a version of the world based on past learning rolls out in front of us. Because our world is always shaped by these layers of processing, we never experience the world without them and thus we naturally assume that the world we experience and the objective world are one and the same. The hidden layers—as a matrix of implicit emotional, procedural, cognitive, and sensory-motor memories—create our reality a millisecond before the arrival of our conscious self. The survival value of being able to predict negative possibilities has resulted in a brain that is biased toward living in the future. One of the reasons why some psychotherapies have come to focus on the "here and now" is to counteract this neural bias.

Our hidden layers present to us a picture of the world with an agenda based on what has worked in the past. These hidden layers carry forward the past in a way that determines our experience of the present and sets a trajectory toward the future (Freyd, 1987). They highlight some aspects of experience while diminishing others, direct us to orient to certain aspects of the environment, and completely block awareness of others. By definition, the hidden layers are never directly seen. They are like black holes, known only by the effects of their gravity on other celestial bodies. Therapists are experts at inferring the architecture of the hidden layers by interpreting their effects on their patients' stories, the symptoms from which they suffer, and the lives they lead.

The hidden layers can make the same experience a source of pleasure for one person and a source of dread for another. The carryover of past learning into a present where it is irrelevant or destructive is certainly a major flaw in the design compromise between speed and flexibility. Early attachment experiences organize lasting schemas (within hidden layers) which, in turn, shape our experience of those around us throughout life. The degree of integration between emotional and verbal networks will determine whether or not we become aware of our emotions or can put them into words.

Perceptual Biases and Self-Deception

The power and consistency of perceptual and cognitive distortions in everyday human interactions provide considerable evidence for the existence of hidden processing (Levy, 1997). The fact that errors in judgment fall into consistent patterns suggests that they reflect stable neural organization. Some distortions particularly relevant to psychotherapy are biases in the way we process information about ourselves and others. Some are the result of our limited perspective on a complex environment; others may have evolved to decrease our anxiety about the many dangers inherent in our uncertain world. Although serving positive functions, they can also create problems in relating to others and understanding ourselves. While the illusions of continuity and control may help us to organize our experience, some distortions may simply be a function of the limitations of perspective.

Because we see a complex world from a single vantage point, our perception has an inherent egocentric bias. Our *egocentric bias* leads us to believe that everyone who sees the world differently is simply wrong or misguided. This becomes obvious when dealing with individuals with psychosis or severe character disorders. They create a world from hidden layers so idiosyncratic that it is easy to see the contribution of their unique neural processing. An individual experiencing paranoia will always find a clue to a conspiracy. Someone suffering from obsessive-compulsive disorder will discover many potential sources of contamination. For those of us without such obvious symptoms, the distortions created by the hidden layers are less obvious and more difficult to detect (except, of course, for spouses). Unlike symptoms, they are invisible to their owners because they are the woof and warp of the fabric of their character (Reich, 1945).

The *fundamental attribution error* (Heider, 1958) refers to our tendency to explain the behavior of others based on aspects of their character as opposed to environmental or situational variables. When explaining our own behaviors, we tend to do the opposite, understanding the environment as having a greater impact on our behavior. We fail a test because we didn't have time to study or because the professor wasn't very good; others fail because they are not very bright. An extension of this bias leads to another phenomenon referred to as *blaming the victim* (Ryan, 1971). Individuals who are victimized by illness, poverty, or attackers are seen as having done something to bring on their problems. How often do you hear it said that a rape victim wore provocative clothing or that people in poverty are too lazy to get a job? On the other hand, we see our own problems as the result of outside forces beyond our control.

Another phenomenon that reflects the functioning of the hidden layers is referred to by social psychologists as *belief perseverance*. Put simply, belief perseverance is our tendency to attend to facts that support our beliefs while we ignore those that contradict our beliefs (Lord, Ross, & Lepper, 1979). We experience this phenomenon on a daily basis in both psychotherapy and everyday interactions. The hidden layers are conservative in the sense that they hold onto a way of understanding the world that has, thus far, led to survival (Janoff-Bulman, 1992). This may, in part, explain why many people with negative beliefs about themselves hold onto those beliefs with such tenacity, and why racial prejudice often continues despite evidence to the contrary.

These aspects of hidden layer processing are vital to psychotherapy. In many forms of treatment, we attempt to reverse belief perseverance and attribution biases, and undermine the conservative nature of the hidden layers. By encouraging patients to be open to new ideas and decrease attributions of causation to environmental factors, we guide them to experiment with new behaviors and take responsibility for their actions. These techniques are vehicles to create safe emergencies so that neural networks can be expanded and integrated. *Belief perseverance is the enemy of neural plasticity.*

Defense mechanisms and perceptual biases may serve a number of survival optimizing functions (Nesse & Lloyd, 1992). Repression, denial, and humor certainly support social cooperation and lead us to put a positive spin on the behavior of family and friends (as well as overlooking bad behavior). These same distortions and defenses help regulate internal states by reducing anxiety and shame while decreasing awareness of depressing and demoralizing realities (Nesse & Lloyd, 1992). Both reality and distortions are double-edged swords: They can contribute to either mental health or mental illness.

A more unique contribution of evolutionary psychology is the idea that self-deception aids in the deception of others. In other words, if we believe our deceptions, we are less likely to give away our real thoughts and intentions via nonverbal signs and behaviors. Behaviors and feelings that are opposite of our true desires (reaction formation) are quite effective in deceiving others. It has been noticed, for example, that "people are remarkably reluctant to consider impure motives in a loud moralist" (Nesse & Lloyd, 1992, p. 611). The best con men are often so convincing that their victims refuse to believe they have been cheated, despite considerable monetary evidence.

Hidden Layers and the Freudian Unconscious

Prior to the complex elaboration of the neocortex, survival of the organism depended on instincts and reflexes dedicated to what Pribram playfully called the "four Fs": fighting, fleeing, feeding, and sex (Pribram, 1960). With the expansion of the cerebral cortex and the eventual emergence of the conscious mind, new domains of social relationships and inner experience emerged. The same networks that mediated the four Fs were conserved as the infrastructure of later-developing systems of emotion and cognition. The result is a psyche organized by our ability to tolerate anxiety, stress, and arousal in our inner and outer worlds. Our defense mechanisms appear to modulate the experience of inner anxiety as our physical bodies interact with the environment to negotiate physical survival.

The hidden layers of the psychodynamic unconscious—reflected in defense mechanisms such as repression, denial, humor, and intellectualization—target thoughts and feelings that are kept from awareness through motivated forgetting, modifications, and distortions of experience. Freud recognized that we can see the workings of the unconscious in the way we organize and understand ambiguous stimuli. That is, in a condition of reduced external structure, our hidden layers organize the world, make predictions, highlight certain thoughts and feelings, and ignore others. This is all performed in keeping with past learning, and conducted below the level of consciousness. You will remember that Freud referred to this phenomenon as the projective hypothesis.

The therapist employs the projective hypothesis by using a number of strategies to read the hidden architecture of the unconscious. Therapists try, as much as possible, to remain a "blank screen" in order to allow their clients to project feelings and thoughts onto them. This is why therapists are often less interested in answering clients' questions than they are in discovering what the clients' imagined answers might be. In a similar manner, projective tests like the Rorschach present an ambiguous or incomplete stimulus to the client in order to discover how he or she will organize the material.

Another example of a projective technique is free association, in which a client is told to say whatever comes to mind. Because of the uninhibited nature of dreams, Freud called them "the royal road to the unconscious." Freud, like many others, recognized that the narratives we construct are fictions that may not be conducive to psychological or physical health. The "talking cure" is based on the premise that the more accurate the information included in the narrative of the self (organizing conscious experience), the easier more painful experiences can be processed and the need for damaging defenses reduced.

Narratives and Development

Narrative storytelling is the primary model humans possess for the sequential and meaningful integration of human action (Oatley, 1992). Narratives are a vehicle of explaining behavior and defining both the social and private selves. Narratives are emotionally meaningful, causally linked sequences of actions and consequences that aid in the organization, maintenance, and evaluation of behavior (Fivush, 1994). Narratives also serve to educate children in the tales, myths, and legends of their families and cultures (Howard, 1991: Malinkowski, 1984). The organization and coherence provided by narratives offer the opportunity for teaching, repairing, updating, and creating new stories. The new story can then serve as a blueprint for new behavior. The power of stories to heal suffering and confusion has been understood by shamans since prehistory (Frank, 1963). The technique of creating new stories about the self has been pivotal to many forms of psychotherapy.

Narratives come to regulate the experience and expression of emotional behavior, and are one aspect of the internal representation of mothers' organizing and soothing effects. They are soothing to the degree to which they evoke sensations of safety and well-being or provide an optimistic memory for the future during distress in the present. A small child who is struggling with accomplishing some task may say to himself, "I think I can, I think I can," remembering the tiny train trying to make it uphill. This metaphoric evocation of a story, which combines an emotional situation with a desired outcome, can instill the expectation and confidence that, like the little train, the child will succeed. Narratives and stories serve as blueprints for behavior and goal attainment. As such, they help to organize the moment-to-moment experiences that are required to establish and attain goals. In this way, narratives help to anchor us in our bodies through time.

Humans may be the first primates able to regulate their own affect. The cerebral cortex makes this possible through the internalization of the group and significant others via mental representations. These representations are tied to somatic, emotional, and behavioral memories. Within the early symbiotic bond between mother and child, the mother's store of conscious and unconscious procedural, emotional, and conscious memory is transferred to the child through a constant stream of obvious and subtle interactions. The mother shapes the structures of the social and fearful brains, and determines the child's affective core and eventual self-image through patterns of attachment. Later, when the child goes through the process of differentiation, much of the mother's inner world has already been transferred to the child's hidden processing layers.

Although Neisser divided the individual, social, and conceptual selves, this division is of questionable validity given that the individual and conceptual selves emerge from the first dyad. This emergence is never fully complete, because the self is a matrix of learning and memory reflective of and shaped by social interactions (Cacioppo & Berntson, 1992). The internalization of the mother and other important figures, and the impact of those around us on our internal state, also speak to this essential truth. Psychotherapists refer to these representations as *inner objects*, networks of sensory, emotional, and conceptual memories of significant others. These inner objects can be a source of comfort, distress, or indifference. The self is primarily constructed and populated by those with whom we have had relationships. It can therefore be more accurately thought of as a matrix of memories in the space between individuals and the environment. Gergen (1994) expressed the idea that the act of having memories is to engage in a "cultural practice."

Parents organize memory and create the story of the self with their children (Nelson, 1993). By the age of two-and-a-half, narratives between parents and children are co-constructed at the rate of 2.2 per hour in everyday conversation (Miller & Sperry, 1988). These narratives not only connect parent and child, but also contain an evaluation of what is discussed. In this way, narratives expand the capacity of the social brain to appraise the significance and value of increasingly complex social situations through time.

The ways in which parents construct narratives help to shape their children's sense of self and the world (Ochs & Capps, 2001). For example, gender differences in the content and nature of narrative have been discovered across cultural groups. The work of Miller and her colleagues (Miller & Sperry, 1988) suggests that narratives with boys include angry emotions and often reflect autonomy of self and actions. Girls, on the other hand, are guided to create narratives about the self in which their identity is embedded in a social context. Girls are taught to take responsibility for the feelings of others. If, in fact, the self is organized and experienced primarily through narratives, the experience of self of males and females must be quite different.

Parents also differ in their own emotional development, psychological health, and self-reflective capacities. We will see in the construction of the social brain the correlation between self-reflective capacity and secure attachment patterns. Fonagy and colleagues (Fonagy, Steele, Steele, Moran, & Higgitt, 1991) explored the development of a prereflective self, including the social self of the left-hemisphere interpreter, and a reflective self that includes the "internal observer" of mental life. Parents teach children how to be self-reflective by including their own internal state in interactions and by encouraging children to share their own. Children who have been taught to tell stories that include mental states demonstrate a greater frequency of secure attachment. Being able to understand and consider the mental states of oneself and others has been shown to decrease dependency on defensive strategies (Fonagy et al., 1991), most likely reflecting increased neural integration of multiple processing networks.

Research suggests that what is created in parent–child narratives about experience is not just a story; embedded within the storytelling is the selection of information to be included, how it will be processed and understood, and if it will be egocentric or have multiple subjective centers (empathic capacity). Thus, the way narratives are structured contains a theory of mind of the self and others. It follows that the more complex and coherent a narrative, the more neural network participation and integration will occur (Siegel, 1999). Narrative seen in this light is not unlike a music score for an orchestra, as it organizes and times the participation of many instruments. The breadth and complexity of this score determines the instruments used, their coordination, and the quality of the final performance. Parents and children write this score together in the context of family and culture.

Narratives and Neural Network Integration

Advanced scientific principles and formulas may dominate left-hemisphere processing but have little integrative effect across brain systems. This may be why in psychotherapy, understanding alone is the booby prize. Although we all appreciate and respect the scientific perspective, most of us would agree that we do not operate through linear and logical processes. For example, the disjointed nature of our experience leads us to be suspicious of autobiographies presented as smooth and well-organized narratives (Albright, 1994). We relate to stories containing confusion, emotional crises, and moral dilemmas because they draw us in at many levels, both intellectually and emotionally. This is the power of poetry and the allure of literature.

Although it has been suggested that therapists "traffic in stories" because of a lack of advanced scientific principles (Oatley, 1992), it may be that these stories—with their imprecise and hybrid nature—are the most accurate tools available for the work of neural network integration at the highest level (Rossi, 1993). The combination of a goal-oriented and linear storyline, with verbal and nonverbal expressions of emotion, activates and utilizes processing of both left and right hemispheres, as well as cortical and subcortical processing. This simultaneous activation may be what is required for wiring and rewiring through the simultaneous or alternating activation of feelings, thoughts, behaviors, and sensations. The imprecision of stories may be a key to their success in the integration of neural systems with such diverse processing strategies.

Each form of psychotherapy teaches its own perspective on how the self should be understood. The co-construction of a new narrative in psychotherapy is centered around the therapist's beliefs and the client's goals (Spence, 1982). In a sense, each therapy orientation has its own language, heroes, sets of myths, and stories told by its adherents. In this way, clients from the same therapist form a kind of siblinghood, because they share an inner world shaped by the therapist's metaphors. This is certainly a bonding point in families as well. Husbands and wives have been shown to participate in co-constructing their mutual reality in "creative remembering" (Ross & Buehler, 1994), including altering their views of their previous relationships (Berger & Kellner, 1964).

The malleability of memory, so problematic in a courtroom, can serve a great benefit in therapy if understood in its proper context (remember Sheldon's tricycle). Therapy is not just the rewriting of a client's story; it is the teaching of a method, a process of integration, an assessment and recalibration of perception, and a set of principles for future organization. In this way, therapy is both a form of reparenting and the learning of a strategy for reediting the self.

Summary

The self is a matrix of learning and memory organized and encoded within hidden layers of neural networks. Although we can't see its workings directly, we can see the reflection of its organization through perceptual biases, the defenses of the Freudian unconscious, and distortions in the way we understand experience. The self is primarily a social construction, reflecting not just our place in society but ways of being, thinking, and feeling that support our connection with the group. In the next chapter, we will explore the sculpting of the brain in the context of social relationships, with a special focus on early attachment between parent and child.

The Interpersonal Sculpting
of the Social Brain

In the orphanage, the child becomes sad,
and many of them die of sadness.
(from the 1760 diary of a Spanish bishop,
quoted by Rene Spitz, 1946)

As we all know, humans have a prolonged period of dependency during development. From the first moments of our lives, we exist within a complex matrix of social relationships. This elaborate social relatedness is organized and controlled by neural networks of bonding and attachment, play, predicting others' intentions, and being able to see the world through others' eyes. These skills and abilities are required to survive within our social world and to form lasting relationships.

Precursors to the development of these advanced skills and their complex neural networks are our basic reflexes. Smiling, orienting toward others, shared gaze, looking where others are looking, and imitating facial gestures and movements are all driven by instinct and serve to jumpstart processes of bonding and communication. Early bonding experiences gradually evolve into long-term patterns of attachment and our ability to experience, tolerate, and regulate emotions. Networks of the social brain dedicated to attachment and interaction are also primary components of the neural substrate of emotion, and form the core of personality (Price, Carmichael, & Drevets, 1996).

In this chapter, we will look at aspects of both the neurobiology and interpersonal sculpting of neural networks dedicated to social behavior. This vast and constantly expanding area of study bridges from primitive reflexes to the most complex schema of attachment and self-identity. Understanding core processes of how the social brain becomes organized is of intense interest to psychotherapists attempting to impact these neural systems.

Neonatal Reflexes Priming the Social Brain

Over 20 involuntary reflexes have been identified in the newborn. Many of these reflexes, controlled at birth by the brainstem, are gradually inhibited and then replaced by cortical circuits controlling voluntary behavior. These reflexes have been selected by evolution to increase the newborn's chances of survival by enhancing its physical and emotional connection to the mother. Some examples—like the rooting and sucking reflexes—help the infant obtain nurturance, while the Palmar Grasp (automatic hand grasp) and the Moro Reflex (reaching out of the arms) help the child to hold onto the mother.

Bonding in the first few weeks occurs at a very primitive level, with smell and touch playing primary roles. Although specific words are meaningless, the tone and prosody of the voice hold center stage. A mother instinctually embraces her baby after birth, maximizing contact area of the skin and helping the infant's hypothalamus establish a set point for temperature regulation. The infant and mother gaze into each other's eyes, linking their hearts and brains, while nursing establishes the lifelong relationship between nutritional and emotional nurturance. Endorphin levels in both mother and child rise and fall as they touch, separate, and touch again, providing them with alternating rushes of well-being and distress.

Orienting of the head to the sound of the mother's voice increases the possibility of eye contact. Seeking circles and complex figures directs eye contact toward the mother's face and eyes. Prolonged, shared, and emotionally stimulating gazes stimulate the growth of networks of attachment and the entire brain (Schore, 1994). Reflexive smiling evokes smiling from caretakers, further stimulating and engaging the infant in the attachment and brain-building process. In recent years, the image of the infant as a passive recipient of stimulation has been replaced with a view of the infant as a competent participant in getting its needs met by reacting to and impacting on specific aspects of the social environment.

Within the first hours after birth, newborns will open their mouths and stick out their tongues in imitation of adults (Meltzoff & Moore, 1983, 1993). Within 36 hours of birth, neonates are able to discriminate among happy, sad, and surprised facial expressions at a rate that exceeds chance (Field, Woodson, Greenberg, & Cohen, 1982). Looking at happy faces causes newborns to widen their lips, whereas sad faces elicit pouting. Surprised models elicit wide-open mouth movement. Infants, it seems, look primarily at the mouth for happy and sad faces, whereas they alternate between the eyes and mouth in response to expressions of surprise. This suggests that they are capable of selecting different visual targets based on the information presented to them (Field et al., 1982).

The Importance of Eyes

The eyes are a primary point of orientation for infants, and play a significant role in bonding and social interactions throughout life. Throughout the animal kingdom, eyes play a crucial role in determining the safety and danger of others. Both bird and butterfly wings have evolved to have eyelike spots, causing avoidance behaviors in predators (Blest, 1957). Gaze aversion, or "visual cutoff," is an important social behavior that indicates dominance hierarchy in both humans and primates. The "Are you lookin' at me?" monologue of Robert DeNiro in *Taxi Driver* is a familiar example of the relationship between eye gaze and dominance. Direct eye gaze is a threat signal in primates (De Waal, 1989), and the recognition that we are being looked at results in an increase in heart rate in humans (Nichols & Champness, 1971; Wada, 1961). What must it be like for primates trapped in zoos who have hundreds of human primates staring at them every day?

During early infancy, mutual gaze between caretaker and child is a primary mechanism for promoting brain growth and organization. Escalating positive emotions generated within reciprocal interactions activate dopaminergic and opioid systems; these build the brain and increase tolerance for higher levels of positive affect and arousal. During the second year of life, the eyes and facial expressions come to be used to inhibit toddler activities. Looks of disapproval or disgust from the adult while the toddler is in a state of arousal result in the experience of shame (Schore, 1994). Because shame is neurobiologically toxic for older infants, it is important for parents to reconnect with their children in order to avoid prolonged states of shame. In his remarkable work, *Affect Regulation and the Origin of the Self*, Allan Schore (1994) described the process of the transduction of these early interactions into the organization and functioning of the nervous system.

The neurobiological and evolutionary significance of eye contact is important for developing an implicit theory of the intention of the other. Elaborate neural circuits have evolved to monitor the direction of eye gaze of potentially dangerous others in order to anticipate their next move. Shared direction of gaze is also important in group communication. The classic example of this is how we look up when we see other people doing so; in these situations, the eyes serve as a source of social communication. The connection among the eyes, visual system, and emotion can be easily witnessed in the delight a child takes in extended games of peek-a-boo.

Thanks to the neurochemistry of bonding, the smiles and laughter elicited from a child during peek-a-boo are just as addicting for adults. There is a surge of good feeling in both children and caretakers with each reappearance of the eyes.

Eye contact is a powerful tool in both childrearing and psychotherapy. In their gradual movement away from parents, toddlers will check back visually to see the expression on a parent's face. If the parent looks calm, the child will feel confident to explore further. A frightened look from the parent may result in the child seeking proximity and decreasing his or her exploration. This is one of the many mediums through which a parent's internal world is automatically transferred to the child—a process referred to as *social referencing* (Gunnar & Stone, 1984).

In therapy, the way a patient experiences your gaze (as caring or threatening) is an aspect of transference that may provide important cues to early bonding experiences. Some patients request that the therapist not "stare" at them because it makes them uncomfortable. Other might feel that a similar gaze makes them feel attended to and cared for. Although some patients prefer to lay down and look away from the therapist, others want to "keep an eye on you." All of these reactions reflect the eyes' ability to trigger the patient's learning history within implicit networks of the social brain. The role of the amygdala in the visual system provides a direct line for triggering danger signals to the body. The eyes and the information they communicate are windows to our interpersonal histories as well as our souls.

The Neurochemistry of Bonding

The neurochemistry underlying mother–child bonding is very complex: The warm and happy feelings; the desire to hold, touch, and nurse; the pain of separation and the joy and excitement of reunion all have neurochemical correlates that allow us to experience these wonderful feelings. Through a biochemical cascade, mother–child interactions stimulate the secretion of oxytocin, prolactin, endorphins, and dopamine, which create positive and rewarding feelings. These biochemical processes, in turn, stimulate the structural maturation of the Ofc (Panksepp, 1998; Schore, 1994).

The secretion of *endogenous opioids*, such as endorphins, results in a sense of well-being, pain reduction, and elation. These opiates are strongly reinforcing and serve to shape our preferences from early on in life (Kehoe & Blass, 1989). Research with primates suggests that the activation of the opioid systems of mother and child propels and regulates the attachment process. When primates engage in grooming behavior, endorphin levels increase in both parent and child (Keverne, Martens, & Tuite, 1989). During separation, the administration of nonsedating morphine has the same soothing effect on the infants as does the reappearance of the mother.

Higher levels of endorphins make us feel safe and relaxed, whereas low levels stimulate behavior designed to increase proximity, caretaking, and a sense of safety. When naltrexone (a drug that blocks the effects of endogenous opioids) was administered to infant primates, their clinging behavior increased (Kalin et al., 1995). This same effect has been demonstrated in rodents (Panksepp, Nelson, Siviy, 1994) and in dogs as measured by increases in tail wagging (Knowles, Conner, & Panksepp, 1989). Opioids are central to the initial shaping of early bonding experiences, promoting a core sense of safety and well-being in the child. The internalization of the mother involves an intricate network of visceral, motor, sensory, and emotional memories that can be invoked in times of stress and can support the ability to regulate affect. Most likely, endogenous opioids contribute to the positive emotional aspects of the *internalized mother*.

Proto-Conversation

Mother and child engage in complex and reciprocal interactions even before birth. Communication occurs through sound, movement, and touch while their shared biochemical environment informs the child about his or her mother's state of arousal and sense of safety. After birth, the earliest interplay begins the process of transmitting the communication style of the mother, family, and culture. The social and emotional context of interactions over the first year of life serve as the interpersonal and emotional scaffolding for the semantic language to follow. The growth spurt of the right hemisphere during this time provides the neural substrate for the development of the emotional components of language. Damage to the right hemisphere later in life impacts the social and emotional aspects of language while leaving grammar intact.

Close examination of the bidirectional *proto-conversation* (Bateson, 1979) between a mother and her baby demonstrates that infants have far more influence on their mothers than previously thought. A baby does not simply react to its mother, but instead learns how to affect the mother's feelings and behaviors. Both mother and infant adjust to each others gestures, behaviors, and sounds in a sort of lyrical song and dance (Trevarthen, 1993). The availability, attunement, and emotionality organizing the mother's interactions are internalized during this right-hemisphere-to-right-hemisphere linkup with her baby (Schore, 1994). This is the language of inter-subjectivity, in which the child learns from the mother about the fundamental safety or dangerousness of the world. Proto-conversation creates the psychological, social, and emotional context from which narratives will gradually emerge.

Sensitive Periods

You may remember from an earlier chapter that a sensitive period is a window of time when exuberant growth and connectivity occur in specific neural networks. The onset and conclusion of these time windows are genetically and environmentally triggered, and correspond with the rapid development of skills and abilities organized by that particular network. The rapid rate of neural growth makes learning during sensitive periods relatively easy when compared to learning outside of these times. One of the best examples of this occurs when children begin to learn language during the second and third years of life. Another is the development of the right hemisphere over the first 18–36 months, and the shaping of circuits involved with attachment and affect regulation (Schore, 1994). Although the social brain is capable of growing and evolving throughout life, attachment patterns are apparent by the end of the first year (Ainsworth, Blehar, Waters, & Wall, 1978).

The strength of learning during these sensitive periods results in early experiences having a disproportionately powerful role in sculpting the networks of attachment and affect regulation. Because this early learning is essentially unconscious, it has the additional power of organizing our background affect, our views of the world, and relationships prior to the development of conscious awareness. Early suboptimal experiences of bonding and attachment become imprinted within the circuits of the social brain and are carried into adulthood.

Nowhere are these organizing principles more evident than in psychotherapy. Clients continue to see themselves, the world, and others as a function of their experiences in early relationships, despite much evidence to the contrary. This anachronistic world view is mediated through the power of negative learning during the early development of the social brain, and is resistant to change. Self-identity is an emotional and conceptual spin-off of the self experienced in a relationship; in other words, the individual emerges from the dyad. The core sense of self, world, and others generated from negative early experiences affects all domains of life, making the individual vulnerable to deficits in social and occupational functioning, physical illness, and psychopathology later in life.

The Neural Networks of the Social Brain

The neural structures of the social brain include the amygdala, the anterior cingulate, the orbitofrontal areas of the prefrontal cortex, and the frontal portions of the temporal lobes. These structures have expanded and networked in parallel with the explosion of social and emotional information necessary for survival within increasingly larger primate groups.

The *orbital area of the prefrontal cortex* (Ofc) is considered the apex of the limbic system, differentiating it from the other areas of the frontal cortex in both its connectivity to other structures and its neuroanatomical organization (Fuster, 1997). In many ways, it is as much an extension of the limbic system as it is a portion of the cortex (Mesulam & Mufson, 1982). Its position as a convergence zone for polysensory and emotional information, and its direct connection with the hypothalamus, point to its importance as an association area that mediates information concerning our external and internal worlds. Its inhibitory role in autonomic functioning highlights its contribution to the organization of higher-order behavior and affect regulation (Fuster, 1985; Schore, 1994).

Lesions to the Ofc result in difficulties reading emotional facial expressions necessary for social interactions. The Ofc also participates in allowing us to use the facial expressions of others to serve as primary or secondary reinforcers of our behavior (Zald & Kim, 2001). In other words, the Ofc helps link our motivational states to the expressed likes and dislike of others, allowing us to attune with and respond to others' feelings and needs. These processes are accomplished in conjunction with the other centers of the social brain.

The *amygdala*, working in concert with the Ofc, is also a core component of the social brain in humans. You will remember from our discussion on memory that the amygdala is an organ of appraisal of safety and danger, and mediates many aspects of the fight-or-flight response. In primates, the amygdala has been shown to be sensitive to the sight of other monkeys interacting (Brothers, Ring, & Kling, 1990). Damage to the amygdala creates difficulties in many important aspects of social judgment and communication, such as reading emotional facial expressions, determining which way another person is looking (Adolphs, Tranel, Damasio, & Damasio, 1994; Young, et al.,

1995), and estimating the approachability and trustworthiness of others (Adolphs, Tranel, & Damasio, 1998). You will remember that the amygdala's direct connection with the autonomic nervous system serves to translate its appraisals into immediate bodily reactions related to fight and flight. This is the neural substrate of our intuitions about the trustworthiness of others.

Cells in the amygdala of macaque monkeys have been found to be selectively sensitive to approach movements (Brothers et al., 1990). Given the importance of immediate reaction to the approach behavior of other primates, it is logical that part of the amygdala's role in appraisal for danger has to do with the immediate detection of potentially dangerous approach behavior and the rapid signaling to the sympathetic branch of the autonomic nervous system. Neurons in the temporal lobes have also been shown to detect eye contact, open mouth, and identity—all vital in primate survival (Brothers & Ring, 1993). Damage to the amygdala and adjacent structures can result in a loss of status in the group hierarchy, encountering alien troops without fear, and abnormal friendliness to experimenters (Kluver & Bucy, 1938). These behaviors suggest a loss of judgment regarding group and species etiquette, familiarity (visual agnosia), and potential social danger. Findings in case studies with human patients suggest similar effects (Hayman, Rexer, Pavol, Strite, & Myers, 1998; Lee et al., 1998).

In more primitive mammals, where feeding and social communication are primarily organized by olfaction, the amygdala is chiefly involved with the sense of smell. As primates evolved, the lateral areas of the amygdala expanded and connected with cross-modal sensory areas, especially vision. Visual scanning became increasingly important in social interactions as primates came to stand upright and group size expanded. This process also corresponded with the shift from a primarily nocturnal existence to being creatures of the day. As the role of the amygdala shifted from olfaction to the other senses, the primacy of vision, and especially the emotionally expressive face, took on a central role in interactive communication (Schore, 1994). In fact, damage to the amygdala has been shown to result in deficits of nonverbal visual memory (Tranel & Hyman, 1990). The importance of vision in social communication is evident in metaphor; if we are attracted to people, we give them "the eye"; if we threaten them, we "stare them down."

The Ofc and amygdala are key components of the neurology of both attachment and fear. The amygdala's primitive appraisal abilities are utilized in conjunction with the frontal lobes' ability to comprehend the reward or punishment value of complex stimuli (O'Doherty et al., 2001). The close connection between attachment and affect regulation is the result of the role of the Ofc in the inhibition and organization of emotional experience. The organization of attachment patterns and the regulation of emotions are behaviorally associated because they are, in essence, two ways of understanding the same process. Attachment is, at its primitive biological core, a means of survival and hence a means of controlling anxiety.

The *anterior cingulate* is an association area of visceral, motor, tactile, autonomic, and emotional information. It first appeared during evolution in animals in which maternal behavior, play, and nursing have a role in social bonding and attachment. The cingulate evolved at a stage when sound became involved with communication between predator and prey, potential mates, and mother and child (MacLean 1985). Destruction of the anterior cingulate results in mutism, a loss of maternal responses, and probable infant death due to neglect (Joseph, 1996). Amphibians and reptiles, lacking a cingulate, are able to form groups but appear to lack long-term social and emotional bonds.

The *temporal lobes* integrate sensation, emotion, and behavior (Adams et al., 1997). The senses are integrated, organized, and combined with primitive drives and emotional significance in a top-down linkup of all three levels of the triune brain. Specific areas of the temporal lobes combine highly processed information from the different senses and integrate them with affective and somatic input from the amygdala. This is a good example of an association area. The convergence of information allows for rapid survival reactions to complex environmental input, such as facial expressions. Cells involved in reading facial expressions (and others dedicated to the identification of faces) are located in adjacent areas of the temporal lobes (Desimone, 1991; Hasselmo, Rolls, & Baylis 1989).

These neural structures serve as the core of the social brain. Developing from birth, the architecture of the social brain contains our implicit and procedural memories of our early interpersonal learning history. It stores information about the safety and danger of others, what we can expect when they come close, and if we can depend on them for nurturance and support. The social brain edits our experience, interpreting the ongoing stream of social information in light of implicit memories of events from long ago.

It is within this neural system that early interpersonal experiences are organized into schemas for attachment (Bowlby, 1969). *Attachment schemas* are implicit procedural memories reflecting sensory, motor, affective, and cognitive memories of caretaking experiences. These memory networks become evoked in subsequent interpersonal experiences throughout life. Attachment schemas serve to direct our attention toward or away from others by providing us with ongoing and unconscious input about approach/avoidance decisions. Another way to think about these schemas is that they contain a prediction of the likelihood that being with others will result in a positive or negative emotional state. These schemas are manifest in the selection of significant others, the emotions experienced within relationships, and many of the crises that lead individuals and couples into treatment.

The power of these networks becomes evident as we move among different interpersonal contexts. Although many of us may feel like competent adults when we are with coworkers, we may experience ourselves quite differently when we are home for the holidays. Our emotions, behaviors, and even our self-image may shift dramatically in the presence of our parents, despite our advanced age. These experiential shifts may parallel neural network shifts triggered by the strength of memories within the social brain. Research with schizo-phrenic patients in the presence of critical and noncritical family members demonstrated different levels of physiological arousal related to each parent (Tarrier, Vaughn, Lader, & Leff, 1979). Relationships serve as regulators of internal physiological processes which is why separation or bereavement can result in a temporary (and sometimes permanent) loss of regulatory capacity (Hofer, 1984, 1987).

Mirror Neurons

Using microscopic sensors, neuroscientists are able to record the firing of single neurons in monkeys' brains. This recording can take place while they are aware, alert, and interacting with other monkeys. Through such methods, neurons have been discovered in the premotor areas of the frontal cortex, which fire when another primate or the experimenter is observed engaging in a specific behavior, such as grasping an object with a hand (Jeannerod, Arbib, Rizzolatti, & Sakata, 1995). Some of these neurons are so specific they only fire when an object is grasped in a certain way by particular fingers (Rizzolatti & Arbib, 1998). What is even more interesting is that these same neurons fire when the monkey performs the same action itself (Gallese, Fadiga, Fogassi, & Rizzolatti, 1996): Neuron see, neuron do.

These neurons have been dubbed *mirror neurons* because they fire in response to an observation of a highly specific relationship between an actor and some object, and also fire when the action is performed (mirrored) by the observer. Despite the fact that the activity of individual neurons is being measured, one must remember that a mirror neuron is but one neuron in a complex network of thousands or perhaps millions of interconnected neurons. It is more correct to think of mirror neurons as being a single point of measurement of far-reaching and complex neural networks.

Although single-cell recording from healthy human subjects is not possible for ethical reasons, scanning brain activity has been used to extend these findings to humans. One such study demonstrated that areas in the human brain analogous to those containing mirror neurons in primates (premotor cortex and Broca's area) are activated during both the observation and the execution of hand actions (Nishitani & Hari, 2000). Support for the relationship between these areas in the monkey and Broca's area in humans comes from recent PET studies, showing activation in Broca's area during the active or imagined carrying out of hand movements (Bonda, Petrides, Frey, & Evans, 1994; Decety, 1994; Grafton, Arbib, Fadiga, & Rizzolatti, 1996).

The facts that mirror neurons fire when the same action is observed or performed by monkeys and that the same systems appear to exist in humans lead to some interesting hypotheses related to their role in learning and communication. The implications are clear when it comes to procedural learning via modeling the behaviors of others. It has always been known that both humans and primates can learn by observation. Because mirror neurons activate for both observation and action, they can provide a core neural mechanism for motor learning. Also, because these neurons have been found in Broca's area in humans, mirror neurons may be involved in the recognition and expression of phonetic gestures and actions (Gallese et al., 1996).

Mirror neurons may additionally play a role in the organization and synchronization of such group behaviors as hunting and dancing. At a primitive level, mirror neurons and their associated networks within the social brain provide a means for linking brains and bodies through shared observation. Shared actions and turn taking may be the genesis of proto-conversation and semantic language. Some language learning may be triggered by these mirror neurons within Broca's area, as the sounds and lip movements of caretakers are imitated. The alternation of mirroring and turn taking seen in mother–infant interactions may be a contemporary reflection of the early evolution of language.

It is logical to assume that the facial expressions, gestures, and posture of another will activate similar sensory-motor circuits in the observer. These motor systems, in turn, activate networks of emotion associated with such actions. Seeing a sad child cry makes us reflexively frown, tilt our heads, say "aawwhhhh," and feel sad with them. Watching a defeated athlete walk slowly off the field with his or her head down can lead us to feel sad and, perhaps, trigger a memory of a time we suffered defeat ourselves. In these and other ways, mirror neurons may bridge the gap between sender and receiver, helping us understand one another and enhance the possibility of empathic attunement (Wolf, Gales, Shane, & Shane, 2000; Wolf, in press). The internal emotional associations linked to mirror circuitry are activated via outwardly expressed gestures, posture, tone, and other pragmatic aspects of communication. Our own internal state—generated via mirroring—can become our intuitive "theory" of the internal state of the other.

Recognition and Face Neurons

Our temporal lobes, including neurons dedicated to mirroring and faces, are essential to our ability to have relationships with other people. Besides being able to recognize faces and the behaviors of others, we need to experience other people as being different from inanimate objects. You are probably familiar with autism and Asperger syndrome; both disorders are characterized by profound deficits in the ability to relate to others. In interacting with individuals suffering from these disorders, I have been left with the feeling that, to them, I am no different from any other object in the environment. Not surprisingly, research has demonstrated that these patients process faces in an area of the right temporal lobe normally used to process objects (Schultz et al., 2000). This finding reflects one of the many possible neuroanatomical mechanisms underlying these disorders of relatedness. Perhaps the same findings may hold true for patients with psychopathy, another disorder of relatedness.

An important function of the social brain is to recognize faces and assign appraisal (emotional) value to them. The first part of this process is the very complex task of face recognition and knowing that a face viewed from different angles is the *same* face. This task, easy for even a child's brain, has defied computer programmers for decades. Although the recognition of faces most likely involves both hemispheres in humans, it is a function more suited to the visual-spatial mechanisms of the right hemisphere and its holistic processing strategies.

Research with primates has demonstrated that a particular region of the temporal cortex contains cells that are responsive to faces, their identity, and their various expressions (Perrett et al., 1984). These are key components of the social brain in that they relate the visual recognition of others to arousal, emotion, and motor reactions (Perrett, Rolls, & Cann, 1982). Neurons activated by faces have also been detected in the amygdala (Leonard, Rolls, Wilson, & Baylis, 1985), pointing to the collaboration of various structures within the social brain. The temporal cortex contributes primarily to the complex recognition task (the countless combination of facial features), while the amygdala and the Ofc contribute the affective or appraisal element to the processing of the social brain. Together they give us the ability to approach the friendly faces of friends and keep our distance from potential enemies.

Capgras Syndrome: A Disconnection Within the Social Brain

Sometimes the circuits of recognition and emotion become unintegrated, resulting in unusual experiences and even more unusual explanations. A few years ago, Craig, a young man in his early 20s, came in for a therapy session. Craig had been released from hospital just a few weeks earlier. As he walked across my office, I could see that his movements were slowed by the heavy medications he took to keep his hallucinations at bay. The previous September, Craig had gone away for his first year of college; sometime during December things went wrong in his brain. His parents were called and told that their son had locked himself in his room, thrown all of his and his room-mate's possessions out of the window, and was listening to the same song 24 hours a day. They raced to his school to find him in the middle of what was his first schizophrenic episode.

I asked him how things were since he left the hospital, and he told me that they were pretty good. Craig enjoyed having access to his stereo and guitar, and was spending a large part of the day trying to improve his technique. His overall impression was that things were going well. He reported that he wasn't experiencing the paranoia or hearing voices as he had before he was hospitalized. His sleep and appetite were adequate, and he felt like he would soon be able to return to school. He enjoyed his neighborhood and spending time with his old high school buddies. After describing his life at home he said, "There's only one problem, doc. I don't feel comfortable being at home because my parents and brother have been replaced by doubles."

"Doubles?" I asked him. "What do you mean doubles?"

He went on to explain that he had gotten a strange feeling about his parents and younger brother when they came to visit him in the hospital. He figured it was just that he had been through a hard time and that the medication made it difficult for him to think straight. But once he got home he found out the source of his feelings. His family had been replaced by doubles. I gave my best quizzical therapist expression and asked what made him think they were doubles. Craig described how they were excellent copies and that he even asked them questions he thought only his real parents could answer and, sure enough, they knew the answers. When I pressed the question again he replied with some annoyance, "Don't you think I would know if they were my real parents?"

This syndrome of impostors, called Capgras syndrome (Serieux & Capgras, 1909), can occur alone, but usually appears in tandem with some other brain dysfunction such as schizophrenia (Odom-White, de Leon, Stanilla, Cloud, & Simpson, 1995), temporal lobe epilepsy (Ardila & Rosseli, 1988), or head injury (Weston & Whitlock, 1971). Although the neurobiology of Capgras syndrome is not definitively understood, there has been ongoing speculation that it is related to a disconnection among perception, affect, and analysis (Alexander, Stuss, & Benson, 1979; Merrin & Silberfarb, 1979). An EEG study found "abundant and severe EEG abnormalities" in 21 Capgras patients in the area of the temporal lobes, leading the authors to suggest that the delusion of impostors may be caused by a "dysrhythmia" of brainwaves (Christodoulou & Malliara-Loulakaki, 1981).

Capgras syndrome does not appear to be a problem with the recognition of faces. Craig recognized that the people he was living with were physically identical to his real parents. The problem Craig was having seemed to be that they no longer *felt* like his parents — the emotional "glow" of recognition was missing (Hirsten & Ramachandran, 1997). Based on the circuitry of the social brain, we can hypothesize that, for some reason, there has been a disconnection, or lack of coherence, among the face recognition circuits of the temporal lobes and the appraisal/emotional contribution of the amygdala, Ofc, and other limbic circuitry. With this connection disrupted, the emotional experience connected to a familiar face is absent, leading the patient to search for an explanation.

Most of us have felt the firing of these familiarity circuits in an exaggerated form when we run into a friend or family member. Seeing someone familiar in an unusual place or at an unexpected time heightens it even further. Our "shock" of recognition leads the more histrionic among us to shake our heads and say, "Oh my God, what are you doing here?" Craig was experiencing what amounts to the opposite of this experience. He expected to feel something when he saw his family that he didn't. This is probably what he was referring to when he said "Don't you think I would know if they were my real parents?" The Capgras experience may be the opposite of the déjà vu feeling, where something feels familiar but is actually new. Déjà vu represents the firing of familiarity circuits (probably in the amygdala) at a random time and in an unfamiliar setting. Strong déjà vu experiences are often reported by patients with temporal lobe epilepsy.

I would suspect that the delusion of impostors is the contribution of the left-hemisphere interpreter trying to construct a logical narrative to explain the unlikely combination of seeing one's parents but not feeling the expected emotional familiarity (Maher, 1974). The process of developing the delusion of impostors may be similar to the process that schizophrenics go through when they have the experience of thoughts being inserted into their heads. They attempt to give this highly unusual sensory experience a logical explanation. The very absurdity of the explanation parallels the bizarre nature of the experience. In the face of experiencing their thoughts as being inserted in their heads, patients ask themselves, "Who would have the technology to do such a thing as broadcast thoughts into my head?" When I worked in Boston, they often concluded that MIT was the culprit, whereas patients with similar delusions in Los Angeles pointed the finger at Cal Tech.

Building the Social Brain

Now that we have an idea of some of the neural structures comprising the social brain, we can turn our attention to the interpersonal processes that stimulate and shape these structures. The building of each brain reflects the coming together of our evolutionary history, the generations preceding our birth, and the unique pairing of parent and child (Eisenberg, 1995). Nature and nurture are not in opposition in this process, but instead work in a cooperative and reciprocal manner, maximizing adaptation to each ecological and psychosocial niche. Parents' capabilities for attachment begin to take shape in their own childhoods. As a child, a young girl may begin to imagine someday having children of her own. The shaping of the virtual child is influenced by her fulfilled and unfulfilled needs. The empathy and care she has received and the assistance she has gained in articulating and understanding her own inner world will influence her future parenting abilities. A mother's childhood can determine whether she is prepared to emotionally provide for her newborn or if she will require her child to give to her the love and attention she herself failed to receive as a child (Miller, 1981).

Early bonding and attachment experiences not only build the networks of the social brain, they also promote the building of the brain as a whole through the energy and excitement generated within the attachment bond. Physical and emotional interactions between mother and child result in a cascade of biochemical processes, stimulating and enhancing the growth and connectivity of neural networks throughout the brain (Schore, 1994). Face-to-face interactions activate the child's sympathetic nervous system and increase oxygen consumption and energy metabolism. Higher levels of activation correlate with increased production and availability of norepinephrine, endorphins, and dopamine, enhancing both the child's energy and his or her pleasure (Schore, 1997a). The vital importance of the early interactions to the building of the entire brain may help to explain the actual deaths of institutionalized children who have been deprived of early interaction (Spitz, 1946).

Attunement and Reciprocity

Attunement and reciprocity are qualitative aspects of bonding that reflect mutual awareness, emotional resonance, and turn taking. The mother's ability to resonate with the infant's internal states, and translate them into actions and words appropriate to the child's stage of development, will eventually lead to the child's ability to connect internal states with words. The early emotional regulation, established via mother–infant synchrony, contributes to the organization and integration of neural networks and the eventual development of self-regulation in the child (Siegel, 1999). Emotional mother–infant synchrony during the first year is predictive of the toddler's self-control at two years, even when temperament, IQ, and maternal style are factored out of the equation (Feldman, Greenbaum, & Yirimiya, 1999).

Stage-appropriate attunement and scaffolding of basic functions will maximize neural growth and network coherence. For the newborn, this may be reflected in stroking and cuddling; in a four-year-old, it means helping him or her to learn to share with a sibling. A 16-year-old, on the other hand, needs assistance with creating and staying focused on goals for the future. As the child grows, the pairing of feelings with words enhances the integration of vertical and horizontal networks dedicated to language and emotions. The activation of increasing levels of excitement, paired with a sense of safety, expands the child's ability to tolerate feelings and regulate his or her emotional world. The combined sense of safety, freedom from anxiety, and the excitement generated via attunement provides the affective background for the experience of vitality and spontaneous expression. This also applies to the optimal psychotherapeutic process.

The building of the social brain between 18 and 24 months is driven by the attunement between the right hemisphere of the parent and the right hemisphere of the child (Schore, 2000). It is through this process that the unconscious of the mother is transferred to the unconscious of the child. In this way, the parents' unconscious is the child's first reality. The right-hemisphere-biased circuits of the social brain come on line at birth, and appear to have their sensitive periods during the first two years of life (Chiron et al., 1997). The mother appears to regress to a state of preoccupation with her infant in the last months of pregnancy, and continues in this state for the first few months of her infant's life (Winnicott, 1963). This maternal preoccupation involves an increased sensitivity to the visceral and emotional experience of the child in order to attune to its primitive communications. The fact that this occurs nonverbally also supports the notion that it is a process organized by the unconscious functioning of the right hemisphere. The mother's purposeful regression allows her to lend her capacity to translate bodily states into words and actions that are soothing to the infant.

It is not uncommon for women late in their pregnancy or in the first months after giving birth to report that they feel they have lost IQ points. Although these changes are often attributed to hormonal alterations and sleep deprivation, they may also be related to a shift in bias to the right hemisphere. A shift to right-hemisphere-biased processing may allow the mother an increased level of emotional and physiological sensitivity to enhance the "intuitive" elements of attachment. A shift of brain coherence toward the right hemisphere would explain the decrease in linear semantic processing and memory abilities reported by new mothers and mothers-to-be. Although a "right shift" might be very useful for attunement with an infant, it could be detrimental to functions best performed by the left. Finding the right words, remembering appointments, and following logical arguments may all suffer to some degree during this period, and these functions are what most people think of as aspects of intelligence.

On the other hand, mothers, like people in general, tend to take their emotional intelligence for granted. Many new mothers report an increasing need during the first year to get out into the world of adults or back to work. This need may parallel a shift back to previous levels of right–left balance. Given that right-hemisphere bias and left-hemisphere hypometabolism have been shown in depressive reactions, these natural shifts to right-biased processing may, in some cases, be causal in the development of postpartum depression.

Shame

During the first year of life, parent–child interactions are mainly positive, affectionate, and playful. Due to limited skills and mobility, the infant stays in close proximity to the caretaker, who provides for the infant's many bodily and emotional needs. As the infant transforms into a toddler, a parent's role comes to include protecting the toddler from falling down stairs, being eaten by the dog, or drinking fabric softener. The toddler's increasing motor coordination and exploratory drive confronts caretakers with many new challenges. For these and many more reasons, parents find themselves saying "No!" on a constant basis beginning in the early part of the second year (Rothbart, Taylor, & Tucker, 1989). Affection and attunement, experienced as unconditional during the first year, come to be tied to specific types of behavior.

Shame, appearing early in the second year of life, is a powerful inhibitory emotion and a primary mechanism of social control (Schore, 1991). The same face-to-face interactions that stimulated excitement, exhilaration, and brain growth during the first year now include information on the recognition of disapproval and disappointment. Shame is represented physiologically in a rapid transition from a positive to negative affective state and from sympathetic to parasympathetic dominance. This shift is triggered by the expectation of attunement in a positive state, only to find disapproval and misattunement in the face of the caretaker (Schore, 1994). Behaviorally, people in a shame state look downward, hang their head, and round their shoulders. This same state (submission) exists in your pet dog when he hunches over, pulls his tail between his legs, and slinks away as you scowl at him for committing a canine faux pas. Similar postures reflect loss, depression, and helplessness in humans.

During early socializing experiences, shame is an emotional reflection of a loss of connection with the caretaker, drawing its power from the primal need to stay connected for survival. Prolonged and repeated shame states result in physiological dysregulation and negatively impact the development of networks of affect regulation and attachment centered in medial prefrontal areas and other circuitry of the social brain (Schore, 1994).

Starting from a state of shame, the return to attunement with parents creates a rebalancing of autonomic functioning, supports affect regulation, and contributes to the gradual development of self-regulation. Repeated and rapid return from shame to attuned states consolidates into an expectation of positive outcomes during difficult social interactions. These repeated repairs are stored as visceral, sensory, motor, and emotional memories, making the internalization of positive parenting a full-body experience. Children left in a shamed state for long periods of time may develop permanently dysregulated autonomic functioning.

Because shame is a powerful, preverbal, and physiologically based organizing principle, the overuse of shame in the process of parenting can predispose children to developmental psychopathology related to affect regulation and identity (Schore, 1994). As part of his therapeutic programs, John Bradshaw (1990) referred to "inner child work" as addressing the long-standing power of these early shame experiences, which he calls "toxic shame." Joseph (1996) used a similar term, "childlike central core," when referring to a right-hemisphere and limbic system network containing implicit memories related to these early parent–child interactions. Schore (1994) rightly differentiated shame from the later-occurring phenomenon of guilt. Guilt is a more complex, language-based, and less visceral reaction that exists in a broader psychosocial context. Guilt is more closely related to unacceptable behaviors, whereas shame is an emotion about the self that is internalized before the ability to distinguish between one's behavior and self is possible.

Winnicott and the Emergence of the Person

In building a bridge between the development and integration of neural networks during parenting and psychotherapy, we will use the work of the English pediatrician and psychoanalyst Donald Winnicott. Winnicott developed some basic principles that both predate and parallel the findings from attachment research. He also coined terms such as *good-enough mothering*, *holding environment*, and *transitional object*, which have become part of the basic lexicon of child development. His ideas have been highly influential both because of their connection to everyday experience and their freedom from obscure jargon. Winnicott provided, from a psychological perspective, an understanding for growth and integration of the person that can also be applied to the nervous system.

Winnicott described the core of mothering as providing a *facilitating and holding environment* that embodies both the mother's empathic abilities and respect for the autonomy of the child. He clearly recognized the mother's devotion and adaptation to the child, allowing her to offer herself as an evolving scaffolding for her child's growth. Winnicott defined the early and intense focus on the baby as *primary maternal preoccupation*, and understood it to include the mother's absorption in the experiences with her baby and her attunement to its primitive developmental state. Winnicott saw this preoccupation as a biologically mediated process beginning in the last trimester of pregnancy and gradually diminishing as the child's need for it becomes less intense. As the baby develops, the facilitating environment evolves to adapt to his or her new needs and abilities (Winnicott, 1963). The *good-enough mother*, in Winnicott's thinking, was a mother who is able to do an adequate job in this difficult, complex, and always changing process of adaptation (Winnicott, 1962).

Winnicott believed that to talk of an infant separate from a mother was an abstraction. What actually exists is a symbiotic infant–mother dyad within which the child is nurtured, its social brain is formed, and from which the infant eventually emerges. Because an internalized mother always remains an organizing principle of the social brain, it could be said that, at some level, we carry the representation of the mother–infant dyad within us throughout our lives. A central component of development depends on the mother's ability to mirror her child. *Mirroring* is the process by which a mother attunes to her child's inner world and gives form to his or her formless fantasies, thoughts, and needs. Mirroring serve the purpose of taking the disorganized processes within the child, organizing them for the child, and making them part of the dyadic interaction. In this way, the child learns about his or her inner world.

As the mother gradually recovers from her preoccupation with her child and again becomes interested in other areas of life, the child is forced to gradually come to terms with some of its own limitations. In an appropriately attuned parent, this gradual failure of adaptation should parallel the infant's increasing abilities, frustration tolerance, and affect regulation. Winnicott used the term *impingement* to describe maternal failures of adaptation. These can take the form of not appropriately anticipating the child's needs, interfering with its need for quiet and calm, and overestimating or underestimating its abilities. Gradual minor impingements force the infant to grow, whereas major impingements (experiences that far surpass the infant's ability to cope) can result in derailment of positive adaptation and the solidification of defense mechanisms. Everyone experiences impingements all the time; patients regularly experience them during psychotherapy. Our ability to experience, cope with, and learn from impingements is an important component of ego strength.

Minor impingements are situations of moderate stress that the child repeatedly confronts and masters. These situations, balancing challenges and safety, most likely maximize neural growth and integration. Less-secure children have experienced more severe and consistent impingements and have been provided with less emotional scaffolding. *Major impingements* overwhelm the child's ability to cope and integrate experience in a cohesive manner, resulting in dissociated networking and functional abilities. Minor impingements are learning-enhancing experiences, whereas major impingements result in decreased neural integration and learning, and hamper the child's development.

True Self/False Self

One of Winnicott's most clinically useful concepts has been the idea of the development of a true and false self. The *true self* represents those aspects of the self that develop in the context of manageable impingements, support, encouragement, and acceptance by the caretaker. Respect for the autonomy and separateness of the child leads the parent to be motivated to discover the child's interests, as opposed to imposing his or her own on the child. The true self reflects brain and bodily networks that can tolerate negative feelings and integrate them into conscious awareness. This true self is reflected in our ability to seek out what feels right for us in our activities, ourselves, and relationships with others.

Secure attachments and a sense of a safe world create the context for the development of the true self. Winnicott's true self is obviously one in which neural network development and integration have been maximized, affect is well regulated, and emotions and conscious awareness are seamlessly woven together. The true self reflects neural integration and access across modes of information processing, and an awareness of the difference between reflexive and reflective forms of language. The true self embodies an open and ongoing dialogue among the heart, the mind, and the body.

What Winnicott called a *false self* results from expectations and impingements for which the child is developmentally unprepared. When parents use their children for their own emotional needs, the child can become compulsively attuned to the parents and create a false self that regulates the parents' needs. This can occur due to parental distraction, psychopathology, or a lack of respect for or awareness of the child's autonomy. Without assistance in developing his or her self-reflective capacity, such children live through reflexive social behavior and never learn that they have feelings and needs of their own that need to be expressed and nurtured.

Prolonged impingements result in chronic emotional dysregulation; this fosters the development of defense mechanisms and character disorders. This false self is enhanced in the presence of emotionally dysregulated or traumatized parents who look to the child for regulation in a reversal of the mirroring process (see Chapter 10 describing the self in exile). The false self also reflects dissociated neural processing, lack of adequate affect regulation, and the inhibition of sensations and emotions necessary for the formation of the true self.

The Consolidation of the Self

In Winnicott's view, too many impingements prevent the infant from experiencing what he called *formless quiescence*, by which he referred to those moments of safety that teach the child that the world can be a safe place. It is in these quite moments that the experience of self is consolidated, neural networks integrate, and fantasy and reality delicately blend. In the context of too many impingements, children must be prepared to respond to unsettling feelings or demands by others. They lose touch with their own spontaneous needs and gestures because they are irrelevant to moment-to-moment survival or the caretakers' expectations and demands. Both the internal neural architecture of the social brain and the co-constructed narratives come to reflect the needs of the parent; the growth of the child's self is put on temporary or permanent hold. Constant vigilance to the environment thwarts the organization of a coherent subjective perspective and ongoing sense of self.

Winnicott felt that a major achievement of attachment and bonding was *the capacity to be alone,* a concept learned through the experience of being alone in the presence of an available mother. The capacity to be alone reflects the ongoing transfer of affect regulation from mother to child. Security of attachment creates enough of a sense of safety to allow feelings to spontaneously "bubble up" with the confidence that they will be manageable and understandable (Miller, Alvarez, & Miller, 1990). This is the context in which the best possible integration of cognitive and emotional processes can occur. This context will minimize the need to employ the types of defenses that result in unintegrated neural systems and the psychological dissociation of memories, feelings, and knowledge. Good-enough mothering results in the development of a belief in a benign world (Winnicott, 1958).

Winnicott felt that *manic defenses* are one result of a lack of the capacity to be alone. If manic defenses are chronically employed, they can become a way of life and keep children and adults from experiencing the psychological ground for neural integration. Impulsive behaviors and thoughts, disconnected from self-reflective processes, serve the purpose of avoiding awareness of unaddressed feelings and needs; to these individuals, *to feel is to feel bad* (Miller, Alvarez, & Miller, 1990). The experience of the inner world is paired with discomfort, sadness, isolation, and shame from a time before conscious awareness. This early stimulus–response pairing serves as an unconscious assumption or background affect throughout life. Sadly, many children with manic defenses are mistakenly diagnosed with Attention Deficit Disorder.

In clinical practice, we see that borderline patients lack the capacity to be alone. These patients have a catastrophic reaction to real or imagined separation that is experienced as a threat to their very survival. This reaction could be an implicit memory of overwhelming abandonment fears from childhood; these adults react in a manner one would expect of young children who have not yet developed object constancy or affect regulation. There is little memory across different affective states and an inability to draw on memories of positive relationships for self-soothing. It is as if the child within such patients has been dissociated from the rest of their development, and awaits proper parenting. These reactions in borderline patients may be our best window to the chaotic and often frightening emotional world of early childhood.

People with manic defenses often mask their inability to be alone by stirring up a whirlwind of activities, social interactions, and phone calls. Adults often come into therapy who, despite their outward success, report feelings of despair and emptiness unconnected to any current events or interpersonal losses. Exploration of their histories usually points to patterns of insecure attachments in which achievement served as a medium for security and acceptance. Constantly escalating levels of activity are reinforced by the avoidance of the negative feelings that would bubble up when the patients were quiet or alone. These people often have a hard time relaxing or taking a vacation because the lack of distractions leaves them open to the intrusion of uncomfortable feelings.

Winnicott's description of the maturation of the infant, within the facilitating environment of the parent, provides a general sketch for the interpersonal building of the brain. Optimal brain growth requires an environment that adapts to its changing developmental capabilities. The growth and integration of the brain needs to be protected from too much stimulation or being expected to perform beyond its developmental capacity. Both excitement and quiescence are vital alternating states in this process. Winnicott understood therapy to be a process of controlled regression to a childhood state in order to succeed in developmental processes that were thwarted in early life (St. Clair, 1986). This is a core component of rebuilding the social brain in psychotherapy.

Attachment

Just as Winnicott observed and worked with mother-infant pairs in his consulting office, John Bowlby (1969) performed naturalistic observations of both primates in the wild and children in orphanages. Also a psychoanalyst, Bowlby was interested in mother–child bonds and the impact of separation and loss on children. Based on his observations, he developed the concepts of *attachment figures*, *proximity seeking*, *secure base*, and *safe haven*. Bowlby's observation of behavior can be interwoven with Winnicott's theorizing about the infant's inner experience during the processes of attachment and individuation.

Bowlby's work, which highlighted the importance of specific caretakers, resulted in a shift in the care of institutionalized children. Children who had previously been cared for by whomever was available were now assigned consistent caretakers to encourage bonding with specific figures. Subsequently, Mary Ainsworth and her student, Mary Main, developed research methods allowing them to test Bowlby's theories in the laboratory. The decades of attachment research inspired by Bowlby provides us with some fascinating tools to study the sculpting of the social brain during early childhood.

Bowlby suggested that early interactions create *attachment schemas* that provide predictions concerning subsequent human interactions. Schemas are implicit memories that organize within networks of the social brain, based on experiences of safety and danger with caretakers during early sensitive periods. These schema are especially apparent in stressful situations because of the central role of attachment in affect regulation. They also trigger rapid and unconscious approach-avoidance decisions in interpersonal situations. Attachment is mediated by the homeostatic regulation of the social brain, the autonomic nervous system, and a cascade of biochemical processes that parallel states of positive and negative emotions.

Research in attachment began with Ainsworth's attempt to see if Bowlby's naturalistic observations could be identified and measured in a consistent and valid way (Ainsworth et al., 1978). This was done in the context of in-home observations of the interactions of mother–child dyads. These observations led to the development of three broad categories of parent–child interactions. The next stage of this research was to determine whether the children of mothers in these categories displayed differences in their attachment behaviors. The research method developed to study the attachment behavior of the children was the infant strange situation (ISS).

The ISS is an experimental setup consisting of placing an infant and its mother in a room, then having a stranger join them (Ainsworth et al., 1978). After a period of time, the mother exits the room, leaving the child alone with the stranger. After another brief period, the mother returns. The child's *reunion behavior* is rated to determine his or her attachment style. The child being left alone, combined with the introduction of an unknown other, mirrors a situation in nature that would evoke distress calls from an infant for its mother to return. The attachment schema of the child, or their expectation of soothing, should be reflected in their reunion behavior. Does the child seek comfort from the mother or ignore her? Does the child have a hard time being comforted? Does the child feel better and go back to play or is he or she anxious and uneasy, clingy, or withdrawn? These and other behaviors are the focus of the ISS scoring system and reflect the mother's ability to regulate the affect of the child, as well as the child's internalization of the mother's soothing capacity. Because the amygdala is a core component of both the social and fearful brains, attachment schemas are essentially interwoven with the biological core of the experience of fear, anxiety, safety, and danger.

Four categories of the infants' reactions to their mothers' return have been derived from the ISS: *secure, avoidant, anxious-ambivalent,* and *disorganized.* A strong relationship was found between these categories of infant reunion behavior and those originally derived from the in-home observations of mothers during the first year of life. Infants rated as securely attached sought proximity under stress, were quickly soothed, and returned to play or exploratory behavior. These children, comprising approximately 70% of the sample, seemed to expect that their mothers would be attentive, helpful, and encouraging of their continued autonomy. It is believed that infants internalized their mothers' sense of safety and comfort provided by their general tendency to be available and sensitive to their child's feelings and needs. These mothers were seen as effective in their interactions with their children and had become "a background context for seeking stimulation elsewhere" (Stern, 1995).

Avoidantly attached children, who tended to have mothers who were rejecting, unavailable and distant, ignored their mothers when they returned to the room. The avoidantly attached child would only glance over to his or her mother as she came in, or would shun contact altogether. These children appeared to lack an expectation that their mother would be a source of soothing and safety. Avoidantly attached children seemed to have learned that they are better off not engaging with their mothers. They find that it is easier to regulate their own emotions than to seek comfort from their mothers. They seem to have learned that the stress for which they need soothing may well be compounded by misattunement or dismissal.

Children rated as anxious-ambivalently attached sought proximity but were not easily soothed and were slow to return to play. Anxious-ambivalent children—often had inconsistently available mothers—may have their stress worsened by their mothers' stress. Their slow return to play and emotional regulation may reflect the lack of a sense of internalized safety. Finally, there were a group of children who engaged in chaotic and even self-injurious behaviors. These chaotic behaviors were demonstrated in conjunction with secure, avoidant, and anxious-ambivalent behaviors and were often paired with mothers who were rated as suffering from unresolved grief or trauma. The dysregulation and chaos of the mothers' internal worlds had been transferred to their children's and could be observed in their children's behavior.

During later research, a fourth category was determined called disorganized. These children demonstrated disorganized behavior on reunion such as approach-withdrawal, turning in circles, or falling to the ground. These children are thought to have had alarm states induced by the parents. In this biological paradox, the child's brain has an innate drive to move towards the attachment figure. However, since the parent is the source of alarm, the child is faced with an unsolvable problem. Hence, disorganization is the only option. Parents of children in this category are thought to demonstrate frightened, frightening, and disorganized behavior to their children.

Parents Talk of Their Childhoods

The relationship between parenting styles and attachment behaviors raises the question of parents' own early attachment history. It is assumed that the parenting styles of adults are somehow shaped by childhood experiences. Because explicit adult memories of childhood are normally distorted or contaminated by so many factors, a more subtle measure needed to be developed. Implicit memory systems needed to be tapped in order to circumvent distortions of the left-hemisphere interpreter and the various mechanisms of defense. An interesting research tool that seems to have succeeded in this difficult task is the *adult attachment interview* (AAI; Main & Goldwyn, 1998).

The AAI consists of open-ended questions about childhood relationships and early experiences. This is a particularly interesting measure in that it contains not only a way to gather information about what individuals remember of their childhood, but also provides a linguistic analysis of the coherence of the narrative's organization and presentation. Coherence analysis includes an examination of both the logic and understandability of the narrative to the listener. Scoring takes into account the integration of emotional and experiential materials, gaps in memory and information, and the overall quality of the subject's presentation (Hesse, 1999).

In a sense, the AAI bypasses the left-hemisphere interpreter by examining the quality of the job that the brain is doing in synthesizing the various cognitive and emotional components of explicit and implicit memory (Siegel, 1999). Siegel proposed that coherence of the text and presentation of the AAI narrative most likely parallel neural network coherence and integration. The coherence of the presentation of information—reflecting the level of early affect regulation—provides a window to the nature of a person's attachment experiences. In essence, the AAI asks about childhood experiences and reflects how the person has come to make sense of their lives, put feelings into words, resolve traumatic experiences, and integrate the various networks of information processing across emotion, sensation, and behavior in conscious awareness.

Four categories again emerge from research with the AAI, correlating with the results of both in-home observations of mothers and the infant strange situation. Mothers and fathers who were associated with securely attached children tended to have both detailed episodic memories of childhood and a balanced perspective between the good and the bad aspects of their own parents and childhood experiences. They were able to describe these experiences in a coherent narrative that was understandable and believable to the listener (Main, 1993). This group, called autonomous, demonstrated good integration of cognition and emotion.

The second group of parents, associated with avoidantly attached children, demonstrated a *lack of recall* for childhood events and an overall dismissive attitude toward the impact of relationships in their childhoods. This group is said to have a "dismissing" state of mind with respect to attachment. The narratives of these parents were incoherent, based on a lack of information, and they tended to demonstrate an idealization or condemnation of their own parents. With these parents, there was a sense that they were defending against their histories through denial and repression. This lack of recall could also be the result of a disruption in the integration of the cognitive and emotional elements of autobiographical memory.

A third group of parents, rated as *enmeshed* or *preoccupied*, tended to have anxious/ambivalently attached children, and had incoherent narratives with lots of verbal output that lacked boundaries between past and present events. These parents appeared preoccupied, pressured, and had a harder time keeping the perspective and knowledge of the listener in mind. Finally, some parents are placed also in an *unresolved/disorganized* fourth group. Their narratives may appear like any of the other three groups except that during the discussion of trauma or loss, they become disoriented and/or disorganized. The consistency and organization of their narratives were disrupted with emotional intrusions and missing information about their experiences of trauma or loss. These narratives had the least cognitive and emotional integration, and reflected the disruptions of neural integration secondary to trauma, dissociative defenses, and unresolved grief.

Interestingly, the positive or negative nature of a parent's childhood is not the predictive feature correlating with his or her own child's attachment pattern. What does appear to matter is the coherence of the narrative created, not the exposure to trauma or loss during childhood. This strongly suggests that the processing, working through, and integration of childhood experiences is the relevant variable in a parent's ability to be a safe haven for his or her children. This *earned autonomy*, through a parent's own healing of childhood wounds, appears able to interrupt the transmission of negative attachment patterns from one generation to the next (Siegel, 1999).

The power of the relationship between parent and child attachment patterns was demonstrated by Fonagy and his colleagues (Fonagy et al., 1991a) when they administered AAIs to women who were pregnant with their first child and the fathers-to-be. When the children reached their first birthday, their attachment patterns were rated in the infant strange situation. In 75% of these cases, the child's attachment pattern was predicted by the nature of the parent's narrative during the AAI before the child's birth. Parents of infants who came to be securely attached were able to provide a fluid narrative, provide examples of interactions, had few memory gaps, and presented little idealization of the past. These parents did not seem to have significant defensive distortions, were able to express negative feelings without being overwhelmed, and listeners tended to believe what the parents were saying (Fonagy et al., 1991a).

Attachment Patterns and Neural Integration

It is hypothesized that parents who are rated as autonomous in the AAI have higher levels of neural integration between cognitive and emotional processing networks (Siegel, 1999). This inference is based on the fact that they are able to utilize and organize cognitive and emotional memory functioning to a higher degree than are parents who have nonsecure adult attachment states of mind. They do not appear to be suffering the effects of unresolved trauma or dissociative defenses, and have attained a high degree of affect regulation. They are able to remember and make sense of their own childhoods, have resolved negative and traumatic experiences, and are available to their children both verbally and emotionally. Their children develop attachment schemas within the social brain that make them secure in the expectation that their parents are a safe haven who will soothe and assist them. Not surprisingly, parents' emotional availability to themselves appears to parallel their emotional availability to children.

The three other patterns demonstrated in the attachment research all seem to reflect a lower level of psychological (and hence neurological) integration, and more primitive defenses that characterize these disconnections. The lack of recall and black-and-white thinking of the dismissing parent likely reflect blocked and unintegrated neural coherence. This brain organization then results in decreased attention and emotional availability to the child. The enmeshed parent has difficulty with boundaries between him- or herself and others, as well as between past memories and present experiences. These internal and interpersonal issues then lead to inconsistent availability and a flood of words that can alternately regulate or dysregulate the child. Thus the child, who is also anxious and ambivalent, will seek proximity but have a difficult time returning to play because of the schema of unpredictable availabilty and the confusing and emotionally dysregulating nature of the parent's messages and emotions.

Recent research suggests that attachment patterns formed in childhood may be relatively stable into adulthood. They have been shown to impact experiences of romantic love, interpersonal attitudes, and the sense of self (Brennan & Shaver, 1995; Hazan & Shaver, 1990). Adults who were once children of anxious parents tend to return repeatedly to their parents throughout their lives for a sense of comfort and security, only to be disappointed. Many of these children become parents to their own parents, soothing and taking care of the people they wish would care for them. A metaphor I use in therapy is the repeated return to an empty well. Each time the bucket is lowered there is the hope that it will contain the nurturance they need when it is raised. Each time the bucket comes up empty, it reinforces the basic lack of dependability of relationships and safety in the world.

The transduction of attachment schemas into neurobiological structure is believed to be primarily organized by the orbitofrontal cortex (Schore, 1994). The Ofc processes the punishment and reward value of complex stimuli (O'Doherty et al., 2001; Tremblay & Schultz, 1999): in this case, the parent or parents. In its role in affect regulation, the Ofc (via the networks of the social brain) mediates emotional responses (Hariri et al., 2000) and coordinates the activation and balance of the sympathetic and parasympathetic branches of the autonomic nervous system (Price et al., 1996). Secure attachments represent the optimal balance of sympathetic and parasympathetic arousal, whereas their imbalance correlates with insecure attachment patterns (Schore, 1994). The balance of these two systems becomes established early in life and translates into enduring patterns of arousal, reactivity to stress, and possible vulnerability to adolescent and adult psychopathology.

Parasympathetic dominance is proposed to be correlated with an avoidant style, a low level of emotional expression, and the avoidance of eye contact. It is a mode of withdrawal from the world and from others that blocks exploration of the environment and seeking emotional support. Sympathetic dominance may correlate with anxious/ambivalent attachment patterns characterized by irritability, acting-out behavior, and decreased ability to recover from stress. These children receive from their caretakers unregulated doses of affect that are overstimulating and underorganized. They experience difficulties with poor impulse control, hostility, and fears of abandonment (Schore, 1994).

By far the most disorganizing pattern appears when the parent has unresolved trauma or loss. The transmission of traumatic experiences through play in children and verbal recounting of the trauma by adults has been consistently reported (Terr, 1990). In normal social interactions, the trauma-related behaviors of victims will lead them to be avoided by other children. A child with a traumatized mother who creates alarming experiences for the child has no choice but to stay with and depend on the source of the alarm. The child's safe haven is replaced with repetitive *trauma by proxy* and emotional dysregulation. This process creates a new generation of victims. In research with Holocaust survivors, indications of parental trauma were found in the biochemistry of their non-traumatized children (Yehuda et al., 2000; Yehuda & Siever, 1997). Children with avoidant and disorganized attachment schema have also been shown to have higher levels of stress hormones (Spangler & Grossman, 1993).

Attachment research suggests that adults can create secure attachment for their children despite their own negative experiences as children. Earned autonomy, through enhanced integration of early experiences, results in the ability to serve as a safe haven for one's children. Thus, the powerful shaping experiences of childhood can be modified through subsequent personal relationships, psychotherapy, and self-awareness. The ability to consciously process stressful and traumatic life events appears to correlate with more secure attachment, flexible affect regulation, and increased availability to narrative memory. The integration of neural circuitry across cognitive, behavioral, sensory, and emotional domains is the proposed neuroanatomical substrate of this earned autonomy (Siegel, 1999). A healing environment, such as *good-enough psychotherapy*, in which trauma is processed and resolved, supports this reintegrative process.

When a child is left in silence due to his or her parents' inability to verbalize experienced events and internal experience, the child does not develop the capacity to understand and manage his or her own inner and outer world. The ability of language to integrate neural structures and organize experience at a conscious level is left unutilized. When trauma occurs early in a child's life in the absence of a healing environment, the effect of the trauma and the ensuing silence is to increase stress while depriving him or her of an important aspect of emotional regulation. Language, in combination with emotional attunement, is a central tool in the therapeutic process; it creates the opportunity to blend words with feelings, a means of neural growth and neural network integration.

Parent–child talk, in the context of emotional attunement, provides the ground for the co-construction of narratives. When verbal interactions include reference to sensations, feelings, behaviors, and knowledge, they provide a medium through which the child's brain is able to integrate the various aspects of its experience in a coherent manner. The organization of autobiographical memory in a manner to include processing from multiple neural networks enhances self-awareness, increases the ability to solve problems, cope with stress, and regulate affect. This integrative process—so important to parenting—is what psychotherapy attempts to reestablish.

Narrative Co-Construction

Co-constructed narratives form the oral traditions of ancient and modern tribes as well as parent–child relationships. They are an important mechanism of transmission of historical and family culture. The participation of caretakers and children in describing shared experiences organizes memory, embeds it within a social context, and assists in the process of linking feelings and actions to others and the self. The cocreation and repetition of stories help the child to develop and practice recall abilities and have their memories shaped by the input of others (Nelson, 1993). This mutual shaping of memory between child and caretaker can serve both positive and negative ends. Positive outcomes include teaching the importance of accuracy of memory, imparting of cultural values, and shaping the child's view of him- or herself based on his or her role in the story. Negative outcomes include the transfer of the caretakers' fears and anxieties into the child's narratives so that they become central and repetitive themes in the experience of the child (Ochs & Capps, 2001).

When caretakers cannot tolerate certain emotions or feelings, they will be excluded from narratives or shaped into other, more acceptable forms. These narratives become a blueprint for the dissociation of neural processing and the building of an identity that does not include a conscious awareness of these emotions. Narratives that struggle to integrate frightening experiences with words can serve as the context for healing by simultaneously creating cortical activation and increasing descending control over subcortically triggered emotions. As it turns out, there appears to be a relationship among the complexity of a child's narratives, self-talk, and the security of the child's attachment.

Main and her colleagues (Main, Kaplan, & Cassidy, 1985) studied a group of six-year-old children who, at one year, were assessed in the infant strange situation. They discovered that secure attachments with primary caretakers correlated with a number of abilities found to be less common in children with insecure attachment patterns. Securely attached children engaged in self-talk during toddlerhood and spontaneous self-reflective remarks at age six. They also appreciated that their thoughts were private and not accessible to their parents and others. Finally, it was found that securely attached children tended to make comments about their thinking process and their ability to remember things about their history.

These processes of "mind" reflect the co-construction of narratives with parents and the utilization of these narratives in the expression and development of the experience of self and self-identity. They also point to a more sophisticated ability to meta-cognize (think about thinking); this represents a high level of cortical and linguistic self-regulation. These children are taught to internalize the self-regulatory mechanisms of their parents. Insecurely attached children were often found to lack these skills and abilities. As you might expect, child abuse correlates with less secure attachment patterns in children and a decreased ability to talk about their internal states (Beeghly & Cicchetti, 1994).

Fonagy and his colleagues (1991b) studied the relationship between infant security and reflective self-functioning in mothers and fathers. They found a high correlation between a measure of self-reflection and narrative coherence. In fact, when reflective self-function was controlled for in the statistical analysis, coherence no longer related to infant security. This suggests that the relationship between coherence and reflective self-functioning is powerful, and that the ability to reflect on the self (or the sophistication of the language of self-reflection) plays an important role in the integration of multiple processing networks of memory, affect regulation, and organization. In discussing these results, the researchers suggested that "The caregiver who manifests this capacity at its maximum will be the most likely to be able to respect the child's vulnerable emerging psychological world and reduce to a minimum the occasions on which the child needs to make recourse to primitive defensive behavior characteristic of insecure attachment" (p. 208).

If a child is able to achieve this ability from someone other than the primary caretaker, he or she may be able to earn a higher level of integration and security than would be predicted by his or her parents' rating on the adult attachment interview (Siegel, 1999). This may come from other significant people in the child's environment who are able to attune to the child's world and assist in the child's articulation of his or her emotional life. These feelings may, in part, explain some of the earned autonomy seen in parents with negative childhood experiences but with coherent narratives and the ability to provide a safe haven to their children. Earned autonomy is convincing evidence that early negative experiences can be reintegrated and repaired later in life. Personal growth can heal and the social brain can remain plastic.

Summary

Humans spend their lives embedded within an intricate web of complex social relationships. We are attuned to the sensations and emotions of those around us even before birth. Primitive brainstem reflexes—such as smiling, grasping, and sucking—jump-start the bonding process. These reflexes are gradually added to, and later superseded by, networks of the developing limbic and cortical regions of the brain.

Two powerful elements contributing to both the evolution and sculpting of the human brain are emotional attunement and the use of language. These two interactive processes stimulate the brain to grow, organize, and integrate. The internalized mother, our attachment schema, and our ability to guide and regulate our thoughts and emotions, are determined by the shaping of the networks of our social brains through emotional attunement and the co-construction of narratives.

The power of early relationships to influence adult experiences has been long recognized. Psychoanalysis and other forms of psychodynamic psychotherapy have studied this relationship in great depth. While it remains unclear how much change is possible subsequent to the early formation of these neural systems, increasing our understanding of the underlying processes of the social brain may offer new insights for the practice of psychotherapy.

PART IV

THE DISORGANIZATION
OF EXPERIENCE
AND PSYCHOPATHOLOGY

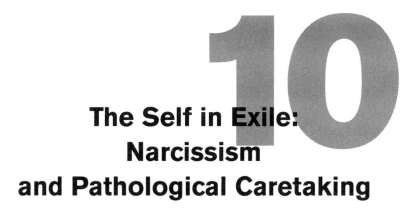

The Self in Exile:
Narcissism
and Pathological Caretaking

E ach of us is born twice: first from our mother's body over a few
hours, and again from our parents' psyche over a lifetime. As
we have seen, the organization of the social brain is initially
sculpted via parent–child interactions. These interactions shape the
infrastructure of our moment-to-moment experience of the world
and especially other people. As the child's brain continues to form,
self-awareness and self-identity gradually emerge. As we have seen,
consciousness and identity are complex functions constructed from
the contributions of multiple (primarily nonconscious) neural networks. Pathological states highlight the fact that the self is a fragile
construction of the brain. Furthermore, there is significant flexibility in the location, experience, and organization of the self and the
body.

Victims of rape and torture frequently report out-of-body experiences during their traumatic experiences. A young woman named
Joanne described to me, in great detail, how she watched herself
being raped from behind a closet door across the room from where
it was actually happening. Another client, Mark, who had been bru-
tally attacked while getting into his car after work, described watching himself being repeatedly stabbed from across the street. The

perception of the self is also vulnerable to alteration and distortion. Anorectic clients, their bones protruding through their skin and their health in serious jeopardy, insist that they feel and look fat. Patients with multiple personalities are perhaps the most complex example of the plasticity of self, because they generate many different sub-personalities associated with different affective states.

Narcissism, a common form of "self" disturbance, appears to be related to a reversal of the mirroring process during childhood. The narcissistic child's social brain and sense of self are not shaped by their own emerging emotions and sensibilities; rather, they are determined by the parents' own need for nurturance, attunement, and affect regulation. This is Winnicott's false self, embedded in the networks of the left-hemisphere interpreter, filtering out emotional input from the right hemisphere and the body. In this chapter, we will explore the reversal of the mirroring process and the adult conditions of pathological caretaking and codependency that emerge from these early suboptimal attachment experiences.

Silent Hammers

Jerry, a successful writer, came to therapy complaining of depression and exhaustion. His long work hours, frequent deadlines, and last-minute emergency rewrites kept him in a constant state of tension. His personal life centered around his girlfriend, Cara, whom he described as "high maintenance" and likened to a second job. Jerry experienced his life as a relentless struggle to please everyone he knew. Despite his depression, Jerry felt guilty about coming to therapy, and expressed fear about wasting my time; he felt that he was the *helper*, not the one who received help. "After all," he stated, "you could be seeing someone who really needs the help."

After a few sessions, it became clear to me that Jerry had spent the first half of his 39 years taking care of his immature and self-centered parents. All of his subsequent relationships appeared to follow the same pattern. Although he described his romantic relationships in positive terms, he reported almost as an aside that he always felt deprived of attention and nurturance. The same held true in his relationships with coworkers and employers. It was clear he was exhausting himself by attempting to meet the needs of others in order to gain the love and attention for which he longed. These futile efforts would invariably end in sadness, resentment, and angry withdrawal. Although he was exhausted from trying so hard and failing so completely, Jerry still maintained the hope that his work would someday pay off.

Working with Jerry was both fascinating and frustrating. He questioned nearly everything I said, betraying his hidden distrust of my ability to help him. On the other hand, his flair for the dramatic resulted in interesting and entertaining stories during almost every session. He seemed to have an uncanny ability to intuit my interests. At times, I lapsed into being the audience for his one-man show. I soon realized that Jerry experienced me as just another person to entertain and take care of while he secretly waited to receive care in return. At the same time, he resisted every attempt I made to show care and concern for him.

Jerry was hesitant to discuss his childhood, saying that he remembered little of his life before he left for college. Our sessions consisted primarily of stories of his interactions with unappreciative others and his trying to enlist my understanding and support for his side in their conflicts. He was both comforted by my compassion and annoyed with my continued suggestions that he pay attention to his inner emotional world, especially when engaged with others. As the weeks passed, I grew increasingly frustrated. However, the intensity of his defenses reflected his emotional vulnerability, and I needed to be careful not to move too quickly. On the other hand, if I went too slowly, he might fill with resentment and terminate therapy just as he had with so many other relationships.

At some point, I suggested that he write something about himself. Jerry agreed and soon created a story about a little man named Hal who sat at a control panel in his head. Hal was a sort of ship's captain at the helm of the *U.S.S. Jerry*. When Jerry was alone, Hal would monitor the other people in Jerry's life. A wall full of t.v. screens kept track of where they were, what they were doing, and whether Jerry was in their thoughts. When he would come into contact with another ship, like his girlfriend Cara, Hal would select a holographic image of Jerry specifically for that person. Hal had a screen to monitor Jerry from the perspective of the other ship, in order to make sure that the hologram was having the proper effect. Hal's purpose was best described by the show business adage: "Give the people what they want."

I was impressed by the clarity of the story of Hal. Jerry was telling me that his sense of self was organized around his theory of the minds of others. There was nothing about Hal that had anything to do with Jerry's own thoughts, feelings, or needs. Jerry only knew he needed to know the needs of others; for him, this was love; this was life. I realized Hal reflected the early sculpting of Jerry's social brain by his parents: This is how Jerry survived childhood. The story of Hal was a reflection of implicit memory, symbolically representing the core emotional drama from his early life. It was a drama lived in the absence of conscious awareness of its existence or its power over him. Despite the apparently obvious nature of this story, Jerry would not entertain interpretations. He seemed to have great difficulty experiencing the world from his own point of view. In Jerry's conscious experience, he was Hal.

A few sessions later, Jerry used another metaphor to describe his inner world. He described himself as a house on a typical movie set: a perfectly detailed facade with great curb appeal but without a finished interior; there was no true place to live. If you looked behind the facade there were only exposed 2x4s and bare floors. He said, "A good director knows how to place his cameras so as to maintain the illusion of a real building." In a moment of receptivity and trust, he told me that his goal for therapy was to finish building and decorating the interiors so that he didn't have to worry about camera angles. Jerry was tired of feeling like a fraud in a world of real people. I could feel his inner world shifting as his feelings of emptiness were surfacing into consciousness.

I told Jerry, "As we grow, the story of who we are gets written in collaboration with those around us, especially our parents. They watch us and listen to us and try and put words to what they see us struggling to express. This helps us know our own self and write our story. When parents didn't get this as children, or are suffering with some problem, they may look to their children to help them find themselves."

I think this is what may have happened with Jerry's parents. He learned to be sensitive to them and attend to their needs when they should have been helping him write his story. In a sense, Jerry's story got written by default; in serving others he was hoping to find himself, and he was still searching all these years later. I suggested to Jerry that even his choice of writing as a career may have been an expression of his desire to write his story. Although there are many good and honorable aspects to serving others, I told him that it may be more important to write a new story where his own needs would be balanced with the needs of others.

Jerry asked, "Is this why, when people ask me how I am, the first thing I think about is how others in my life feel?" I nodded as I watched the muscles in his face relax. A new understanding of a familiar behavior was emerging, and his inner world was being reorganized. After a period of silence, he said softly, "I even do it with you, don't I? I pay you to take care of me and I end up entertaining you and protecting you from my needs." The session was over and he walked silently out of the office. I wondered if he could withstand the stress of these insights and would return for our next session.

He did come back, and with a sly expression he uncharacteristically touched my shoulder as he passed. "You're gonna think you're pretty smart when I tell you this one." I noticed his voice had changed; it was no longer the voice of an entertainer. Jerry was sharing this experience from a different place within himself. On the previous Friday, he had gone out with Cara and didn't get back to Cara's apartment until 3:00 A.M. The combination of alcohol and exhaustion caused him to fall asleep as his head hit the pillow. After what seemed like a few minutes, he was jarred from sleep by the banging of hammers outside the bedroom window. He picked up his throbbing head and saw on the clock that it was not yet 7:00 in the morning. "I felt like my head was going to explode!"

Jerry's face became increasingly tense as he described the murderous fantasies passing through his mind. He imagined going outside and "punching out" the entire team of construction workers. Just at the moment he was about to jump up and run outside, Cara pushed her head up from the pillow. She looked at Jerry with an expression of exhausted rage and said, "I'm going to go out there and kill those guys." Apparently, they had been waking her up this way for most of the week.

Falling back on my office couch and letting out a sigh, Jerry described how her words triggered something altogether familiar and totally unconscious. With eyes wide open he said, "When I heard Cara's anger I became a different person. My exhaustion vanished, I felt energized and alive! I completely forgot about the construction workers. My total focus instantaneously shifted to how to make Cara feel better." He described jumping up as if well rested and on holiday and saying to Cara, "A little breakfast will make you feel better." He became oblivious to the sound of the hammers and bounded into the kitchen as Cara pulled the pillows over her head.

Ten minutes later, Jerry was at the stove brewing coffee, frying eggs, making toast, about to call out "Breakfast is served," when he again heard the hammers. He said, "I was amazed that I hadn't heard them since I had gotten out of bed." He realized that they hadn't stopped, but from the moment he had seen the anger on Cara's face, he was completely involved in activities to cope with her feelings, utterly ignoring his own. He realized that attending to Cara's distress catapulted him out of his own distress.

As he stood, spatula in hand, these feelings triggered a long-forgotten memory. He remembered coming home from school to find his mother crying, head down in her arms on the kitchen table. Jerry remembered his terror as he went over and stood beside her. She didn't respond when he asked her what was wrong; she just continued sobbing. He didn't know what to do or who to call. His father had left them months before, and his mother had grown more silent and withdrawn with each passing week. He stood motionless, not knowing if she was even aware of his presence.

He tried to engage her in conversation, telling her about his day at school. He even told some jokes he thought she might disapprove of in the hope of getting her angry enough to chase after him. She remained silent, crushed by the weight of her sadness, loss, and fear. Jerry recalled growing increasingly desperate and afraid as time passed. He stood motionless as the afternoon light turned to dusk. He eventually came up with the idea to cook for her and went over to the stove to fry her some eggs, the only thing he knew how to make. After collecting what he needed, he pulled a chair over to the stove and started to cook. This seemed to get her attention. She came over and they cooked together in silence.

During our first few sessions, Jerry had mentioned his parents' divorce, his father's drinking, and his mother's depression. He characterized his home as "a vault of silence" with very little interaction or shared activities. The family took no meals or vacations together; most of their energy was taken up with day-to-day survival. He spoke of these things in passing, with little emotion and an insistence that his childhood had no connection with his adult difficulties. He said he had coped with his family situation by burying himself in books and writing stories, for which he has been rewarded ever since. This memory provided evidence for what I had suspected; Jerry had grown up with too much stress and too little parenting. He had lost himself in everyone else's stories but had not received the emotional freedom or support he needed to write his own.

Jerry came away from the experience of the hammers and the memories they triggered with a new perspective. He could see, from this and other childhood memories that began to emerge, how he was constantly frightened by the emotional instability and distance of both of his parents. It was also clear that he, like Hal, was constantly monitoring the feelings and needs of others. As a child, he felt as if his life depended on it. I was especially fascinated with the fact that his own anger, frustration, and exhaustion disappeared in the face of Cara's negative feelings. He later told me that he figured this was why he felt so uncomfortable and vulnerable when he wasn't in a relationship. Never having learned how to regulate his own feelings, it was safer to stay in the minds and hearts of others.

The power of these insights were emotionally unsettling for Jerry, and it took him many weeks to get back on track. As he regained his equilibrium, we began to apply his new insights to more aspects of his life. Thinking back on his romantic partners, he realized that they were never as good at anticipating or attending to his needs as he was to theirs. This imbalance led him to feel unloved and uncared for. At one point, he stood up abruptly and shouted, "I blamed them for not being as 'sick' as I am." Jerry came to understand that feeling like an empty shell was connected to not knowing his own feelings. He said, "My feelings were never important when I was a kid. It's my feelings that are going to furnish those rooms inside of me and I have to have my own feelings to feel whole."

These experiences were a turning point in Jerry's treatment. We created a common language and used it to explore Jerry's inner world. Hal gradually replaced some of the old monitors with new ones designed to track his own feelings. Eventually, Hal and his monitors became unnecessary. Jerry feared he was being too selfish by considering his own needs, and he actually did lose some "friends" who relied on his constant and unilateral attention. Cara and Jerry grew closer, however, and she admitted that she liked Jerry better when he didn't try to make her happy all the time. Jerry slowly recovered from his pathological caretaking.

Jerry's difficulties highlight a number of principles related to the development and organization of the brain that were examined in previous chapters. During childhood, Jerry's brain adapted to a demanding and nonnurturing emotional environment. From early in life, his survival depended on being highly aware of the feelings and needs of his parents. The neural systems of his social brain came to be hypersensitive to his parents' facial expressions, body language, and behaviors as he attempted to monitor their emotions and behave in ways that regulated their feelings and bonded them to him. Systems normally used to help a child come to experience him- or herself were usurped to monitor other people in his life. This was how Hal was born. Jerry's mirroring skills continued to be utilized in adulthood with his friends, employers, and therapist through emotional caretaking and entertaining stories.

Because Jerry didn't have help processing and integrating his own emotions during childhood, they remained chaotic, frightening, and overwhelming long into his adult years. Caretaking came to be reinforced not only by those he attracted, but by the avoidance of his own disorganizing emotions through attending to the feelings of others. Caretaking evolved into a form of affect regulation as well as a way of connecting to others via a false self (Hal). This was demonstrated by the instantaneous inhibition of his feelings of anger at the construction workers when he realized Cara was awake and upset. From early in development, hidden layers of neural processing organized the inhibition of his own feelings and directed his social brain to focus on the internal state of others. This neural network organization was in place prior to Jerry's development of self-conscious awareness, making this way of experiencing the world completely unconscious and an a priori assumption in his life.

Through these processes, Jerry's evolving sense of self was shaped through the eyes, minds, and hearts of others. Left-hemisphere-processing networks, which inhibit affect and participate in the creation of stories about the self, allowed Jerry to become a functional adult with a successful writing career. His ability to describe himself symbolically, first as a monitoring robot and then as a director planning camera angles, reflects his subconscious awareness of his self-organization. Without assistance in connecting these insights to the organization of his conscious self, they remained correct but useless bits of information contained within dissociated neural networks.

Interpretations—such as the one Jerry made connecting his cooking eggs for Cara and taking care of his mother—triggered emotions of sadness and loss. Making his defenses conscious appeared to activate the emotional networks that the defenses had been inhibiting. The higher-association areas involved in the organization of conscious awareness appear capable of the type of plasticity required to make interpretations result in qualitative changes of experience. Implicit memories of early childhood—stored within networks of the social brain—were experienced emotionally and expressed in Jerry's feeling unworthy of my help and distrustful of the ability of others to help him. These were echoes of his disappointment and hurt in reaction to his parents' inability to assist him when he was needy.

His insecure attachment resulted in a complex array of emotional and behavioral adaptations. Jerry's lack of conscious recall for much of his childhood was one example. Another was his unconscious expectation that expressions of his needs would be met by more emotional pain. All of the factors seen in Jerry's struggle to attain love and caring reflect his brain's adaptation to a childhood full of impingements and the absence of an integrated and integrating other. Jerry's parents did not assist him to create a narrative identity centered around his own experience. In therapy, I helped Jerry to apply his considerable creative skills to write a story of self.

Pathological Caretaking

Pathological caretaking is an aspect of a disturbance of self referred to as *narcissism* (Miller et al., 1990). Narcissism is characterized by a two-sided self: one reflecting an inflated sense of self-importance, the other reflecting emptiness and despair. The origin of this formation of the self occurs when a child is looking for love and attunement and instead discovers the mother's own predicament (Miller, 1981). The child, robbed of self-discovery, compensates by caring for the parents under a real or imagined threat of abandonment. The bright and sensitive child attunes to and regulates the parents' emotions, and comes to reflect what the parents want from him or her. The child will usually appear mature beyond his or her years, and identifies with the ability to regulate those around him or her. Because of their power to regulate the affect of one or both parents, such children are filled with a sense of inflated self-importance. Miller and Winnicott call this a *particular manifestation of the false self*, well described by Jerry as both a theatrical facade and an inner robot monitoring others.

The other side of narcissism reflects those aspects of the child's emotional world that have found no mirroring. This true self, or the part that is unique to the individual, is left undeveloped and eventually forgotten. This emotional core (or inner child) awaits parenting. This core aspect of the emotional self is the implicit emotional memory of abandonment and how contingent the love received was on taking care of others. This is the source of the depression, the sense of being a fraud, and the lack of an emotional connection with life.

The development of the social brain (and the subsequent formation of the sense of self) becomes dedicated to the prediction of and attunement to the moods and needs of the parent and others. This ability serves to ward off abandonment anxiety while truncating the development of the understanding, expression, and regulation of one's own feelings. Such children grow into self-awareness with the others' emotions experienced as their own, and an overwhelming sense of responsibility, or even compulsion, to regulate the emotions of those around them. In Jerry's case, it helped him to avoid his own poorly understood and dysregulated emotional world.

Pathological caretaking is a specific manifestation of narcissism. The caretaking of others serves as a substitute for self-soothing abilities and inner emotional organization. Pathological caretakers come to therapy primarily because they are depressed and exhausted by their inability to create a boundary between themselves and the needs of others. Being alone is difficult when they are not exhausted, because they need others to regulate their internal world; but being with others is such hard work. For these people, a battering or abusive relationship is far less frightening than isolation. Caretakers are difficult clients because they have learned during early attachment relationships that help is not forthcoming when they are in distress. Caretakers like Jerry have learned that, in the face of inner needs, it is best to put them out of mind and keep "giving the people what they want."

Alice Miller: Archaeologist of Childhood Experience

The central importance of parental relationships in shaping the social brain is nowhere better articulated than in a series of elegantly simple works by the Viennese psychotherapist Alice Miller. Her work with what she called "gifted children" targeted adults, like Jerry, who were raised by parents whose emotional needs were greater than their ability to attune to their children. Taking a stand against her analytic colleagues, Miller reshaped the therapeutic role into one of advocate for the child within her adult patients. Reaching back through the years to reconnect with long-forgotten childhood experiences, Miller reinterpreted much of her clients' adult behavior as a reflection of their adaptational histories. In observing the nonverbal reenactment of implicit memory, Miller formed hypotheses concerning what her clients had been exposed to, how their young brains had adapted, and what it would take to unearth the abandoned "true self."

Miller's archaeological view of memory included the awareness that memory from different developmental stages will reflect different modes of processing and understanding. In her role of advocate, she saw therapy as a process wherein therapists help clients to unearth their history, not from the point of view of the adult but instead from that of the child. Memories in these subcortical networks do not age as years go by; they remain in their initial form. Miller came to this formulation from clinical experience rather than a knowledge of the multiple systems of explicit and implicit memory.

Miller used the term *double amnesia* to describe the process by which such children have had to first forget certain parts of themselves (e.g., feelings, thoughts, and fantasies) that could not be accepted or tolerated in their family. The second layer of forgetting is to forget that these feelings had been forgotten. These two layers of forgetting ensured that such children would not slip back into wanting what could not be had. Given our knowledge of the multiple systems of memory and their dissociability, Miller's double amnesia is most likely grounded in both the disconnection between systems of implicit and explicit memory, and constructing a self-narrative that excludes reference to personal needs.

The lack of assistance in the construction of a self-narrative, combined with the heightened anxiety and vigilance necessary for survival with narcissistic caretakers, leads to a deficit in the consolidation of autobiographical memory. The memories are not repressed, but rather are unorganized by hippocampal cortical systems that would allow them to be accessible to conscious consideration. In this light, Miller's work is a reconstruction of the past, based on available conscious memory in combination with nonverbal expressions from implicit systems of memory. Such patients' present experiences are examined for emotional truths, then traced back through a hypothesized trajectory. The patients' considerable empathic ability can be utilized to their advantage by asking how they think some other child might feel in a situation similar to their own. This method, used a number of times, is often successful.

For Miller, gifted children were those who were exquisitely sensitive to the cues of parents and who had the innate ability to mold themselves to their parents' messages. These are the children who come to be called "codependent" and may make up the bulk of service professions such a doctors, nurses, social workers, and therapists. Jerry—with his sensitivity, intellect, and wit—certainly appeared to fit into this category.

Although the gifted child described by Miller may be quite functional, he or she often feels empty and devoid of vitality. Because their vitality and true self are not acceptable, these aspects of gifted children are inhibited and banished from awareness. This creates a vulnerability, not only to disturbances in personality but also to the unconscious transmission of "mirror reversal" to the next generation. Parents who have not been adequately parented themselves look to their children for the nurturance and care they were unable to receive years before. Miller stated, "What these mothers had once failed to find in their own mothers they were able to find in their children, someone at their disposal who can be used as an echo, who can be controlled, is completely centered on them, will never desert them, and offers full attention and admiration" (Miller, 1981, p. 35).

A child's instinct to bond with his or her parents drives them to do so regardless of the terms and conditions. When such children look into their mother's eyes and find no reflection but, rather, "the mother's own predicament," they will mold themselves (if able) to their mother's psychic needs. Compulsive compliance—initially adaptive in response to narcissistic or abusive caretakers—becomes maladaptive in relationship to others and the development of the self (Crittenden & DiLalla, 1988). The gifted child doesn't rebel, and that becomes the problem. Unable to attend to their own emotional memories, and thus, unable to construct the story of their lives, these children constantly search for someone who needs to be nurtured.

Miller felt that the child within the adult patient always needs an advocate, because it is completely helpless in childhood to resist the coercion of the parents' unconscious. Our brains are designed to take our parents' behavior as a given, and our job is to adapt to the environmental contingencies. Remember that the child's first reality is the parents' unconscious, transferred via right-hemisphere to right-hemisphere attunement well before the articulation of self-identity. Because it is implanted in early implicit memory, it is never experienced as anything other than the self. Miller was quick to describe the tragedy for the parents who may be well aware of the pain from their own childhood and may have vowed to never make their children feel as they did. The intergenerational transmission continues because it is reflexive and unconscious, and because each generation, at some level, protects the image of the parents and guards against the pain of their own unfulfilled emotional needs.

Although the patient does not generally have explicit memory for early relationships with his or her parents, Miller posits that these learning experiences are implicitly recorded in how the patient thinks of and treats him- or herself. The strictness and negativity of how patients talk of themselves (superego) will betray their parents' negative attitudes toward them years before (Miller, 1983). These implicit emotional and behavioral memories—in the form of attitudes, anxieties, and self-statements—contribute to the continued repression of real emotions and needs. These early memories are stored in hidden layers, and shape all of our thoughts and feelings.

For children, punishment also implies guilt. Therefore, abuse and neglect equate with their own innate badness or evil. Miller reported about a teacher who told her that several children in her class, after seeing a film about the Holocaust, said, "But the Jews must have been guilty or they wouldn't have been punished like that" (Miller, 1983, p. 158). This assumption of guilt on the part of children both protects the parent and serves as the core of a negative self-image. Because this self-image is organized and stored by implicit systems of affective memory, the child's later-developing identity forms around this a priori negative core. Caretaking and compulsive perfectionism also reflect the ongoing attempt to compensate for the certainty of unworthiness.

René Magritte and His Mother

A chilling example of this reversal of the mirroring process is demonstrated in a painting by the surrealist Rene Magritte, entitled the *The Spirit of Geometry* (see Figure 10.1). It depicts a mother holding a child but with a startling twist: Their heads and faces have been exchanged. Magritte was the eldest of three boys in a middle-class household in turn-of-the-century Belgium. His mother suffered

Figure 10.1   The Spirit of Geometry, René Magritte

Magritte's image of a mother and her son may reflect an implicit emotional memory of his relationship with his mother (© 2002 C. Herscovici, Brussels/Artists Rights Society (ARS), New York).

from depression throughout his childhood, and made multiple suicide attempts. She was, in fact, locked in her room each night for her own protection. One cold February morning, she managed to slip out of her room and drowned in the Sambre river.

Based on his adult life, it is fair to assume that René was a bright and sensitive child, and that he suffered from a lack of positive maternal attention for most or all of his childhood. To lose his mother to suicide at the age of 14 serves as an additional severe blow to the child's sense of safety. This painting suggests that the young Magritte looked into his mother's eyes and found fatigue, depression, and emptiness. In her eyes he read "You be the mommy, I'll be the baby," and he complied.

In retrospect, a biographer suggested that Magritte himself seemed only at peace when he was "tormented by problems" (Gablik, 1985). Much of the body of Magritte's surrealist work presents us with the message that the world is not what it appears to be. Although Magritte repeatedly stated that his early experiences had no bearing on his artistic work, it is difficult to imagine that the loss, betrayal, and abandonment from his childhood didn't reverberate in his many works, warning us not to be fooled by the assumptions on which we depend.

Summary

The separation between the true and false selves reflects the brain's ability to develop dissociated tracks of experience. Early trauma and stress in nonhealing environments can even result in the formation of multiple separate personalities, now referred to as *dissociative identity disorder* (DID). It is logical to assume that these different experiential states are encoded within different patterns of neural network activation. The existence of pathological caretaking, DID, and other disorders of the self demonstrate the fragile and flexible nature of the self, its vulnerability to fragmentation and exile, and its inclination to adapt to pathological conditions.

Pathological conditions and our own everyday experiences teach us that the self is a mental construction in the service of adaptation. The purpose of both the brain and the self is survival. For each of us, the organization of our own self—including our personality, defenses, coping styles, and the like—reflects the conditions to which we have had to adapt. Put another way, all aspects of the self are forms of implicit memory stored in neural networks that organize emotion, sensation, and behavior. These networks are sculpted in reaction to real or imagined threats as the brain strives to predict and control danger.

Primitive neural mechanisms of fear and anxiety used in the avoidance of physical danger have been conserved through evolution and applied to the domains of subjective experience. Stress, fear, anxiety, and trauma are central to our experience because our brains have been shaped by its reactions to inner and outer signals of threat. We now turn our attention to the neurobiology and psychology of stress, and the positive and negative effects it has on the adapting brain and self.

11

The Anxious
and Fearful Brain

The behavior of all organisms is based on approaching what is life sustaining and avoiding what is dangerous. Throughout evolution, the success of rapid and accurate approach–avoidance decisions determines if an organism lives to reproduce and carry its genes forward to the next generation. Because vigilance and approach–avoidance reactions are a central mechanism of the process of natural selection, evolution favors anxious genes (Beck et al., 1979).

The neural circuitry involved in fear and anxiety, although biased toward the right hemisphere, involves both hemispheres and all levels of the triune brain. The most primitive subcortical fight-or-flight circuitry, shared with our reptilian ancestors, interacts with the most highly evolved association areas of the cerebral cortex. This results in the capacity to experience anxiety about everything from an unexpected tap on the shoulder on a dark night to an existential crisis. The connection between every kind of anxiety and the core biological mechanisms of physical survival supports the philosophical notion that all anxiety, at its core, may be the fear of death (Tillich, 1974).

It is clear that the processes of appraisal and rapid approach–avoidance behavior have been a central determinant of natural selection throughout evolution. As such, later evolving systems are based in and shaped by more primitive survival mechanisms. This is a key aspect of the organization of the hidden layers during evolution and their specific programming during an individual's lifetime. Some anxieties appear to be hard wired, specific to primates, and linked to both our present and past survival needs. Fear of spiders, snakes, open and closed spaces, and heights all harken back to the survival reflexes of our forest-dwelling ancestors.

The amygdala plays a central role in the expression and regulation of anxiety and fear. It has been conserved and expanded during evolution to accommodate increasingly complex cognitive, sensory, and emotional input into survival decisions. Its central role in appraisal and the triggering of the biochemical cascade of the fight-or-flight response leads it to be involved in networks of memory, affect regulation, and social relatedness. From an evolutionary perspective, our complex neural systems have all been sculpted to better serve the prime directive of survival.

Anxiety and fear are the conscious emotional aspects of the body's ongoing appraisal of what is dangerous and life threatening. They tell the body that it should be prepared to take action. Anxiety can be triggered by countless conscious or unconscious cues and has the power to shape our behaviors, thoughts, and feelings. At its most adaptive, anxiety encourages us to step back from the edge of a cliff, cross the street when unsavory characters are coming our way, and doublecheck to see if we signed our tax forms before we seal the envelope. At its least adaptive, it unconsciously steers us away from actions like taking important and appropriate risks, pushing ourselves to reach personal goals, or engaging in new and potentially beneficial behaviors.

The response to stress, or *general adaptation syndrome* (Selye, 1979), results in a multitude of biological and psychological changes designed to prepare the body for fight-or-flight situations. Energy is mobilized through increased cardiovascular and muscular tone, whereas digestion, growth, and immune responses are inhibited. As part of the stress response, a cascade of biochemical changes occur in the hypothalamus, pituitary, and adrenal glands (the HPA axis), as well as in the sympathetic nervous system. These biochemicals mediate the physical and psychological changes experienced during stress and crisis. Increased levels of glucocorticoids, epinephrine, and endogenous opioids are particularly relevant to a discussion of the psychological impact of stress and trauma, in that they alter cognition as well as affect the storage of traumatic and nontraumatic memory. We experience the effects of the general adaptation syndrome in situations such as automobile accidents, at crucial moments during sporting events, or when faced with public speaking. The dangers can be real, imagined, or experienced vicariously.

With the expansion of the cerebral cortex and the emergence of imagination, we have become capable of feeling anxious about potential outcomes and situations that can never exist. We can now worry about monsters living under our beds and the eventual expansion of the sun and incineration of the earth. Because our imaginal capabilities have allowed for the construction of the self, we can also become anxious about potential threats to our psychological survival. The expectation of rejection by another can result in social withdrawal; the fear of forgetting one's lines in a play can result in stage fright. Psychotherapists deal with a wide variety of anxiety disorders based in the fear of what can feel like social death. Systems of physical survival have been conserved in the evolution of consciousness and the ego, to be triggered when threats to these abstract constructions are activated.

Consciously experienced anxiety provides the opportunity to face and work through one's fears. The common wisdom of getting back on the horse that threw you is advice clearly aimed at preventing the use of avoidance as a way to control anxiety. Unfortunately, anxiety can be paired with all kinds of environmental cues and behaviors, as well as internal sensations, emotions, and thoughts. These pairings, stored in hidden neural layers, shape behavior outside of conscious awareness. Compounding the problem, the left-hemisphere interpreter provides a rationale supporting and reinforcing avoidance; "Its inhuman to ride horses!" "Who needs planes?" "Why go out when it is comfortable at home?" The avoidance of thoughts and feelings associated with feared stimuli both reflects and perpetuates a lack of integration among neural networks. Facing what is feared is a core component of all forms of psychotherapy.

We see this, for example, with adult women who were sexually or emotionally abused as children. These women often come to therapy with chronic and severe weight problems. They do well on diets until they begin to be noticed by men. Attracting attention is unconsciously associated in their hidden layers with the pain, fear, and shame of childhood relationships. These negative emotional reactions lead these women to return to behavioral patterns associated with an avoidance of such feelings. The act of eating is doubly reinforcing because it provides nurturance, while gaining back the weight serves to protect these women from the experiences that led to their negative emotional memories.

Thus, what started out as a straightforward survival-based alarm system, can also become a nuisance. This is another downside of the design compromises between speed and accuracy mentioned earlier (Mesulam, 1998). Evolution designed a brain that reacts quickly to a variety of subtle environmental cues. These same capabilities have negative consequences when applied to a complex and largely nonconscious psychological environment. An understanding of the neuroscience of anxiety and fear is helpful in both the conceptualization and treatment of most clinical disorders. In the following pages, we will explore some basic neuroscience research relevant to development, psychopathology, and psychotherapy. We will look at the two loops of fear circuitry outlined by Joseph LeDoux, the role of the amygdala in the appraisal and regulation of fear and anxiety proposed by Michael Davis, and Robert Sapolsky's work on the negative impact on the brain of long-term stress.

Fast and Slow Fear Networks

LeDoux (1994) demonstrated through his research that there are two interrelated yet separable fear circuits in laboratory animals. The conservation of these systems during evolution allows us to apply these findings to humans. The two systems (which for present purposes we will call *fast* and *slow*) each play a somewhat different role in the overall reaction to a feared stimulus or a dangerous situation. Besides being an accurate model for laboratory research, LeDoux's theory can be clinically useful for anxious and fearful clients by helping them to understand the neurobiological mechanisms of what they are experiencing.

The *fast system*, which is reflexive and acts immediately, sends information directly from the sense organs (eyes, ears, skin, nose, tongue) through the thalamus to the amygdala. The amygdala evaluates the sensory input and immediately translates it into bodily responses related to fight-or-flight reactions via its connections with the autonomic nervous systems. The thalamus may contribute to stimulus appraisal by containing crude representations of things often encountered in the environment, such as species-specific fears. These subcortical structures play an executive function in this rapid appraisal and response because the increased time it would take to include the cortex in these decisions might have too large a survival cost.

The *slow system* sends sensory information from the thalamus on to hippocampal and cortical circuits for further evaluation. This system is slower because it contains more synaptic connections and involves conscious processing. Cortical circuits of memory and executive processing examine the information more carefully, compare it to memories of other similar situations, and make voluntary decisions concerning how to proceed. The hippocampus aids the cortex by contextualizing the particular situation in time and space. This slow system in humans—with its apex in the orbitofrontal cortex—has the additional task of making sense of the behavioral and visceral reaction already set into motion by the fast systems. In this way, our conscious executive functions discover the decisions that have already been made by our unconscious executives. Figure 11.1 depicts the neural circuits of the fast and slow fear networks.

This dual circuitry helps us to understand why we often react to things before thinking and then wonder why we acted so strongly (and why we have to apologize for things we knew better than to do).

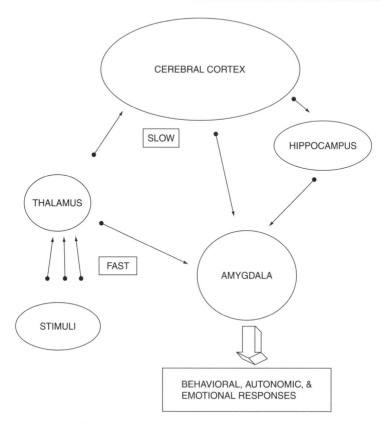

Figure 11.1   Fast and slow fear circuits

A depiction of the two pathways of information to the amygdala—one directly from the thalamus and the other through the cortex and hippocampus (adapted from LeDoux, J. Emotion, memory, and the brain. Copyright © 1994 by Scientific American, Inc. All rights reserved).

The fast fear network is at the center of the hidden layers of processing, shaping their connections and determining our behavior. In therapy, we usually attempt to utilize the conscious linguistic structures of the slow circuit to inhibit and modify the reflexes and emotional appraisals of the fast circuit. Coupled with relaxation techniques and psychoeducation, exposure to a feared stimulus often serves to recondition fast circuits and enhance the regulatory input of the slow cortical circuits. Put another way, cognitive and behavioral interventions, when successful, increase the integration of the fast and slow circuits so that the fast circuit can respond in more adaptive ways.

There are many examples of these two systems in action. I walked into the basement one day to look for a tool when, out of the corner of my eye, I saw a small brown shape near my foot. There are plenty of little critters in my neighborhood and they often crawl, burrow, or fly into my house. My heart skipped a beat and I immediately jumped back. My heart rate increased, my eyes widened, and I became tense, ready to act. Moving backward, I oriented toward the brown shape, saw that it looked more like a small piece of wood than a rodent, and began to relax. After a few seconds, my heart rate and level of arousal were back to normal; the potential danger had passed.

Analyzing this experience on the basis of the two systems, my peripheral vision saw the shape and my amygdala appraised it in an overgeneralized fashion to be a threat. My amygdala activated a variety of sympathetic responses including startle, increased respiration, and avoidance. In the split second while my body was reacting, I reflexively oriented my head toward the shape, which brought it to the fovea of my retina, providing my hippocampus and cortex with more detailed visual information; they then appraised the shape differently (and more accurately) than did my skiddish amygdala. I suppose that a species-specific fear accounts for such a strong reaction to an animal weighing just a few ounces. This example, trivial as it may be, leads to a more serious application of LeDoux's theory to interpersonal relationships.

As the core of the neural networks of our social brain, the amygdala organizes the appraisals of what we have learned from our history of interpersonal relationships. In interpersonal situations, our amygdala reflexively and unconsciously appraises others in the context of our past experiences. From moment to moment, the hidden layers of our fast systems (organized by past learning) shape the nature of our present experience. This is one mechanism by which our early social learning and attachment shape our experiences. In this way, our learning history creates the present. Put another way, by the time we become conscious of others, our brain has already organized ways to think about them. In the case of prejudice, skin color, gender, and other salient attributes create a set of presuppositions on which we unconsciously base our interpretations of other people. At the opposite extreme, love at first sight is the triggering of past emotional memories and projecting them onto another person, resulting in a sort of positive prejudice.

The Amygdala's Role in Anxiety and Fear

Although we are genetically programmed to become anxious about things like snakes or abandonment, fear can be learned by pairing any thought, feeling, action, or sensation with a noxious stimulus such as electric shock or public shame. Learning to be anxious can occur at conscious and unconscious levels related to both internal and external stimuli. Like the hippocampus, the lateral areas of the amygdala are capable of long-term potentiation (LTP) involved in reinforcing connections among neurons. Remember that LTP is the process through which the association among neurons becomes strengthened and learning is established. The amygdala can learn, throughout life, to pair any stimulus with anxiety or fear.

There is an abundance of research supporting the amygdala's role in the experience of fear. Individuals with panic disorder have increased neural activity in the right temporal lobe and amygdala (Reiman et al., 1989). Electrical stimulation of the amygdala's central nucleus results in the experience of anxiety and fear, whereas destruction of the amygdala will eliminate anxiety reactions altogether (Carvey, 1998). In fact, the destruction of the amygdala in animals results in an inability to acquire a conditioned fear response.

As we saw earlier in our discussion of memory, the hippocampus and amygdala organize interacting but dissociable systems of memory. Bechara and colleagues (1995) reported that a patient with bilateral amygdala (left and right) damage was unable to acquire a conditioned autonomic response to sensory stimuli. The patient was, however, able to consciously remember the conditioning situation because his hippocampi were still intact. Another patient with bilateral damage to the hippocampus showed no conscious memory for the conditioning situation but did acquire autonomic and behavioral conditioning. The authors concluded that the amygdala is "indispensable" for coupling emotional conditioning with sensory information (Bechara et al., 1995).

The neural projections from the amygdala to numerous anatomical targets cause the multiple physical expressions of anxiety, fear, and panic. Projections from the amygdala to the lateral hypothalamus result in sympathetic activation responsible for increased heart rate and blood pressure. The amygdala's stimulation of the trigeminal facial motor nerve even causes the facial expressions of fear (Davis, 1992). The amygdala is also essential in reading the fearful facial expressions of others (Baird et al., 1999). As you can see from Figure 11.2, the amygdala is well connected, making the fear response a powerful whole-body experience.

The triggering of these physiological and emotional reactions in the absence of real danger results in *panic attacks*. People suffering panic attacks often go to emergency rooms thinking they are having a heart attack. The triggering of the autonomic nervous system by the amygdala causes a racing heart, sweating, and other physiological symptoms as the body prepares for fight-or-flight. Psychologically, victims report a sense of impending doom, feelings of unreality, and the thought that they must be going crazy because they are feeling so terrified in the absence of any specific danger. Panic attacks are often triggered by stress or other conflicts in the sufferer's life, but he or she seldom makes the connection between these events and the panic attacks. The associations are contained within hidden neural layers. They are experienced as "coming out of the blue," leaving victims to struggle to comprehend what is happening and why.

The amygdala's tendency toward generalization results in the triggering of panic by an increasing number of internal and external

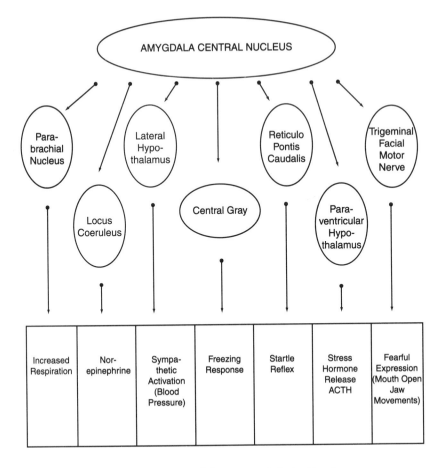

Figure 11.2 Some targets of the amygdala in the fear response

Some of the many anatomical targets of the amygdala in the fear response, and their biological and behavioral contributions.

cues (Douglas & Pribram, 1966). Because panic attacks are experienced as unpredictable and life threatening, they result in an increasing limitation of activities. *Agoraphobia,* or fear of open spaces, develops as victims of panic attacks associate fear with an increasing number and variety of situations. Hoping to avoid these attacks, sufferers restrict their activities to the point where they eventually become housebound. The behavior of these individuals become shaped by their fear and they gradually come to avoid most of life.

The development and connectivity of the amygdala have many implications for both early child development and psychotherapy. Without the inhibitory impact of the later-developing hippocampal–cortical networks, early fear experiences are likely to be overwhelming full-body experiences. Because the amygdala is operational at birth, the experience of fear may be the strongest early emotion. Part of the power of early emotional learning may be a function of the intensity of these uninhibited and unregulated negative affects in shaping early neural infrastructure. The infant is very dependent on caretakers to modulate these powerful experiences. Because the networks of amygdala-mediated memory are dissociable from those of the later-developing hippocampal systems, early memory and overwhelming traumatic memory from later in life can be stored without cortical involvement or control. They will not be consciously remembered, but instead will emerge as intuitive knowledge.

The Locus Coeruleus and Norepinephrine

One important projection from the amygdala connects it with the locus coeruleus (LC). The LC is a small structure with extensive projections throughout the brainstem, midbrain, and cerebral cortex. It is, in fact, connected with a greater variety of brain areas than is any other portion of the brain so far discovered (Aston-Jones, Valentino, VanBockstaele, & Meyerson, 1994). The LC is the brain's primary generator of norepinephrine (NE), which drives the activity of the sympathetic branch of the autonomic nervous system responsible for the fight-or flight response. One effect of NE is to enhance the firing of cells that are highly relevant based on past learning (past fear responses), while inhibiting cells involved in baseline activities.

This means that stimulation of the LC prepares us for danger by activating circuits involved in dealing with stress. We become alert and vigilant, scan for danger, and maintain a posture of tense readiness. Activation of the LC during trauma heightens memory for danger; it creates a sort of "print now" command for amygdala memory circuits (Livingston, 1967). *Print now* refers to a traumatic memory imprinted because of the biochemical activation that occurs during stress. The pathways containing these traumatic memories become hyperpotentiated, meaning that they are more easily triggered by less severe subsequent stressors. During times of lowered hippocampal–cortical involvement (e.g., intoxication or near-sleep states), traumatic memories may be triggered. Translated into human and clinical terms, this means that surges of NE during periods of safety may result in past traumatic associations (anxiety, startle, visual images, etc.) being brought to awareness and overshadowing contemporary experiences.

Stimulating the LC in animals results in a disruption of ongoing behavior and triggering of an orienting reflex (like the one I had to the small piece of wood). This is seen in patients with posttraumatic stress disorder who respond to trauma-related cues decades after their experience. LC activity in primates results in a high degree of vigilance while interrupting sleep, grooming, and eating. Through a series of connections, the central nucleus of the amygdala stimulates the LC, which, in turn, is thought to be a major control area of the sympathetic nervous system (Aston-Jones et al., 1994). An understanding of the biochemistry and functioning of the LC is an important component of any theory of the cause of anxiety disorders (Svensson, 1987).

The Recovery of Fears and Phobias Under Stress

Jacobs and Nadel (1985) proposed the existence of two systems of learning and memory involved in fears and phobias. These two systems parallel LeDoux's model of the fast and slow fear circuitry. The *taxon system* (fast system or amygdaloid system) is responsible for the acquisition of skills and rules, and the conditioning of stimulus-response connections. This system is context free, meaning that it contains no information about the location, time, or perspective from which learning took place. Taxon learning generalizes broadly and is primarily nonconscious. This is the system in which early learning of fear, safety, and attachment is organized and stored. The taxon system is represented in implicit and procedural memory.

The *locale system*—with the hippocampus and the cortex at its core—is responsible for cognitive maps necessary for external context, mental representations, and the pairing of memories with the situations in which they were learned. The development of the locale memory system parallels that of hippocampal–cortical circuits. Thus, although there is a great deal of learning during infancy (especially in the networks of the fearful and social brains), there is no source attribution or autobiographical narrative.

For example, a child may develop a general wariness for the world because of his or her mother's fearful look when strangers approach but will not recognize the source of his or her own apprehension in these situations later in life. We enter middle childhood with neural networks programmed by early learning experienced as basic emotional givens. Under nontraumatic conditions in adults, learning involves the integration of taxon and locale systems. This integration connects sensory-motor and emotional memories to contextualized, semantic, autobiographical components of memory. For children and traumatized adults, the taxon system may function independently, resulting in an adaptive dissociation among various systems of memory and conscious awareness.

Jacobs and Nadel (1985) contended that stress both changes the inner biological environment activating the taxon system and suppresses the inhibitory effects of the locale system. These changes result in the emergence of earlier fears or frightening experiences that had been successfully inhibited. This theory certainly parallels the voluminous research demonstrating the contribution of stress to the emergence or worsening of psychiatric and physical disorders. Jacobs and Nadel suggested that stress impairs or downgrades the functioning of the locale system, causing us to fall back on the more primitive organization of taxon (amygdaloid) systems. From a psychoanalytic perspective, this process may be understood as regression to more primitive defense mechanisms under stress. This process also parallels the return of neonatal reflexes (the cortical release signs discussed in chap. 4) in patients with Alzheimer's disease or other forms of brain damage.

Despite the apparent extinction of a phobia or fear, the original memory is maintained and can become reactivated under stress. This neural explanation addresses the Freudian notion of *symptom substitution*, in which one fear or source of anxiety may be replaced by another after successful treatment of the first. In other words, a new trigger reactivates the still intact underlying neural circuitry. Thus, as Jacobs and Nadel suggested, the therapist may not only need to generate stress as a part of treatment (to activate and have access to these circuits) but also continue treatment well after behavioral manifestations are eliminated. The inclusion of stress management training is also supported by this hypothesis. If the overall level of stress can be decreased, the likelihood of reactivation of primitive fear circuitry also decreases.

We are all guided by anxiety and fear, most of it unconscious and subclinical. Successful psychotherapy for anxiety, fears, and phobias has been shaped by the necessity of integrating fast and slow circuits, taxon and locale systems, and affect and cognition. Educating patients about panic leads to increased participation of the cortex during anxiety states. *Stress inoculation*, or the cognitive preparation for future stress, leads to an increasing opportunity for descending inhibition of the amygdaloid circuits by the hippocampal–cortical networks. Exposure, response prevention, and relaxation training result in the counterconditioning of unconscious associations stored in amygdaloid memory systems. This model of memory applies to all clinical situations, regardless of the presence of panic or anxiety disorders.

Drowning in a Sea of Doom

Tina's cardiologist suggested that she see a psychotherapist after a third visit to the emergency room. Each time, seemingly out of nowhere, Tina would become breathless and lightheaded; her heart would race until she felt as if it were going to burst from her chest. Convinced she was having a heart attack, Tina would call for the paramedics. As she waited for the ambulance, Tina reported feeling like she was drowning in "sea of doom." She would imagine her teenaged children growing up without her, and have vivid memories of her own mother's death when she was a child. These feelings and images—together with the fear of death—would make her even more frightened. She told me that waiting for the ambulance felt like "an eternity."

Tina, who was actually in excellent health, was repeatedly told she was having panic attacks. It took three of these embarrassing episodes to convince her to seek therapy. She came to my office feeling defeated and very frightened; she felt like she was losing a lifelong battle to stay in control. During our first session, I learned that Tina had a difficult childhood, including abandonment by her father, prolonged financial difficulties, and the death of her mother when Tina was 15. She finished high school while living with an aunt, put herself through college, and became a successful real estate agent. A four-year marriage had left her with two children, now in their teens, to raise on her own. Tina's identity was that of a survivor and hard worker who did not allow herself to depend on others. The panic attacks had shaken her self-confidence and created a fear of returning to the chaos, pain, and dependency of her childhood. She had hoped for a medical explanation to avoid having to revisit many difficult memories.

I began treatment by educating Tina about her body's fear response and why it felt to her like she was having a heart attack. Her racing heart, lightheadedness, rapid breathing, and sense of danger were the result of the amygdala's multiple signals to the brainstem to prepare to fight or run. Gaining conscious regulation of her amygdala's alarm circuitry was the first order of business. We discussed strategies to ward off these attacks by slowing her breathing and employing relaxation techniques. During sessions, I would have Tina make herself anxious and then assist her in calming down. This provided her with a sense of mastery in regulating amygdala activation.

Understanding what was happening in her body and knowing that her life was not in danger, relieved some of her fear.

The second phase of treatment focused on addressing the long-standing lifestyle issues that kept her in a chronic state of heightened agitation. We examined the amount of responsibilities she carried and her lack of relaxation and recreation. Tina's financial fears led her to overbook her work schedule to the point of exhaustion. I learned that Tina constantly criss-crossed the Los Angeles freeway system, travelling between 30,000 and 40,000 miles each year. Between showing homes and shuttling her children from school to their various activities, we calculated that she was behind the wheel up to six hours a day, usually behind schedule. She began to understand the panic attacks as her body's way of telling her to make some changes and reduce her level of stress. Regular exercise, decreasing her sales territory, and making alternative arrangements for some of her children's transportation needs proved to be the most helpful solutions in these areas.

As these interventions became more routine, we explored the impact of her childhood experiences on both her self-image and lifestyle. Tina harbored the fear that she would die like her mother, leaving her children alone in the world. She tried to do everything she could for them, and save all the money they would need to go to college, all the time thinking that she would not be around for long. Her financial planning was detailed and over the years she had followed through with it almost to the letter. The problem was that it had originally been created for two incomes; now she was doing it on her own. She came to see that her fear of death might become a self-fulfilling prophecy. Tina also came to realize that her heart was still broken over her mother's death, and that she had never allowed herself to grieve her loss. She had been in a chronic state of stress since her mother's death, and grief was a luxury she had felt she could not afford.

The Hippocampus, Glucocorticoids, and Stress

The human brain is well equipped to use anxiety to shape new learning and survive brief periods of stress without negative results. Most traumatic experiences can be coped with and resolved through the help of caring and empathic others in the natural course of life. Individuals come to therapy when anxiety and stress have been chronic or have spiraled out of control. Patients have often experienced years—or even a lifetime—of anxiety, stress, and repeated trauma. The adaptation to these chronic dysregulated states has resulted in a disorganization of their experience. Thought of in another way, the experience of these patients' lives has organized around stress and trauma. Their views of themselves and the world, their personalities and relationships, and the architecture of their brains all reflect their coping and adaptation.

In a series of studies, Robert Sapolsky explored the relationship between stress and the hippocampus. His research is particularly important because it may help explain some of the negative lifetime effects of childhood trauma. Working with rats and vervet monkeys, Sapolsky and his colleagues demonstrated that stress results in what appears to be permanent hippocampal damage and functional impairment (Sapolsky, 1990; Sapolsky, Uno, Robert, & Finch, 1990). Remember that the hippocampus is involved in the consolidation and storage of explicit memory, reality testing, and inhibition of the amygdala. Studies of adults with PTSD related to combat exposure and childhood abuse show their hippocampi to be significantly smaller than those of comparison patients without PTSD (Bremner, Southwick, Johnson, Yehuda, & Charney, 1993; Bremner et al., 1995; 1997).

The biological link between prolonged stress and hippocampal damage appears to be mediated via glucocorticoids. *Glucocorticoids* (GC) are hormones secreted by the adrenal gland as part of the body's stress response. They participate in the fight-or-flight response of the sympathetic nervous system. Glucocorticoids promote the break down of complex compounds into basic fatty and amino acids so that they can be used for immediate energy. Perhaps most damaging to long-term growth are GCs' role in disrupting the immune and inflammatory responses, as well as cellular growth and reproduction. Long-term biological well-being is sacrificed for immediate survival.

The emergency reaction of the fight-or-flight response is akin to throwing everything on a ship overboard to avoid sinking, or burning the furniture in winter to avoid freezing to death. The focus on immediate survival supersedes all medium- and long-term plans and goals. These biological processes need to be reversed as soon as possible after the crisis has passed to allow the body to recover and return to the job of repair and long-term maintenance. It is apparent that this system was designed to cope with the risks involved with brief periods of stress in emergency situations; it was not designed to be maintained for weeks or years at a time.

The hippocampus, rich in GC receptors, has a negative feedback role with the adrenal gland to inhibit GC production. If the hippocampus detects too many GCs, it sends a message (via the hypothalamus or the pituitary) to the adrenal gland to slow down GC production (Sapolsky, Krey, & McEwen, 1984). Chronic stress results in prolonged high levels of GCs in the bloodstream, possibly resulting in decreased hippocampal volume and changes in the structure of neural dendrites (Woolley, Gould, & McEwen, 1990). It is hypothesized that higher levels of stress hormones increase the vulnerability of the hippocampus to a number of potential metabolic insults (Sapolsky, 1985). At this point it is unclear if this reflects permanent damage to the hippocampus or a reversible inhibition of the growth of new neurons. In either case, less hippocampal mass means fewer GC receptors which, in turn, means less negative feedback to the adrenal gland. Loss of volume in the hippocampus appears to be related to long-term, cumulative GC exposure (Sapolsky et al., 1990).

Rats and humans differ in a number of ways besides whisker length. The increased size of the human brain and its additional processing capacity make it possible for us to worry about many more dangers than those that preoccupy rats. The expansion of our brains has allowed for us to create complex situations such as traffic jams and overburdened schedules, generating ever-increasing levels of stress. Stress that is experienced as inescapable tends to have a greater negative impact. Ironically, hippocampal damage—which can result in memory impairment, affect dysregulation, and decreased reality testing—makes life even more difficult, creating even higher levels of stress.

Research suggests that prolonged childhood stress can have life-long effects on functioning related to hippocampal damage, immunological suppression, and other stress-related impairments. High base levels of glucocorticoids may be a primary reason why chronically stressed individuals have higher rates of physical illness. Although we like to think of childhood as a time of innocence and play, many children grow up in a state of constant distress. Parental physical or mental illness, community violence, poverty, and many other factors can result in this unfortunate situation.

Stress and Maternal Care

A number of studies suggest that the nature and amount of early maternal care and handling may have a strong influence on the establishment of hippocampal GC receptor density, as well as other stress modulating functions in adulthood (Meaney et al., 1989; Plotsky & Meaney, 1993). If early care can stimulate the creation of more GC receptors in the hippocampus, this will allow the hippocampus to downregulate the amount of GCs in reaction to stress; this results in a decreased reaction to subsequent stress and greater protection of the hippocampus. If this is the case, it would serve as a mediating biochemical factor in the creation of secure attachment, decreased reaction to future stress, and increased physical and psychological health.

Research has shown that rats handled during infancy exhibit more open field activity (Levine, Haltmeyer, Karas, & Denenberg, 1967), increased gene expression, and higher concentrations of GC receptors on their hippocampi than do nonhandled controls (Meaney et al., 1989, 2000). The amount of licking and grooming behavior provided to rat pups in the first 10 days of life correlated with decreased biological responses to acute stress, greater GC feedback sensitivity (Liu et al., 1997), and many other positive changes in the complex reactions of the hypothalamic-pituitary-adrenal axis to stress (Jacobson & Sapolsky, 1991; Viau, Sharma, Plotsky, & Meaney, 1993). These changes remained well into the rats' adult lives, suggesting that the establishment of these early physiological setpoints may be stable over a lifetime. Nonhandled rats developed both hippocampal cell loss and deficits of their spatial memory as they aged. This means that they were not as good at maze running, which, in the wild, would translate into less food and greater danger (Sapolsky, 1990). These effects of early stress, found to be preventable by adrenalectomy in middle-aged rats, support the theory that these negative changes are mediated via high levels of GCS.

Summary

The fearful brain has two interconnected systems responsible for different aspects of fear processing. The fast system—with the amygdala at its core—makes rapid, reflexive, and unconscious decisions to provide for immediate survival. This system develops first and organizes learning related to attachment and affect-regulation. Also called the taxon system, the fast system involves sensory-motor and affective memories typical of early life and later traumatic memories. The slow system, based in hippocampal–ortical networks, contextualizes and makes conscious what is being processed. The slow system's job is to regulate the activity of the amygdala by modulating its output based on a more complex appraisal of potentially dangerous situations. This slow locale system contextualizes experience in time and space, and supports conscious awareness via cortical connectivity.

These two systems, reflecting both top-down and left–right circuits, can become dissociated during prolonged periods of stress or trauma. In psychotherapy, we attempt to activate both fast and slow circuits, taxon and locale systems, and implicit and explicit forms of memory to inform and educate each about the other. When emotional taxon networks are inhibited, we use techniques to trigger them so that they can be activated and integrated with slow locale circuits. When these same networks are out of control, we recruit locale circuits to contextualize them in time and space and allow them to be tamed by the descending, inhibitory capabilities of cortical processes. The overall goal is the activation and integration of both systems.

Early trauma results in both hippocampal impairment and long-term psychological difficulties. Hippocampal impairment decreases its ability to inhibit the emotions triggered by amygdaloid memory systems; deficits in reality testing and short-term memory will make the process of integration more difficult. Longer periods of relationship building and pragmatic interventions focused on stress reduction and the development of coping skills may be necessary prerequisites for successful long-term therapy. Patients who have suffered metabolic disruptions, head trauma, seizures, or periods of anoxia may have hippocampal compromise (Lombroso & Sapolsky, 1998). Mountain climbers, divers, or individuals with heart disease may suffer prolonged periods of oxygen deprivation and sustain hippocampal damage (Regard, Oelz, Brugger, & Landis, 1989). High-dose GC administration for autoimmune diseases may also result in hippocampal and other neural damage (Sapolsky, 1996). All of these factors must be kept in mind when gathering medical and psychosocial information.

Impairment of the hippocampus from early and chronic stress may make the therapeutic process more difficult for many clients. For example, Stein and his colleagues (Stein, Koverla, Hanna, Torchia, & McClarty, 1997) found that adult women who had experienced childhood abuse had significantly reduced left hippocampal volume. They also found that the amount of reduction was significantly correlated with increased dissociative symptoms. This relationship suggests that the left hippocampus may play a role in the memory functions related to the integration of memories into a cohesive narrative (Stein et al., 1997). The hippocampus is also thought to be involved in the flexible incorporation of new information into existing structures of memory (Eichenbaum, 1992). If this is the case, early abuse may not only correlate with the lack of assistance of caretakers in the co-construction of coherent narratives about the self, it may also result in damage to neural structures required to organize cohesive narratives and the story of the self that will persist into adult life.

12

The Impact of Trauma on the Brain

For each of us there is a point at which anxiety and fear cross the line into trauma. Trauma can cause severe disturbances in the integration of cognitive and emotional processing. The neurobiological reactions to these experiences appear to lie on a continuum of intensity. The earlier, more severe, and more prolonged the trauma, the more negative and far reaching the effects (De Bellis, Baum, Birnmaher, Keshavan, Eccard, Boring, et al., 1999; De Bellis, Keshavan, Clark, Casey, Giedd, Boring, et al., 1999). Unresolved and unintegrated trauma may result in a disorder known as *posttraumatic stress disorder* (PTSD). PTSD is comprised of a set of symptoms that reflect the physiological dysregulation and lack of integration of multiple networks of implicit and explicit memory (Siegel, 1999).

We have all heard the sayings "What doesn't kill you makes you stronger" and "Time heals all wounds." These bits of common wisdom conjure up pictures of difficult and traumatic experiences that, once overcome, result in greater levels of physical and emotional well-being. Although trials and tribulations can certainly build character, they can also create permanent biological, neurological, and psychological compromise. Trauma produces a wide variety of homeostatic dysregulations that interfere with all realms of personal and interpersonal functioning (Perry, Pollard, Blakley, Baker, & Vigilante, 1995). Support for the negative impact of trauma comes from research that has shown that cumulative lifetime trauma increases the likelihood of developing PTSD (Yehuda et al., 1995). A history of previous assaults also increases the chances of developing PTSD following rape (Resnick, Yehuda, Pitman, & Foy, 1995). Likewise, childhood abuse increases the chances of developing PTSD after adult combat exposure (Bremner, Southwick, Johnson, Yehuda, & Charney, 1993). It has also been shown that severe stress reactions during combat make subsequent negative reactions to mild and moderate stress more likely (Solomon, 1990).

The effects of early and severe trauma are widespread, devastating, and difficult to treat. Because of the importance of a context of safety and bonding in the early construction of the brain, childhood trauma compromises core neural networks. It stands to reason that the most devastating types of trauma are those that occur at the hands of caretakers. Physical and sexual abuse by parents not only traumatizes children, but also deprives them of healing interactions. The wide range of effects involved in the adaptation to early unresolved trauma results in the phenomena of *complex posttraumatic stress disorder.*

Trauma is biochemically encoded in the brain in a variety of ways, including changes in the availability and effects of neurotransmitters and neuromodulators. Neuroanatomic encoding occurs through changes in structures like the hippocampus, and in the coordination and integration of neural network functioning. These changes in neurobiological mechanisms are reflected in the victim's physiological, psychological, and interpersonal experiences (see, e.g., Carroll, Rueger, Foy, & Donahoe, 1985). Deficits in psychological and interpersonal functioning then create additional stress which further compromises neurobiological structures. In this way, adaptation to trauma, especially early in life, becomes a "state of mind, brain, and body" around which all subsequent experience organizes.

Expanding the Definition of Trauma

Trauma is not limited to surviving life-threatening experiences (as the standard diagnostic manual appears to suggest; American Psychiatric Association, 2000). For a young child, trauma may be experienced in the form of separation from parents, looking into the eyes of a depressed mother, or being in a household with a high level of marital tension (Cogill, Caplan, Alexandra, Robson, & Kumar, 1986). For an adolescent, chronic stress and trauma may come from the incessant teasing of peers or taking care of the needs of an alcoholic parent. For an adult, chronic loneliness, the loss of a pet, or a constant sense of shame or failure may have the same impact. Although it is impossible to understand the nature of prenatal and infant experience, we can assume that the infant is stressed well before the brain develops the capacity for consciousness. While we can't ask if it is stressed, we can assess whether an infant's body is experiencing biochemical changes indicative of a stress response (Gunnar, 1992, 1998).

There is a distinct possibility that stress is possible even before birth; an unborn child may become stressed as a result of the shared biological environment with its mother. Studies suggest that maternal stress is associated with their children's lower birthweight, irritability, hyperactivity, and learning disabilities (Zuckerman, Bauchner, Parker, & Cabral, 1990). Rats born to stressed mothers show more clinging to the mother, less locomotion, and decreased environmental exploration (Schneider, 1992). Prenatal stress may also result in permanent alterations in dopamine activity and cerebral lateralization, making offspring more susceptible to both anxiety and limiting their functioning into adulthood (Field et al., 1988). Children of Holocaust survivors have an increased prevalence of PTSD despite similar rates of exposure to traumatic events when compared to children of non-Holocaust survivors. This suggests that they experienced a transferred vulnerability through interactions with their traumatized parents (Yehuda, 1999).

Maternal depression may actually serve as a highly stressful or traumatic experience for infants and children. Tiffany Field and her colleagues found that infants whose mothers were depressed during the infant's first year of life demonstrate biochemical, physiological, and behavioral dysregulation. These children show more neurophysiological and behavioral signs of stress and depression, including greater activation in their right frontal lobes, higher levels of norepinephrine, lower vagal tone, and higher heart rates and cortisol levels (Field, 1997; Field et al., 1988). These infants tend to develop behaviors and biological processes that mirror their depressed mothers. Just like their depressed mothers, such infants engage less in interactive behaviors (e.g., orienting toward and gazing at others) that are so vitally important for healthy development. Infants of depressed mothers behave this way even with other adults, making it more difficult for them to successfully interact with nondepressed others (Field et al., 1988).

In another study, it was found that depressed mothers were angry at their infants more of the time and were more likely to poke at them, disengage from them, and spend less time in "matched states" (Field, Healy, Goldstein, & Guthertz, 1990). These results suggest that infants are modeling on their mother's behavior, exhibiting resonance with their depressed states, and reacting to the negative behaviors directed toward them. Based on biological, physiological, and behavioral data, having a depressed mother is a stressful and potentially traumatic experience for an infant. Fortunately, it has been shown that interventions with depressed mothers and their infants have had positive results. For example, remission of maternal depression and teaching mothers to massage their infants on a regular basis resulted in improvement of the infants' symptoms (Field, 1997).

We would not consider these infants traumatized in the usual sense, and often think of infants as extremely resilient. On a biological level, however, the experience of having a depressed mother may result in the same changes as would occur in an adult exposed to a life-threatening situation. After all, infants' lives—and the building of their brains—depend on positive interactions with their parents. The loss of maternal presence, engagement, and vitality may all be experienced (at a biological level) as life threatening to an infant.

Neurotransmitter and Hormonal Changes

As we saw in chapter 11, states of acute stress result in predictable patterns of biochemical changes. There are increases in the levels of norepinephrine, dopamine, endogenous opioids, and glucocorticoids, and a decrease in serotonin. When stress is prolonged or chronic, changes occur in the baseline production, availability, and homeostatic regulation of these neurochemicals. These changes result in long-term behavioral and psychological alterations. Each of these substances serves a different purpose in the stress response and contributes in different ways to the long-term impact of PTSD.

As we have seen, increased levels of norepinephrine (NE) prepare us for fight-or-flight readiness and reinforce the biological encoding of traumatic memory. Higher levels of NE correlate with an increase in the experience of anxiety, arousal, and irritability. Heightened long-term activation of NE results in an increase in the level of tension and a heightened or unmodulated startle response (Butler et al., 1990; Ornitz & Pynoos, 1989). Besides being stronger, the startle response is also more resistant to habituation in response to subsequent milder and novel stressors (Nisenbaum, Zigmond, Sved, & Abercrombie, 1991; Petty, Chae, Kramer, Jordan, & Wilson, 1994; van der Kolk, 1994). Consistent startle experiences also enhance the victim's impression of the world as a dangerous and unsettling place. This is a good example of a feedback loop between physiological and psychological processes. An increased level of dopamine (activating the frontal cortex) correlates with hypervigilance, paranoia, and perceptual distortions when under stress. Symptoms of social withdrawal and the avoidance of new and potentially dangerous stimuli (neophobia) are shaped by the anxiety of these biochemical changes.

Lower levels of serotonin have been found in traumatized humans and in animals after being subjected to inescapable shock (Anisman, 1978; Usdin, Kvetnansky, & Kopin, 1976). Chronically low levels of serotonin are correlated with higher levels of irritability, depression, aggression, arousal, and violence (Coccaro, Siever, Klar, & Maurer, 1989). Prisoners convicted of violent crimes have lower serotonin levels when compared to criminals convicted of nonviolent crimes.

Endogenous opioids, which relieve pain in fight-or-flight situations, can have a profound effect on reality testing and memory processing when released in response to a variety of emotional situations unrelated to danger. Higher opioid levels result not only in analgesia, but also in emotional blunting and difficulties with reality testing. Most likely, they are also involved with dissociative reactions and the experience of depersonalization and derealization, both of which provide an experience of distance from the traumatized body (Shilony & Grossman, 1993). Opioids are also related to self-harm in adults abused as children (van der Kolk, 1994), a topic we will soon address.

As we have seen, high levels of glucocorticoids have a catabolic effect on the nervous system and are thought to be responsible for decreased volume of the hippocampus (Wantanabe, Gould, & McEwen, 1992) and related memory deficits (Bremner, Scott, Delaney, Southwick, Mason, Johnson, et al., 1993; Nelson & Carver, 1998). Patients with PTSD related to childhood physical and sexual abuse have been shown to have hippocampi that are 12% smaller than those of comparison subjects (Bremner et al., 1997). Another study showed that right hippocampi were 8% smaller in patients with combat-related PTSD. Glucocorticoids sacrifice long-term conservation and homeostasis for short-term survival. Chronically high levels have negative effects on brain structures and the immune system. Traumatized individuals thus have higher rates of physical illness, which enhances their experience of being fragile and vulnerable individuals.

These biochemical and neuroanatomical changes are paralleled by such symptomatology as emotional dyscontrol, social withdrawal, and lower levels of adaptive functioning. Together, these and other negative effects of trauma result in a person whose functioning is compromised in some or all areas of life. The impact of trauma depends on a complex interaction of the physical and psychological stages of development during which it occurs, the length and degree of the trauma, and the presence of vulnerabilities or past traumas. The impact of a wide variety of traumatic experiences is woven into the structure of personality, often making it difficult to identify and treat.

The Symptoms of Posttraumatic Stress Disorder

Trauma results in a variety of psychological and physiological processes reflecting the reaction of the mind and body to threat. The pattern of reaction to trauma is predictable and connected to a variety of well-understood biological processes. Reaction to trauma tends to gradually diminish within a context of resolving the traumatic situation, gathering support from others, and having the ability to talk through the experience; these allow for regaining a sense of psychological control and biological homeostasis. An awareness of the importance of these healing processes has led to the development and testing of interventions made at different intervals following traumatic situations (Mitchell & Everly, 1993).

Talking through the traumatic experience in the context of supportive others creates the neurobiological conditions for the reestablishment of neural coherence. The co-construction of narratives drives the integration of cognition, affect, sensation, and behaviors. These are the very channels that can stay dissociated when early trauma, such as child sexual abuse, is never discussed or processed. The suffering of Holocaust survivors and combat veterans is often exacerbated by the psychological and political dynamics that encouraged them to remain silent about their horrifying experiences. Co-constructed narratives in an emotionally supportive environment can provide the necessary matrix for the psychological and neurobiological integration required to avoid dissociative reactions.

When the trauma is severe, prolonged, or happens to a vulnerable individual, PTSD can develop. PTSD is caused by the loss of the regulation of the neurobiological processes dedicated to the appraisal and response to threat. There are three main symptom clusters in PTSD: hyperarousal, intrusion, and avoidance. These three groups of symptoms reflect the dysregulation of the central nervous system in response to unintegrated stress. Put another way, these symptoms demonstrate the loss of integration among neural networks controlling cognition, sensation, affect, and behavior.

Hyperarousal reflects a stress induced dysregulation of the amygdala and autonomic nervous system, resulting in an exaggerated startle reflex, agitation, anxiety, and irritability. That jumpy feeling we get when we drink too much caffeine gives us a taste for this experience. Chronic hyperarousal leads one to experience the world as a more dangerous and hostile place. Constant or uncontrollable agitation makes us less desirable as companions and thus, less able to benefit from the companionship of others.

Intrusions occur when traumatic experiences break into consciousness and are experienced as happening in the present. These may manifest in flashbacks resulting in a veteran hitting the ground in response to a car backfiring, or a rape victim having a panic attack while making love to her husband. These are activations of subcortical systems cued by stimuli reminiscent of the initial trauma. You may remember from the chapters on memory and fear that the amygdala both controls this activation and tends to generalize from the initial stimuli to a wide variety of cues. There is no sense of distance from the trauma in time or place, because the cortico–hippocampal networks have not been able to contextualize the somatic, sensory, and emotional memories within networks of autobiographical memory.

Avoidance is the attempt to defend against dangers by limiting contact with the world, withdrawing from others, and narrowing the range of thoughts and feelings. Avoidance can take the form of denial and repression, and, in more extreme instances, dissociation and amnesia. The power of avoidance was highlighted by the research of Williams (1994), who found that 38% of adult women who had suffered documented sexual abuse when they were children had no memory of the event. Compulsive activities can also aid in avoiding negative affect, as can alcohol and drug abuse, both so common in victims of trauma. Avoidance serves short-term anxiety reduction but perpetuates the lack of neural network integration. The passage of time does not cure trauma, nor does it diminish the intensity of flashbacks.

When experienced in combination, these symptoms result in a cycle of activation and numbing reflecting the body's memory of the trauma (van der Kolk, 1994). Instead of serving to mobilize the body to deal with new external threats, traumatic memories become the stimuli for continuing emotional responses. Someone suffering from PTSD is, in essence, in a continual loop of unconscious self-traumatization, coping, and exhaustion. When these symptoms are experienced on a chronic basis, they can devastate every aspect of the victim's life, from physical well-being to the quality of relationships to the victim's experience of the world.

Complex Posttraumatic Stress Disorder

Complex PTSD occurs in the context of prolonged inescapable stress and trauma. It is complex because of its extensive physiological effects and its impact on all areas of development and functioning (Herman, 1992). Enduring personality traits and coping strategies evolving from traumatic states tend to increase the individual's vulnerability to more trauma. This can manifest through engagement in abusive relationships, poor judgment, or a lack of adequate self-protection. Long-term PTSD has been shown to correlate with the presence of what are called "neurological soft signs" pointing to subtle neurological impairments (Gurvits et al., 2000). These neurological signs could suggest a vulnerability to the development of PTSD, or they could reflect the impact of the long-term physiological dysregulation caused by PTSD (Green, 1981).

When confronted with threat under normal circumstances, the processes related to arousal and the fight-or-flight response become activated; the threat is dealt with and soon passes. Children are not well equipped to cope with threat in this way. Fighting and fleeing may actually decrease their chances for survival because their survival depends on dependency. When a child first cries for help but no help arrives, or when trauma is being inflicted by a caretaker, he or she may shift from hyperarousal to dissociation (Perry et al., 1995). Traumatized children who are agitated may be misdiagnosed as suffering from attention deficit disorder, while the numbing response in infants can be misinterpreted as a lack of sensitivity to pain. This may also be true for women who are often unable to outrun or outfight male attackers.

Until recently, surgery was performed on infants without anesthesia because their gradual lack of protest was mistakenly interpreted as insensitivity to pain as opposed to a traumatic reaction to it (Zeltzer, Anderson, & Schecter, 1990). Recent survey research suggests that less than 25% of physicians performing circumcision on newborns use any form of analgesia (Wellington & Rieder, 1993), despite physiological indications that neonates are experiencing stress and pain during and after the procedure (Hoyle et al., 1983). These practices appear to be a holdover of beliefs that newborns either don't experience or don't remember pain (Marshall, Stratton, Moore, & Boxerman, 1980). It makes sense that an appreciation for the possibility of PTSD reactions in neonates and young children has lagged behind other areas.

Research with rats has demonstrated that exposure to inescapable shock serves to sensitize their hippocampi to subsequent releases of norepinephrine under stress (Petty et al., 1994). This suggests that after prolonged, inescapable shock, rats (and most likely humans) react more strongly to subsequent stress that is milder in nature. This neurobiological shift results in small stressors being experienced as more extreme. Petty and his colleagues suggest that this may help to explain the coping difficulties seen in victims of PTSD when confronted with mild to moderate stress (Petty et al., 1994). Think back to Sheldon, whom I described in chapter 5; he still suffered from anxiety 60 years after his childhood experiences during World War II.

Dissociation allows the traumatized individual to escape the trauma via a number of biological and psychological processes. Increased levels of endogenous opioids create a sense of well-being and a decrease in explicit processing of overwhelming traumatic situations. Psychological processes such as derealization and depersonalization allow the victim to either avoid the reality of his or her situation or watch it as an observer. These processes provide the experience of leaving the body, traveling to other worlds, or immersing oneself into other objects in the environment. Hyperarousal and dissociation in childhood establish an inner biopsychological environment primed to establish boundaries between different emotional states and experiences for a lifetime. If it is too painful to experience the world from inside one's body, self-identity can become organized outside the physical self.

Early traumatic experiences determine biochemical levels and neuroanatomical networking, thus impacting experience and adaptation throughout development. The tendency to dissociate and disconnect various tracks of processing creates a bias toward unintegrated information processing across conscious awareness, sensation, affect, and behavior. General dissociative defenses resulting in an aberrant organization of networks of memory, fear, and the social brain contribute to deficits of affect regulation, attachment, and executive functioning (van der Kolk et al., 1996). The malformation of these interdependent systems results in many disorders that spring from extreme early stress. Compulsive disorders related to eating or gambling, and somatization disorders in which emotions are converted into physical symptoms, can all be understood in this way. PTSD, borderline personality disorder, and self-harm can all reflect complex adaptation to early trauma (Saxe et al., 1994; van der Kolk et al., 1996).

I Am Not Crazy!

Jesse was referred to me by her neurologist after months of extensive medical and neurodiagnostic testing. Her team of doctors could find no physical causes for the debilitating pain she experienced in her head and throughout her upper body. Alternative forms of treatment, such as chiropractic and acupuncture, were also tried without symptomatic relief. Jesse came to see me on the insistence of her husband, and she was not the least bit happy about it. Sitting opposite me with her arms crossed and her jaw set, she glared at me and said, "I am not crazy!"

Life had been going well for Jesse. She had a solid marriage and a happy and healthy four-year-old daughter. She found her work as an executive in a small computer firm interesting, and she liked her colleagues who told her that they appreciated her contributions to the business. Approximately a year earlier, she had started to develop pain in her head, hands, arms, and back, and began a fruitless search for a medical explanation. The pain became the center of her attention as her interest and ability in being an executive, friend, wife, and mother gradually diminished. By the time she came for therapy, she had been spending most of her days taking medication, sneaking away for naps, and withdrawing to her room whenever she could find an excuse. There was no longer any fun or relaxation in her life, and her husband had become seriously concerned.

We were slow in developing a therapeutic relationship, given her resistance and fear of being seen as "crazy." She reluctantly shared about her troubled childhood. Jesse felt she had obviously gotten over her traumatic past based on her later success at work and in her marriage. As she told me of her mother's physical abuse at the hands of her father, she remained confident that there was no connection between her present physical pain and the emotional pain of her youth. Unfortunately, a common occurrence in her childhood was to be locked in her room by her father before he would begin to beat her mother. She would lie in bed feeling horrified by their screams, her mother's cries to Jesse to help her, and the long ominous silences that always followed.

Jesse remembered that she would pound on the door and yell to get her father's attention. As she grew older, however, she gave up her outward protests and instead lay in bed crying and clutching her head. Jesse said that she found herself driving her nails into her head and shoulders, drawing blood, and eventually scarring herself. She showed me some of the scars she still carried. In listening to these terrible reminiscences, I felt that her pain symptoms might well be implicit somatic memories of these experiences. The stresses in her present life, including the fact that her own daughter was reaching the age she had been when she first became aware of the beatings, could all serve as triggers for these memories. From a psychological perspective, her pain could be seen as a form of loyalty or connection to her mother through suffering.

I decided not to share these interpretations because of Jesse's resistance to the possible psychological origins of her pain. Instead, I continued to encourage her to talk about her childhood in as much detail as she could tolerate. She also told me of her mother's prolonged battle with cancer when Jesse was a teenager, and how she nursed her through the final months. In my work with Jesse, I avoided any talk of her physical pain and continued to refocus her on sharing childhood experiences with me.

In the process of repeatedly sharing stories from her childhood, her memories became increasing more detailed and her emotions more available and better matched to the situations she described. Jesse expressed her rage at her father for his violent behavior and she was able to realize that she was also angry at her mother for not leaving him when Jesse was young. As she went through these memories and put them into the perspective of her current life, Jesse was gradually able to feel that she could connect with her mother through happiness instead of joining her in suffering.

We both came to notice that the intensity of her pain and the time she spent focusing on it gradually diminished. Toward the end of our last session, she thanked me for helping her and said that although she didn't understand how or why, her physical and emotional pain did seem to be connected. Our unspoken agreement was that I wasn't allowed to be the one to suggest this possibility. Jesse winked at me and said, "You are a tricky fellow."

Traumatic Memory

It has long been recognized that moderate amounts of stress enhance learning and memory by increasing vigilance and heightening attention, whereas high levels impair learning and memory (Yerkes & Dodson, 1908). Trauma is a state of high arousal that impairs integration across many domains of learning and memory. The neural networks in the limbic system and cortex involved in memory are influenced by several systems of ascending fibers that modulate arousal (Squire, 1987). In this way, stressful, threatening, and traumatic memories are emphasized based on instinctual and learned appraisal of their dangerousness. Each of these systems has its own neurotransmitters, which have different effects on the encoding and storage of memory. We have already discussed NE, serotonin, dopamine, glucocorticoids, and endogenous opioids, all of which impact memory processes in different ways.

When NE is administered to rats after an aversive event, low doses enhance retention whereas high doses impair retention (Introini-Collison & McGaugh, 1987); this supports Yerkes and Dodson's theory that moderate levels of arousal enhance memory whereas high levels impair memory. In a study by Cahill and his colleagues (Cahill, Prins, Weber, & McGaugh, 1994), subjects were read emotionally evocative and neutral stories and shown related slides.

Half of the subjects were given propranolol (a drug that decreases the effects of the NE) and the others were not. Results demonstrated that subjects who received propranolol had significantly impaired memory for the emotion-arousing stories but not for the neutral stories.

Activation of the amygdala (and the related physiological and biological changes) is at the heart of the modulation of emotional and traumatic memory (Cahill & McGaugh, 1998). The release of norepinephrine during the stress response serves to heighten the activation of the amygdala, thus reinforcing and intensifying memories for traumatic events (McGaugh, 1990). Individuals with PTSD have had their amygdaloid memory systems imprinted with trauma at such an extreme level that their memories are resistant to cortical integration (van der Kolk et al., 1996). Extreme trauma results in the inhibition of neural networks (cortico–hippocampal) that could contextualize and attenuate them. When we think of trauma overwhelming the defenses, we can also think in terms of an intense activation of subcortical networks serving to inhibit the participation of the hippocampus and cortex in the memory process.

Traumatic experience can disrupt the storage (encoding) of information and the integration of the various systems of attention and memory (Vasterling, Brailey, Constans, & Sutker, 1998; Yehuda et al., 1995; Zeitlin & McNally, 1991). *Memory encoding* for conscious explicit memory can be disrupted when the hippocampus is blocked or damaged by glucocorticoids or is inhibited by heightened amygdala functioning. This could lead to a lack of conscious memory for traumatic and highly emotional events (Adamec, 1991; Schacter, 1986; Squire & Zola-Morgan, 1991). *Memory integration* can be impaired by disruption of the cortico–hippocampal tracks dedicated to the integration of new memories into existing memory networks. Remember that these systems also provide contextualization in time and space, and integration of sensory, affective, and behavioral memory with conscious awareness.

Thus, although we may have very accurate physiological and emotional memories for a traumatic event, the factual information may be quite inaccurate given the inhibition of cortico–hippocampal involvement during the trauma. Add to this the tendency of the left-hemisphere interpreter to confabulate a story in the absence of accurate information, and we may have what represents the underlying mechanisms of the malleability of memory.

Traumatic Flashbacks and Speechless Terror

Flashbacks are commonly reported by individuals who have experienced trauma. They are described as full-body experiences of aspects of the traumatic event, including physiological arousal and sensory stimulation. In a sense, the victim of a flashback is transported back in time to the traumatic experience. Flashbacks are so intense that they overwhelm the reality constraints of the contemporary situation and send the victim into an all-too-familiar and recurrent nightmare.

The power of traumatic flashbacks was driven home for me one day in a therapy session with a professional football player who stood nearly twice my size. When recalling his early abuse, he began to cry softly as he spoke of one particularly painful experience from childhood. He described in agonizing detail his small body growing limp after repeated blows from his father's fists. This explicit memory cued an implicit memory, a flashback; suddenly, he was standing over me and breathing heavily. Despite my alarm, I managed to sit quietly, eventually asking him what he was feeling. While looking into my eyes he asked me in a child's voice to please not hurt him anymore. His fear of me in contrast to our relative sizes was a stark demonstration of primitive memory systems overriding normal conscious processing.

Traumatic flashbacks are memories of a quite different nature than are those of nontraumatic events. To begin with, they are stored in more primitive circuits with less cortical and left-hemisphere involvement. Because of this, they are strongly somatic, sensory, and emotional, as well as inherently nonverbal (Krystal, Bremner, Southwick, & Charney, 1998). The lack of cortical–hippocampal involvement results in an absence of the localization of the memory in time, so when it is triggered it is experienced as occurring in the present (Siegel, 1995). Flashbacks are also repetitive and stereotypic, often seeming to proceed at the pace in which the events originally occurred. This suggests that although the cortex may condense and abbreviate memories in narrative and symbolic form, these subcortical networks may store memories in more concrete, stimulus-response chains of sensations, behaviors, and emotions.

In flashbacks, the amygdala-mediated fear networks (primarily in the right hemisphere) are activated. The amygdala's dense connectivity with the visual system most likely accounts for the presence of visual hallucinations during flashbacks. This is compared with the hallucinations in schizophrenia that involve the temporal lobes and are usually auditory in nature. Bereaved individuals often report seeing their loved ones sitting in their favorite chair or walking across the room in some familiar way. Those who have been attacked will sometimes think they see their attacker out of the corner of their eye. These emotionally charged visual hallucinations and illusions most likely reside in these amygdala-mediated systems.

Rauch and colleagues (1996) explored the neurobiology of intense fear using patients with PTSD. They took eight patients suffering from PTSD and exposed them to two audiotapes: One was emotionally neutral and the other was a script of a traumatic experience. While they were listening to these tapes, measures of patents' heart rate and regional cerebral blood flow (RCBF) were measured via PET scans. RCBF was greater during traumatic audiotapes in right-sided structures including the amygdala, orbitofrontal cortex, insular, anterior and medial temporal lobe, and the anterior cingulate cortex. These are the areas thought to be involved with intense emotion.

An extremely interesting and potentially important clinical finding was a decrease in RCBF in Broca's area (left inferior frontal and middle temporal cortex; Rauch et al., 1996). These findings suggest active inhibition of language centers during trauma. Based on these results, *speechless terror*—often reported by victims of trauma—may have neurobiological correlates consistent with what we know about brain architecture and brain–behavior relationships. This inhibitory effect on Broca's area will impair the encoding of conscious memory for traumatic events at the time they occur. It will then naturally interfere with the development of narratives that serve to process the experience and lead to neural network integration and psychological healing. Activating Broca's area and left cortical networks of explicit episodic memory may be essential in psychotherapy with patients suffering from PTSD and other anxiety-based disorders.

Activating Broca's Area During a Flashback

Jan, seeing me for a one-time consultation, reported that she had suffered from severe physical and sexual abuse from early childhood into her late teens. She told me over the phone that she was having flashbacks of increasing frequency in recent years; it had gotten to the point where she was having three or four a day. Although her therapist had encouraged her to express them as much as possible, Jan felt like she was getting worse instead of better. Expressing her feelings only triggered more frequent and intense flashbacks. She reported becoming less and less functional, which made her decide that she needed a different approach to therapy.

Jan arrived at my office with a stack of diaries and *The Wall Street Journal* under her arm. It was hard to believe that this was the same person I had spoken to over the phone. My first thought was that dissociation is an amazing defense. Jan was a well-dressed woman in her mid-40s who was obviously bright and had a good deal of self-insight. The childhood experiences she recounted in my office were horrendous, and I marveled at her very survival. Her intelligence and sheer will to live were remarkable. It seemed obvious, however, that her repeated reexperiencing of these memories was not helping. The nature of these memories was not changing over time, nor were the emotions evoked by her memories diminishing. In this case, they seemed to retraumatize her each time she experienced them.

She began by talking about her work, and then described the psychotherapy and other forms of treatment in which she had engaged. Approximately 10 minutes into the session, as she was discussing the family members who had abused her, she began to have one of the flashbacks she had described over the phone. Jan reported pain in various parts of her body and contorted as if what she was describing was happening to her at this very moment. After 20 seconds, she began to gag as a part of the memory of the sexual abuse she experienced decades earlier. She was reexperiencing these painful episodes not only as pictures in her mind, but as somatic memories throughout her body.

As she curled into the fetal position on the couch and gasped for breath, my mind raced trying to think of some way to help. Remembering the research done by Rauch and his colleagues, I thought that I should somehow try and activate Broca's area. I began to speak to Jan in a firm but gentle voice, loud enough to reach her in the midst of her traumatic reenactment but not so loud as to frighten her and add to her trauma. I wondered if it mattered which ear I spoke into, wondering which ear has a more direct connection to the left hemisphere language centers. I moved closer to her (careful not to get too close) and repeated over and over, "This is a memory, it isn't happening now. You are remembering something that happened to you many years ago. It was a terrible experience but it is over. It is a memory, it is not happening now."

As I repeated these and similar statements, I was concerned that Jan would be unable to breathe or that my presence might cause her more fear. The words of one of my supervisors flashed through my mind: "Whatever you do, don't panic." I was also encouraged by the fact that she had survived this many times. After 10 minutes (which seemed to me like 10 hours), she appeared to calm down and return to the present. Jan reported that she heard me speaking as if I were far away, but focused on my voice and words as best she could. It was as if I were there in the past with her, calling to her from a safe future where she would be away from all these people who hurt her.

At the end of the session she thanked me and left; I didn't hear from her for a number of months. When she called one afternoon, she reported that since her visit with me, the nature of these flashbacks had changed. She said she had wanted to wait before she called me because she didn't expect that the change she experienced after our session would last. Given her dozen-plus years in a variety of unhelpful treatments, it was easy to be sympathetic to her negative expectations. Jan described that since our session, the flashbacks had changed in a number of ways. She began by saying that they were less physically intense, that the bodily sensations were not as strong as before. Along with this, they were also less frequent; on a few occasions she had even been able to stop one that was coming on by thinking of her version of my words during the session: "This is just a memory, you are safe now, no one can hurt you."

Perhaps most interesting was the fact that during these flashbacks she was now able to remember that she was not a child, that she was not to blame, and it was those who were hurting her who were bad. These thoughts were the sorts of things her other therapists had told her in the past, but only recently could she process them during her flashbacks. I told her that I felt these were signs that the experiences were beginning to be connected to her conscious adult self, and that now she was able to fight and care for herself even in the face of her past. I encouraged her to keep talking throughout the flashback experiences and bring with her as much assertiveness, anger, and power as she could muster. After a few minutes, we ended our conversation and I sat back thinking that neuroscience *could* actually be applied to psychotherapy.

It is impossible for me to know with any certainty whether what I had done with Jan during our one meeting had anything to do with the changes in her flashbacks. If it did, perhaps the active ingredient was the simultaneous activation of the left-hemisphere verbal areas along with the emotional centers of the right hemisphere and limbic structures that stored the flashbacks. Being simultaneously aware of inner and outer worlds may support a higher level of cortical functioning, resulting in increased network integration. In other words, this process results in a memory configuration that is no longer "implicit only" but instead becomes integrated with the contextualizing properties of explicit systems of memory (Siegel, 1995).

The speechless terror, which has been recognized as part of posttraumatic reactions since ancient times, now has a neural correlate consistent with what is known about brain functions. Why does Broca's area become inhibited during trauma? Why would evolution select silence in times of crisis? Perhaps when one is threatened it is better to either run or fight or simply keep quiet and hope to stay undetected. In other words, evolution has taught the brain to "Shut up and do something!" when in danger. The freezing reaction of animals (being still and quiet when they sense a predator) allows them to be less visible (because a still and silent target is more difficult to spot). Spoken language is fundamentally "sound" that primitive fear circuitry has selected to silence. Perhaps those early prehumans who hung around for conversation and negotiation with predators didn't fare well enough to pass down as many genes as did those who either kept quiet, fought, or ran away.

The Addiction to Stress and Self-Harm

Another phenomenon with a possible biochemical mechanism is an addiction to stress experienced by some patients with PTSD. They report that they feel calm and competent in life-threatening situations but find it difficult to cope with normal day-to-day life. A large portion of the initial work with these patients is designed to help them both decrease the creation of stress and, paradoxically, tolerate the anxiety related to the absence of stress. They need to learn how to function in a nontraumatic state. This can usually be accomplished through some combination of stress-reduction techniques, medication, and psychotherapy.

These phenomena point to the possibility that extreme and prolonged stress—significant enough to result in a chronic PTSD reaction—may motivate the creation of new trauma. The new trauma would, in turn, stimulate the production of endogenous opioids that would lead to an increased sense of well-being. A so-called "normal" life leaves traumatized persons a blank screen onto which their dysregulated psyches can project fearful experiences, leaving patients such as these in a state of constant vigilance, arousal, and fear (Fish-Murry, Koby, & van der Kolk, 1987). Trauma and stress as coping strategies provide them with a shift from being anxious and wary to being calm and competent. Because these individuals are so physically worn down by this lifestyle, they often present with depression, exhaustion, and a variety of medical conditions. It is as if they have a drug addiction, except that it is completely unconscious and they are their own pharmacy.

At a biochemical level, endogenous opioids (e.g., the endorphins discussed in the neurochemistry of bonding and trauma) also appear to be involved in severe cases of self-harm and suicide (van der Kolk, 1988). This same chemical system mediates the distress calls of baby primates and mothers' response to these calls. Infants become distressed when their mothers are absent, and are soothed and calmed upon their mother's return. The return of the mother is correlated with the release of endorphins creating the sense of well-being. Endorphins are also released after injury to provide analgesia for pain, allowing us to continue fighting or escaping (Pitman et al., 1990). This system, originally used to cope with pain, was adapted by later-evolving networks of attachment and bonding.

The addiction to stress has a related but more severe variant: self-mutilation and other forms of self-harm. Adults who engage in repeated self-harm almost always describe childhoods that included abuse, neglect, or a deep sense of shame. This correlation has led many theorists to explore the psychodynamic significance of self-harm as a continued involvement with destructive parents. Suicide has been described as the final act of compliance with the parents' unconscious wish for the death of the child (Green, 1978). The association between self-harm and disorders of attachment has been noted and primarily explained through psychological models.

Self-injurious behaviors in humans are often responses to real or imagined abandonment and loss. Research has demonstrated that the frequency of self-harm decreases when people who engage in this behavior are given a drug to block the effects of these endogenous opioids (Pitman et al., 1990; van der Kolk, 1988). Abstracting from the animal model, this would suggest that the state of distress activated by the experience of abandonment is reversed via the release of endorphins caused by the injury. The analgesic effects of these morphine-like substances may account for the reports of reduced anxiety. People who engage in self-harm report a sense of calm and relief after cutting, burning, or hurting themselves. These self-injurious behaviors may be a form of implicit memory that is reinforced, in part, by the endogenous opioid system.

Repeated suicide attempts are often reinforced by the rapid attention of health care professionals, family, and friends. When woven into the personality as a means of affect regulation, this attention-getting behavior results in a kind of characterological suicidality (Schwartz, 1979). This behavior parallels the distress calls of primates whose endorphin levels drop in the absence of the mother. The reappearance of the mother results in a raising of these endorphin levels and the infant discontinues its cry. Characterological suicidality can serve a similar biochemical regulatory purpose if this system was inadequately formed during childhood. Although there are many sound psychological explanations for the relationship of childhood abuse with self-harm and suicidality in adulthood, the process may have a biochemical mechanism that could benefit from pharmacological interventions designed to block the impact of endogenous endorphins.

The Brain and Borderline Personality Disorder

According to Freud, participation in analysis requires sufficient ego strength to withstand the stress of therapy while simultaneously maintaining contact with reality. Based on this assumption, Freud did his best to make sure that his prospective clients were not psychotic. Psychotic individuals are characterized by severe distortions of reality, disorders in their thinking processes, and decompensation under stress. They are also unable to differentiate their transference and other projective processes from reality. These are all reflections of low ego strength. Despite Freud's best efforts to filter out these people, every so often he got a surprise! People who appeared to be average neurotics seemed to become psychotic in the context of the therapeutic relationship. Freud came to refer to these people as having psychic structures on the *borderline* between neurotic and psychotic.

Over the years, the conception of a borderline psychic structure evolved into what is now called a *borderline personality disorder* (BPD). As we have already seen, BPD may represent one variant of complex PTSD. The strongest evidence for this concept is the frequent occurrence of early abuse, trauma, and the use of dissociative symptoms in these individuals. Patients who carry this diagnosis are characterized by:

1. Hypersensitivity to real or imagined abandonment.
2. Disturbances of self-identity.
3. Intense and unstable relationships.
4. Alternating idealization and devaluation of themselves and others (black-and-white thinking).
5. Compulsive, risky, and sometimes self-damaging behaviors.

Although there are a number of theories concerning its cause, many feel that the etiology of BPD stems from problems in early life related to bonding, attachment, and a sense of safety. Research also suggests that affective disorders in these patients and their parents occurs above chance levels. Overall, both their reported history and their symptoms suggest that early attachment was experienced as highly traumatic, emotionally dysregulating, and possibly life threatening.

In my work with these patients, I have always felt that they may provide us with a window to the intense and chaotic experience of infancy. As we have seen (and this is where our neuroscientific knowledge comes in handy), the amygdala is highly functional at birth. Remember that the amygdala is at the center of neural networks involving both fear and attachment. The hippocampal and cortical networks that eventually organize and inhibit the amygdala grow gradually through childhood. Because of this developmental timetable and the prolonged dependence on others for survival, relationships must sometimes be as overwhelmingly frightening to infants as we see they are to patients with BPD.

The symptoms that emerge in this disorder cause patients to create problematic and chaotic relationships that can lead them through a lifetime of serial abandonments. It is even common for therapists to abandon these patients because of their intense criticism and hostility. I find that remembering that such patients are essentially frightened children helps me to maintain a therapeutic posture. Their primitive fear, rage, and shame are a form of implicit posttraumatic memory from a very early stage of development that are activated by real or imagined criticism or abandonment. When these memory networks become activated in treatment, they are so primitive and powerful that the patient is unable to maintain contact with reality. We also see the same phenomena in PTSD flashbacks, most likely stored in the same implicit memory systems. This confused Freud, because he believed that everyone was either neurotic or psychotic. Here was a horse of a different color: primitive and highly complex PTSD.

Examining BPD in light of the neuroscience we have reviewed in previous chapters, here are a few of the neurobiological processes that may be involved in how these symptoms become encoded within neural networks:

1. Amygdaloid memory systems are traumatically primed during early attachment experiences to react to any possible indication of abandonment by triggering sympathetic fight-or-flight

reaction and raising baseline levels of norepinephrine and stress hormones.

2. Orbitofrontal systems are inadequately developed during attachment to engage in healthy self-soothing and the inhibition of fear activation by circuits of the amygdala.

3. Orbitofrontal systems develop separate tracks of positive and negative experiences that are never integrated.

4. Orbitofrontal dissociation may result in disconnection between right- and left-hemisphere and top-down processing, partly accounting for rapid and radical shifts between positive and negative appraisals of relationships.

5. The networks of the social brain are unable to internalize images from early interactions with caretakers to provide self-soothing and affect regulation.

6. Rapid fluctuations between sympathetic and parasympathetic states result in baseline irritability and sympathetic survival responses to real or imagined abandonment.

7. Chronic high levels of stress hormones compromise hippocampal functioning, decreasing the brain's ability to control amygdala functioning and exacerbating emotional dyscontrol.

8. Amygdaloid dyscontrol heightens the impact of early memory on adult functioning, increasing the contemporary impact of early bonding failures.

9. Hippocampal compromise decreases reality testing and memory functioning, contributing to the inability to maintain positive or soothing memories during states of high arousal.

10. Early bonding failures lead to lower levels of serotonin, resulting in greater risk of depression, irritability, and decreased positive reinforcement from interpersonal interactions.

11. Self-harm during dysregulated states results in endorphin release and a sense of calm, putting these individuals at risk for repeated self-abusive behavior.

These are just some of the factors that may be involved in the neurobiology of BPD. Because this diagnosis has so far been outside the purview of neurology, little brain research has been done with BPD patients. Neuropsychological findings with these patients, however, does suggests dysfunction in the frontal and temporal lobes (Paris, Zelkowitz, Guzder, Joseph, & Feldman, 1999; Swirsky-Sacchetti et al., 1993). Executive and memory functions within these brain networks do not provide adequate organization for these patients. We have learned that these functions are built and sculpted in the context of early relationships; it makes sense that they are impaired in BPD patients. The central concept in the treatment of these individuals is structure and limit setting, combined with flexibility and patience (just as it is with raising children). The therapist must provide an external scaffolding within which the client can rebuild these brain networks of memory, self-organization, and affect regulation. On another level, the therapist serves as an external neural circuit to aid in the integration of networks left unintegrated during development.

Neural Network Integration

Unresolved trauma results in information-processing deficits that disrupt integrated neural processing. In fact, the experience of dissociative symptoms immediately after a trauma is predictive of the later development of PTSD (Koopman et al., 1994; McFarlane & Yehuda, 1996). Conscious awareness is split from emotional, and physiological processing. A lack of integration of right- and left-hemisphere functions subsequent to stress may also disrupt processes of interpersonal bonding and bodily regulation (Henry, Satz, & Saslow, 1984). Children victimized by psychological, physical, and sexual abuse have been shown to have a significantly greater probability of demonstrating brainwave abnormalities in the left frontal and temporal regions

(Ito et al., 1993). Brainwave dyscoherence may put individuals at higher risk for the development of all forms of psychiatric disorders (Teicher et al., 1997).

The biochemical changes that occur secondary to trauma enhance primitive (subcortical) stimulus–response pairing of conditioned responses related to sensation, emotion, and behavior. These same changes undermine cortical systems dedicated to the integration of learning across systems of memory into a coherent and conscious narrative (Siegel, 1996). As we understand more about the neurobiological processes underlying PTSD, we will better learn how to treat and possibly prevent this debilitating yet curable mental illness.

Therapies of all kinds, especially those within the cognitive schools, have proven successful in the reintegration of neural processing subsequent to trauma. Systematic desensitization, exposure, and response prevention can all enhance these integrative processes. Recognition of the risks to neural network integration posed by overwhelming stress and trauma has resulted in the development of some newer treatments such as critical incident stress debriefing (CISD; Mitchell & Everly, 1993). Using our present model, CISD may help to prevent PTSD by enhancing the interconnections among neural networks—at risk for dissociation—soon after trauma.

CISD moves through phases of processing cognitive and emotional aspects of experience, using both psychoeducation to enhance an understanding of the body's reaction to stress and group process to provide a context for reality testing and normalization of posttraumatic reactions. The sequential activation of networks of cognition, emotion, sensation, and behavior are encouraged in the context of support and conceptual understanding of the entire process. This is a new treatment modality for PTSD, and conclusive research concerning the efficacy of its timing and various components remains to be done.

Summary

The brain's reaction to trauma provides us with a window to the general processes of learning and plasticity. The brain does indeed change in reaction to environmental events. This helps us to understand why the safe emergency of psychotherapy is able to alter neural networks organized in a manner not conducive to mental health. From the first moments of life, stress shapes our brains in ways that lead us to remember experiences most important for survival. Most of our learning experiences are not traumatic but rather subtle, nondramatic, and unconscious. The interactions between parent and child, the politics of the schoolyard, and experiences of small victories and losses all contribute to shaping who we will become.

In the final chapter, we will review some of the basic principles that have emerged from our exploration of neuroscience and psychotherapy, especially as they apply to the future of both fields.

PART V

THE REORGANIZATION
OF EXPERIENCE

Teaching Old Dogs
New Tricks

The sophistication of the human brain reflects millions of years of evolutionary adaptation. During evolution, old structures were conserved and modified while new structures coalesced and expanded. Countless interactive networks and design compromises created fertile ground for the disruption of smooth integration of neural systems. Disruption in the coordination of these neural systems is the neurobiological substrate of psychological distress and mental illness.

The very complexity of the development and functioning of the brain is also what makes it such a fragile structure. Assuming that the trillions of component parts arrive in their proper places and work according to their genetic templates, there are a host of other challenges to integrated psychological functioning. The discontinuity of conscious and unconscious processes, multiple memory systems, differences between the hemispheres, hidden processing layers, and multiple executive structures are all potential sources of dissociation and dysregulation.

Evolution is driven and directed by the physical survival of the species, not by the happiness of individuals. Thus, much of the brain's functioning is centered around primitive reflexive fight-or-flight mechanisms as opposed to conscious and compassionate decision making. Because of this, the conscious and unconscious management of fear and anxiety is a core component of our personalities, attachment relationships, and identities. The considerable degree of postnatal brain development and the disproportionate emphasis on early childhood experiences in the sculpting of the brain add to our vulnerability to psychological distress.

The human brain is at risk for dysregulation and disorganization. The history of our species, as well as our religious and philosophical beliefs, bear witness to our fragility and constant struggle to make sense of experience. Psychotherapy and the psychological perspective permeate contemporary culture because they address our struggle to create order out of chaos. Although different modes of therapy vary in their focus on cognition, emotion, behavior, and sensations, all attempt to reintegrate and rebalance processes organized in neural networks that have become dysregulated. In this regard, their commonalities far outweigh their differences.

We are only beginning to understand the relationship between the symptoms of mental illness and their underlying neurobiological processes. Fortunately, we have many interesting leads and enthusiastic researchers concentrating on increasing our knowledge. As this knowledge grows, neuroscience will come to have greater impact on the diagnosis and treatment of mental disorders. In the future, psychiatric diagnosis may be made on the basis of dysregulation of specific neural networks along with expressed symptoms. Treatment will also come to focus on specific networks and our conception of viable and successful interventions will expand.

The growth and integration of neural networks is the biological mechanism of all successful learning, including parenting, teaching, and psychotherapy. Expanding consciousness, regulating and controlling unnecessary or destructive impulses, weaving emotions with thoughts in conscious experience, and developing appropriate boundaries with others all involve increased and enhanced communication among an array of processing networks. Life- and brain-changing experiences can occur through religious conversion, climbing a mountain, or having a child. Challenges that force us to expand our awareness, learn new information, or push beyond assumed limits can all change our brains.

Psychotherapy

Psychotherapists are clinical neuroscientists who create an individually tailored enriched environment to enhance brain development. We use a combination of language, empathy, emotion, and behavioral experiments to promote neural integration. Therapists are skilled at teaching clients to become aware of their unconscious processing. We read, interpret, and reflect the nonverbal communication of the right hemisphere expression in the body. Illusions, distortions, and defenses are explored and examined for accuracy. Implicit memory—in the form of attachment schema, transference, and superego—are made conscious and analyzed. Fears, phobias, and traumas are activated along with any other thought processes we might stimulate. This process allows for the linkage among explicit and implicit circuits, conscious awareness, and the inhibition and control of anxiety and fears. Regardless of the client or his or her particular problem, psychotherapy teaches a method to help us better understand and use our brains.

Important factors in the therapeutic process have been identified as an emotionally safe and empathic relationship, the activation of anxiety and stress, and the use of language. *A safe and empathic relationship* establishes an emotional and neurobiological context conducive to the work of neural reorganization. It serves as a buffer and scaffolding within which a client can better tolerate the stress required for neural reorganization. We have already seen that birds are able to learn their "songs" after sensitive periods when exposed to other birds singing, but are unable to learn the same songs heard from a tape recorder (Baptista & Petrinovich, 1986). Under certain conditions, birds require positive social interactions and nurturance in order to learn (Eales, 1985). These studies, combined with what we know about changes in biochemistry during interpersonal interactions, suggest that a positive and attuned interpersonal relationship enhances neural plasticity and learning (Schore, 1994).

The importance of stress in the process of change is recognized by most psychotherapists. Releasing the emotions connected to a painful memory, facing a feared situation, or experimenting with new interpersonal relationships all involve some sort of stress, anxiety, or fear. Although this has been accepted clinically, we now have evidence to suggest that emotion and stress stimulate the biochemical environment for neural plasticity. Optimal levels of arousal and stress result in increased production of neurotransmitters and neural growth hormones that enhance LTP, learning, and cortical reorganization (Cowan & Kandel, 2001; Zhu & Waite, 1998). Stress and emotional expression have been incorporated into psychotherapy because of their impact on these underlying biological processes.

Dissociation in reaction to trauma represents an uncontrolled and negative expression of neural plasticity. Trauma undoubtedly changes us in many ways, from basic startle functions to attachment and self-identity. In therapy, we use moderate levels of stress to access these mechanisms of plasticity in a controlled way with specific goals. The safe emergency of therapy provides both the psychological structure and the biological stimulus for rebuilding the brain. Much of neural integration and reorganization takes place in the association areas of the frontal, temporal, and parietal lobes, which serve to coordinate, regulate, and direct multiple neural circuits. They are the brain's switchboard operators, able to use language, stories, and narratives to link the functioning of systems throughout the brain and body.

The importance of language and the co-construction of autobiographical narratives are grounded in the co-evolution of the cerebral cortex, language, and our complex social structures. Put another way, language and significant social relationships build and shape the brain through evolution as well as during the development of the individ-

ual. Because of this, language in the context of an emotionally meaningful relationship like psychotherapy is a key to resculpting neural
networks. Through the use of autobiographical memory, we can create narratives that bridge processing from various neural networks
into a cohesive and integrated story of the self. Narratives allow us to
combine—in conscious memory—our knowledge, sensations, feelings, and behaviors supporting underlying neural network integration (Siegel, 1999).

The co-construction of narratives with parents serves as a
medium of transfer of the internal world of the parent to child, from
generation to generation. These narratives reflect the implicit values,
problem-solving strategies, and world view of the parents. They also
serve to define us to ourselves and guide us through a complex world.
The more inclusive the narrative is, the greater our ability to continue
to integrate multiple neural networks on an ongoing basis. Research
in attachment has demonstrated that the coherence and inclusiveness
of narratives correlate with secure attachment (Main, 1993).

In the process of evolution, different levels of language have
emerged to reflect various layers of conscious awareness:

1. A reflexive social language, or the language of the left-hemisphere interpreter, serves the purpose of creating a logically
   cohesive and positive presentation to the social world. This
   language evolved from grooming and hand gestures with the
   primary goal of social coordination.
2. An internal language, also reflexive, allows us to have a stream
   of private thoughts, plan and guide behavior, and deceive others. There also appears to be an unconscious aspect of internal language that serves as a mechanism for preserving early
   learning. These are the often critical voices we hear in our
   heads, reflecting the imprint of early shame experiences.
3. A third language, one of self-reflection, appears to be far less
   reflexive and arises in states of openness, low defensiveness,
   and a feeling of safety.

Although the first two levels of language occur spontaneously, self-reflective language most likely requires higher levels of neural network integration; self-reflection requires both higher levels of affect regulation and cognitive processing. Reflexive language keeps us in the moment, reacting to stressors in the midst of survival. Reflective language demonstrates our ability to escape from the present moment, gain perspective on our reflexive reactions, and make decisions about what and how we would like to change. This is the language of the *therapeutic alliance*.

Three levels of awareness sharing a common lexicon result in a great deal of confusion. Many people in and out of therapy report feeling crazy because of the simultaneous and contradictory beliefs they struggle with on a day-to-day basis. Psychotherapy often involves the sorting out of these tracks of consciousness in order to provide us with a clearer idea of just what is going on in there. Whether it is a struggle with a fear of success or contamination, we separate those aspects of brain functioning that approach and those that avoid, and attempt to negotiate a compromise. Although this is usually the function of the executive regions of the cortex, they often need help. Narrative co-construction is an excellent mechanism for this process.

Psychotherapy and Neural Optimism

Psychotherapy has survived for more than 100 years in the absence of an accepted brain-based theory of the mind. Instead, it has used attunement, emotion, stress, and language as tools to change the brain. We have seen that psychotherapy needed to develop independently from brain-based sciences because of the old view of the brain as a predetermined and static entity. This neurological fatalism is essentially incompatible with both the practice and goals of psychotherapy.

Contemporary neuroscience does not support such neurological fatalism; instead, it explores a brain that is constantly adapting to new information, threats, challenges, shame, and excitement. If the brain is seen from the perspective of neural optimism, what can we learn? How valid is the notion of sensitive periods, and how plastic is the brain? Can plasticity be enhanced, and how much of an effect can the environment have on changing the brain in positive ways? These questions are central to psychotherapy, because we rely on the brain's ability to change well after traditional "critical periods" have passed.

Are Sensitive Periods Critical?

Research on imprinting of parental figures in geese (Lorenz, 1991) and the importance of sensitive periods in the development of the visual cortex in cats (Hubel & Wiesel, 1962) have been standard fare in undergraduate education and popular science for decades. Unfortunately, the way these studies have been portrayed created the impression that the timing of brain growth is almost entirely under genetic control, and that imprinting during sensitive periods becomes permanently and indelibly etched into our neural architecture (Rutter & Rutter, 1993).

The neurological fatalism with which we entered the 1990s may have resulted from a misunderstanding of these two bodies of research and the belief that new neurons could not be created after birth. It has been suggested that extracting the concepts of imprinting and critical periods from ethology and applying them to human development is inappropriate and misleading (Michel & Moore, 1995). Learning in humans, at all points during development, is far more complex than the original conceptions of imprinting and critical periods would lead us to believe.

Recall that critical or sensitive periods are times of exuberant growth in neural networks, corresponding with the rapid development of the skills and abilities to which they are dedicated (Chugani, 1998; Fischer, 1987). Although there is no doubt that these periods exist, what is now being questioned is the indelibility of learning during these periods, the nature of learning during nonsensitive periods, and the modification of the timing of these periods. As neuroscience finds more examples of neurogenesis and changes in neural structure in the mature brain, the importance of sensitive periods has increasingly fallen into question (Bornstein, 1989). There is increasing recognition that the brain retains different kinds of plasticity throughout life.

The research on neural plasticity has historically focused on the brain's ability to adapt after early brain injury (Goldman, 1971; Goldman & Galkin, 1978; Henry et al., 1984). Today, plasticity is understood to be a basic principle of healthy brains at any age (within certain limits). Rather than being characterized as lacking plasticity, the adult brain is now seen as having an increased tendency toward neural stabilization (Stiles, 2000) while maintaining its potential for plastic reorganization. This vital shift in perspective has led to a rapid expansion of interest in and exploration of the neurobiological mechanisms of learning and change (Rosenzweig, 2001).

Neural Plasticity

You will remember that changes in synaptic strength in response to some inner or outer stimulus are the basis for learning. The process of long-term potentiation (LTP) prolongs excitation of cell assemblies that are synchronized and interconnected in their firing patterns (Hebb, 1949). This is only a small piece of a vastly complex set of processes and interactions resulting in the connection, timing, and organization of the firing within and between the billions of individual neurons interconnected in neural networks.

Plasticity reflects the ability of neurons to change the way they behave and relate to one another as they adapt to changes in environmental demands (Buonomano & Merzenich, 1998). This can occur in the modulation of signal transmission across synapses, changes in the organization of local neural circuits, and in the relationship between different functional neural networks (Trojan & Pokorny, 1999). It has been demonstrated that the portions of the cortex involved in sensory and motor functions reorganize in response to changing uses, after injury, and during skill learning (Braun et al., 2000; Elbert et al., 1994; Karni et al., 1995). Violinists have larger cortical representations in areas dedicated to the fingers of the left hand than do nonstring players (Elbert et al., 1995) with Braille readers demonstrating similar patterns of cortical plasticity (Sterr et al., 1998a, 1998b).

These and other studies have demonstrated *use-dependent* plasticity in sensory-motor cortical areas. Because of their early maturation and organization, sensory-motor areas have been thought to have the earliest sensitive periods and the most permanent neural organization. The extensive plasticity discovered in these regions suggests that executive and association areas of the frontal cortex (which form later and are characterized by their sensitivity to changing environmental demands) should demonstrate even more neural plasticity in the forms of neurogenesis, synaptogenesis, and altered synaptic connections (Beatty, 2001; Gould, Reeves, et al., 1999b; Hodge & Boakye, 2001; Mateer & Kerns, 2000). In fact, a recent study found continuing increases in white matter volume in the frontal and temporal lobes of males well into the fifth decade of life (Bartzokis et al., 2001). Because executive processes are more complex, abstract, and depend on the contributions of many integrated neural networks, they are more challenging to investigate in detail.

The fact that most of us are able to learn new skills and remember new information throughout life is the clearest evidence for ongoing neural plasticity. The activation and organization of the cortex appears capable of continual change. Plasticity demonstrates flexibility in the expansion and contraction of cortical representation with alternating stimulation and deprivation (Polley, Chen-Bee, & Frostig, 1999). In other words, the brain is capable of shifting between alternate states in response to changes in stimulation, and is capable of far more and faster functional reorganization than previously thought (Ramachandran, Rogers-Ramachandran, & Stewart, 1992). The study of the speed, degree, and nature of neural plasticity is a vast new scientific frontier (Classen, Liepert, Wise, Hallett, &

Cohen, 1998), and the potential to modify or enhance plasticity has profound implications for neurosurgery, education, rehabilitation from brain injury, and psychotherapy (Johansson, 2000).

Enriched Environments

It has been known for decades that enriched and stimulating early environments (when compared to unstimulating environment) have a long-term impact on both neural architecture and neurochemistry. Research has demonstrated that when rats are raised in complex and challenging environments, they show increases in many aspects of brain building. The effects of enriched environments in experimental animals include an increase in the:

1. Weight and thickness of cortex (Bennett, Diamond, Krech, & Rosenzweig, 1964; Diamond et al., 1964).
2. Weight and thickness of hippocampi (Kempermann et al., 1998; Walsh, Budtz-Olsen, Penny, & Cummins, 1969).
3. Length of neuronal dendrites (Kolb & Whishaw, 1998).
4. Formation of synapses among neurons (Kolb & Whishaw, 1998).
5. Activity of glial cells (Kolb & Whishaw, 1998).
6. Levels of neural growth hormones (Ickes et al., 2000).
7. Levels of neurotransmitters (Nilsson et al., 1993).
8. Level of vascular activity (Sirevaag & Greenough, 1988).
9. Level of metabolism (Sirevaag & Greenough, 1988).
10. Amount of gene expression (Guzowski, Setlown, Wagner, & McGaugh, 2001).
11. Levels of nerve growth factor and in the hippocampus and visual cortex (Torasdotter, Metsis, Hendriksson, Winblad, & Mohammed, 1998).

In essence, an enriching environment enables the animal to build and shape a more enriched, complex, and potentially resilient brain. There is no reason to believe that these results are not applicable to humans given the commonality of the fundamental working principles of our underlying neurobiology.

The ability of the environment to stimulate brain growth is so robust that it occurs even in situations of malnutrition. If rats are malnourished, enriched environments will still result in heavier brains than in well-fed but less-stimulated rats. These findings exist despite the fact that the malnourished rats' bodies are significantly lighter due to less caloric intake (Bhide & Bedi, 1982). Although nutritional and environmental deprivation often go hand in hand for most human children, some deficits may be reversed in adulthood. Enriched environments have been shown to result in synaptic plasticity in adult rats (Altman, Wallace, Anderson, & Das, 1968); exposing adult rats to training and enriched environments can ameliorate the effects of earlier nervous system damage (Kolb & Gibb, 1991; Schrott et al., 1992; Schwartz, 1964; Will, Rosenzweig, Bennett, Herbert, & Morimoto, 1977) and genetically based learning deficits (Schrott, 1997). It has also been suggested that an enriched environment may improve poststroke recovery in humans (Ulrich, 1984).

Although controlled studies of nutritional and environmental deprivation are not possible with humans, some naturally occurring situations offer similar insights into the power of environmental enrichment. A study of Korean children adopted by families in the United States found that environmental enrichment counteracted their early malnutrition and deprivation. On measures of height and weight, these children eventually surpassed Korean averages, while their I.Q. scores reached or exceeded values for American children (Winick, Katchadurian, & Harris, 1975). In another study of brain samples after death, a consistent relationship was found between the length of dendrites in Wernicke's area and the subjects' level of education (Jacobs et al., 1993). These studies support findings from animal research suggesting that environmental enrichment can counteract early deprivation, and that education results in measurable differences in brain morphology over a lifetime. At this point in our understanding we need to balance our optimism concerning later enrichment with an awareness that we still do not know what aspects of early learning may be permanent. Continued research in neural plasticity should occur simultaneously with optimizing the experience of children during sensitive periods.

Enhancing Plasticity

As noted earlier, therapy is a safe emergency because of the supportive structure in which stressful learning takes place. A client's sense of safety is enhanced by the therapist's skill, knowledge, and confidence. It is also quite possible that the caring, encouragement, and enthusiasm of the therapist supports and reinforces learning through the enhanced production of dopamine, serotonin, norepinephrine, and other endogenous endorphins that support neural growth and plasticity (Kilgard & Merzenich, 1998; Kirkwood, Rozas, Kirkwood, Perez, & Bear, 1999) and optimize the biochemical conditions for neural plasticity (Barad, 2000).

Therapists often lament the fact that parents do not do a better job during sensitive periods of brain development when their behaviors have such a powerful impact on their childrens' young brains. It has been proposed earlier that the therapeutic context may enhance the brain's ability to rewire through concurrent emotional and cognitive processing. Successful therapeutic techniques may be successful because of their very ability to change brain chemistry in a manner that enhances neural plasticity. As more is learned about the biological mechanisms of sensitive periods, the possibility of controlling them emerges. What if neuroscientists could learn how to reinstate sensitive periods during psychotherapy with adults?

Huang and his colleagues (1999) found that the sensitive period of the visual cortex was accelerated in certain genetically altered mice. It turns out that one of the genetic differences in these mice results in the earlier secretion of brain-derived neurotrophic factor (BDNF), a neural growth hormone. Kang and Schuman (1995) found that BDNF and NT-3 (another neurotrophic factor) enhanced LTP activity when added to an adult hippocampus.

In a related study, it was found that a strain of mice who had higher levels of N-methyl-D-aspartate (NMDA) receptors had enhanced ability in learning and memory tasks (Tang et al., 1999). NMDA is a neurotransmitter involved in the formation of associations among neurons and has been shown to be necessary for cortical reorganization (Jablonska et al., 1999). NMDA receptors have also been shown to be necessary for the initiation of LTP in monkeys (Myers et al., 2000). The effects of cholinergic stimulation suggest it also plays a role in neural plasticity through the activation of neural growth hormones (Cowan & Kandel, 2001; Zhu & Waite, 1998). This area of research may lead to pharmacological interventions that could enhance the brain's ability to learn during certain critical phases of psychotherapy.

Just a few years ago, the conventional wisdom in neuroscience was that we were born with all the neurons we would ever have. More recent research has found an increasing number of areas within the brain where new neurons are generated. *Stem cells*, the basic structure for many types of cells, have been found to renew themselves indefinitely. Stem cells in the adult brain have so far been found in the olfactory bulb and a portion of the hippocampus called the *dentate gyrus* (Jacobs et al., 2000). When the biological processes stimulating and shaping these stems cells are understood, neurosurgeons may be able to add new brain tissue to damaged areas, thus enhancing recovery (Hodge & Boakye, 2001).

The underlying biochemistry of the processes of neuronal growth is also being discovered and may someday be utilized to enhance and support plasticity (Akaneya, Tsumoto, Kinoshita, & Hatanaka, 1997; Barde, 1989) and treat neurodegenerative disorders such as Alzheimers; and Parkinson's diseases (Carswell, 1993). The acceleration or reestablishment of sensitive periods, the enhancement of learning and memory via biochemical adjustments, and the cultivation of new cells all suggest the future possibility of intentional and strategic enhancement of neural plasticity.

Summary

The human brain is astonishingly complex. Billions of neurons and trillions of synaptic connections have organized over evolutionary history in intricate and often hidden relationships. Furthermore, each individual brain simultaneously reflects an adaptation to its unique environment, utterly dependent on caretakers—both healthy and unhealthy—for decades. The neural complexity and design compromises made during evolution, combined with the ups-and-downs of development, render the brain extremely vulnerable to dysregulation. Psychotherapy was born because of this vulnerability.

The power of psychotherapy to change the brain rests in its ability to recognize and alter unintegrated or dysregulated neural networks. As psychotherapy has progressed through the last century, the need for a balance between an empathic relationship and an exposure to manageable stress has been a repeated theme. In this interpersonal and emotional context, the use of language based learning in the form of co-constructed narratives, psychoeducation, and reality testing have also proven central to successful treatment.

As knowledge of neural plasticity and neurogenesis increases, so will our ability to impact and alter the brain. The possibility exists that sensitive periods can be reinstated in the context of psychotherapy, and that stress can be utilized in a controlled manner to "reedit" emotional memories (Post et al., 1998). Although the practical application of these principles to humans remains on the distant horizon, the possibilities of psychotherapy's involvement in brain sculpting are obvious. It is not too much of a stretch to say that psychotherapists are already enhancing plasticity without the help of genetic manipulation or chemical interventions.

In the recent shift to neural optimism, critical periods of neural development are being reconsidered as important but, perhaps, not the final word on neural structure. The impact of enriched environments has demonstrated the brain-building capacity of positive experiences throughout the lifespan. More recent research in neural plasticity (e.g., use-dependent plasticity, neurotransmitter alteration, stem cell implantation) suggests that new experiences, and future potential biological interventions, may be capable of providing us with many tools with which to rebuild the brain. Psychotherapy is on the verge of an exploding new paradigm: The psychotherapist as neuroscientist.

The Psychotherapist as Neuroscientist: An Emerging Paradigm

Psychotherapy, sometimes denigrated as "just talk," is
in its own way as "biological" as the use of drugs.
(Andreasen, 2001)

As the dialogue between psychotherapy and neuroscience continues
to expand, an increasing number of scientific findings will be applied
to clinical theory and practice. Simultaneously, identification of factors related to change in psychotherapy may suggest new areas of
research into learning and plasticity. The synthesis of paradigms is a
slow and often laborious process requiring repeated shuttling
between the two models. Their gradual evolution into a cohesive
whole results from the generation and testing of countless individual
hypotheses. In this final chapter we will explore just a few of these
ideas as we shuttle back and forth between psychotherapy and neuroscience.

Interpretations and Plasticity

You may remember from chapter 3 that interpretation in psychodynamic modes of treatment is sometimes referred to as the "therapist's scalpel." In making an interpretation, the therapist points out some unconscious aspect of the patient's experience. This often takes the form of bringing to consciousness defenses he or she is using to avoid negative feelings. For a client who employs humor in order to avoid feelings of abandonment after a divorce, it might entail reminding him that he is experiencing many signs of depression or that his eyes are moist. For another who is enraged at a minor slight by a coworker, an interpretation might consist of connecting her present feelings to emotional memories of abuse from a previous relationship. In both of these cases, the therapist addresses what appears to be a disconnection among different tracks of cognitive, emotional, sensory, and behavioral processing.

When an interpretation is accurate and delivered in an appropriate and well-timed manner, a number of things occur. The client generally becomes quiet; there is a change in facial expression and sometimes posture. Very often the client will begin to more fully experience the emotion against which he or she was defending. There is a shift from fluent reflexive language to speaking in a slower and more self-reflective manner. Some clients report becoming confused or disoriented, whereas others describe physiological symptoms of anxiety or panic. Borderline clients can demonstrate extreme reactions to interpretations, including emotional and functional decompensation. They may become extremely emotional, leave the consulting room, and engage in self-injurious behavior. Patients like these appear unable to regulate the emotional discharges that result when their defenses are made conscious.

What is actually happening in the brain during and after an accurate and well-timed interpretation? The emotion evoked supports the success of interpretations (and other therapeutic interventions) through both increased activation of subcortical circuits containing negative memories and biochemical changes that enhance plasticity in cortico–hippocampal association areas. The concurrent availability of negative subcortical memories and the enhanced ability of the cortex to create new connections allows for the possibility of reorganizing the matrix of neural networks to bring together (associate) the multiple networks containing various components of a particular memory. Like breaking and resetting a bone that has healed badly, in this process memory systems are, in a sense, loosened so that they can be reformed in a more positive way. This allows for painful implicit memories to be accessible to cortical networks for contextualization in time and space, and the emotional aspects to be regulated and inhibited in situations in which they are no longer relevant.

The confusion and disorientation described and exhibited by many clients appears to be a less-intense version of the dissociation that occurs immediately after overwhelming trauma. As we have already seen, the experience of stress and trauma appears to enhance neural plasticity. Dissociation secondary to trauma reflects the disruption of systems of learning, memory, and neural network organization when levels of stress are too high for too long (Chambers et al., 1999). Stress is a biological state conducive to the reorganization of neural networks. From the point of view of natural selection, learning is a matter of life and death.

Thus, although we usually understand dissociation primarily from the perspective of a psychological defense (Ludwig, 1983), it can also be viewed as an exaggeration of the fundamental processes of learning when pushed beyond their adaptive limits. We might imagine that cortical association areas should be particularly active in dissociative processes. In fact, changes in regional cerebral blood flow (RCBF) in the temporal lobes across personalities have been found in two different case reports of patients with dissociative identity disorder (Mathew, Jack, & West, 1985; Saxe, Vasile, Hill, Bloomingdale, & van der Kolk, 1992). Frontal and temporal regions also show decreased activity when new learning stops and experience is guided by past learning, such as during PTSD flashbacks (Rauch et al., 1996).

The emotional and behavioral shifts occurring in reaction to an interpretation may reflect these underlying neurobiological processes. Bringing a defense to consciousness activates both the cortical networks that organize the defense and the subcortical networks that contain the negative memories and associated affect. This disinhibition results in the emotional and physiological arousal seen in therapy as the amygdala becomes reactivated and alerts the body to the old danger. This may also be the mechanism for regression through the reactivation of old sensory-motor-affective memories stored in normally inhibited amygdaloid systems. There is most likely a shift in hemispheric bias from left to right, correlated with the breakthrough of negative emotions. This left-to-right shift may account for the cessation of reflexive social language of the left-hemisphere interpreter and a shift to greater self-awareness.

Interpretations need to undergo a process called *working through*, referring to the fact they need to be stated, restated, and applied to multiple situations and circumstances (parallel to relapse prevention in cognitive therapies). This process serves to connect new learning to multiple memory networks, and may need to reach a certain critical mass of connections throughout the brain to become reflexive. Working through reflects the expansion and stabilization of new associative matrices of memory. It is also reflected in the co-construction of a new narrative containing altered aspects of behavior, feelings, and self-identity that was previously unintegrated within autobiographical memory or conscious awareness. These self-narratives serve as a way to retain new learning in consciousness and have it continue to shape new ways of being.

Psychopathology and Neuroscience

Functional brain imaging has opened a window to the living human brain in the acts of motor tasks, experiencing symptoms, imagining a feared situation, or telling a lie. An examination of areas activated during different tasks has enhanced our understanding of which neural networks participate in various functions. Although both scanning technology and its application to psychopathology are still in their infancy, there have been many important and provocative initial findings. As scanning techniques become more precise and the hardware more affordable, they will no doubt become incorporated into psychotherapy. As a part of initial assessment, they could help therapists pinpoint areas of neural activation and inhibition. Treatment planning will come to include specific psychotherapeutic and pharmacological intervention to enhance growth and integration of affected networks. Regular scans during the course of therapy may someday replace psychological tests as ways of fine-tuning the therapeutic process and measuring treatment success.

The foundation for this futuristic perspective is already being established. Associations between psychiatric symptoms and changes in the relative metabolism of different areas of the brain are being found. We have already seen lower levels of metabolism in the left-prefrontal cortex of depressed patients (Baxter et al., 1985, 1989) and increased metabolism in the right-prefrontal and limbic region of patients with PTSD (Rauch et al., 1996). The importance of the right-frontal region in PTSD is supported by clinical evidence such as the onset of PTSD after injury to the right-frontal area (Berthier, Posada, & Puentes, 2001) and a "cure" of PTSD symptoms after a right-frontal-lobe stroke (Freeman & Kimbrell, 2001). The inhibition of Broca's area during intense fear states is already a focus of cognitive behavioral forms of treatment, and a reactivation of the language centers may become a standard measure of success in the treatment of PTSD and other anxiety-related disorders. All these findings support the existence of specific circuitry involved in the recognition, reaction, and regulation of anxiety and fear in the aftermath of traumatic experiences.

This is far different than the old localization theories that attributed different disorders to specific areas of the brain. We now understand that each region of the brain exists within multiple neural systems with highly complex interrelationships and homeostatic functions. It is actually the relationship between clinical symptoms and activity levels of specific components of neural networks that is being measured. This is also the case in single-cell recordings of neurons, which respond to mirroring processes and facial recognition. These measuring procedures tap into highly complex and distributed processes with very simple recording devices. All of these physiological and neurobiological measures need to be thought of as correlates of brain–behavior relationships suggesting further exploration.

The neurobiology of obsessive compulsive disorder (OCD) has been of particular interest in this regard. A neural circuit thought to mediate OCD includes the orbitofrontal cortex (Ofc) and subcortical structures called the *caudate nucleus, globus pallidus,* and *thalamus.* This cortical–subcortical circuit, involved with the primitive recognition of and reaction to contamination and danger, becomes locked into an activation loop in patients with OCD (Baxter, 1992). It is hypothesized that the Ofc, or some other component of the OCD circuit, activates the circuit with a worry signal. This signal results in decreased inhibition to the thalamus, which in turn increasingly excites the Ofc and caudate (Baxter, 1992). The result is a feedback loop that is highly resistant to inhibition or shutting down.

Functional scan studies have demonstrated that improvement of OCD symptoms is correlated with decreased activation of the Ofc and caudate nucleus (Rauch et al., 1994). Especially interesting to psychotherapists is the fact that these changes in brain metabolism are the same whether patients are successfully treated with psychotherapy or medication (Baxter et al., 1992; Schwartz et al,. 1996). This is the first research that actually demonstrated the impact of successful psychotherapy on brain metabolism. Although psychotherapy and medication are the first choice of treatment, they are not always successful. Scan-guided psychosurgery for patients who do not respond to any other forms of treatment can disrupt runaway feedback by cutting neural links within the OCD circuit (Biver et al., 1995; Irle, Exner, Thielen, Weniger, & Ruther, 1998; Rubino et al., 2000).

Because individual symptoms can have so many underlying causes, diagnoses aided by an understanding of neural network involvement promise to add specificity and accuracy to the diagnostic process. Increased specificity will naturally lead to increasingly specific psychotherapeutic and pharmacological interventions. Tourette's Syndrome—a disorder characterized by involuntary vocalizations and motor tics—often occurs in individuals who also suffer with OCD, enuresis, and/or ADHD. This is not a coincidence! These disorders share underlying neural circuitry and neurotransmitters (Cummings & Frankel, 1985). They all stem from problems with the inhibition of subcortical impulses by the frontal cortical areas. Thus, structural, regulatory, or biochemical abnormalities in these related top-down networks can result in all four conditions. When this circuit is more fully understood, symptoms of OCD, ADHD, enuresis, and Tourette's may all become subsets of some future diagnosis referred to by the neural networks responsible for these functions.

Another example of the potential impact of neuroimaging on diagnosis is demonstrated in the work of Daniel Amen, M.D. Combining clinical experience and SPECT scans (which measure blood flow in the brain), Amen proposed six different subtypes of ADHD. He suggested that each ADHD type is reflective of different patterns of suboptimal neural activity and regulation (Amen, 2001) requiring various combinations of treatment including medication, exercise, cognitive retraining, education, and emotional support. Because attention and concentration result from the coordination of multiple neural circuits, they can be disrupted by a variety of underlying causes. Thus, although the symptoms expressed in patients with ADHD may look very similar, they can be caused by dysregulation in different networks that contribute to attention. Armed with an understanding of the functions and neurochemistry of each neural network, multifaceted treatments can be created to attempt to readjust them. Regardless of whether Dr. Amen's theories stand up to controlled research, the use of neural network activity in diagnosis is a promising methodological improvement.

The Centrality of Stress

Although stress is a normal part of life, we have seen that early, chronic, and severe stress can result in significant and permanent damage at all stages of development (Glaser, 2000; O'Brien, 1997; Sapolsky, 1996). An emerging concept in treatment is to attempt to buffer victims of stress from neural compromise by chemically blocking the glucocorticoids suspected of causing the damage (Liu et al., 1997; Meaney et al., 1989; Wantanabe, Gould, Daniels, Cameron, & McEwen, 1992) or providing people with experiences to ameliorate their effects. For example, research by Morgan and his colleagues (Morgan et al., 2000) has shown that the neurotransmitter neuropeptide-Y (NPY) is found in the amygdala in higher concentrations in individuals who respond more favorably to high levels of stress (Morgan et al., 2000). Artificially increasing NPY levels may decrease anxiety and buffer the nervous system from some of the damaging effects of stress.

In rats, increased licking of the pups by the mother decreases the pups' subsequent response to stress, as measured by HPA activation (Liu et al., 1997). Although I doubt that encouraging human mothers to lick their children will be of much help, human infants have demonstrated the same sort of decreases in stress hormones as a result of maternal massage (Field et al., 1996) and within secure attachments (Spangler & Grossman, 1993). Maternal depression is a severe stressor for infants, and results in higher levels of stress hormones. Aggressive treatment of depression in new mothers, along with teaching them how to massage their infants on a regular basis, may counteract some of the negative impact of maternal depression on children. Therapy focused on resolving attachment difficulties of mothers prior to giving birth may also be helpful in reducing stress in their infants.

Maternal separation is also extremely stressful for human and primate infants and is reflected in their increased hypothalamic-pituitary-adrenal (HPA) activation (Gunnar, 1992). An increased understanding of maternal separation may lead to better advice about the advisability of and means of coping with infant–mother separation. In unavoidable situations such as illness or death, the ability to lessen the impact of stress hormones via interpersonal and chemical interventions may create the possibility of avoiding yet more difficulty and stress later in life. Given the amount of exposure in our society to stressful events such as abuse, neglect, abandonment, and community violence, the impact of severe stress on the developing brain should be a serious public health concern (Bremner & Narayan, 1998).

Early stress leads to a vulnerability for depression later in life. This, in part, is mediated by deficient organization of frontal circuitry and the establishment of lower levels of excitatory neurotransmitters and growth hormones during critical periods (Schore, 1994). We see the results of this developmental process both in the tendency to lower metabolic activation in the prefrontal cortex and the amygdala (Drevets et al., 1992), and the alleviation of these symptoms when neurotransmitter levels are artificially increased. Early childhood experiences leading to a right-hemisphere bias in cortical function may also play a role in the development of depression. As we discussed in the chapter on laterality, magnetic stimulation of the left hemisphere of depressed patients and the right hemisphere of patients with mania have shown promising results (Grisaru et al., 1998; Klein et al., 1999; Teneback et al., 1999) and may serve as a future alternative to electroconvulsive therapy (Pascual-Leone et al., 1996).

In line with these findings, activation of the left hemisphere through sensory stimulation results in a higher degree of self-serving attributions and positive affect (Drake & Seligman, 1989). Relative left-frontal activation appears to be linked to a state of mind of "self-enhancement," which may decrease risk for psychopathology and be manipulated in such a manner as to decrease depression (Tomarken & Davidson, 1994). The more we understand the relationship between laterality and affect, the more we may be able to incorporate techniques of selective activation of right and left hemispheres into multimodal treatments for mood disorders and other psychiatric difficulties. Psychotherapists may soon employ techniques and devices designed to enhance left–right hemisphere balance in treatment.

Posttraumatic stress disorder (PTSD) is primarily mediated and maintained by neurobiological processes outside of conscious control. In chapter 2, we looked at a way to apply data concerning the inhibition of Broca's area (Rauch et al., 1996) in treating a patient with posttraumatic flashbacks. The activation of Broca's area in the face of high levels of affect appears to be an important mechanism of action in most interventions with patients suffering from PTSD and other anxiety disorders. We know that the Ofc can alter activity in the amygdala; this is essentially what we are doing when we try to help clients employ cortical, reality-based cognition in addressing their fears.

Chemical blockade or disruption of particular circuits involving the amygdala may decrease some of the symptoms of PTSD—such as startle (Lee & Davis, 1997) and freezing (Goldstein, Rasmusson, Bunney, & Roth, 1996)—and mitigate some of their long-term, retraumatizing effects. The ability to decrease the impact of amygdala activation on frontal areas may be relevant to schizophrenia as well as PTSD, given that both appear to involve the amygdala in its role in the release of dopamine for activation of the frontal cortex. It has even been suggested that stimulation of the amygdala could lead to the extinction of conditioned fear (Li, Weiss, Chaung, Post, & Rogawski, 1998).

Understanding the role of LTP and other forms of plasticity in the amygdala, as well as its role in fear conditioning, may provide another avenue for future interventions in psychosis and PTSD (LaBar, Gatenby, Gore, LeDoux, & Phelps, 1998; Rogan & LeDoux, 1996; Rogan, Staubli, & LeDoux, 1997).

Integrating Neural Networks

Despite new theories connecting neural communication and psychopathology, no major form of psychotherapy has emerged with the stated goal of neural network integration. This being said, some atypical techniques have been used involving left–right and top-down integration as an active element. Two such interventions that may be relevant are the caloric test and EMDR.

In chapter 6, we discussed the phenomenon of sensory neglect. This occurs when there is damage to the right-parietal lobe (assumed to be responsible for the integration of sensory and motor information from both sides of the brain). Stimulation with cold water to the left ear results in rapid side-to-side eye movements serving to activate regions of the temporal lobes (Friberg et al., 1985). Although there has been one report of permanent remission of sensory neglect with the cold water treatment (Rubens, 1985), for most the "cure" is only temporary. The bilateral activation of attentional centers in reaction to the caloric test results in increased integration of previously dissociated attention and information-processing systems (Bisiach et al., 1991).

In the treatment of PTSD with EMDR, past traumatic events are recalled and processed with a protocol that involves the focus of attention on ideas, self-beliefs, emotions, and bodily sensations with the addition of periodic stimulation of patients through either watching the therapist's hand going back and forth in front of them, having their legs touched alternately, or other forms of stimulation alternating from one side of the body to the other (Shapiro, 1995). This bilateral (to both sides) and alternating stimulation may serve to activate attention centers in both temporal lobes in a manner similar to the caloric test. This alternating activation may, in fact, enhance neural network connectivity and the integration of traumatic memories into normal information processing.

Techniques such as EMDR and the caloric text may thwart or reverse the brain's adaptive tendency toward the dissociation of networks of emotion and cognition when faced with trauma. Bilateral stimulation may enhance the consolidation of the traumatic memory with cortical–hippocampal circuits providing contextualization in time and place. Activation of these same circuits creates the possibility of inhibiting subcortical sensory-affective memory circuits (Siegel, 1995). Thus, the right–left stimulation of attention may simultaneously trigger integration of affect with cognition, sensation, and behavior throughout the brain.

Once the relationships among neural circuits are more fully understood, psychotherapists may employ these and other noninvasive techniques to stimulate emotional networks for patients who demonstrate a disconnection between cognition and emotion. Could activation of right-hemisphere regions of affect be stimulated during therapy with alexithymic patients to aid in the integration of emotional processes with left-hemisphere linguistic circuitry? Could activation of the left hemisphere during emotional dyscontrol in borderline patients enhance their ability to gain cognitive perspective and control on their emotional reactions?

For conditions involving too much emotional inhibition, new learning may be stimulated by creating moderate levels of affect in therapy; this learning, in turn, may create a biochemical environment more conducive to plasticity in emotional circuits (Bishof, 1983; Chambers et al., 1999). This may be the underlying neurobiology of Freud's belief that affect has to occur in the treatment in order for it to produce change. Simultaneous activation of neural networks of emotion and cognition may result in binding the two in such a way as to allow for the conscious awareness and integration of emotion.

Treatment Rationales and Combinations

The fundamental premise put forth in this book is that any form of psychotherapy is successful to the degree to which it enhances positive experiential change and underlying neural network growth and integration. I expect future research to continue to support this hypothesis. Furthermore, evolving technologies will provide us with increasingly accurate ways of measuring activity within the brain and awareness of the significance of what we are measuring. Understanding and measuring neural network activity may establish a common currency for us to select, combine, and evaluate treatments. It will, one hopes, help us to move past debates between competing schools of thought to a more scientific approach to psychotherapy.

One classic and hard-fought debate about treatment continues between supporters of *psychotherapy* and those who prefer *psychopharmacology*. Despite the fact that research supports the efficacy of both individually and in combination, abuses highlighted in the popular press fuel strong antagonistic feelings against both. Patients who come to see me for psychotherapy are often adamant in their refusal to consider medication. Some feel frightened or criticized if I suggest a medication evaluation; such reactions have led me to approach the issue of medication very carefully. This is one situation in which education about the growth and functioning of the brain is especially useful. As we have seen, experience builds the neural structures of the brain and establishes levels of the neurotransmitters that activate them. In this context, medication can help to establish neural network balance and integration that then enhances the benefits of psychotherapy.

The neurotransmitters powering the frontal cortex (e.g., serotonin, dopamine, and norepinephrine) are stimulated through positive experiences and social interactions. Patients suffering from anxiety disorders and depression limit or eliminate both of these activities, further downregulating their production. This downward spiral is often difficult to break with psychotherapy alone. The right medication can make more of these neurotransmitters available to decrease symptoms of anxiety and depression, thus decreasing focus on fears and negative thoughts. I encourage patients at this point to work on altering their lives in ways that stimulate the activation of these neural networks. In this way, if they choose to discontinue the medication, they have established behaviors and interpersonal relationships that may, in fact, have the same effects on brain functioning.

Many patients who suffer brain damage due to accidents participate in multimodal treatment programs that include physical, cognitive, and psychosocial components of *rehabilitation*. Most generally, the approach to rehabilitation after brain injury is first to assess which systems have been damaged and which have been spared. The next step is to develop a program that plays to such patients' strengths and attempts to compensate for their weaknesses. Interventions focus on compensating for damaged neural networks that no longer function adequately. Because of the architecture of the brain, traffic and industrial accidents often result in damage to the frontal cortex. Because of this damage, disorders of attention, concentration, memory, executive functioning, and emotional regulation are all common in neurological rehabilitation settings. Not coincidentally, these same difficulties are common in many forms of psychopathology.

The traditional split between mind and brain has resulted in the separate development of the fields of psychotherapy and rehabilitation. When psychological difficulties are conceptualized in the context of a brain–behavior relationship, the possibility of an integration of techniques from cognitive rehabilitation into psychotherapy becomes possible. Abnormalities of frontal-lobe functioning are seen in many forms of psychiatric illnesses, such as OCD, PTSD, depression, and ADHD. All of these disorders result in problems similar to those suffered by patients with brain injury. Patients with these and other "psychiatric" diagnoses may benefit from the adjunctive use of cognitive prosthetics developed in a neurological rehabilitation settings (Parente & Herrmann, 1996).

An example of this was given in chapter 5, when I discussed how I employed simple memory strategies to assist my patient Sophia in remembering her appointments. My working assumption was that a combination of decreased hippocampal volume due to chronic stress (Bremner, Scott, Delaney, Southwick, Mason, Johnson, et al., 1993) and hypometabolism in the temporal lobes related to depression (Brody et al., 2001) created real, brain-related memory dysfunctions. The success of cognitive–behavioral treatments with depressed and anxious patients underlines the importance of enhancing the frontal

functions of reality testing, focused attention, and social skills training to reestablish affect regulation (Schwartz, 1996).

Similar rehabilitation techniques may also help with borderline
patients, given that neuropsychological findings with these patients
also suggests damage or dysfunction in frontal and temporal regions
(Paris et al., 1999; Swirsky-Sacchetti et al., 1993). This may help
explain why borderline patients require increased levels of structure
to scaffold erratic executive control and emotional stability.
Manipulation and organization of the physical environment, sensory
stimulation, and the type and amount of activity all impact brain
functioning. Psychoeducation and enlisting family and friends in the
therapeutic process (as utilized extensively in rehabilitation after
brain damage) are potential mechanisms of change.

Diagnostic and treatment approaches focused on cognitive
deficits serve to decrease shame and help to create a stronger treatment alliance. Highly structured skill-building techniques, in the
context of support and understanding, may provide disorganized
patients with the opportunity for early and clearly measurable success experiences. As our understanding of neural networks related to
memory, affect, and behavior expands, prosthetic aids to these systems will be created and applied in the psychotherapy context.
Increasing interdisciplinary coordination of this kind will require
more comprehensive training for psychotherapists, not only in neuroscience but also in cognition, memory, and rehabilitation science.
Removing the traditional barriers between psychotherapy and rehabilitation may lead to a higher quality of care and greater treatment
success.

Knowing Our Brains

Many of us, myself included, have difficulty programming a VCR or
making our "user-friendly" computers work properly. Fortunately,
we have manuals and experts to consult when we finally surrender to
our ignorance. The worst-case scenarios are that we simply don't

record the right television program or have to bribe a friend to explain our computer to us. At the same time, we constantly use what is perhaps the most complex structure in the universe with little thought or attention as to how it works.

Although we are only at the dawn of understanding the brain, an appreciation of its evolutionary history, developmental sculpting, and design flaws can help us use it more wisely. Practical things—like understanding the neural damage resulting from drugs, stress, and early deprivation—should influence everything from personal decision making to public policy. Our tendencies to distort reality in the direction of personal experience and egocentric needs should lead us to examine our beliefs and opinions more carefully. I am convinced that understanding our brains will help us to better know our minds.

Because we now know that mind and brain, and nature and nurture, are one and the same, all of the disorders we have thought of as "psychological" need to be reframed to include neurobiological correlates and mechanisms. On the other hand, if brain-based problems are a central component of a particular client's difficulties, the "most illuminating interpretation" may not be as valuable as accurate neurobiological knowledge (Yovell, 2000). Self-awareness is a relatively new phenomenon in evolutionary history. It is also just recently that we have become aware of the fact that our brains organize the totality of our experience. Psychotherapy increases neural integration through challenges that expand our experience and perspective of ourselves and the world. The challenge of expanding consciousness is to move beyond reflex, fear, and prejudice to a mindfulness and compassion for ourselves and others. Understanding the promise and limitations of our brains is but one essential step in the evolution of human consciousness.

References

Adamec, R. E. (1991). Partial kindling of the ventral hippocampus: Identification of changes in limbic physiology which accompany changes in feline aggression and defense. *Physiology and Behavior, 49,* 443–454.

Adams, R. D., Victor, M., & Ropper, A. H. (1997). *Principles of neurology.* New York: McGraw-Hill.

Adolphs, R., Tranel, D., & Damasio, A. (1998). The human amygdala in social judgment. *Nature, 393,* 470–474.

Adolphs, R., Tranel, D., Damasio, H., & Damasio, A. (1994). Impaired recognition of emotion in facial expressions following bilateral damage to the human amygdala. *Nature, 372,* 669–672.

Ahern, G. L., Schomer, D. L., Kleefield, J., Blume, H., Rees-Cosgrove, G., Weintraub, S., & Mesulam, M. M. (1991). Right hemisphere advantage for evaluating emotional facial expressions. *Cortex, 27,* 193–202.

Ainsworth, M. D. S., Blehar, M. C., Waters, E., & Wall, S. (1978). *Patterns of attachment: A psychological study of the strange situation.* Hillsdale, NJ: Erlbaum.

Akaneya, Y., Tsumoto, T., Kinoshita, S., & Hatanaka, H. (1997). Brain-derived neurotrophic factor enhances long-term potentiation in rat visual cortex. *The Journal of Neuroscience, 17*(17), 6707–6716.

Albright, D. (1994). Literary and psychological models of the self. In U. Neisser & R. Fivush (Eds.), *The remembered self: Construction and accuracy in the self-narrative* (pp. 19–40). New York: Cambridge University Press.

Alexander, G. E., DeLong, M. R., & Strick, P. L. (1986). Parallel organization of functionally segregated circuits linking basal ganglia and cortex. *Annual Review of Neuroscience, 9,* 357–381.

Alexander, M. P., Stuss, D. T., & Benson, D. F. (1979). Capgras syndrome: A reduplicative phenomenon. *Neurology, 29,* 334–339.

Allman, J., & Brothers, L. (1994). Faces, fear, and the amygdala. *Nature, 372,* 613–614.

Altman, J., Wallace, R. B., Anderson, W. J., & Das, G. D. (1968). Behaviorally induced changes in length of cerebrum in rats. *Developmental Psychobiology, 1*(2), 112–117.

Amaral, D. G., Veazey, R. B., & Cowan, W. M. (1982). Some observations on the hypothalamo-amygdaloid connections in the monkey. *Brain Research, 252,* 13–27.

Amen, D. G. (2001). *Healing ADD: The breakthrough program that allows you to see and heal the six types of attention deficit disorder.* New York: Putnam.

American Psychiatric Association (2000). *Diagnostic and statistical manual of mental disorders, (4th Ed.)* Washington, DC: Author.

Andreasen, N. C. (2001). *Brave new brain: Conquering mental illness in the era of the genome.* New York: Oxford University Press.

Anisman, H. (1978). Neurochemical changes elicited by stress: Behavioral correlates. In H. Anisman & G. Bignami (Eds.), *Psychopharmacology of aversively motivated behavior* (pp. 119–171) New York: Plenum.

Ardila, A., & Rosseli, M. (1988). Temporal lobe involvement in Capgras Syndrome. *International Journal of Neuroscience, 43,* 219–224.

Arnsten, A. F. T. (2000). Genetics of childhood disorders: XVIII. ADHD, Part 2: Norepinephrine has a critical modulatory influence on prefrontal cortical function. *Journal of the American Academy of Child and Adolescent Psychiatry, 39*(9), 374–383.

Ashcraft, M. H. (1994). *Human memory and cognition.* New York: HarperCollins.

Aston-Jones, G., Valentino, R. J., VanBockstaele, E. J., & Meyerson, A. T. (1994). Locus coeruleus, stress, and PTSD: Neurobiology and clinical parallels. In M.M. Murburg (Ed.), *Catecholamine function in Posttraumatic Stress Disorder: Emerging concepts* (pp. 17–62). Washington, DC: American Psychiatric Press.

Bagby, R. M., & Taylor, G. J. (1997). Affect dysregulation and alexithymia. In G. J. Taylor, R. M. Bagby, & J. D. A. Parker (Eds.), *Disorders of affect regulation: Alexithymia in medical and psychiatric illness* (pp. 26–45). Cambridge, UK: Cambridge University Press.

Baird, A. A., Gruber, S. A., Fein, D. A., Maas, L. C., Steingard, R. J., Renshaw, P. F., Cohen, B. M., & Yurgelun-Todd, D. A. (1999). Functional magnetic resonance imaging of facial affect recognition in children and adolescents. *Journal of the American Academy of Child and Adolescent Psychiatry, 38*(2), 195–199.

Baptista, L. F., & Petrinovich, L. (1986). Song development in the white-crowned sparrow: Social factors and sex differences. *Animal Behavior, 34,* 1359–1371.

Barad, M. (2000, Feb.). *A biological analysis of transference.* Paper presented at the UCLA Annual Review of Neuropsychiatry, Indian Wells, CA.

Barbas, H. (1995). Anatomic basis of cognitive-emotional interactions in the primate prefrontal cortex. *Neuroscience and Biobehavioral Reviews, 19*(3), 499–510.

Barde, Y.-A. (1989). Trophic factors and neuronal survival. *Neuron, 2,* 1525–1534.

Bargh, J. A., & Chartrand, T. L. (1999). The unbearable automaticity of being. *American Psychologist, 54*(7), 462–479.

Bartzokis, G., Beckson, M., Lu, P. H., Nuechterlein, K. H., Edwards, N., & Mintz, J. (2001). Age-related changes in frontal and temporal lobe volumes in men. *Archives of General Psychiatry, 58,* 461–465.

Bateson, M. C. (1979). The epigenesis of conversational interaction: A personal account of research development. In M. Bullowa (Ed.), *Before speech: The beginning of human communication* (pp. 63–77). Cambridge, UK: Cambridge University Press.

Baxter, L. R. (1992). Neuroimaging studies of obsessive-compulsive disorder. *Psychiatric Clinics of North America, 15*(4), 871–884.

Baxter, L. R., Phelps, M. E., Mazziotta, J. C., Schwartz, J. M., Gerner, R. H., Selin, C. E., & Sumida, R. M. (1985). Cerebral metabolic rates for glucose metabolism in mood disorders. *Archives of General Psychiatry, 42,* 441–447.

Baxter, L. R., Schwartz, J. M., Bergman, K. S., Szuba, M. P., Guze, B. H., Mazziotta, J. C., Alazraki, A., Selin, C. E., Feng, H. K., Munford, P., & Phelps, M. E. (1992). Caudate glucose metabolic rate changes with both drug and behavior therapy for obsessive-compulsive disorder. *Archives of General Psychiatry, 40,* 681–689.

Baxter, L. R., Schwartz, J. M., Phelps, M. E., Mazziotta, J. C., Guze, B. H., Selin, C. E., Gerner, R. H., & Sumida, R. M. (1989). Reduction of prefrontal cortex glucose metabolism common to three types of depression. *Archives of General Psychiatry, 46,* 243–250.

Beatty, J. (2001). *The human brain: Essentials of behavioral neuroscience.* Thousand Oaks, CA: Sage.

Bechara, A., Damasio, H., Tranel, D., & Damasio, A. (1997). Deciding advantageously before knowing the advantageous strategy. *Science, 275,* 1293–1295.

Bechara, A., Tranel, D., Damasio, H., Adolphs, R., Rockland, C., & Damasio, A. R. (1995). Double dissociation of conditioning and declarative knowledge relative to the amygdala and hippocampus in humans. *Science, 269,* 1115–1118.

Beck, A. T. (1976). *Cognitive therapy and emotional disorders.* New York: International University Press.

Beck, A. T., Rush, A. J., Shaw, B. F., & Emery, G. (1979). *Cognitive therapy of depression.* New York: Guilford.

Beeghly, M., & Cicchetti, D. (1994). Child maltreatment, attachment, and the self-system: Emergence of an internal state lexicon in toddlers at high social risk. *Development and Psychopathology, 6,* 5–30.

Bell, M. A., & Fox, N. A. (1992). The relations between frontal brain electrical activity and cognitive development during infancy. *Child Development, 63,* 1142–1163.

Benes, F. M. (1989). Myelination of cortical–hippocampal relays during late adolescence. *Schizophrenia Bulletin, 15*(4), 585–593.

Bennett, E. L., Diamond, M. C., Krech, D., & Rosenzweig, M. R. (1964). Chemical and anatomical plasticity of brain. *Science, 146,* 610–619.

Benson, F. D. (1994). *The neurology of thinking.* New York: Oxford University Press.

Berger, P. L., & Kellner, M. (1964). Marriage and the construction of reality. *Diogenes, 46,* 1–24.

Berthier, M. L., Posada, A., & Puentes, C. (2001). Dissociative flashbacks after right frontal injury in a Vietnam veteran with combat-related posttraumatic stress disorder. *The Journal of Neuropsychiatry and Clinical Neurosciences, 13*(1), 101–105.

Bhide, P. G., & Bedi, K. S. (1982). The effects of environmental diversity on well-fed and previously undernourished rats: I. Body and brain measurements. *The Journal of Comparative Neurology, 207*, 403–409.

Bishof, H. (1983). Imprinting and cortical plasticity: A comparative review. *Neuroscience and Biobehavioral Reviews, 7*, 213–225.

Bischoff-Grethe, A., Proper, S. M., Mao, H., Daniels, K. A. & Berns, G. S. (2000). Conscious and unconscious processing of nonverbal predictability in Wernicke's area. *The Journal of Neuroscience, 20*(5), 1975–1981.

Bisiach, E., & Luzzatti, C. (1978). Unilateral neglect of representational space. *Cortex, 14*, 129–133.

Bisiach, E., Rusconi, M. L., & Vallar, G. (1991). Remission of somatoparaphrenic delusions through vestibular stimulation. *Neuropsychologia, 29*(10), 1029–1031.

Biver, F., Goldman, S., Francois, A., DeLaPorte, C., Luxen, A., Gribomont, B., & Lotstra, F. (1995). Changes in metabolism of cerebral glucose after stereotactic leukotomy for refractory obsessive-compulsive disorder: A case report. *Journal of Neurology, Neurosurgery & Psychiatry, 58*(4), 502–505.

Black, J. E. (1998). How a child builds its brain: Some lessons from animal studies of neural plasticity. *Preventive Medicine, 27*, 168–171.

Blest, A. (1957). The function of eyespot patterns in the Lepidoptera. *Behavior, 11*, 209–256.

Blonder, L. X., Bowers, D., & Heilman, K. M. (1991). The role of right hemisphere in emotional communication. *Brain, 114*, 1115–1127.

Bohning, D. E. (2000). Introduction and overview of TMS physics. In M. S. George & R. H. Belmaker (Eds.), *Transcranial magnetic stimulation in neuropsychiatry* (pp. 13–44). Washington, DC: American Psychiatric Press.

Bonda, E., Petrides, M., Frey, S., & Evans, A. C. (1994). Frontal cortex involvement in organized sequences of hand movements: Evidence from a positron emission tomography study [abstract]. *Social Neuroscience Abstracts, 20*, 7353.

Bornstein, M. H. (1989). Sensitive periods in development: Structural characteristics and causal interpretations. *Psychological Bulletin, 105*(2), 179–197.

Bowen, M. (1978). *Family therapy in clinical practice.* New York: Jason Aronson.

Bowlby, J. (1969). *Attachment.* New York: Basic.

Bradley, S. (1990). Affect regulation and psychopathology: Bridging the mind-body gap. *Canadian Journal of Psychiatry, 35*, 540–547.

Bradshaw, J. (1990). *Homecoming: Reclaiming and championing your inner child.* New York: Bantam.

Braun, C., Scweizer, R., Elbert, T., Borbaumer, N., & Taub, E. (2000). Differential activation in somatosensory cortex for different discrimination tasks. *The Journal of Neuroscience, 20*(1), 446–450.

Bremner, J. D., & Narayan, M. (1998). The effects of stress on memory and the hippocampus throughout the life cycle: Implications for childhood development and aging. *Development and Psychopathology, 10*, 871–885.

Bremner, J. D., Randall, P., Scott, T. M., Bronen, R. A., Seibyl, J. P., Southwick, S. M., Delaney, R. C., McCarthy, G., Charney, D. S., & Innis, R. B. (1995). MRI-based measurement of hippocampal volume in patients with combat-related posttraumatic stress disorder. *American Journal of Psychiatry, 152*(7), 973–981.

Bremner, J. D., Randall, P., Vermetten, E., Staib, L., Bronen, R. A., Mazure, C., Capelli, S., McCarthy, G., Innis, R. B., & Charney, D. S. (1997). Magnetic resonance imaging-based measurement of hippocampal volume in posttraumatic stress disorder related to childhood physical and sexual abuse: A preliminary report. *Biological Psychiatry, 41*, 23–32.

Bremner, J. D., Scott, T. M., Delaney, R. C., Southwick, S. M., Mason, J. W., Johnson, D. R., Innis, R. B., McCarthy, G., & Charney, D. S. (1993). Deficits of short-term memory in posttraumatic stress disorder. *American Journal of Psychiatry, 150*(7), 1015–1019.

Bremner, J. D., Southwick, S. M., Johnson, D. R., Yehuda, R., & Charney, D. S. (1993). Childhood physical abuse and combat-related posttraumatic stress disorder in Vietnam veterans. *American Journal of Psychiatry, 150*(2), 235–239.

Brennan, K. A., & Shaver, P. R. (1995). Dimensions of adult attachment, affect regulation, and romantic relationship functioning. *Personality and Social Psychology Bulletin, 21*(3), 267–283.

Brewin, C. R., Dalgleish, T., & Joseph, S. (1996). A dual representation theory of post traumatic stress disorder. *Psychological Research, 103*, 670–686.

Brodal, P. (1992). *The central nervous system.* New York: Oxford University Press.

Brody, A. L., Saxena, S., Stoessel, P., Gillies, L. A., Fairbanks, L. A., Alborzian, S., Phelps, M. E., Huang, S. C., Wu, H. M., Ho, M. L., Ho, M. K., Au, S. C., Maidment, K., & Baxter, L. R. (2001). Regional brain metabolic changes in patients with major depression treated with either paroxetine or interpersonal therapy. *Archives of General Psychiatry, 58*, 631–640.

Brothers, A., & Ring, B. (1993). Mesial temporal neurons in the macaque monkey with responses selective for aspects of social stimuli. *Behavioral Brain Research, 57*, 53–61.

Brothers, A., Ring, B., & Kling, A. (1990). Response of neurons in the macaque amygdala to complex social stimuli. *Behavioral Brain Research, 41*, 199–213.

Brothers, L. (1997). *Friday's footprint.* New York: Oxford Press.

Bruner, J. S. (1990). *Acts of meaning.* Cambridge, MA: Harvard University Press.

Bruner, J. S. (1994). The "remembered" self. In U. Neisser & R. Fivush (Eds.), *The remembered self: Construction and accuracy in the self-narrative* (pp. 41–54). New York: Cambridge University Press.

Buonomano, D. V., & Merzenich, M. M. (1998). Cortical plasticity: From synapses to maps. *Annual Review of Neuroscience, 21*, 149–186.

Butler, R. W., Braff, D. L., Rauch, J. L., Jenkins, M. A., Sprock, J., & Geyer, M. A. (1990). Physiological evidence of exaggerated startle response in a subgroup of Vietnam veterans with combat-related PTSD. *American Journal of Psychiatry, 147*(10), 1308–1312.

Cacioppo, J. T., & Berntson, G. G. (1992). Social psychological contributions to the decade of the brain. *American Psychologist, 47*(8), 1019–1028.

Cahill, L., & McGaugh, J. L. (1998). Mechanisms of emotional arousal and lasting declarative memory. *Trends in Neuroscience, 21*(7), 294–299.

Cahill, L., Prins, B., Weber, M., & McGaugh, J. L. (1994). Beta-adrenergic activation and memory for emotional events. *Nature, 371*, 702–704.

Cappa, S., Sterzi, R., Vallar, G., & Bisiach, E. (1987). Remission of hemineglect and anosognosia during vestibular stimulation. *Neuropsychologia, 25*(5), 775–782.

Carroll, E. M., Rueger, D. B., Foy, D. W., & Donahoe, C. P. (1985). Vietnam combat veterans with posttraumatic stress disorder: Analysis of marital and cohabitation adjustment. *Journal of Abnormal Psychology, 94*, 329–337.

Carswell, S. (1993). The potential for treating neurodegenerative disorders with NGF-inducing compounds. *Experimental Neurology, 124*, 36–42.

Carvey, P. M. (1998). *Drug action in the central nervous system.* New York: Oxford University Press.

Casey, B. J., Castellanos, F. X., & Giedd, J. N. (1997). Implications of right frontostriatal circuitry in response inhibition and attention-deficit/hyperactivity disorder. *Journal of the American Academy of Child and Adolescent Psychiatry, 36*, 374–383.

Ceci, S., & Bruch, M. (1993). Suggestibility of the child witness: A historical review and synthesis. *Psychological Bulletin, 113*, 403–439.

Chambers, R. A., Bremner, J. D., Moghaddam, B., Southwick, S. M., Charney, D. S., & Krystal, J. H. (1999). Glutamate and posttraumatic stress disorder: Toward a psychobiology of dissociation. *Seminars in Clinical Neuropsychiatry, 4*(4), 274–281.

Changeux, J. P., & Danchin, A. (1976). Selective stabilization of developing synapses as a mechanism for the specification of neuronal networks. *Nature, 264*, 705–712.

Chapman, L. F., Walter, R. D., Markham, C. H., Rand, R. W., & Crandall, P. H. (1967). Memory changes induced by stimulation of hippocampus or amygdala in epilepsy patients with implanted electrodes. *Transactions of the American Neurological Association, 92*, 50–56.

Charney, D. S., Nestler, E. J., & Bunney, B. S. (1999). *Neurobiology of Mental Illness.* New York: Oxford University Press.

Chiron, C., Jambaque, I., Nabbout, R., Lounes, R., Syrota, A., & Dulac, O. (1997). The right brain is dominant in human infants. *Brain, 120*, 1057–1065.

Christman, S. D. (1994). The many sides of the two sides of the brain. *Brain and Cognition, 26*, 91–98.

Christodoulou, G. N., & Malliara-Loulakaki, S. (1981). Delusional misidentification syndromes and cerebral "dysrhythmia." *Psychiatrica Clinica, 14*, 245–251.

Chugani, H. T. (1998). A critical period of brain development: Studies of cerebral glucose utilization with PET. *Preventive Medicine, 27*, 184–188.

Chugani, H. T., & Phelps, M. E. (1991). Imaging human brain development with positron emission tomography. *The Journal of Nuclear Medicine, 32*(1), 23–26.

Chugani, H. T., Phelps, M. E., & Mazziotta, J. C. (1987). Positron emission tomography study of human brain functional development. *Annals of Neurology, 22*, 487–497.

Classen, J., Liepert, J., Wise, S. P., Hallett, M., & Cohen, L. G. (1998). Rapid plasticity of human cortical movements representation induced by practice. *Journal of Neurophysiology, 79,* 1117–1123.

Cobb, S. (1944). *Foundations of neuropsychiatry.* Baltimore, MD: The Williams and Wilkins Company.

Coccaro, E. F., Siever, L. J., Klar, H. M., & Maurer, G. (1989). Serotonergic studies in patients with affective and personality disorders. *Archives of General Psychiatry, 46,* 587–598.

Cogill, S. R., Caplan, H. L., Alexandra, H., Robson, K. M., & Kumar, R. (1986). Impact of maternal postnatal depression on cognitive development of young children. *British Medical Journal, 292,* 1165–1167.

Coplan, J. D., & Lydiard, R. B. (1998). Brain circuits in panic disorder. *Biological Psychiatry, 44*(12), 1264–1276.

Coren, S., & Porac, C. (1977). Fifty centuries of right-handedness: The historical record. *Science, 198,* 631–632.

Corina, D. P., Vaid, J., & Bellugi, U. (1992). The linguistic basis of left hemisphere specialization. *Science, 255,* 1258–1260.

Cowan, W. M., & Kandel, E. R. (2001). A brief history of synapses and synaptic transmission. In W. M. Cowan, T. C. Sudhof, & C.F. Stevens (Eds.), *Synapses* (pp. 1–87). Baltimore: Johns Hopkins University Press.

Cozolino, L. J. (1997). The intrusion of early implicit memory into adult consciousness. *Dissociation 10*(1), 44–53.

Crick, F. (1994). *The astonishing hypothesis: The scientific search for the soul.* New York: Scribner's Sons.

Critchley, H., Daly, E., Phillips, M., Brammer, M., Bullmore, E., Williams, S., Van Amelsvoort, T., Robertson, D., David, A., & Murphy, D. (2000). Explicit and implicit mechanisms for processing of social information from facial expressions: A functional magnetic resonance imaging study. *Human Brain Mapping, 9,* 93–105.

Crittenden, P. M., & DiLalla, D. L. (1988). Compulsive compliance: The development of an inhibitory coping strategy in infancy. *Journal of Abnormal Child Psychology, 16*(5), 585–599.

Cummings, J. L. (1993). Frontal-subcortical circuits and human behavior. *Archives of Neurology, 50,* 873–880.

Cummings, J. L. (1985). *Clinical neuropsychiatry.* New York: Grune and Stratton.

Cummings, J. L., & Frankel, M. (1985). Gilles de la Tourette Syndrome and the neurological basis of obsessions and compulsions. *Biological Psychiatry, 20,* 1117–1126.

Cutting, J. (1992). The role of the right hemisphere in psychiatric disorders. *British Journal of Psychiatry, 160,* 583–588.

Damasio, A. R. (1999). *The feeling of what happens.* New York: Harcourt Brace.

Damasio, A. R. (1994). *Descartes' error.* New York: Putnam.

Damasio, H., Grabowski, T., Frank, R., Galaburda, A. M., & Damasio, A. R. (1994). The return of Phineas Gage: Clues about the brain from the skull of a famous patient. *Science, 264,* 1102–1105.

Davidson, R. J. (1999). The neurobiology of personality and personality disorders. In D. S. Charney, E. J. Nestler, & B. S. Bunney (Eds.), *Neurobiology of mental illness* (pp. 841–854). New York: Oxford University Press.

Davis, M. (1992). The role of the amygdala in fear and anxiety. *Annual Review of Neuroscience, 15*, 353–375.

Dawson, G., Panagiotides, H., Klinger, L. G., & Hill, D. (1992). The role of frontal lobe functioning in the development of self-regulatory behavior. *Brain and Cognition, 20*, 152–175.

DeBell, C., & Jones, R. D. (1997). As good as it seems: A review of EMDR experimental research. *Professional Psychology: Research and Practice, 28*(2), 153–163.

De Bellis, M. D., Baum, A. S., Birmaher, B., Keshavan, M. S., Eccard, C. H., Boring, A. M., Jenkins, F. J., & Ryan, N. D. (1999). A. E. Bennett research award. Developmental traumatology. Part I: Biological stress systems. *Biological Psychiatry, 45*(10), 1259–1270.

De Bellis, M. D., Keshavan, M.S., Clark, D. B., Casey, B. J., Giedd, J. N., Boring, A. M., Frustaci, K., & Ryan, N. D. (1999). A. E. Bennett research award. Developmental traumatology. Part II: Brain development. *Biological Psychiatry, 45*(10), 1271–1284.

decasper, A. J., & Fifer, W. P. (1980). Of human bonding: Newborns prefer their mothers' voices. *Science, 208*, 1174–1176.

Decety, J. (1994). Mapping motor representations with positron emission tomography. *Nature, 371*, 600–602.

de Lanerolle, N. C., Kim, J. H., Robbins, R. J., & Spencer, D. D. (1989). Hippocampal interneuron loss and plasticity in human temporal lobe epilepsy. *Brain Research, 495*, 387–395.

Dennett, D. C. (1991). *Consciousness explained*. Boston: Little, Brown.

Desimone, R. (1991). Face-selective cells in the temporal cortex of monkeys. *Journal of Cognitive Neuroscience, 3*, 1–8.

Devinsky, O. (2000). Right cerebral hemisphere dominance for a sense of corporeal and emotional self. *Epilepsy and Behavior, 1*, 60–73.

Devinsky, O., Morrell, M. J., & Vogt, B. A. (1995). Contributions of anterior cingulate cortex to behavior. *Brain, 118*, 179–306.

De Waal, F. (1989). *Peacemaking among primates*. New York: Penguin.

Diamond, M. C., Krech, D., & Rosenweig, M. R. (1964). The effects of enriched environment on the histology of the rat cerebral cortex. *Journal of Comparative Neurology, 123*, 111–119.

Diamond, M. C., Law, F., Rhodes, H., Lindner, B., Rosenzweig, M. R., Krech, D., & Bennett, E. L. (1966). Increases of cortical depth and glia numbers in rats subjected to enriched environments. *Journal of Comparative Neurology, 128*, 117–126.

Diamond, M. C., Scheibel, A. B., Murphy, G. M., & Harvey, T. (1985). On the brain of a scientist: Albert Einstein. *Experimental Neurology, 88*, 198–204.

Dias, R., Robbins, T. W., & Roberts, A. C. (1996). Dissociation in prefrontal cortex of affective and attentional shifts. *Nature, 380*, 69–72.

Dimond, S. J., & Farrington, L. (1977). Emotional response to films shown to the right or left hemisphere of the brain measured by heart rate. *Acta Psychologica, 41*, 255–260.

Dolan, R. J. (1999). On the neurology of morals. *Nature Neuroscience, 2*(11), 927–929.

Douglas, R. J. (1967). The hippocampus and behavior. *Psychological Bulletin, 67*(6), 416–442.

Douglas, R. J., & Pribram, K. H. (1966). Learning and limbic lesions. *Neuropsychologia, 4*, 197–220.

Drake, R. A. (1984). Lateral asymmetry of personal optimism. *Journal of Research in Personality, 18*, 497–507.

Drake, R. A., & Seligman, M. E. P. (1989). Self-serving biases in causal attributions as a function of altered activation asymmetry. *International Journal of Neuroscience, 45*, 199–204.

Drevets, W. C. (1998). Functional neuroimaging studies of depression: The anatomy of melancholia. *Annual Review of Medicine, 49*, 341–361.

Drevets, W. C., Videen, T. O., Price, J. L., Preskorn, S. H., Carmichael, S. T., & Raichle, M. E. (1992). A functional anatomical study of unipolar depression. *The Journal of Neuroscience, 12*(9), 3628–3641.

Dunbar, R. I. (1992). Neocortex size as a constraint on group size in primates. *Journal of Human Evolution, 20*, 246–293.

Dunbar, R. I. (1993). Coevolution of neocortical size, group size and language in humans. *Behavioral and Brain Science, 16*, 681–735.

Dunbar R. I. (1996). *Grooming, gossip, and the evolution of language.* Cambridge, MA: Harvard University Press.

Eales, L. A. (1985). Song learning in zebra finches: Some effects of song model availability on what is learnt and when. *Animal Behavior, 37*, 507–508.

Edelman, G. M. (1987). *Neural Darwinism.* New York: Basic.

Edelman, G. M. (1989). *The remembered present: A biological theory of consciousness.* New York: Basic.

Eichenbaum, H. (1992). The hippocampal system and declarative memory in animals. *Journal of Cognitive Neuroscience, 4*(3), 217–231.

Eisenberg, L. (1995). The social construction of the human brain. *American Journal of Psychiatry, 152*(11), 1563–1575.

Elbert, T., Flor, H., Birbaumer, N., Knecht, S., Hampson, S., Larbig, W., & Taub, E. (1994). Extensive reorganization of the somatosensory cortex in adult humans after nervous system injury. *NeuroReport, 5*, 2593–2597.

Elbert, T., Pantev, C., Wienbruch, C., Rockstroh, B., & Taub, E. (1995). Increased cortical representation of the fingers of the left hand in string players. *Science, 270*, 305–307.

Eliot, L. (1999). *What's going on in there.* New York: Bantam.

Eliot, T. S. (1950). *The cocktail party.* New York: Harcourt, Brace and Company.

Ellenberger, H. F. (1970). *The discovery of the unconscious.* New York: Basic.

Ellis, A. (1962). *Reason and emotion in psychotherapy.* Secaucus, NJ: Lyle Stuart.

Emde, R. N., Biringen, Z., Clyman, R. B. & Oppenheim, D. (1991). The moral self of infancy: Affective core and procedural knowledge. *Developmental Review, 11*, 251–270.

Erdelyi, M. H. (1994). Dissociation, defenses, and the unconscious. In D. Spence (Ed.), *Dissociation: Culture, mind, and body* (pp. 3–20). Washington, DC: American Psychiatric Press.

Eriksson, P. S., Perfileva, E., Bjork-Eriksson, T., Alborn, A. M., Nordborg, C., Peterson, D. A., & Gage, F. H. (1998). Neurogenesis in the adult human hippocampus. *Nature Medicine, 4*, 1313–1317.

Eslinger, P. J. (1998). Neurological and neuropsychological bases of empathy. *European Neurology, 39*, 193–199.

Falkai, P., & Bogerts, B. (1986). Cell loss in the hippocampus of schizophrenics. *European Archives of Psychiatry and Neurological Sciences, 236*, 154–161.

Faraone, S. V., & Biederman, J. (1999). The neurobiology of attention deficit hyperactivity disorder. In D. S. Charney, E. J. Nestler, & B. S. Bunney (Eds.), *Neurobiology of mental illness* (pp. 788–801). New York: Oxford University Press.

Feinberg, T. E. (2001). *Altered egos: How the brain creates the self.* New York: Oxford University Press.

Feinberg, T. E., & Shapiro, R. M. (1989). Misidentification-reduplication and the right hemisphere. *Neuropsychiatry, Neuropsychology, and Behavioral Neurology, 2*(1), 39–48.

Feldman, R., Greenbaum, C. W., & Yirimiya, N. (1999). Mother–infant affect synchrony as an antecedent of the emergence of self-control. *Developmental Psychology, 35*(5), 223–231.

Field, T. M. (1997). The treatment of depressed mothers and their infants. In L. Murry & P. J. Cooper (Eds.), *Postpartum depression and child development* (pp. 221–236). New York: Guilford.

Field, T. M., Grizzle, N., Scafidi, F., Abrams, S., Richardson, S., Kuhn, C., & Schanberg, S. (1996). Message therapy for infants of depressed mothers. *Infant behavior and development, 19*, 107–112.

Field, T. M., Healy, B., Goldstein, S., & Guthertz, M. (1990). Behavior-state matching and synchrony in mother–infant interactions of nondepressed vs depressed dyads. *Developmental Psychology, 26*(1), 7–14.

Field, T. M., Healy, B., Goldstein, S., Perry, S., & Bendell, D. (1988). Infants of depressed mothers show "depressed" behavior even with nondepressed adults. *Child Development, 59*, 1569–1579.

Field, T. M., Woodson, R., Greenberg, R., & Cohen, D. (1982). Discrimination and imitation of facial expressions by neonates. *Science, 218*, 179–181.

Fine, M. L. (1989). Embryonic, larval and adult development of the sonic neuromuscular system in the oyster toadfish. *Brain, Behavior and Evolutions, 34*, 13–24.

Firth, U. (1998). Literally changing the brain. *Brain, 121*(6), 1011–1012.

Fischer, K. W. (1987). Relations between brain and cognitive development. *Child Development, 58*, 623–632.

Fischer, K. W., Shaver, P. R., & Carnochan, P. (1990). How emotions develop and how they organize development. *Cognition and Emotion, 4,* 81–127.

Fish-Murry, C. C., Koby, E. V., & van der Kolk, B. A. (1987). Evolving ideas: The effects of abuse on children's thought. In B. A. van der Kolk (Ed.), *Psychological trauma* (pp. 89–110). Washington, DC: American Psychiatric Press.

Fivush, R. (1994). Constructing narrative, emotion, and self in parent–child conversations about the past. In U. Neisser & R. Fivush (Eds.), *The remembered self: Construction and accuracy in the self-narrative* (pp. 136–157). New York: Cambridge University Press.

Fonagy, P., Steele, H., & Steele, M. (1991). Maternal representations of attachment during pregnancy predict the organization of infant–mother attachment at one year of age. *Child Development, 62,* 891–905.

Fonagy, P., Steele, M., Steele, H., Moran, G. S., & Higgitt, A. C. (1991). The capacity to understand mental states: The reflective self in parent and child and its significance for security of attachment. *Infant Mental Health Journal, 12*(3), 201–218.

Fox, N. A. (1991). If it's not left it's right: Electroencephalograph asymmetry and the development of emotion. *American Psychologist, 46*(8), 863–872.

Frank, J. (1963). *Persuasion and healing.* New York: Schoken.

Freeman, T. W., & Kimbrell, T. (2001). A "cure" for chronic combat-related post-traumatic stress disorder secondary to a right frontal lobe infarct: A case report. *The Journal of Neuropsychiatry and Clinical Neurosciences, 13*(1), 106–109.

Freud, S. (1895). Project for a scientific psychology. *New introductory lectures in psychoanalysis: Standard edition, 22,* 3–182.

Freud, S. (1912). *The dynamics of transference.* Standard Edition. London: Hogarth Press. 12, pp. 99–108.

Freyd, J. J. (1987). Dynamic mental representations. *Psychological Reviews, 94,* 427–438.

Friberg, L., Olsen, T. S., Roland, P. E., Paulsen, O. B., & Lassen, N. A. (1985). Focal increase of blood flow in the cerebral cortex of man during vestibular stimulation. *Brain, 108,* 609–623.

Frick, R. B. (1982). The ego and the vestibulocerebellar system: Some theoretical perspectives. *Psychoanalytic Quarterly, 51,* 93–122.

Fuster, J. M. (1985). The prefrontal cortex and temporal integration. In A. Peters & E. G. Jones (Eds.), *Cerebral cortex. Vol 4. Association and auditory cortices* (pp. 151–171). New York: Plenum.

Fuster, J. M. (1996). Frontal lobe and the cognitive foundation of behavioral action. In A. R. Damasio (Ed.), *Neurobiology of decision-making* (pp. 47–61). Berlin: Springer-Verlag.

Fuster J. M. (1997). *The prefrontal cortex.* Philadelphia: Lippincott-Raven Publishers.

Fuster, J. M., Bonder, M., & Kroger, J. K. (2000). Cross-modal and cross-temporal association in neurons of frontal cortex. *Nature, 405,* 347–351.

Gablik, S. (1985). *Magritte.* New York: Thames and Hudson.

Galin, D. (1974). Implications for psychiatry of left and right cerebral specialization: A neurophysiological context for unconscious processes. *Archives of General Psychiatry, 31,* 572–583.

Galin, D., Johnstone, J., Nakell, L., & Herron, J. (1979). Development for the capacity for tactile information transfer between hemispheres in normal children. *Science, 204,* 1330–1331.

Gallese, V., Fadiga, L., Fogassi, L., & Rizzolatti, G. (1996). Action recognition in the premotor cortex. *Brain, 119,* 593–609.

Gazzaniga, M. S. (1989). Organization of the human brain. *Science, 245,* 947–952.

Gazzaniga, M. S. (1995). Consciousness and the cerebral hemispheres. In M. S. Gazzaniga (Ed.), *The cognitive neurosciences* (pp. 1391–1400). Cambridge, MA: MIT Press.

Gazzaniga, M. S., LeDoux, J. E., & Wilson, D. H. (1977). Language, praxis, and the right hemisphere: Clues to some mechanisms of consciousness. *Neurology, 27,* 1144–1147.

Gedo, J. E. (1991). *The biology of clinical encounters: Psychoanalysis as a science of mind.* Hillsdale, NJ: Analytic Press.

Gergen, K. J. (1994). Mind, text, and society: Self-memory in social context. In U. Neisser & R. Fivush (Eds.), *The remembered self: Construction and accuracy in the self-narrative* (pp. 136–157). New York: Cambridge University Press.

Geschwind, N., & Galaburda, A. M. (1985). Cerebral lateralization: Biological mechanisms, associations and pathology: I. A hypothesis and a program for research. *Archives of Neurology, 42,* 428–459.

Gibson, J. J. (1966). *The senses considered as perceptual systems.* Boston: Houghton Mifflin.

Gilliland, B. E., & James, R. K. (1998). *Theories and strategies in counseling and psychotherapy.* Boston: Allyn & Bacon.

Gitlin, M. J. (1996). *The psychotherapist's guide to psychopharmacology.* New York: Free Press.

Glaser, D. (2000). Child abuse and neglect and the brain—A review. *Journal of Child Psychiatry and Allied Disciplines, 41*(1), 97–116.

Gloor, P. (1978). Inputs and outputs of the amygdala: What the amygdala is trying to tell the rest of the brain. In K. E. Livingston & O. Hornykiewicz (Eds.), *Limbic mechanisms: The continuing evolution of the limbic system concept* (pp. 189–209). New York: Plenum.

Goel, V., Grafman, J., Sadato, N., & Hallett, M. (1995). Modeling other minds. *NeuroReport, 6,* 1741–1746.

Goldberg, E., & Costa, L. D. (1981). Hemispheric differences in the acquisition and use of descriptive systems. *Brain and Language, 14,* 144–173.

Goldman, P. S. (1971). Functional development of the prefrontal cortex in early life and the problem of neural plasticity. *Experimental Neurology, 32,* 366–387.

Goldman, P. S., & Galkin, T. W. (1978). Prenatal removal of frontal association cortex in the fetal rhesus monkey: Anatomical and functional consequences in postnatal life. *Brain Research, 152,* 451–485.

Goldman-Rakic, P. S. (1987). Development of cortical circuitry and cognitive function. *Child Development, 58,* 601–622.

Goldstein, L. E., Rasmusson, A. M., Bunney, B. S., & Roth, R. H. (1996). Role of the amygdala in the coordination of behavioral, neuroendocrine, and prefrontal cortical monoamine responses to psychological stress in the rat. *The Journal of Neuroscience, 16*(15), 4787–4798.

Goleman, D. (1995). *Emotional intelligence.* New York: Bantam.

Golomb, J., de Leon, M. J., Kluger, A., George, A. E., Tarshish, C., & Ferris, S. H. (1993). Hippocampal atrophy in normal aging: An association with recent memory impairment. *Archives of Neurology, 50*(9), 967–973.

Goodman, R. R., Snyder, S. H., Kuhar, M. J., & Young, W. S. III. (1980). Differential of delta and mu opiate receptor localizations by light microscope autoradiography. *Proceedings of the National Academy of Sciences USA, 77,* 2167–2174.

Gould, E., McEwen, B. S., Tanapat, P., Galea, L. A. M., & Fuchs, E. (1997). Neurogenesis in the dentate gyrus of the adult tree shrew is regulated by psychosocial stress and NMDA receptor activation. *Journal of Neuroscience, 17*(7), 2492–2498.

Gould, E., Reeves, A. J., Graziano, M. S. A., & Gross, C. G. (1999). Neurogenesis in the neocortex of adult primates. *Science, 628,* 548–552.

Gould, E., Tanapat, P., Hastings, N. B., & Shors, T. J. (1999). Neurogenesis in adulthood: A possible role in learning. *Trends in Cognitive Sciences, 3,* 186–191.

Gould, S. J. (1977). *Ontogeny and phylogeny.* Cambridge, MA: The Belknap Press of Harvard University.

Grafton, S. T., Arbib, M. A., Fadiga, L., & Rizzolatti, G. (1996). Localization of grasp representations in human by positron emission tomography. 2: Observation compared with imagination. *Experimental Brain Research, 112,* 103–111.

Green, A. (1978). Self-destructive behavior in battered children. *American Journal of Psychiatry, 135,* 551–579.

Green, A. (1981). Neurological impairments in maltreated children. *Child Abuse and Neglect, 5,* 129–134.

Greenough, W. T. (1987). Experience effects on the developing and mature brain: Dendritic branching and synaptogenesis. In N. A. Krasnegor, E. M. Blass, M. A. Hofer, & W. P. Smotherman (Eds.), *Perinatal development: A psychobiological perspective* (pp. 195–221). Orlando: Academic Press.

Grisaru, N., Chudakov, B., Yaroslavsky, Y., & Belmaker, R. H. (1998). Transcranial magnetic stimulation in mania: A controlled study. *American Journal of Psychiatry, 155*(11), 1608–1610.

Gross, C. G. (2000). Neurogenesis in the adult brain: Death of a dogma. *Nature Review of Neuroscience, 1*(1), 67–73.

Gunnar, M. R. (1992). Reactivity of the hypothalamic-pituitary-adrenocortical system to stressors in normal infants and children. *Pediatrics, 90*(Suppl 3), 491–479.

Gunnar, M. R. (1998). Quality of care and buffering of neuroendocrine stress reactions: Potential effects on the developing human brain. *Preventive Medicine, 27,* 208–211.

Gunnar, M. R., & Stone, C. (1984). The effects of positive maternal affect on infant responses to pleasant, ambiguous, and fear-provoking toys. *Child Development, 55,* 1231–1236.

Gurvits, T. V., Gilbertson, M. W., Lasko, N. B., Tarhan, A. S., Simeon, D., Maclin, M. L., Orr, S. P., & Pitman, R. K. (2000). Neurological soft signs in chronic posttraumatic stress disorder. *Archives of General Psychiatry, 57*, 181–183.

Guzowski, J. F., Setlow, B., Wagner, E. K., & McGaugh, J. L. (2001). Experience-dependent gene expression in the rat hippocampus after spatial learning: A comparison of the immediate-early genes Arc, c-fos, and zif268. *The Journal of Neuroscience, 21*(14), 5089–5098.

Halgren, E., Walter, R. D., Cherlow, D. G., & Crandall, P. H. (1978). Mental phenomena evoked by electrical stimulation of the human hippocampal formation and amygdala. *Brain, 101*, 83–117.

Hampden-Turner, C. (1981). *Maps of the mind.* New York: MacMillian.

Hariri, A. R., Bookheimer, S. Y., & Mazziotta, J. C. (2000). Modulating emotional responses: Effects of a neocortical network on the limbic system. *Neuroreport, 11*(1), 43–48.

Harlow, J. (1868). Recovery from the passage of an iron bar through the head. *Publication of the Massachusetts Medical Society, 2*, 329–346.

Hasselmo, M. E., Rolls, E. T., & Baylis, G. C. (1989). The role of expression and identity in the face-selective responses of neurons in the temporal visual cortex of the monkey. *Behavior Brain Research, 32*, 203–218.

Hayman, L. A., Rexer, J. L., Pavol, M. A., Strite, D., & Meyers, C. A. (1998). Kluver-Bucy syndrome after bilateral selective damage of amygdala and its cortical connections. *The Journal of Neuropsychiatry and Clinical Neurosciences, 10*(3), 354–358.

Hazan, C., & Shaver, P. R. (1990). Love and work: An attachment-theoretical perspective. *Journal of Personality and Social Psychology, 59*(2), 270–280.

Hebb, D. O. (1949). *The organization of behavior: A neuropsychological theory.* New York: Wiley.

Heider, F. (1958). *The psychology of interpersonal relations.* New York: Wiley.

Hendin, H., Haas, A. P., Houghton, W., Schwartz, M., & Wallen, V. (1984). The reliving experience in Vietnam veterans with posttraumatic stress disorder. *Comprehensive Psychiatry, 25*(2), 165–173.

Henry, R. R., Satz, P., & Saslow, E. (1984). Early brain damage and the ontogenesis of functional asymmetry. *Early Brain Damage, 1*, 253–275.

Herman, B. A., & Panksepp, J. (1978). Effects of morphine and naloxone on separation distress and approach attachment: Evidence for opiate mediation of social effect. *Pharmacology, Biochemistry and Behavior, 9*, 213–220.

Herman, J. L. (1992). Complex PTSD: A syndrome in survivors of prolonged and repeated trauma. *Journal of Traumatic Stress, 5*(3), 377–391.

Herschkowitz, N., Kegan, J., & Zilles, K. (1997). Neurobiological basis of behavioral development in the first year. *Neuropediatrics, 28*, 296–306.

Hesse, E. (1999). The adult attachment interview: Historical and current perspectives. In J. Cassidy & P. R. Shaver (Eds.), *Handbook of attachment: Theory, research, and clinical applications* (pp. 395–433). New York: Guilford.

Hirsten, W., & Ramachandran, V. S. (1997). Capgras syndrome: A novel probe for understanding the neural representation of the identity and familiarity of persons. *Proceedings of the Royal Society of London, 264*, 437–444.

Hiscock, M., Isrealian, M., Inch, R., Jacek, C., & Hiscock-Kalil, C. (1995). Is there a sex difference in human laterality? II. An exhaustive survey of visual laterality studies from six neuropsychology journals. *Journal of Clinical and Experimental Neuropsychology, 17*, 590–610.

Hobson, R. P. (1991). Against the theory of "theory of mind." *British Journal of Developmental Psychology, 9*, 33–51.

Hodge, C. J., & Boakye, M. (2001). Biological plasticity: The future of science in neurosurgery. *Neurosurgery, 48*(1), 2–16.

Hofer, M. A. (1984). Relationships as regulators: A psychobiologic perspective on bereavement. *Psychosomatic Medicine, 46*(3), 183–197.

Hofer, M. A. (1987). Early social relationships: A psychobiologist's view. *Child Development, 58*(3), 633–647.

Hoppe, K. D. (1977). Split-brains and psychoanalysis. *Psychoanalytic Quarterly, 46*, 220–244.

Hoppe, K. D., & Bogen, J. E. (1977). Alexithymia in twelve commissurotomized patients. *Psychotherapy and Psychosomatics, 28*, 148–155.

Howard, G. S. (1991). Culture tales: A narrative approach to thinking, cross-cultural psychology, and psychotherapy. *American Psychologist, 46*(3), 187–197.

Hoyle, R. L., Bromberger, B., Groversman, H. D., Klauber, M. R., Dixon, S. D., & Snyder, J. M. (1983). Regional anesthesia during newborn circumcision: Effect on infant pain response. *Clinical Pediatrics (Philadelphia), 22*, 813–818.

Huang, Z. J., Kirkwood, A., Pizzarusso, T., Porciatti, V., Morales, B., Bear, M. F., Maffei, L., & Tonegawa, S. (1999). BDNF regulates the maturation of inhibition and the critical period of plasticity in mouse visual cortex. *Cell, 98*, 739–755.

Hubel, D. H., & Wiesel, T. N. (1962). Receptive field binocular interaction and functional architecture in the cat's visual cortex. *Journal of Physiology, 160*, 106–154.

Hurley, R. A., Taber, K. H., Zhang, J., & Hayman, L. A. (1999). Neuropsychiatric presentation of multiple sclerosis. *The Journal of Neuropsychiatry and Clinical Neurosciences, 11*(1), 5–7.

Huttenlocher, P. R. (1994). Synaptogenesis in the human cerebral cortex. In G. Dawson & K. W. Fischer (Eds.), *Human behavior and the developing brain* (pp. 137–152). New York: Guilford.

Ickes, B. R., Pham, T. M., Sanders, L. A., Albeck, D. S., Mohammed, A. H., & Grandholm, A. C. (2000). Long-term environmental enrichment leads to regional increases in neurotrophin levels in rat brains. *Experimental Neurology, 164*(1), 45–52.

Ingvar, D. H. (1985). Memory for the future: An essay on the temporal organization of conscious awareness. *Human Neurobiology, 4*, 127–136.

Introini-Collison, I., & McGaugh, J. L. (1987). Naloxone and beta-endorphin alter the effects of post-training epinephrine on retention of an inhibitory avoidance response. *Psychopharmacology, 92*, 229–235.

Irle, E., Exner, C., Thielen, K., Weniger, G., & Ruther, E. (1998). Obsessive-compulsive disorder and ventromedial frontal lesions: Clinical and neuropsychological findings. *American Journal of Psychiatry, 155*(2), 255–263.

Ito, Y., Teicher, M. H., Glod, C. A., Harper, D., Magnus, E., & Gelbard, H. A. (1993). Increased prevalence of electrophysiological abnormalities in children with psychological, physical, and sexual abuse. *Journal of Neuropsychiatry, 5*(4), 401–408.

Jablonska, B., Gierdalski, M., Kossut, M., & Skangiel-Kramska, J. (1999). Partial blocking of NMDA receptors reduces plastic changes induced by short-lasting classical conditioning in the SL barrel cortex of adult mice. *Cerebral Cortex, 9,* 222–231.

Jacobs, B., Schall, M., & Scheibel, A. B. (1993). A quantitative dendritic analysis of Wernicke's area in humans: II. Gender, hemispheric, and environmental factors. *Journal of Comparative Neurology, 327,* 97–111.

Jacobs, B., & Scheibel, A. B. (1993). A quantitative dendritic analysis of Wernicke's area in humans: I. Lifespan changes. *Journal of Comparative Neurology, 327,* 97–111.

Jacobs, B. L., van Praag, H., & Gage, F. H. (2000). Depression and the birth and death of brain cells. *American Scientist, 88,* 340–345.

Jacobs, W., & Nadel, L. (1985). Stress-induced recovery of fears and phobias. *Psychological Review, 92*(4), 512–531.

Jacobson, L., & Sapolsky, R. (1991). The role of the hippocampus in feedback regulation of the hypothalamic-pituitary-adrenocortical axis. *Endocrine Reviews, 12*(2), 118–134.

Janoff-Bulman, R. (1992). *Shattered assumptions: Towards a new psychology of trauma.* New York: Free Press.

Jason, G., & Pajurkova, E. (1992). Failure of metacontrol: Breakdown in behavioral unity after lesions of the corpus callosum and inferomedial frontal lobes. *Cortex, 28,* 241–260.

Jaynes, J. (1976). *The origin of consciousness in the breakdown of the bicameral mind.* Boston: Houghton Mifflin.

Jeannerod, M., Arbib, M. A., Rizzolatti, G., & Sakata, H. (1995). Grasping objects: The cortical mechanism of visuomotor transformation. *Trends in Neuroscience, 18,* 314–320.

Johansson, B. B. (2000). Brain plasticity and stroke rehabilitation. *Stroke, 31,* 223–230.

Johnson, M. (1987). *The body in the mind.* Chicago: University of Chicago Press.

Joseph, R. (1996). *Neuropsychiatry, neuropsychology, and clinical neuroscience.* Baltimore: Williams & Wilkins.

Kalin, N. H., Larson, C., Shelton, S. E., & Davidson, R. J. (1998). Asymmetric frontal brain activity, cortisol, and behavior associated with fearful temperament in rhesus monkeys. *Behavioral Neuroscience, 112,* 286–292.

Kalin, N. H., Shelton, S. E., & Lynn, D. E. (1995). Opiate systems in mother and infant primates coordinate intimate contact during reunion. *Psychoneuroendocrinology, 20*(7), 735–742.

Kalin, N. H., Shelton, S. E., & Snowdon, C. T. (1993). Social factors regulating security and fear in infant rhesus monkeys. *Depression, 1,* 137–142.

Kandel, E. R. (1998). A new intellectual framework for psychiatry. *American Journal of Psychiatry, 155*(4), 457–469.

Kang, H., & Schuman, E. M. (1995). Long-lasting neurotrophin-induced enhancement of synaptic transmission in the adult hippocampus. *Science, 267,* 1658–1662.

Karni, A., Meyer, G., Jezzard, P., Adams, M. M., Turner, R., & Ungerleider, L. G. (1995). Functional MRI evidence for adult cortex plasticity during motor skill learning. *Nature, 377*, 155–158.

Katz, L. C., & Shatz, C. J. (1996). Synaptic activity and the construction of cortical circuits. *Science, 274*, 1133–1138.

Keenan, J. P., McCutcheon, B., Freund, S., Gallup, G. G., Sanders, G., & Pascual-Leone, A. (1999). Left hand advantage in a self-face recognition task. *Neuropsychologia, 37*, 1421–1425.

Kehoe, P., & Blass, E. M. (1989). Conditioned opioid release in ten-day-old rats: Reversal of stress with maternal stimuli. *Developmental Psychobiology, 19*(4), 385–398.

Kempermann, G., Kuhn, H. G., & Gage, F. H. (1997). More hippocampal neurons in adult mice living in an enriched environment. *Nature, 386*, 493–495.

Kempermann, G., Kuhn, H. G., & Gage, F. H. (1998). Experience-induced neurogenesis in the senescent dentate gyrus. *Journal of Neuroscience, 18*, 3206–3212.

Keverne, E. B., Martens, N. D., & Tuite, B. (1989). Beta-endorphin concentrations in cerebrospinal fluid of monkeys are influenced by grooming relationships. *Psychoneuroendocrinology, 18*(4), 307–321.

Kilgard, M. P., & Merzenich, M. M. (1998). Cortical map reorganization enabled by nucleus basalis activity. *Science, 279*, 1714–1718.

Kimble, D. P. (1968). Hippocampus and internal inhibition. *Psychological Bulletin, 70* (5), 285–295.

Kirkwood, A., Rozas, C., Kirkwood, J., Perez, F., & Bear, M. F. (1999). Modulation of long-term synaptic depression in visual cortex by acetylcholine and norepinephrine. *Journal of Neuroscience, 19*, 1599–1609.

Klein, E., Kreinin, I., Chistyakov, A., Koren, D., Mecz, L., Marmur, S., Ben-Shachar, D., & Feinsod, M. (1999). Therapeutic efficacy of right prefrontal slow repetitive transcranial magnetic stimulation in major depression. *Archives of General Psychiatry, 56*, 315–320.

Kluver, H., & Bucy, P. C. (1938). An analysis of certain effects of bilateral temporal lobectomy in the rhesus monkey, with special reference to "psychic blindness." *The Journal of Psychology, 5*, 33–54.

Knight, R. T., & Grabowecky, M. (1995). Escape from linear time: Prefrontal cortex and conscious experience. In M.S. Gazzaniga (Ed.), *The cognitive neurosciences* (pp. 1357–1371). Cambridge, MA: MIT Press.

Knowles, P. A., Conner, R. L., & Panksepp, J. (1989). Opiate effects on social behavior of juvenile dogs as a function of social deprivation. *Pharmacology, Biochemistry and Behavior, 33*, 533–537.

Kohut, H. (1984). *How does analysis cure?* Chicago: University of Chicago Press.

Kolb, B., & Gibb, R. (1991). Environmental enrichment and cortical injury: Behavioral and anatomical consequences of frontal cortex lesions. *Cerebral Cortex, 1*, 189–198.

Kolb, B., & Whishaw, I. Q. (1998). Brain plasticity and behavior. *Annual Review of Psychology, 49*, 43–64.

Konig, P., & Engel, A. K. (1995). Correlated firing in sensory-motor systems. *Current Opinions in Neurobiology, 5*, 511–519.

Koopman, C., Classen, C., & Spiegel, D. (1994). Predictors of posttraumatic stress symptoms among survivors of the Oakland/Berkeley, Calif. firestorm. *American Journal of Psychiatry, 151*(6), 888–894.

Krystal, J. H., Bremner, J. D., Southwick, S. M., & Charney, D. S. (1998). The emerging neurobiology of dissociation: Implication for treatment of posttraumatic stress disorder. In J. D. Bremner & C. R. Marmar (Eds.), *Trauma, memory, and dissociation* (pp. 321–363). Washington, DC: American Psychiatric Press.

LaBar, K. S., Gatenby, J. C., Gore, J. C., LeDoux, J. E., & Phelps, A. E. (1998). Human amygdala activation during conditioned fear acquisition and extinction: A mixed-trial FMRI study. *Neuron, 20*, 937–945.

Lachmann, F. M., & Beebe B. A. (1996). Three principles of salience in the organization of the patient-analyst interaction. *Psychoanalytic Psychology, 13*(1), 1–22.

Langer, E. J. (1978). Rethinking the role of thought in social interaction. In J. H. Harvey, W. Ickes, & R. F. Kidd (Eds.), *New directions in attribution research* (Vol. 2, pp. 35–58). Hillsdale, NJ: Erlbaum.

Langs, R. (1976). *The bipersonal field.* New York: Jason Aronson.

LeDoux, J. E. (1986). Sensory systems and emotion: A model of affective processing. *Integrative Psychiatry, 4*, 237–243.

LeDoux, J. E. (1994). Emotion, memory and the brain. *Scientific American, 270*, 32–39.

LeDoux, J. E. (1996). *The emotional brain.* New York: Simon & Schuster.

LeDoux, J. E., Romanski, L. M., & Xagoraris, A. E. (1989). Indelibility of subcortical emotional memories. *Journal of Cognitive Neuroscience, 1*, 238–243.

LeDoux, J. E., Wilson, D. H., & Gazzaniga, M. S. (1977). A divided mind: Observations on the conscious properties of the separated hemispheres. *Annals of Neurology, 2*, 417–421.

Lee, G. P., Bechara, A., Adolphs, R., Arena, J., Meador, K. J., Loring, D. W., & Smith, J. R. (1998). Clinical and physiological effects of stereotaxic bilateral amygdalotomy for intractable aggression. *The Journal of Neuropsychiatry and Clinical Neurosciences, 10*, 413–420.

Lee, Y., & Davis, M. (1997). Role of the hippocampus, the bed nucleus of the stria terminalis and the amygdala in the excitatory effect of corticotropin-releasing hormone on the acoustic startle reflex. *The Journal of Neuroscience, 17*(16), 6434–6446.

Leonard, C. M., Rolls, E. T., Wilson, F. A. W., & Baylis, G. C. (1985). Neurons in the amygdala of the monkey with responses selective for faces. *Behavioral Brain Research, 15*, 159–176.

Levine, S., Haltmeyer, G. C., Karas, G. G., & Denenberg, V. H. (1967). Physiological and behavioral effects of infantile stimulation. *Physiology and Behavior, 2*(1), 55–59.

Levy, D. A. (1997). *Tools of critical thinking.* Boston: Allyn & Bacon.

Levy, J., Trevarthen, C., & Sperry, R. W. (1972). Perception of bilateral chimeric figures following hemispheric disconnection. *Brain, 95*, 61–78.

Lewicki, P., Hill, T., & Czyzewska, M. (1992). Nonconscious acquisition of information. *American Psychologist, 47*(6), 796–801.

Li, H., Weiss, S. R. B., Chaung, D. M., Post, R. M., & Rogawski, M. A. (1998). Bidirectional synaptic plasticity in the rat basolateral amygdala: Characterization of an activity-dependent switch sensitive to the presynaptic metabotropic glutamate receptor antagonist 2S-alpha-ethyglutamic acid. *The Journal of Neuroscience, 18*(5), 1662–1670.

Liu, D., Diorio, J., Tannenbaum, B., Caldji, C., Francis, D., Freedman, A., Sharma, S., Pearson, D., Plotsky, P. M., & Meaney, M. J. (1997). Maternal care, hippocampal glucocorticoid receptors, and hypothalamic-pituitary-adrenal responses to stress. *Science, 277,* 1659–1662.

Livingston, R. B. (1967). Reinforcement. In G. C. Quarton, T. Melnick, & F. O. Schmitt (Eds.), *The neurosciences* (pp. 568–576). New York: Rockefeller University Press.

Loftus, E. F. (1988). *Memory.* New York: Ardsley House.

Loftus, E. F., Milo, E. M., & Paddock, J. R. (1995). The accidental executioner: Why psychotherapy must be informed by science. *The Counseling Psychologist, 23*(2), 300–309.

Lombroso, P. J., & Sapolsky, R. (1998). Development of the cerebral cortex: Stress and brain development. *Journal of the Academy of Child and Adolescent Psychiatry, 37*(12), 1337–1339.

Lord, C. G., Ross, L., & Lepper, M. (1979). Biased assimilation and attitude polarization: The effects of prior theories on subsequently considered evidence. *Journal of Personality and Social Psychology, 37,* 1231–1247.

Lorenz, K. (1991). *Here am I—where are you: The behavior of the greylag goose.* New York: Harcourt Brace Jovanovich.

Lovell, J., & Kluger, J. (1994). Lost moon: The perilous voyage of Apollo 13. New York: Simon & Schuster.

Ludwig, A. M. (1983). The psychobiological functions of dissociation. *American Journal of Hypnosis, 26*(2), 93–99.

MacLean, P. D. (1985). Brain evolution relating to family, play, and the separation call. *Archives of General Psychiatry, 42,* 405–417.

MacLean, P. D. (1990). *The triune brain in evolution: Role of paleocerebral functions.* New York: Plenum.

Maher, B. A. (1974). Delusional thinking and perceptual disorder. *Journal of Individual Psychology, 30,* 98–113.

Main, M. (1993). Discourse, prediction, and the recent studies in attachment: Implications for psychoanalysis. *Journal of the American Psychoanalytic Association, 41,* 209–244.

Main, M., & Goldwyn, R. (1998). *Adult attachment scoring and classification system.* Unpublished manuscript, University of California at Berkeley.

Main, M., Kaplan, N., & Cassidy, J. (1985). Security in infancy, childhood, and adulthood: A move to the level of representation. In I. Bretherton & E. Waters (Eds.), Growing points of attachment theory and research. *Monographs of the Society for Research in Child Development, 50*(1–2, Serial No. 209, pp. 66–104).

Main, M., & Solomon, J. (1986). Discovery of an insecure/disorganized attachment pattern. In T. B. Brazelton & M. Yogman (Eds.), *Affective development in infancy* (pp. 95–124). Norwood, NJ: Ablex.

Malenka, R. C., & Siegelbaum, S. A. (2001). Synaptic plasticity: Diverse targets and mechanisms for regulating synaptic efficacy. In W. M. Cowan, T. C. Sudhof, & C. F. Stevens (Eds.), *Synapses* (pp. 393–453). Baltimore: Johns Hopkins University Press.

Malinkowski, B. (1984). The role of myth in life. In A. Dundes (Ed.), *Sacred narrative* (pp. 193–206). Berkeley: University of California Press. (Original work published 1926)

Malloy, P., Bihrle, A., Duffy, J., & Cimino, C. (1993). The orbitomedial frontal syndrome. *Archives of Clinical Neuropsychology, 8,* 185–201.

Marr, D. (1971). A theory of archicortex. *Philosophical Transactions of the Royal Society, 262,* 23–81.

Marshall, R. E., Stratton, W. C., Moore, J., & Boxerman, S. B. (1980). Circumcision I: Effects upon newborn behavior. *Infant Behavioral Development, 3,* 1–14.

Martin, A., Wiggs, C. L., Ungerleider, L. G., & Haxby, J. V. (1996). Neural correlates of category-specific knowledge. *Nature, 379,* 649–652.

Mateer, C. A., & Kerns, K. A. (2000). Capitalizing on neuroplasticity. *Brain and Cognition, 42,* 106–109.

Mathew, R. J., Jack, R. A., & West, W. S. (1985). Regional cerebral blow flow in a patient with multiple personality. *American Journal of Psychiatry, 142*(4), 504–505.

Mayberg, H. S. (1997). Limbic-cortical dysregulation: A proposed model of depression. *Journal of Neuropsychiatry, 9*(3), 471–481.

Mayberg, H. S., Liotti, M., Brannan, S. K., McGinnis, S., Mahurin, R. K., Jerabek, P. A., Silva, J. A., Tekell, J. L., Martin, C. C., Lancaster, J. L., & Fox, P. T. (1999). Reciprocal limbic-cortical function and negative mood: Converging PET findings in depression and normal sadness. *American Journal of Psychiatry, 156,* 675–682.

McCarthy, G. (1995). Functional neuroimaging of memory. *The Neuroscientist, 1*(3), 155–163.

McFarlane, A. C., & Yehuda, R. (1996). Resilience, vulnerability, and the course of posttraumatic reactions. In B. A. van der Kolk, A. C. McFarlane, & L. Weisaeth (Eds.), *Traumatic stress: The effects of overwhelming experience on mind, body, and society* (pp. 129–154). New York: Guilford.

McGaugh, J. L. (1990). Significance and remembrance: The role of neuromodulatory systems. *Psychological Science, 1*(1), 15–25.

McGaugh, J. L. (1996, Sept.). *Stress-activated hormonal systems and the regulation of memory storage.* Paper presented at the New York Academy of Sciences meeting on The psychobiology of posttraumatic stress, New York.

McGaugh, J. L., Introini-Collison, I. B., Cahill, L. F., Castellano, C., Dalmaz, C., Parent, M. B., & Williams, C. L. (1993). Neuromodulatory systems and memory storage: Role of the amygdala. *Behavioral Brain Research, 58,* 81–90.

Meaney, M. J., Aitken, D. H., Viau, V., Sharma, S., & Sarrieau, A. (1989). Neonatal handling alters adrenocortical negative feedback sensitivity and hippocampal type II glucocorticoid receptor binding in the rat. *Neuroendocrinology, 50,* 597–604.

Meaney, M. J., Diorio, J., Francis, D., Weaver, S., Yau, J., Chapman, K., & Seckl, J. R. (2000). Postnatal handling increases the expression of CAMP-inducible transcription factors in the rat hippocampus: The effects of thyroid hormones and serotonin. *The Journal of Neuroscience, 20*(10), 3926–3935.

Meltzoff, A. N., & Moore, M. K. (1983). Newborn infants imitate adult facial gestures. *Child Development, 54*, 702–709.

Meltzoff, A. N., & Moore, M. K. (1993). Imitation of facial and manual gestures by human neonates. *Science, 198*, 75–78.

Merlin, D. (1995). The neurobiology of human consciousness: An evolutionary approach. *Neuropsychologia, 33*(9), 1087–1102.

Merrin, E. L., & Silberfarb, P. M. (1979). The Capgras phenomenon. *Archives of General Psychiatry, 33*, 965–968.

Mesulam, M. M. (1981). A cortical network for directed attention and unilateral neglect. *Annals of Neurology, 10*, 309–325.

Mesulam, M. M. (1985). Attention, confusional states, and neglect. In M. Mesulam (Ed.), *Principles of behavioral neurology* (pp. 125–168). Philadelphia: F.A. Davis.

Mesulam, M. M. (1998). From sensation to cognition. *Brain, 121*, 1013–1052.

Mesulam, M. M., & Mufson, E. J. (1982). Insula of the old world monkey, III: Efferent cortical output and comments on function. *Journal of Comparative Neurology, 212*, 38–52.

Meyers, C. A., Berman, S. A., Scheibel, R. S., & Hayman, A. (1992). Case report: Acquired antisocial personality disorder associated with unilateral left orbital frontal lobe damage. *Journal of Psychiatry and Neuroscience, 17*(3), 121–125.

Michel, G. F., & Moore, C. L. (1995). *Developmental psychobiology: An interdisciplinary science.* Cambridge, MA: MIT Press.

Miller, A. (1981). *Prisoners of childhood: The drama of the gifted child and the search for the true self.* New York: Basic.

Miller, A. (1983). *For your own good: Hidden cruelty in child-rearing and the roots of violence.* New York: Farrar, Straus & Giroux.

Miller, H., Alvarez, V., & Miller, N. (1990). *The psychopathology and psychoanalytic psychotherapy of compulsive caretaking.* Unpublished manuscript.

Miller, P. J., & Sperry, L. (1988). Early talk about the past: The origins of conversational stories of personal experience. *Journal of Child Language, 15*, 293–315.

Mitchell, J. T., & Everly, G. S. (1993). *Critical incident stress debriefing: An operations manual for the prevention of trauma among emergency service and disaster workers.* Baltimore, MD: Chevron Publishing.

Morgan, C. A., Wang, S., Southwick, S. M., Rasmusson, A., Hazlett, G., Hauger, R. L., & Charney, D. S. (2000). Plasma neuropeptide-Y concentrations in humans exposed to military survival training. *Biological Psychiatry, 47*, 902–909.

Myers, J. J., & Sperry, R. W. (1985). Interhemispheric communication after section of the forebrain commissures. *Cortex, 21*, 249–260.

Myers, W. A., Churchill, J. D., Muja, N., & Garraghty, P. E. (2000). Role of NMDA receptors in adult primates cortical somatosensory plasticity. *Journal of Comparative Neurology, 418*, 373–382.

Nasrallah, H. A. (1985). The unintegrated right cerebral hemispheric consciousness as alien intruder: A possible mechanism for Schneiderian delusions in schizophrenia. *Comprehensive Psychiatry, 26*(3), 273–282.

Nauta, W. J. H. (1971). The problem of the frontal lobe: A reinterpretation. *Journal of Psychiatric Research, 8*, 167–187.

Nebes, R. D. (1971). Superiority of the minor hemisphere in commissurotomized man for the perception of part-whole relationships. *Cortex, 7*(4), 333–349.

Neisser, U. (1994). Self-narrative: True and false. In U. Neisser & R. Fivush (Eds.), *The remembered self: Construction and accuracy in the self-narrative* (pp. 1–18). New York: Cambridge University Press.

Nelson, C. A., & Carver, L. J. (1998). The effects of stress and trauma on brain and memory: A view from developmental cognitive neuroscience. *Development and Psychopathology, 10*, 793–809.

Nelson, K. (1993). The psychological and social origins of autobiographical memory. *Psychological Science, 4*(1), 7–14.

Nelson, M. D., Saykin, A. J., Flashman, L. A., & Riordan, H. J. (1998). Hippocampal volume reduction in schizophrenia as assessed by magnetic resonance imaging: A meta-analytic study. *Archives of General Psychiatry, 55*, 433–440.

Nesse, R. M., & Lloyd, A. T. (1992). The evolution of psychodynamic mechanisms. In J. H. Barkow, L. Cosmides, & J. Tooby (Eds.), *The adapted mind: Evolutionary psychology and the generation of culture* (pp. 601–626). New York: Oxford University Press.

Newberg, A., Alavi, A., Baime, M., Pourdehnad, M., Santanna, J., & Aquili, E. (2001). The measurement of cerebral blood flow during the complex cognitive task of meditation: A preliminary SPECT study. *Psychiatric Research: Neuroimaging Section, 106*, 113–122.

Newman, D. (1982). Perspective-taking verses context in understanding lies. *Quarterly Newsletter of the Laboratory of Comparative Human Cognition, 4*, 26–29.

Nichols, K., & Champness, B. (1971). Eye gaze and the GRS. *Journal of Experimental Social Psychology, 7*, 623–626.

Nikolaenko, N. N., Egorov, A. Y., & Freiman, E. A. (1997). Representational activity of the right and left hemispheres of the brain. *Behavioral Neurology, 10*, 49–59.

Nilsson, L., Mohammed, A. K. H., Henriksson, B. G., Folkesson, R., Winblad, B., & Bergstrom, L. (1993). Environmental influence on somatostatin levels and gene expression in the rat brain. *Brain Research, 628*, 93–98.

Nisenbaum, L. K., Zigmond, M. J., Sved, A. F., & Abercrombie, E. D. (1991). Prior exposure to chronic stress results in enhanced synthesis and release of hippocampal norepinephrine in response to novel stressors. *The Journal of Neuroscience, 11*(5), 1478–1484.

Nishitani, N., & Hari, R. (2000). Temporal dynamics of cortical representation for action. *Proceedings of the National Academy of Science, 97*(2), 913–918.

Nottebohm, F. (1981). A brain for all seasons: Cyclical anatomical changes in song-control nuclei of the canary brain. *Science, 214*, 138–1370.

Oatley, K. (1992). Integrative action of narrative. In D. J. Stein & J. E. Young (Eds.), *Cognitive science and clinical disorders* (pp. 151–172). New York: Academic.

O'Brien, J. T. (1997). The "glucocorticoid cascade" hypothesis in man. *British Journal of Psychiatry, 170*, 199–201.

Ochs, E., & Capps, L. (2001). *Living narrative: Creating lives in everyday story-telling*. Cambridge, MA: Harvard University Press.

O'Doherty, J., Kringelback, M. L., Rolls, E. T., Hornak, J., & Andrews, C. (2001). Abstract reward and punishment representations in the human orbitofrontal cortex. *Nature Neuroscience, 4*(1), 95–102.

Odom-White, A., de Leon, J., Stanilla, J., Cloud, B. S., & Simpson, G. M. (1995). Misidentification syndromes in schizophrenia: Case reviews with implications for classification and prevalence. *Australian and New Zealand Journal of Psychiatry, 29*, 63–68.

O'Keefe, J., & Nadel, L. (1978). *The hippocampus as a cognitive map*. Oxford, UK: Clarendon.

Olton, D. S. (1986). Hippocampal function and memory for temporal context. In R. L. Isaacson & K. H. Pribram (Eds.), *The Hippocampus* (Vol. 4), (pp. 281–298). New York: Plenum.

Orlinsky, D. E., & Howard, K. J. (1986). Process and outcome in psychotherapy. In S. L. Garfield & A. E. Bergin (Eds.), *Handbook of psychotherapy and behavior change* (pp. 311–381). New York: Wiley.

Ornitz, E. M., & Pynoos, R. S. (1989). Startle modulation in children with posttraumatic stress disorder. *American Journal of Psychiatry, 146*(7), 866–870.

Ouspensky, P. D. (1954). *The psychology of man's possible evolution*. New York: Knopf.

Panksepp, J. (1998). *Affective neuroscience: The foundation of human and animal emotions*. New York: Oxford University Press.

Panksepp, J., Nelson, E., & Siviy, S. (1994). Brain opioids and mother-infant social motivation. *Acta Paediatrica Supplement, 397*, 40–46.

Parente, R., & Herrmann, D. (1996). *Retraining cognition*. Gaithersberg, MD: Aspen.

Paris, J., Zelkowitz, P., Guzder, J., Joseph, S., & Feldman, R. (1999). Neuropsychological factors associated with borderline pathology in children. *Journal of the Academy of Child and Adolescent Psychiatry, 38*(6), 770–774.

Pascual-Leone, A., Rubio, B., Pallardo, F., & Catala, M. D. (1996). Rapid-rate transcranial magnetic stimulation of left dorsolateral prefrontal cortex in drug-resistant depression. *Lancet, 348*, 233–237.

Pascual-Leone, A., Wassermann, E. M., Grafman, J., & Hallett, M. (1996). The role of the dorsolateral prefrontal cortex in implicit procedural learning. *Experimental Brain Research, 107*, 479–485.

Penfield, W., & Perot, P. (1963). The brain's record of auditory and visual experience. *Brain, 86*, 595–696.

Perls, F., Hefferline, R., & Goodman, P. (1951). *Gestalt therapy: Excitement and growth in human personality*. New York: Dell.

Perrett, D. I., Rolls, E. T., & Cann, W. (1982). Visual neurons responsive to faces in the monkey temporal cortex. *Experimental Brain Research, 47*, 329–342.

Perrett, D. I., Smith, A. J., Potter, D. D., Mistlin, A. J., Head, A. D., Milner, A. D., & Jeeves, M. A. (1984). Neurons responsive to faces in the temporal cortex: Studies of functional organization, sensitivity to identity and relation to perception. *Human Neurobiology, 3*, 197–208.

Perry, B. D., Pollard, R. A., Blakley, T. I, Baker, W. L., & Vigilante, D. (1995). Childhood trauma, the neurobiology of adaptation, and "use dependent" development of the brain: How "states" become "traits." *Infant Mental Health Journal, 16*(4), 271–291.

Persinger, M. A., & Makarec, K. (1991). Greater right hemisphericity is associated with lower self-esteem in adults. *Perceptual and Motor Skills, 73*, 1244–1246.

Petty, F., Chae, Y., Kramer, G., Jordan, S., & Wilson, L. (1994). Learned helplessness sensitizes hippocampal norepinephrine to mild stress. *Biological Psychiatry, 35*, 903–908.

Pfrieger, F. W., & Barres, B. A. (1996). New views on synapse-glia interactions. *Current Opinions in Neurobiology, 6*, 615–621.

Pham, T. M., Soderstrom, S., Henriksson, B. G., & Mohammed, A. H. (1997). Effects of neonatal stimulation on later cognitive function and hippocampal nerve growth factor. *Behavioral Brain Research, 86*, 113–120.

Pipp, S., & Harmon, R. J. (1987). Attachment as regulation: A commentary. *Child Development, 58*(3), 648–652.

Pitman, R. K., Orr, S. P., van der Kolk, B. A., Greenberg, M. S., Meyerhoff, J. L., & Mougey, E. H. (1990). Analgesia: A new dependent variable for the biological study of posttraumatic stress disorder. In M.E. Wolf & A.D. Mosnaim (Eds.), *Posttraumatic stress disorder: Etiology, phenomenology, and treatment* (pp. 141–147). Washington, DC: American Psychiatric Press.

Platt, M. L., & Glimcher, P. W. (1999). Neural correlates of decision variables in parietal cortex. *Nature, 400*, 233–238.

Plotsky, P. M., & Meaney, M. J. (1993). Early, postnatal experience alters hypothalamic corticotropin-releasing factor (CRF) MRNA, median eminence CRF content and stress-induced release in adult rats. *Molecular Brain Research, 18*, 195–200.

Plutchik, R. (2001). The nature of emotions. *American Scientist, 89*, 344–350.

Polley, D. B., Chen-Bee, C. H., & Frostig, R. D. (1999). Two directions of plasticity in the sensory-deprived adult cortex. *Neuron, 24*(3), 623–637.

Post, R. M., & Weiss, S. R. B. (1997). Emergent properties of neural systems: How focal molecular neurobiological alterations can affect behavior. *Development and Psychopathology, 9*, 907–929.

Post, R. M., Weiss, S. R. B., Li, H., Smith, A., Zhang, L. X., Xing, G., Osuch, E. A., & McCann, U. D. (1998). Neural plasticity and emotional memory. *Development and Psychopathology, 10*, 829–855.

Pribram, K. H. (1960). The intrinsic systems of the forebrain. In J. Field, H. W. Magoun, & V. E. Hall (Eds.), *Handbook on physiology, neurophysiology II* (pp. 1323–1344). Washington, DC: American Psychological Society.

Pribram, K. H. (1991). *Brain and perception: Holonomy and structure in figural processing.* Hillsdale, NJ: Erlbaum.

Pribram, K. H., & Gill, M. M. (1976). *Freud's "Project" re-assessed: Preface to contemporary cognitive theory and neuropsychology.* New York: Basic.

Price, B. H., Daffner, K. R., Stowe, R. M., & Mesulam, M. M. (1990). The comportmental learning disabilities of early frontal lobe damage. *Brain, 113*, 1383–1393.

Price, J. L., Carmichael, S. T., & Drevets, W. C. (1996). Networks related to the orbital and medial prefrontal cortex: A substrate for emotional behavior? *Progress in Brain Research, 107*, 523–536.

Price, J. M., & Landsverk, J. (1998). Social information-processing as predictors of social adaptation and behavior problems among maltreated children in foster care. *Child Abuse and Neglect, 22*(9), 845–858.

Purves, D., & Lichtman, J. W. (1980). Elimination of synapses in the developing nervous system. *Science, 210*, 153–157.

Purves, D., & Voyvodic, J. T. (1987). Imaging mammalian nerve cells and their connections over time in living animals. *Trends in Neurosciences, 10*, 398–404.

Raine, A., Buchsbaum, M. S., Stanley, J., Lottenberg, S., Abel, L., & Stoddard, J. (1994). Selective reductions in prefrontal glucose metabolism in murderers. *Biological Psychiatry, 36*, 365–373.

Rakic, P. (1985). Limits of neurogenesis in primates. *Science, 227*, 154–156.

Ramachandran, V. S., Rogers-Ramachandran, D., & Stewart, M. (1992). Perceptual correlates of massive cortical reorganization. *Science, 258*, 1159–1160.

Rauch, S. L., Jenike, M. A., Alpert, N. M., Baer, L., Breiter, H. C. R., Savage, C. R., & Fischman, A. J. (1994). Regional cerebral blood flow measured during symptom provocation in obsessive-compulsive disorder using oxygen 15–labeled carbon dioxide and positron emission tomography. *Archives of General Psychiatry, 51*, 62–70.

Rauch, S. L., van der Kolk, B. A., Fisler, R. E., Alpert, N. M., Orr, S. P., Savage, C. R., Fischman, A. J., Jenike, M. A., & Pitman, R. K. (1996). A symptom provocation study of PTSD using PET and script driven imagery. *Archives of General Psychiatry, 53*, 380–387.

Regard, M., Oelz, O., Brugger, P., & Landis, T. (1989). Persistent cognitive impairment in climbers after repeated exposure to extreme altitude. *Neurology, 39*, 210–213.

Reich, W. (1945). *Character analysis.* New York: Simon & Schuster.

Reiman, E. M., Raichle, M. E., Robins, E., Mintun, M. A., Fusselman, M. J., Fox, P. T., Price, J. L., & Hackman, K. A. (1989). Neuroanatomical correlates of a lactate-induced anxiety attack. *Archives of General Psychiatry, 46*, 493–500.

Resnick, H. S., Yehuda, R., Pitman, R. K., & Foy, D. W. (1995). Effects of previous trauma on acute plasma cortisol level following rape. *American Journal of Psychiatry, 152*(11), 1675–1677.

Revonsuo, A. (1999). Binding and the phenomenal unity of consciousness. *Consciousness and Cognition, 8*, 173–185.

Rezai, K., Andreasen, N. C., Alliger, R., Cohen, G., Swayze, V., & O'Leary, D. S. (1993). The neuropsychology of the prefrontal cortex. *Archives of Neurology, 50*, 636–642.

Rizzolatti, G., & Arbib, M. A. (1998). Language within our grasp. *Trends in Neuroscience, 21*(5), 188–194.

Rogan, M. T., & LeDoux, J. E. (1996). Emotion: Systems, cells, synaptic plasticity. *Cell, 85*, 469–475.

Rogan, M. T., Staubli, U. V., & LeDoux, J. E. (1997). Fear conditioning induces associative long-term potentiation in the amygdala. *Nature, 390*, 604–607.

Rogers, C. R. (1942). *Counseling and psychotherapy.* Boston: Houghton Mifflin.

Rolls, E. T. (1999). *The brain and emotion.* New York: Oxford University Press.

Rolls, E. T. (2000). The orbitofrontal cortex and reward. *Cerebral Cortex, 10*(3), 284–294.

Rosenzweig, M. R. (2001). Learning and neural plasticity over the life span. In P. E. Gold & W. T. Greenough (Eds.), *Memory consolidation: Essays in honor or James L. McGaugh* (pp. 275–294). Washington, DC: American Psychological Association.

Ross, E. D. (1981). The aprosodias. *Archives of Neurology, 38*, 561–569.

Ross, E. D., Homan, R. W., & Buck, R. (1994). Differential hemispheric lateralization of primary and social emotions: Implications for developing a comprehensive neurology for emotions, repression, and the subconscious. *Neuropsychiatry, Neuropsychology, and Behavioral Neurology, 7*(1), 1–19.

Ross, M., & Buehler, R. (1994). Creative remembering. In U. Neisser & R. Fivush (Eds.), *The remembered self: Construction and accuracy in the self-narrative* (pp. 205–235). New York: Cambridge University Press.

Rossi, E. L. (1993). *The psychobiology of mind-body healing.* New York: W.W. Norton.

Rothbart, M. K., Taylor, S. B., & Tucker, D. M. (1989). Right-sided facial asymmetry in infant emotional expression. *Neuropsychologia, 27*, 675–687.

Rubens, A. B. (1985). Caloric stimulation and unilateral visual neglect. *Neurology, 35*, 1019–1024.

Rubino, G. J., Farahani, K., McGill, D., Van de Wiele, B., Villablanca, J. P., & Wang-Maithieson, A. (2000). Magnetic resonance imaging-guided neurosurgery in the magnetic fringe fields: The next step in neuronavigation. *Neurosurgery, 46*(3), 643–654.

Rutter, M., & Rutter, M. (1993). *Developing minds: Challenge and continuity across the life span.* New York: Basic.

Ryan, W. (1971). *Blaming the victim.* New York: Pantheon.

Sapolsky, R. M. (1985). A mechanism for glucocorticoid toxicity in the hippocampus: Increased neuronal vulnerability to metabolic insults. *The Journal of Neuroscience, 5*(5), 1228–1232.

Sapolsky, R. M. (1987). Glucocorticoids and hippocampal damage. *Trends in Neuroscience, 10*(9), 346–349.

Sapolsky, R. M. (1990, Jan.). Stress in the wild. *Scientific American*, pp. 116–123.

Sapolsky, R. M. (1996). Why stress is bad for your brain. *Science, 273*, 749–750.

Sapolsky, R. M., Krey, L. C., & McEwen, B. S. (1984). Glucocorticoid-sensitive hippocampal neurons are involved in terminating the adrenocortical stress response. *Proceedings of the National Academy of Science, USA, 81*, 6174–6177.

Sapolsky, R. M., Uno, H., Rebert, C. S., & Finch, C. E. (1990). Hippocampal damage associated with prolonged glucocorticoid exposure in primates. *The Journal of Neuroscience, 10*(9), 2897–2902.

Sarter, M., & Markowitsch, H. J. (1985). The amygdala's role in human mnemonic processing. *Cortex, 21*, 7–24.

Saxe, G. N., Chinman, G., Berkowitz, R., Hall, K., Leiberg, G., Schwartz, J., & van der Kolk, B. A. (1994). Somatization in patients with dissociative disorders. *American Journal of Psychiatry, 151*(9), 1329–1333.

Saxe, G. N., Vasile, R. G., Hill, T. C., Bloomingdale, K., & van der Kolk, B. A. (1992). SPECT imaging and multiple personality disorder. *Journal of Nervous and Mental Disease, 180*(10), 662–663.

Schacter, D. L. (1976). The hypnagogic state: A critical review of the literature. *Psychological Bulletin, 83*(3), 452–481.

Schacter, D. L. (1986). Amnesia and crime. *American Psychologist, 41*(3), 286–295.

Schacter, D. L. (1996). *Searching for memory: The brain, the mind, and the past.* New York: Basic.

Schall, J. D. (2001). Neural basis of deciding, choosing and acting. *Nature Reviews Neuroscience, 2,* 33–42.

Schiffer, F., Teicher, M. H., & Papanicolaou, A. C. (1995). Evoked potential evidence for right brain activity during the recall of traumatic memories. *Journal of Neuropsychiatry and Clinical Neurosciences, 7,* 169–175.

Schmahmann, J. D. (1997). *The cerebellum and cognition.* New York: Academic.

Schmand, B., Smit, J. H., Geerlings, M. I., & Lindeboom, J. (1997). The effects of intelligence and education on the development of dementia: A test of the brain reserve hypothesis. *Psychological Medicine, 27,* 1337–1344.

Schneider, M. L. (1992). Prenatal stress exposure alters postnatal behavioral expression under conditions of novelty challenge in rhesus monkey infants. *Developmental Psychobiology, 25*(7), 529–540.

Schore, A. N. (1991). Early superego development: The emergence of shame and narcissistic affect regulation in the practicing period. *Psychoanalysis and Contemporary Thought, 14,* 187–250.

Schore, A. N. (1994). *Affect regulation and the origin of the self: The neurobiology of emotional development.* Hillsdale, NJ: Erlbaum.

Schore, A. N. (1996). The experience-dependent maturation of a regulatory system in the orbital prefrontal cortex and the origin of developmental psychopathology. *Development and Psychopathology, 8,* 59–87.

Schore, A. N. (1997a). Early organization of the nonlinear right brain and development of a predisposition to psychiatric disorders. *Development and Psychopathology, 9,* 595–631.

Schore, A. N. (1997b). A century after Freud's project for a scientific psychology: Is a rapproachment between psychoanalysis and neurobiology at hand? *Journal of the American Psychoanalytic Association, 45,* 841–867.

Schore, A. N. (2000). Attachment and the regulation of the right brain. *Attachment and Human Development, 2*(1), 23–47.

Schrott, L. M. (1997). Effect of training and environment on brain morphology and behavior. *Acta Paediatrica Scandanavia,* (Suppl.), 422, 45–47.

Schrott, L. M., Denenberg, V. H., Sherman, G. F., Waters, N. S., Rosen, G. D., & Galaburda, A. M. (1992). Environmental enrichment, neocortical ectopias, and behavior in the autoimmune NZB mouse. *Developmental Brain Research, 67,* 85–93.

Schultz, R. T., Gauthier, I., Klin, A., Fulbright, R. K., Anderson, A. W., Volkmar, F., Skudlarski, P., Lacadie, C., Cohen, D. J., & Gore, J. C. (2000). Abnormal ventral temporal cortical activity during face discrimination among individuals with Autism and Asperger syndrome. *Archives of General Psychiatry, 57,* 331–340.

Schuz, A. (1978). Some facts and hypotheses concerning dendritic spines and learning. In M.A.B. Braizer & H. Petsche (Eds.), *Architectonics of the cerebral cortex* (pp. 129–135). New York: Raven.

Schwartz, D. A. (1979). The suicidal character. *Psychiatric Quarterly, 51*(1), 64–70.

Schwartz, J. M. (1996). *Brain lock: Free yourself from obsessive-compulsive behaviors.* New York: ReganBooks.

Schwartz, J. M., Stoessel, P. W., Baxter, L. R., Martin, K. M., & Phelps, M. E. (1996). Systematic changes in cerebral glucose metabolic rate after successful behavior modification treatment of obsessive-compulsive disorder. *Archives of General Psychiatry, 53,* 109–113.

Schwartz, S. (1964). Effects of neonatal cortical lesions and early environmental factors on adult rat behavior. *Journal of Comparative Physiological Psychology, 57,* 72–77.

Scott, A. (1995). *Stairway to the mind: The controversial new science of consciousness.* New York: Springer-Verlag.

Searleman, A. (1977). A review of right hemisphere linguistic capabilities. *Psychological Bulletin, 84*(3), 503–528.

Seidman, L. J., Faracone, S. V., Goldstein, J. M., Goodman, J. M., Kremen, W. S., Toomey, R., Tourville, J., Kennedy, D., Makris, N., Caviness, V. S., & Tsuang, M. T. (1999). Thalamic and amygdala-hippocampal volume reductions in first-degree relatives of patients with schizophrenia: An MRI-based morphometric analysis. *Biological Psychiatry, 46,* 941–954.

Selden, N. R. W., Everitt, B. J., Jarrard, L. E., & Robbins, T. W. (1991). Complementary roles for the amygdala and hippocampus in aversive conditioning to explicit and contextual cues. *Neuroscience, 42*(2), 335–350.

Selye, H. (1979). *The stress of my life.* New York: Van Nostrand.

Semmes, J. (1968). Hemispheric specialization: A possible clue to mechanism. *Neuropsychologia, 6,* 11–26.

Sergent, J. (1986). Subcortical coordination of hemispheric activity in commissurotomized patients. *Brain, 109,* 357–369.

Sergent, J. (1990). Furtive incursions into bicameral minds. *Brain, 113,* 537–568.

Serieux, P., & Capgras, J. (1909). Misinterpretive delusional states. In *Les folies raisonnantes: Le delire d'interpretation* (pp. 5–43). Paris: Balliere.

Shapiro, D., Jamner, L. D., & Spence, S. (1997). Cerebral laterality, repressive coping, autonomic arousal, and human bonding. *Acta Scandanavica Physiologica, 640*(Suppl.) 60–64.

Shapiro, F. (1995). *Eye movement desensitization and reprocessing: Basic principles, protocols, and procedures.* New York: Guilford.

Shatz, C. J. (1990). Impulse activity and patterning of connections during CNS development. *Neuron, 5,* 745–756.

Sheline, Y. I., Gado, M. H., & Price, J. L. (1998). Amygdala core nuclei volumes are decreased in recurrent major depression. *NeuroReport, 9,* 2023–2028.

Sheline, Y. I., Wang, P. W., Gado, M. H., Csernansky, J. G., & Vannier, M. W. (1996). Hippocampal atrophy in recurrent major depression. *Proceedings of the National Academy of Sciences, USA, 93*, 3908–3913.

Shenton, M. E., Kikinis, R., Jolesz, F. A., Pollak, S. D., LeMay, M., Wible, C. G., Hokama, H., Martin, J., Metcalf, D., Coleman, M., & McCarley, R. W. (1992). Abnormalities of the left temporal lobe and thought disorder in schizophrenia: A quantitative magnetic resonance imaging study. *The New England Journal of Medicine, 327*(9), 604–612.

Sherry, D. F., Jacobs, L. F., & Gaulin, S. J. C. (1992). Spatial memory and adaptive specialization of the hippocampus. *Trends in Neuroscience, 15*(8), 298–303.

Sherry, D. F., & Schacter, D. L. (1987). The evolution of multiple memory systems. *Psychological Review, 94*, 439–454.

Shilony, E., & Grossman, F. K. (1993). Depersonalization as a defense mechanism in survivors of trauma. *Journal of Traumatic Stress, 6*(1), 119–128.

Shima, K., & Tanji, J. (1998). Role for cingulate motor area cells in voluntary movement selection based on reward. *Science, 282*, 1335–1338.

Siegel, D. J. (1995). Trauma and psychotherapy: A cognitive sciences view. *Journal of Psychotherapy Practice and Research, 4*, 93–122.

Siegel, D. J. (1996). Cognition, memory, and dissociation. *Child and Adolescent Clinics of North America, 5*(2), 509–536.

Siegel, D. J. (1999). *Developing mind: Toward a neurobiology of interpersonal experience*. New York: Guilford.

Silberman, E. K., & Weingartner, H. (1986). Hemispheric lateralization of functions related to emotion. *Brain and Cognition, 5*, 322–353.

Sirevaag, A. M., & Greenough, W. T. (1988). A multivariate statistical summary of synaptic plasticity measures in rats exposed to complex, social and individual environments. *Brain Research, 441*, 386–392.

Snyder, L. H., Batista, A. P., & Andersen, R. A. (1997). Coding of intention in the posterior parietal cortex. *Nature, 386*, 167–170.

Solomon, Z. (1990). Back to the front: Recurrent exposure to combat stress and reactivation of posttraumatic stress disorder. In M. E. Wolf (Ed.), *Posttraumatic stress disorder: Etiology, phenomenology, and treatment* (pp. 126–138). Washington, DC: American Psychiatric Press.

Sontheimer, H. (1995). Glial influences on neuronal signaling. *The Neuroscientist, 1*(3), 123–126.

Spangler, G., & Grossman, K. E. (1993). Biobehavioral organization in securely and insecurely attached infants. *Child Development, 64*, 1439–1450.

Spear, L. P. (2000). The adolescent brain and age-related behavioral manifestations. *Neuroscience and Biobehavioral Reviews, 24*, 417–463.

Specter, M. (2001, July 23). Rethinking the brain. *The New Yorker*. pp. 42–53.

Spence, D. P. (1982). *Narrative truth and historical truth*. New York: W.W. Norton.

Sperry, W. R. (1968). Hemispheric deconnection and unity in conscious awareness. *American Psychologist, 23*, 723–733.

Sperry, W. R. (1981). Changing priorities. *Annual Review of Neuroscience, 4*, 1–15.

Sperry, R. W., Gazzaniga, M. S., & Bogen, J. E. (1969). Interhemispheric relationships: The neocortical commissures; syndromes of hemisphere disconnection.

In P. J. Vinken & G. W. Bruyn (Eds.), *Handbook of clinical neurology* (Vol. 4, pp 273–290). Amsterdam: North-Holland.

Spitz, R. (1946). Hospitalism: An inquiry into the genesis of psychiatric conditions in early childhood. *The Psychoanalytic Study of the Child, 1*, 53–74.

Springer, S., & Deutsch, G. (1998). *Left brain, right brain: Perspectives from cognitive neuroscience.* New York: W.H. Freeman.

Squire, L. R. (1987). *Memory and brain.* Oxford, UK: Oxford University Press.

Squire, L. R., & Zola-Morgan, S. (1991). The medial temporal lobe memory system. *Science, 253*, 2380–2386.

Starkstein, S. E., & Robinson, R. G. (1997). Mechanisms of disinhibition after brain lesion. *Journal of Nervous and Mental Disease, 185*(2), 108–114.

St. Clair, M. (1986). *Object relations and self psychology.* Monterey, CA: Brooks/Cole.

Stein, M. B., Koverola, C., Hanna, C., Torchia, M. G., & McClarty, B. (1997). Hippocampal volume in women victimized by childhood sexual abuse. *Psychological Medicine, 27*, 951–959.

Stephan, H., & Andy, O. J. (1977). Quantitative comparison of the amygdala in insectivores and primates. *Acta Anatomica, 98*, 130–153.

Stern, D. N. (1985). *The interpersonal world of the infant.* New York: Basic.

Stern, D. N. (1995). *The motherhood constellation.* New York: Basic.

Sterr, A., Muller, M. M., Elbert, T., Rockstroh, B., Pantev, C., & Taub, E. (1998a). Perceptual correlates of changes in cortical representation of fingers in blind multifinger Braille readers. *The Journal of Neuroscience, 18*(11), 4417–4423.

Sterr, A., Muller, M. M., Elbert, T., Rockstroh, B., Pantev, C., & Taub, E. (1998b). Changed perceptions is Braille readers. *Nature, 391*, 134–135.

Stiles, J. (2000). Neural plasticity and cognitive development. *Developmental Neuropsychology, 18*(2), 237–272.

Stolorow, R. D., & Atwood, G. E. (1979). *Faces in a cloud: Subjectivity in psychoanalytic theory.* New York: Jason Aronson.

Stuss, D. T., Gallup, G. G., & Alexander, M. P. (2001). The frontal lobes are necessary for "theory of mind". *Brain, 124*, 279–286.

Sulloway, F. J. (1979). *Freud: Biologist of the mind.* New York: Basic.

Svensson, T. H. (1987). Peripheral, autonomic regulation of locus coeruleus noradrenergic neurons in the brain: Putative implications for psychiatry and psychopharmacology. *Psychopharmacology, 92*, 1–7.

Swirsky-Sacchetti, T., Gorton, G., Samuel, S., Sobel, R., Genetta-Wadley, A., & Burleigh, B. (1993). *Journal of Clinical Psychology, 49*(3), 385–396.

Tang, Y. P., Shimizu, E., Dube, G. R., Rampon, C., Kerchner, G. A., Zhuo, M., Liu, G., & Tsien, J. Z. (1999). Genetic enhancement of learning and memory in mice. *Nature, 401*, 63–69.

Tarrier, N., Vaughn, C. E., Lader, M. H., & Leff, J. P. (1979). Bodily reactions to people and events in schizophrenia. *Archives of General Psychiatry, 36*, 311–315.

Taylor, G. J. (2000). Recent developments in alexithymia theory and research. *Canadian Journal of Psychiatry, 45*, 134–142.

Taylor, M. A. (1999). *The fundamentals of clinical neuropsychiatry.* Oxford, UK: Oxford University Press.

Taylor, S. E., & Brown, J. D. (1988). Illusion and well-being: A social psychological perspective on mental health. *Psychological Bulletin, 103*(2), 193–210.

Teasdale, J. D., Howard, R. J., Cox, S. G., Ha, Y., Brammer, M. J., Williams, S. C. R., & Checkley, S. A. (1999). Functional MRI study of the cognitive generation of affect. *American Journal of Psychiatry, 156*(2), 209–215.

Teicher, M. H., Ito, Y., Glod, C. A., Andersen, S. L., Dumont, N., & Ackerman, E. (1997). Preliminary evidence for abnormal cortical development in physically and sexually abused children using EEG coherence and MRI. *Annals of the New York Academy of Sciences, 821*, 160–175.

ten Cate, C. (1989). Behavioral development: Toward understanding processes. In P. P. G. Bateson & P. Klopfer (Eds.), *Perspectives in ethology* (Vol. 8, pp. 243–269). New York: Plenum.

Teneback, C. C., Nahas, Z., Speer, A. M., Molloy, M., Stallings, L. E., Spicer, K. M., Risch, S. C., & George, M. S. (1999). Changes in prefrontal cortex and paralimbic activity in depression following two weeks of daily left prefrontal TMS. *The Journal of Neuropsychiatry and Clinical Neurosciences, 11*(4), 426–435.

Terr, L. (1990). *Too scared to cry.* New York: Harper & Row.

Thatcher, R. W. (1980). Neurolinguistics: Theoretical and evolutionary perspectives. *Brain and Language, 11*, 235–260.

Thatcher, R. W., Walker, R. A., & Giudice, S. (1987). Human cerebral hemispheres develop at different rates and ages. *Science, 236*, 1110–1113.

Thayer, J. F., & Cohen, B. H. (1985). Differential hemispheric lateralization for positive and negative emotion: An electromyographic study. *Biological Psychology, 21*(4), 265–266.

Tillich, P. (1974). *The courage to be.* New Haven, CT: Yale University Press.

Tomarken, A. J., & Davidson, R. J. (1994). Frontal brain activation in repressors and nonrepressors. *Journal of Abnormal Psychology, 103*(2), 339–349.

Torasdotter, M., Metsis, M., Henriksson, B. G., Winblad, B., & Mohammed, A. H. (1998). Environmental enrichment results in higher levels of nerve growth factor MRNA in the rat visual cortex and hippocampus. *Behavioral Brain Research, 93*, 83–90.

Tranel, D., & Hyman, B. T. (1990). Neuropsychological correlates of bilateral amygdala damage. *Archives of Neurology, 47*, 349–355.

Treisman, A. (1996). The binding problem. *Current Opinions in Neurobiology, 6*, 171–178.

Tremblay, L., & Schultz, W. (1999). Relative reward preference in primate orbitofrontal cortex. *Nature, 398*, 704–708.

Trevarthen, C. (1993). The self born in intersubjectivity: The psychology of an infant communicating. In U. Neisser (Ed.), *The perceived self: Ecological and interpersonal sources of self knowledge* (pp. 121–173). Cambridge, UK: Cambridge University Press.

Trojan, S., & Pokorny, J. (1999). Theoretical aspects of neuroplasticity. *Physiological Research, 48*, 87–97.

Tucker, D. M. (1992). Developing emotions and cortical networks. In M. R. Gunnar & C. Nelson (Eds.), *Minnesota symposia on child psychology, vol. 24. Developmental behavioral neuroscience* (pp. 75–128). Hillsdale, NJ: Erlbaum.

Tucker, D. M., Luu, P., & Pribram, K. H. (1995). Social and emotional self-regulation. *Annals of the New York Academy of Sciences, 769*, 213–239.

Tulving, E. (1985). How many memory systems are there? *American Psychologist,
40*(4), 385–398.

Ulrich, R. (1984). View through a window may influence recovery from surgery.
Science, 224, 420–421.

Ungerleider, L. G. (1995). Functional brain imaging studies of cortical mechanisms
for memory. *Science, 270*, 769–775.

Usdin, E., Kvetnansky, R, & Kopin, I. J. (1976). *Stress and catecholamines.* Oxford,
UK: Pergamon.

Vallar, G., Sterzi, R., Bottini, G., Cappa, S., & Rusconi, M.L. (1990). Temporary
remission of left hemianesthgesia after vestibular stimulation: A sensory neglect
phenomenon. *Cortex, 26*, 123–131.

van der Kolk, B. A. (1988). The trauma spectrum: The interaction of biological and
social events in the genesis of the trauma response. *Journal of Traumatic Stress,
1*(3), 273–290.

van der Kolk, B. A. (1994). The body keeps the score: Memory and the evolving psychobiology of post traumatic stress. *Harvard Review of Psychiatry, 1*, 253–265.

van der Kolk, B. A., Blitz, R., Burr, W., Sherry, S., & Hartmann, E. (1984).
Nightmares and trauma: A comparison of nightmares after combat with lifelong
nightmares in veterans. *American Journal of Psychiatry, 141*, 187–190.

van der Kolk, B. A., & Greenberg, M. S. (1987). The psychobiology of the traumatic
response: Hyperarousal, constriction, and addiction to traumatic reexposure. In
B. A. van der Kolk (Ed.), *Psychological trauma* (pp. 63–87). Washington, DC:
American Psychiatric Press.

van der Kolk, B. A., Pelcovitz, D., Roth, S., Mandel, F. S., McFarlane, A., & Herman,
J. L. (1996). Dissociation, somatization, and affect dysregulation: The complexity of adaptation to trauma. *American Journal of Psychiatry, 153*(7), 83–95.

Van Hoesen, G. W. (1981). The differential distribution, diversity and sprouting of
cortical projections to the amygdala in the rhesus monkey. In Y. Ben-Ari (Ed.),
The amygdaloid complex (pp. 77–90). Amsterdam: Elsevier/North-Holland
Biomedical Press.

Vasterling, J. J., Brailey, K., Constans, J. I., & Sutker, P. B. (1998). Attention and memory dysfunction in posttraumatic stress disorder. *Neuropsychology, 12*(1), 125–133.

Vernadakis, A. (1996). Glia-neuron intercommunications and synaptic plasticity.
Progressive Neurobiology, 49, 185–214.

Viau, V., Sharma, S., Plotsky, P. M., & Meaney, M. J. (1993). Increased plasma ACTH
responses to stress in nonhandled compared with handled rats require basal levels of corticosterone and are associated with increased levels of ACTH secreta-
gogues in the median eminence. *The Journal of Neuroscience, 13*(3), 1097–1105.

Voltaire (1976). *The portable Voltaire.* New York: Viking. von Bonin, G. (1963). *The
evolution of the human brain.* Chicago: University of Chicago Press.

vonBonin, G. (1963). The evolution of the human brain. Chicago: Univeristy of
Chicago Press.

von der Malsburg, C. (1995). Binding in models of perception and brain function. *Current Opinions in Neurobiology, 5*, 520–526.

Wada, J. (1961). Modification of cortically induced responses in brainstem by shift of attention in monkeys. *Science, 133*, 40–42.

Walsh, R. N., Budtz-Olsen, O. E., Penny, J. E., & Cummins, R. A. (1969). The effects of environmental complexity of the histology of the rat hippocampus. *Journal of Comparative Neurology, 137*, 361–366.

Walsh, V., Ashbridge, E., & Cowey, A. (1998). Cortical plasticity in perceptual learning demonstrated by transcranial magnetic stimulation. *Neuropsychologia, 36*(1), 45–49.

Wantanabe, M. (1996). Reward expectancy in primate prefrontal neurons. *Nature, 382*, 629–632.

Wantanabe, Y. E., Gould, E., Cameron, D., Daniels, D., & McEwen, B. S. (1992). Phenytoin prevents stress and corticosterone induced atrophy of CA3 pyramidal neurons. *Hippocampus, 2*, 431–436.

Wantanabe, Y. E., Gould, E., & McEwen, B. S. (1992). Stress induced atrophy of apical dendrites of hippocampal CA3 pyramidal neurons. *Brain Research, 588*, 341–345.

Weiner, I. (1998). *Principles of psychotherapy*. New York: Wiley.

Weingarten, S. M., Cherlow, D. G., & Holmgren, E. (1977). The relationship of hallucinations to the depth structures of the temporal lobe. *Acta Neurochirurgica, 24* (Suppl.) 199–216.

Wellington, N., & Rieder, M. J. (1993). Attitudes and practices regarding analgesia for newborn circumcision. *Pediatrics, 92*(4), 541–543.

Weston, M. J., & Whitlock, F. A. (1971). The capgras syndrome following head injury. *British Journal of Psychiatry, 119*, 25–31.

Wexler, B. E., & Heninger, G. R. (1979). Alterations in cerebral laterality during acute psychotic illness. *Archives of General Psychiatry, 36*, 278–284.

Will, B. E., Rosenzweig, M. R., Bennett, E. B., Herbert, M., Morimoto, H. (1977). Relatively brief environmental enrichment aids recovery of learning capacity and alters brain measures after postweaning brain lesions in rats. *Journal of Comparative Physiological Psychology, 91*, 33–50.

Williams, L. M. (1994). Recall of childhood trauma: A prospective study of women's memories of child sexual abuse. *Journal of Consulting and Clinical Psychology, 62*(6), 1167–1176.

Wilson, F. A. W., O'Scalaidhe, S. P., & Goldman-Rakic, P. S. (1993). Dissociation of object and spatial processing domains in primate prefrontal cortex. *Science, 260*, 1955–1958.

Wilson, F. R. (1998). *The hand*. New York: Vintage.

Winick, M., Katchadurian, K., & Harris, R. C. (1975). Malnutrition and environmental enrichment by early adoption. *Science, 190*, 1173–1175.

Winnicott, D. W. (1958). The capacity to be alone. In *Maturational processes and the facilitating environment* (pp. 29–36). New York: International Universities Press.

Winnicott, D. W. (1962). Ego integration in child development. In *Maturational processes and the facilitating environment* (pp. 56–63). New York: International Universities Press.

Winnicott, D. W. (1963). From dependence to independence in the development of the individual. In *Maturational processes and the facilitating environment* (pp. 83–92). New York: International Universities Press.

Witelson, S. F., Kigar, D. L., & Harvey, T. (1999). The exceptional brain of Albert Einstein. *The Lancet, 353,* 2149–2153.

Wittling, W. (1997). The right hemisphere and the human stress response. *Acta Physiologica Scandinavica, 640* (Suppl.), 55–59.

Wittling, W., & Pfluger, M. (1990). Neuroendocrine hemisphere asymmetries: Salivary cortisol secretion during lateralized viewing of emotion-related and neutral films. *Brain and Cognition, 14,* 243–265.

Wolf, N.S. (In press). *Before and beyond words: The neurobiology of empathy.* Forthcoming from W. W. Norton.

Wolf, N. S., Gales, M. E., Shane, E., & Shane, M. (2000). The developmental trajectory from amodal perception to empathy and communication: The role of mirror neurons in this process. *Psychoanalytic Inquiry, 21*(1), 94–112.

Wolpe, J. (1958). *Psychotherapy by reciprocal inhibition.* Stanford, CA: Stanford University Press.

Woolley, C. S., Gould, E., & McEwen, B. S. (1990). Exposure to excess glucocorticoids alters dendritic morphology of adult hippocampal pyramidal neurons. *Brain Research, 531,* 225–231.

Yapko, M. D. (1994). *Suggestions of abuse.* New York: Simon & Schuster.

Yehuda, R. (1999). Biological factors associated with susceptibility to posttraumatic stress disorder. *Canadian Journal of Psychiatry, 44*(1), 34–39.

Yehuda, R., Bierer, L. M., Schmeidler, J., Aferiat, D. H., Breslau, I., & Dolan, S. (2000). Low cortisol and risk for PTSD in adult offspring of holocaust survivors. *The American Journal of Psychiatry, 157*(8), 1252–1259.

Yehuda, R., Keefe, R. S. E., Harvey, P. D., Levengood, R. A., Gerber, D. K., Geni, J., & Siever, L. J. (1995). Learning and memory in combat veterans with posttraumatic stress disorder. *American Journal of Psychiatry, 152*(1), 137–139.

Yehuda, R., Kahana, B., Schmeidler, J., Southwick, S. M., Wilson, S., & Giller, E. I. (1995). Impact of cumulative lifetime trauma and recent stress on current posttraumatic stress disorder symptoms in holocaust survivors. *American Journal of Psychiatry, 152*(12), 1815–1818.

Yehuda, R., & Siever, L. J. (1997). Persistent effects of stress in trauma survivors and their descendants. *Biological Psychiatry, 41,* 1S-120S.

Yerkes, R. M., & Dodson, J. D. (1908). The relation of strength of stimulus to rapidity of habit formation. *Journal of Comparative and Neurological Psychology, 18,* 459–482.

Young, A. W., Aggleton, J. P., Hellawell, D. J., Johnson, M., Broks, P., & Hanley, J. R. (1995). Face processing impairments after amygdalotomy. *Brain, 118,* 15–24.

Yovell, Y. (2000). From hysteria to posttraumatic stress disorder: Psychoanalysis and the neurobiology of traumatic memories. *Neuropsychoanalysis, 2,* 171–181.

Zald, D. H., & Kim, S. W. (2001). The orbitofrontal cortex. In S. P. Salloway, P. F. Malloy, & J. D. Duffy (Eds.), *The frontal lobes and neuropsychiatric illness* (pp. 33–69). Washington, DC: American Psychiatric Press.

Zeitlin, S. B., Lane, R. D., O'Leary, D. S., & Schrift, M. J. (1989). Interhemspheric transfer deficit and alexithymia. *American Journal of Psychiatry, 146*(11), 1434–1439.

Zeitlin, S. B., & McNally, R. J. (1991). Implicit and explicit memory bias for threat in post traumatic stress disorder. *Behavior Research and Therapy, 29*(5), 451–457.

Zeltzer, L. K., Anderson, C. T. M., & Schecter, N. L. (1990). Pediatric pain: Current status and new directions. *Current problems in pediatrics, 20*(8), 415–486.

Zhu, X. O., & Waite, P. M. E. (1998). Cholinergic depletion reduces plasticity of barrel field cortex. *Cerebral Cortex, 8*, 63–72.

Zola-Morgan, S. M., & Squire, L. R. (1990). The primate hippocampal formation: Evidence for a time-limited role in memory storage. *Science, 250*, 288–290.

Zuckerman, B., Bauchner, H., Parker, S., & Cabral, H. (1990). Maternal depressive symptoms during pregnancy, and newborn irritability. *Developmental and Behavioral Pediatrics, 11*(4), 190–194.

Index